THE BRITISH LABOUR GOVERNMENT AND THE GREEK CIVIL WAR 1945–1949:
THE IMPERIALISM OF 'NON-INTERVENTION'

For Dimitris, my father, who survived it,

and

for Gillian, who survived the writing of it

The British Labour Government and the Greek Civil War 1945–1949: the Imperialism of 'Non-Intervention'

Thanasis D. Sfikas

Ryburn Publishing
KEELE UNIVERSITY PRESS

First published in 1994
by Ryburn Publishing
an imprint of
Keele University Press Ltd
Keele, Staffordshire
© Thanasis D. Sfikas
Composed and originated by
Ryburn Publishing Services
Printed in Bodmin by Hartnolls
for Ryburn Book Production,
Keele University, England

ISBN 1-85331-048-4

Contents

Abbreviations

AKE	Agrotiko Komma Ellados [Agrarian Party of Greece]
AMAG	American Mission for Aid to Greece
AMFOGE	Allied Mission For Observing the Greek Elections
BEM	British Economic Mission
BLO	British Liaison Officer
BMM	British Military Mission
BPM	British Police Mission
BSP	British Sessional Papers
CAB	Cabinet Papers (Minutes and Memoranda)
CC	Central Committee
CHURCHILL–ROOSEVELT	*Churchill–Roosevelt: The Complete Correspondence*, vols. I–III, ed. W.F. Kimball (Princeton: Princeton University Press, 1984)
CIGS	Commander of the Imperial General Staff
COS	Chiefs of Staff
CP	Communist Party
CPSU	Communist Party of the Soviet Union
DBPO	*Documents on British Policy Overseas*, series I, vols. I–II, ed. R. Butler, M.E. Pelly, H.J. Yasamee (London: HMSO, 1984)
DSE	Dimokratikos Stratos Elladas [Democratic Army of Greece]
EAM	Ethniko Apeleftherotiko Metopo [National Liberation Front]
EAM: LV (I)	*EAM: Lefki Vivlos: Mais 1944–Martis 1945* [EAM: White Book: May 1944–March 1945] (Trikala: 1945)
EAM: LV (II)	*EAM: Lefki Vivlos: Paraviaseis tis Varkizas (Flevaris–Iounis 1945)* [EAM: White Book: Violations of Varkiza (February–June 1945)] (Athens: June 1945)
EAM: LV (III)	*EAM: Lefki Vivlos: 'Dimokratikos' Neofasismos, Ioulis–Oktovris 1945* [EAM: White Book: 'Democratic' Neofascism, July–October 1945] (Athens: October 1945)
EDES	Ethnikos Dimokratikos Ellinikos Syndesmos [National Republican Greek League]
ELAS	Ethnikos Laikos Apeleftherotikos Stratos [National People's Liberation Army]
ELD	Enosi Laikis Dimokratias [Union of People's Democracy]
EPE	Ethniki Politiki Enosis [National Political Union]
EPSV	*Episima Praktika ton Synedriaseon tis Voulis* [Official Minutes of the Parliamentary Sessions] (Athens: Ethniko Typografeio, 1946–1949)

6

FO	Foreign Office
FRUS	*Foreign Relations of the United States* (Washington: Government Printing Office, 1969–1976)
GAK	Genika Archeia tou Kratous [General Archives of the State] (Athens)
GES/DIS	Geniko Epiteleio Stratou / Diefthynsi Istorias Stratou [Greek General Staff / Army History Directorate](Athens)
(G) HQ	(General) Headquarters
GNA	Greek National Army
HC Deb.	House of Commons Debates, 5th series (London: 1909ff)
IEE	*Istoria tou Ellinikou Ethnous* [History of the Hellenic Nation], vols. I–XV (Athens: Ekdotiki Athinon, 1978)
JUSMAPG	Joint United States Military Advisory and Planning Group
KKE	Kommunistiko Komma Ellados [Communist Party of Greece]
KKE: EK	*KKE: Episima Keimena* [KKE: Official Documents], vols. V– VI (Athens: Synchroni Epochi, 1981, 1987)
KKE (es.)	Kommunistiko Komma Ellados (esoterikou) [Communist Party of Greece (of the interior)], Eurocommunist
KKE (es.): EK	*KKE (esoterikou): Episima Keimena* [KKE (interior): Official Documents], vol. V (Skopje and Rome: 1973)
MVR	*Ambassador MacVeagh Reports 1933–1947*, ed. J.O. Iatrides (Princeton: Princeton University Press, 1980)
NSC	National Security Council (USA)
PEEA	Politiki Epitropi Ethnikis Apeleftherosis [Political Committee of National Liberation]
PEEA Archives	*Archeio tis Politikis Epitropis Ethnikis Apeleftherosis (PEEA): Praktika Synedriaseon* (Athens: Synchroni Epochi, 1990)
PRO	Public Record Office (London)
SKE	Sosialistiko Komma Ellados [Socialist Party of Greece]
STALIN et al.	Ministry of Foreign Affairs of the USSR: *Correspondence between the Chairman of the Council of Ministers of the Presidents of the USA and the Prime Ministers of Great Britain during the Great Patriotic War of 1941–1945* vols. I–II (Moscow: Progress Publishers, 1958)
TUC	Trades Union Congress
UDC	Union of Democratic Control
UNRRA	United Nations Relief and Rehabilitation Administration
UNSCOB	United Nations Special Committee on the Balkans
USAGG	US Army Group Greece
WO	War Office

The Athenians to the Melians, 416/5 BC

As for us, even assuming that our empire does come to an end, we are not despondent about what would happen next. One is not so much frightened of being conquered by a power which rules over others, as Sparta does (not that we are concerned with Sparta now), as of what would happen if a ruling power is attacked and defeated by its own subjects. So far as this point is concerned, you can leave it to us to face the risks involved. What we shall do now is to show you that it is for the good of our own empire that we are here and that it is for the preservation of your city that we shall say what we are going to say. We do not want any trouble in bringing you into our empire, and we want you to be spared for the good both of yourselves and of ourselves.

Thucydides, V : 91

Preface

This is a study neither of British foreign policy nor of the Greek Civil War. It is both – or, more accurately, it is more than the former and less than the latter. My objectives are to examine British policy towards Greece in 1945–1949, trace the domestic and international origins of the Labour government's conduct, analyse the setting on which it was applied, and show that, contrary to common assumptions, the story of Anglo-Greek relations remained a remarkable one even after the enunciation of the Truman Doctrine. Indicative of the intention to evaluate British policy in its appropriate context is the rejection of titles such as the presumptuous 'British Foreign Policy' or the voracious 'The Greek Civil War'. Indeed, what is missing from the available literature is precisely the interrelation of these two components. Historians who rely exclusively on British records are content with the study of the British outlook, with the result that their strictly perceptual approach often falls short of grasping the *real* situation. By contrast, those who make use of Greek records tend to overlook the domestic and international origins of British policy.

In so far as it pertains to the Greek Civil War – one of the major but less known internal wars in twentieth-century Europe[1] – the undertaking hardly needs justification. Though inaccurate, the official position of the Greek Communist Party (KKE) that the Civil War 'was systematically prepared and imposed ... by international imperialism and the native oligarchy'[2] serves as a useful reminder of the extent of British involvement. The emotionally charged nature of the issue and the inaccessibility of source material have until recently obstructed scholarly investigation. The tackling of aspects of the history of the period is now well under way, but an overall view has yet to emerge. The importance of the British component has both historic and historiographical foundations. The strategic necessity of establishing and maintaining a friendly regime in Athens compelled the British to intervene politically and militarily in Greek affairs and at times assume effective control of the country. The historiographical reasons stem from the treatment of the subject by British historians, whose inability to consult Greek sources renders them dependent upon the labours of Greek or Greek-speaking writers.

A brief commentary on some of the most important items in the current literature on the subject can be found in the bibliographical section of this book. Here two points must be stressed in advance. The first is that the availability of several indispensable books is in sharp contrast with the plethora of publications whose conspicuous bias and depressing lack of scholarship classifies them in the category of works which, as has been noted in a different context, 'do nothing but harm to those who allow themselves to regard them with respect'.[3] The second point is that general accounts of British foreign policy before or during the Second World War reserve for Greece a curiously casual approach which leads to gross factual errors, such as the claim that in 1935 there was a monarchist revolt in Greece,[4] or that in 1945 'Britain had the victor's obligations to occupy Japan, Germany, Austria, Venezia Giulia and Greece'.[5] This shortcoming of British overviews which touch upon Greek history is often carried into books on the Cold War.

Inadvertence, however, is not the worst of perils for the unsuspecting. The dangers lurking for those who are unable to consult Greek sources cannot be overstated. Scholars have to work with whatever is available, but this hardly justifies the claim that the book written by C. M. Woodhouse is 'the best assessment of Greece and the beginning of the cold war'.[6] Another historian, also relying heavily on Woodhouse, opines that in 1941–1944 'the British set about a process of reconciliation ... both among exiles in Cairo and London, and among resistance groups in Greece'; and that in December 1944 the Greek communists made 'a serious bid for power, attacking police stations'.[7] For the majority of authors there seems to be no reason for concern over the peculiarities and the particulars of the Greek context, since British records alone are deemed sufficient to account for, and vindicate, British policy.[8]

In my approach I have tried to eschew overly deterministic interpretations. This applies not only to the ubiquitous British 'imperialism', but, more crucially, to the notion that Communist Parties march unwaveringly towards the accomplishment of their malevolent conspiracies. With this lack of preconception, I have attempted to investigate all the possibly relevant evidence, some of which appears in the bibliography on the subject for the first time. The analysis of the Greek policy of the Labour government is based on the Papers of Ernest Bevin, Lord Attlee, Sir Orme Sargent and other top policy-makers, the records of the British Cabinet and its various Committees, the Foreign Office, the War Office, the House of Commons, and the British Press. Things are less fortunate with Greek sources. Government records are subject to the fifty-year rule, a disadvantage I have tried to offset by looking into the private collections deposited with the General Archives of the State in Athens, the published debates of the Greek Parliament and the Greek Press.

The archives of the Greek Communist Party are closed to investigation, but there are published collections of its documents. Though selectively presented by each of the two Greek communist factions, and often with major chronological gaps, there are three good reasons why these collections are invaluable: they do *not* contradict each other, they bring to light hitherto unknown information, and, to a considerable extent, they can be substantiated by a vast body of indispensable memoirs. Special mention must be made of the immensely interesting and sizable chunk of the KKE archives published in exemplary manner by the Greek historian Filippos Iliou in *Avgi*. Sadly, these records only cover the period up to the end of 1947, hence the policy of the KKE in the last two years of the Civil War is the more problematic area; and more sadly, my attempts to secure access to the material still withheld have been fruitless. All evidence has been interpreted in its own terms and with reference to the meaning it had at the time it was deposited in the record. This platitudinous statement is particularly important in the case of the KKE, where anachronisms lie in ambush for those unaware that post-defeat revelations are marred by a polemical and apologetic disposition.

10

This is a piece of diplomatic history written in the firm belief that diplomacy and its history still count. The processes whereby foreign policies are conceived and evolve merit the most thorough of studies for invariably one of their results is the life or death of thousands of people. Students of the history of the modern Greek state know that only too well, and it is one of the aims of this study to show that in the 1940s Greek internal politics was greatly affected by events occurring, and decisions being taken, well beyond the boundaries of that state.

Although the structure of the book is largely narrative, with the six chapters arranged in a chronological order, the sections of each chapter represent thematic and analytical approaches pertaining to the development of the policy of each group. This was a conscious choice made for a number of reasons. Revisionist scholars accuse their traditionalist colleagues of inadequate theoretical basis, only to receive the couter-charge that revisionists lack academic solidity.[9] This book attempts to cut across these mutual recriminations by way of employing what is good in both schools whilst avoiding their more obvious failings. With regard to the need for a theoretical framework, an attempt has been made to seek a more general pattern within which to situate British policy; and on the Greek side, it is emphasized at the outset that the social, economic and political cleavages of the 1930s were instrumental in the clash which erupted in the following decade. On the other hand, this approach, in so far as it can lay any claim to a theoretical basis, has been supplemented by the consultation of virtually all sources pertinent to the subject. It is hoped that this will assist in eschewing deterministic interpretations and tackling the most unwelcome difficulty besetting the study of recent and controversial historical phenomena. In the case of the Greek Civil War, each side – not only in Greece – possesses an arsenal of actual or presumed facts on which it draws freely and selectively whenever suitable. Against this, an interpretation of Anglo-Greek relations based on *established* facts may contribute to a better understanding of the issue and provide an aid to future scholars engaged in a synthetic treatment of the Greek Civil War proper or a wider study of the beginnings of the Cold War.

There is hardly any need to stress that the foreign policy of the British Labour governments of 1945–1951 is a highly controversial subject.[10] A civil war is so by definition, and the Greek experience is no exception. What enhances the difficulties is that Anglo-Greek relations in the 1940s were a major ingredient in the controversy on both sides. The understanding of some periods is beset by the ideological use of words and perceptions, especially when a communist insurgency is concerned. There is no neutral or apolitical vocabulary. Words themselves become a weapon with a view to isolating and confusing enemies, rallying and motivating friends, and enlisting the support of wavering bystanders. Insurgents are called 'bandits', which denies them the legal status of combatants. Their supporters are labelled 'criminals' or 'traitors'. Government forces become 'enemies of the people' or 'mercenaries', governments themselves 'fascist', 'corrupt' or 'puppet regimes'. Attacks by means of surprise and unusual methods are 'terrorism'.[11] In the face of such perceptual straitjackets, a strictly historical approach, based on the evidence, will separate the analytical 'what happened' from the emotive and judgemental 'what should have happened'. Machiavelli instructed Rafaello Girolami that 'occasionally words must serve to veil the facts. But this must happen in such a way that no one becomes aware of it; or, if it should be noticed, excuses must be at hand, to be produced immediately.'[12] Ultimately, everything depends on whether one can defy these instructions.

The pleasant duty of unfolding the roll of debts must necessarily begin with Professor Martin Blinkhorn of the University of Lancaster, without whose initial encouragement this study would have never been conceived, let alone embarked upon and completed. Naturally, my first debt goes to him for his skilful, kind and patient supervision of my doctoral thesis and his unwavering commitment while I was revising it for publication. Professor John Gooch of the University of Leeds and Dr. Stephen Constantine of the University of Lancaster suggested lines of inquiry which would have otherwise eluded me, thus greatly enriching the scope of my inquiry. In Professor Richard Clogg of London University, I found a perceptive examiner of my doctoral thesis whose comments have proved invaluable during the task of revision. A very special debt of gratitude goes to Professor Ole L. Smith of the University of Gothenburg, who not only read an earlier draft of this book and corrected me where I was wrong, but who overall demonstrated enough generosity to exceed my persistent requests. At a late but crucial meeting Filippos Iliou kindly encouraged me and put my thoughts into perspective.

Assistant Professor S. N. Fassoulakis of the University of Athens has given me unsparing moral and practical support ever since I was an undergraduate student of his ten years ago. At that time my aspiration to postgraduate studies was enthusiastically encouraged by Professor S. E. Tsitsonis of the University of Athens, and Professor Costas Evangelidis, now Deputy-Rector of the University of Athens. To all three I express my deep gratitude.

I am greatly indebted to Dr. Christos Loukos who went out of his way to facilitate my research at the Centre for the Study of Modern Greek History of the Academy of Athens, and to the staff of the General Archives of the State in Athens for the very same reason.

For all the advice I have received, no doubt errors of fact and interpretation will remain in the text. These are all mine, and I can only express in advance my regret if I have been unable to understand and benefit from the comments and suggestions of so many scholars.

From the moment they accepted this book for publication, Richard Clark and Lucia Crothall of Ryburn Publishing have been immensely helpful and understanding during times when my own personal circumstances were trying.

My enormous debt to Gillian Mason is both scholarly and personal, but I must try to respect her dislike of sentimental acknowledgements.

My greatest debt of all, however, will remain a silent one, for no word would ever do justice to the contribution of Daphne, Michalis, Dimitris and Evangelia – my family. I can only say that Dimitris, my father, first gave me an early taste for History and then enlightened my understanding of a period which he himself had experienced as a young man. By far the greatest pleasure in writing this book has been the knowledge that in the end it would be dedicated to him.

Thanasis D. Sfikas
Leigh, Lancashire
May 1993

NOTES

1. W. Laquer, *Guerrilla: A Historical and Critical Survey* (London: 1977), p.286.
2. KKE CC, *Syndomi Istoria tou KKE, Schedio, Meros A: 1918–1949* (Athens: 1988), p.285.
3. G.R. Elton, *The Practice of History* (London: 1967), p.58, n.27. These works range from Cold War hysteria to 'new left' and 'eurocommunist' stories. Among the former, D.G. Kousoulas, *Revolution and Defeat: The Story of the Greek Communist Party, 1918–1949* (London: 1965); E. Averoff Tossizza, *By Fire and Axe: The Communist Party and the Civil War in Greece, 1946–1949* (New Rochelle: 1978), E. O'Ballance, *The Greek Civil War* (London: 1966); A.I. Korandis, *Politiki ke Diplomatiki Istoria tis Ellados 1941–1945* I–II (Athens: 1987). Among the latter, D. Eudes, *The Kapetanios: Partisans and Civil War in Greece 1943–1949* (London: 1972); Ch. Chiclet, *Les communistes grecs dans la guerre* (Paris: 1987). Incisive bibliographical remarks in O.L. Smith, 'The Greek Communists 1941–1949: Review Article', *Epsilon: Modern Greek and Balkan Studies* 2 (1988), 77–101, and P. Papastratis, 'I Istoriografia tis dekaetias 1940–1950', *Synchrona Themata* nos. 35–36–37 (December 1988), 183–7.
4. A. Clayton, *The British Empire as a Superpower, 1919–1939* (London: 1986), p.44.
5. R. Ovendale, ed., *The Foreign Policy of the British Labour Governments, 1945–1951* (Leicester: 1984), p.7.
6. W.R. Louis, *The British Empire in the Middle East 1945–1951* (Oxford: 1984), p.94, n.16. The book in question is C.M. Woodhouse, *The Struggle for Greece 1941–1949* (London: 1976).
7. H. Thomas, *Armed Truce: The Beginnings of the Cold War 1945–1946* (London: 1988), pp.541, 543.
8. For instance: A. Bullock, *Ernest Bevin: Foreign Secretary 1945–1951* (Oxford: 1985); D. Dilks, ed., *Retreat from Power: Studies in Britain's Foreign Policy of the Twentieth Century*, II: *After 1939* (London: 1981); V. Rothwell, *Britain and the Cold War, 1941–1947* (London: 1982). A most notable exception, even if only in outlook, is K.O. Morgan, *Labour in Power 1945–1951* (Oxford: 1985).
9. See R.J. Maddox, *The New Left and the Origins of the Cold War* (Princeton: 1973) and W.F. Kimball, 'The Cold War warmed over', *American Historical Review*, 79 (1974), 1119–36.
10. K.O. Morgan, *op.cit.*, p.284.
11. See J. Shy, and T. Collier, 'Revolutionary War', in P. Paret, ed., *Makers of Modern Strategy: From Machiavelli to the Nuclear Age* (Oxford: 1986), p.821.
12. Quoted by A. Koestler, *Darkness at Noon* (Harmondsworth: Penguin Books, 1987), p.135.

I Prolegomena: 1936–1944

The Athenians to the Melians

The standard of justice depends on the equality of
power to compel and … the strong do what they
have the power to do and the weak accept what
they have to accept.

Thucydides, V : 89

British Power Politics in the Interwar Years, 1919–1939

The destruction of the four great empires of central and eastern Europe at the
end of the First World War left a power vacuum which at first seemed to offer
a continuing guarantee of British world authority. In 1919–1920, when no
global order had emerged to challenge the still dominant Western imperialist
system, the British Empire and Commonwealth remained intact and territorially enhanced: at the end of the Paris Peace Conference Britain proved the
indisputable master of the Mediterranean and the adjacent Arab lands, having
a firm grip upon the Gibraltar Straits, the Suez Canal, the strategic stronghold
of Malta and a vast stretch of territory lying from Egypt to the oilfields of
Iran and Iraq.

The wider structure of British world power rested on colonial possessions,
effective domination of a number of technically independent states – the
informal empire – and naval and commercial supremacy in particular regions.
The British viewed their Empire as a maritime trading global system
safeguarded predominantly by sea power, hence their conception of imperial
defence and security rested largely on the Royal Navy. Although the importance of sea communications had already begun to decline, a trend which
accelerated after 1945, throughout the interwar period almost half of the
effective strength of the Royal Navy was kept in the Mediterranean – the
lifeline of the British Empire.

As Greece's strategic position straddled Britain's imperial sea communications and the routes to her vital oil supplies in the Middle East, in the
immediate wake of the First World War Lloyd George had tried to set
up as a British client an enlarged Greek state dominating the eastern
Mediterranean. Britain's prestige and power in the Near and the Middle East
survived the collapse of the vision in the sands of Asia Minor in 1922, and
for almost a decade her regional supremacy was unchallenged. In 1923 the
temporary presence of the Italians at Corfu – that is, on both sides of the
entrance to the Adriatic – and their growing interest in Malta's domestic
affairs indicated that some watch would have to be kept on Fascist Italy, but

any British suspicions were lulled. Impressed by British power, Mussolini made it clear that his ambitions lay more in the Balkans or at the expense of France and her possessions.

What potential opponents failed to realize in the 1920s was that Britain's imperial status and role as a superpower were gradually being eroded by a weakened financial structure, relative industrial decline, the rise of non-European power, mounting challenges from most regions of the Indian and colonial empires, the loosening of ties with the Dominions, and domestic problems arising from economic difficulties. Realization of these weaknesses came only in the 1930s, when Japan, Germany and Italy presented Britain with growing challenge in areas of both her formal and trading empires. The Ethiopian crisis then provided a new strategic commitment in the Mediterranean, an area hitherto considered to present no major risk, and the British Service Chiefs made operational plans for an attack on the Italian Fleet at Taranto by carrier-borne aircraft. At first Alexandria was thought too remote as a base, and plans to use Navarino in western Greece ('Port X') were prepared. Navarino was to be seized forcibly if the Greeks were unwilling to offer it, but in the event it was considered to be too vulnerable and the project was dropped.

For centuries Britain had placed her faith in the balance of power. Her traditional policy in a European war was to utilize her economic resources and navy to shore up Continental allies against any major state threatening the Continental equilibrium. The German occupation of Czechoslovakia in March 1939 and the Italian seizure of Albania in the following month prompted Britain to accept a substantial military commitment to European operations. The quest for allies had started and Greece, by virtue of her strategic position, was to be one of them.[1] The story of Anglo-Greek relations during the Second World War explains in part the upheaval of the 1940s, yet the best part of the explanation lies in the politics and society of Greece.

Greek Politics and Society, 1919–1936

From the birth of Greece as a modern state in the early nineteenth century and up to the 1950s, foreign intervention has been a recurrent theme in her history. The policy of the great powers was determined by their strategic objectives in the eastern Mediterranean and the Balkans, while the case of the 1940s particularly illustrates the interrelation between such regional interests and the internal social, political and economic developments in the country at the receiving end. On account of her strategic geographic location Greece had often been a source of interest and concern for the great powers, yet the extent and rigour of intervention from abroad in the 1940s was also determined by developments inside the country. The seeds of the civil strife of 1945–1949 lay in the interwar period, when underneath a bitter political schism simmered potentially explosive social and economic cleavages. These were exacerbated in 1941–1944 by the intervention of the Axis, then Britain and, in 1947, the United States of America.

Victories in the Balkan Wars of 1912–1913 and territorial expansion elevated Greece into some sort of a Mediterranean power, but the unity of the Greek people resoundingly collapsed shortly after the outbreak of the First World War. On the elite level the root of the National Schism, which marred Greek politics in the interwar years, lay in the differences between King Constantine I and Eleftherios Venizelos, the Prime Minister and leader of the Liberal Party, over the country's foreign policy vis-à-vis the clash between the Entente and the Central Powers. Personal and family ties with Germany, admiration for her military might, and the belief that the newly-acquired lands should be consolidated and absorbed, led the monarch to advocate a policy of neutrality. Venizelos, on the other hand, was a fervent custodian of Greece's historical connection with Britain and in rapport with Lloyd George since 1912. Impressed by British naval strength in the Mediterranean and convinced that the Entente would win the war, the Greek Prime Minister espoused its cause from the start. The British promise of territorial concessions on the coast of Asia Minor, where a sizable Greek population had existed for centuries, fomented Venizelos's determination, and the rupture between the two men swiftly engulfed the entire Greek people.

The National Schism began with the unconstitutional practices of the King, which twice forced Venizelos to resign, and the establishment of a royalist government (1915); it was deepened by the launching of a coup in Thessaloniki by some Venizelist officers (1916), and eventually by the Entente intervention which ejected Constantine I and reinstated Venizelos (1917). With strong backing from Lloyd George, Greece's participation in the war on the side of the Entente was rewarded by the Treaty of Sèvres (1920), which established a sizable Greek enclave in Asia Minor. A few months later, however, war-weary and resentful of the Anglo-French interventions in the domestic affairs of the country, the Greek people voted the Liberal Party out of office. The reinstatement of Constantine I by the royalist government through a patently rigged plebiscite provided the pretext for inter-allied rivalries to break loose. Greece was isolated, and despite Lloyd George's genuine feelings, in 1922 the aspirations of Greek irredentism were buried in the sands of Asia Minor. The retreating soldiers were followed home by more than a million refugees.[2]

The military defeat by the Turkish Nationalists and the uprooting of Hellenism from Asia Minor added more fuel to the National Schism. The Venizelist Colonels Nikolaos Plastiras and Stylianos Gonatas rebelled and forced Constantine I into exile, while five royalist ministers and the Commander-in-Chief of the army were executed as traitors. In 1923, after an abortive royalist counter-coup and an overwhelming Venizelist victory at the polls, George II, son and successor of Constantine I, went to London on leave of absence pending a plebiscite on the constitutional question. This was conducted in the following year, when a majority of 70% voted for the abolition of the monarchy. The ill-fated Greek Republic had come into being.[3]

From its conception, the Liberal Party constituted a contradictory inter-class alliance of the entrepreneurial bourgeoisie with a potentially radical popular mass base. Ultimately irreconcilable interests had temporarily been assuaged and the alliance had been forged around a programme combining irredentism with social – mostly land – reform. Under the Liberal Party, the entrepreneurial bourgeoisie sided with the Entente because the promise of territorial expansion carried the prospects of lasting political domination of that faction and the rationalization of the state, economy and society, for which Britain was the prime model. The Liberals' major opponent, the royalists, later to become the Populist Party, was also a broadly-based inter-class coalition, with diverse elements brought together by common hostility to modern capitalism, the nineteenth-century bonds created between them under the state bourgeoisie (whose auxiliaries and dependants were largely those in the professions, government and personal services), patronage and protection. This heterogeneous, traditionalist and conservative alliance required no specific political programme, being rather dedicated to the defence of entrenched interests at every level of society.

In 1917–1920 the reversal of his earlier labour policies and the sharp decline in the standards of living, coupled with the appeal of neutralist propaganda, crippled Venizelos's working-class support. Yet throughout the interwar years the Liberals continued to draw the bulk of their strength from the most deprived classes, groups and areas, which represented the numerically largest potential base for radical or even revolutionary social movements. The Liberal Party was thus directly vulnerable to any would-be challenge from the Left. After the collapse of the irredentist aspirations in 1922, Venizelos turned to Republicanism and the capitalist modernization of the country as the means to secure the hegemony of the entrepreneurial bourgeoisie. The Republic was established in 1924, and shortly afterwards land reform and the settlement of the refugees were completed. By the early 1930s, however, the dream of sustained industrial expansion was shattered by the Great Depression, which primarily hit the Venizelist entrepreneurial bourgeoisie. The latter deserted the Liberal Party and rallied behind the Populists, whose reassuring image of conservative house-keeping and economic consolidation seemed to hold the promise of security and stability.[4]

After the recognition of the Republic by the Populist leader Panayis Tsaldaris in 1932, Venizelos declared that the regime and the past were no longer the issues and conducted the election of the following year on the basis of economic policies, where his record had been poor. The Populist victory was followed by an abortive coup by the republican General Plastiras, a royalist attempt to assassinate Venizelos, and, in the end, by increasing talk among government circles of the restoration of the monarchy. This prompted Venizelos and some republican army officers to launch a large-scale coup on 1 March 1935, but that also ended in a shambles. As a result, restoration became a reality when, in November of that year, George II regained his throne through a plebiscite grotesquely falsified even by Greek standards.[5]

After the electoral defeat of 1933, polarization over the question of the regime appeared to offer the Liberal Party the only remedy to a possible break-up of its inter-class coalition. By opting for polarization Venizelos effectively destroyed the chances of a lasting compromise with his opponents. The prospect of civil war, by no means remote, could thus only be averted by

18

the emergence of a third force. In the wake of the March 1935 coup the eminent Liberal Georgios Papandreou broke away and founded the Republican Party, but his attempt, like that of the republican National Unity Party of Professor Panayiotis Kanellopoulos, failed for lack of concrete and novel programmes. The actual third force was the Left.[6]

From 1918 to 1931 the Greek Communist Party (KKE) was gradually transformed from the original mould of a social-democratic mass party to the Bolshevik model. Bitter factional struggles and assorted purges came to a halt in 1931, when the Comintern appointed a new leadership under Nikos Zachariadis. Three years later he was elected Secretary, and in 1935 Secretary-General and leader of the Party. The KKE was born out of the early defection of radical labour from Venizelism, whereas the Agrarian Party (AKE) grew out of highly rising expectations among the beneficiaries of the Liberal land reform and the rural refugee settlement – the new smallholders. Though in the 1920s factionalism and a fragile organizational structure prevented the AKE from championing the peasants' cause, the concrete challenge of the Left emerged during the 1928–1932 Venizelos government. The impact of industrialization and the limited immediate benefits of the Liberals' agricultural policy greatly expanded the field for radical agitation and paved the way for further inroads into Venizelist support. Venizelos responded by elevating anti-communism into the official state ideology. *Any* radical agitation was branded illegal and met with police repression.[7]

Until the mid-1930s the KKE had placed itself on the periphery of Greek politics through its own sectarianism and its reluctant advocacy, following Comintern dictates, of an autonomous Macedonian state. Ironically, the 80,000 Slavo-Macedonians of Greek Macedonia, whom the Greek state often harassed, had not aligned themselves with the KKE, as that would have further aggravated their position.[8] These self-inflicted handicaps were removed in 1934–1935 with the abandonment of the autonomist policy and the adoption of the Popular Front strategy, which enabled the KKE to seize the opportunity afforded by the failure of bourgeois reconciliation. The abortive Venizelist coup of March 1935 demolished the barriers between the Liberals and the Left, for the ensuing anti-Venizelist repression was directed against what was dubbed 'Venizelocommunism'. At the grassroots level spontaneous fraternization became a reality, as republicans of all shades experienced the police brutality which had hitherto been reserved for communists. Moreover, in response to the imminent threat of restoration, a united republican front officially materialized on a national level in the autumn of 1935, when a co-ordinating committee was set up including the entire spectrum from the Liberals to the KKE.[9]

Uneasy at the unholy alliance with the KKE, and apprehensive of a further leftward move of the Liberals' mass support, from his exile in Paris Venizelos declared a trial recognition of the monarchy; the Liberal Party withdrew from the co-ordinating committee, forcing the minor Venizelist parties to follow suit. After the controversial restoration of George II in November 1935, a general election was proclaimed for the following January. All republican parties refused to join in a Popular Front with the KKE, yet the leftward movement of the republican masses appears to have been only temporarily stemmed; it was possibly an instinctive search for guidance and security against the prospect of a monarchist dictatorship that led them to vote for the Liberals. The election, conducted by a caretaker government, was fair but inconclusive. The Populist Party and its royalist allies won 143 seats and the Liberals and their allies 142, with the fifteen deputies of the Communist-dominated Popular Front holding the balance.[10]

The political haggling that followed resulted in an impasse. Developments were precipitated by Venizelos's and the Liberal Party's recognition of the monarchy (which alienated many republicans), the Sofulis-Sklavainas pact and the deaths of Venizelos, the Populist leader Panayis Tsaldaris, and the caretaker Premier. In February 1936 the uncharismatic new Liberal leader Themistoklis Sofulis concluded with the KKE deputy Stelios Sklavainas a pact which contained a government programme in exchange for which the KKE would vote for Sofulis as President of the Parliament and support a future Liberal Cabinet. Sofulis was elected President of the Parliament, and though the rest of the pact was not implemented, its importance was to last. On the Right it might have strengthened the fear of 'Venizelocommunism', but it also provided an unintentional approval of the leftward movement of the Venizelist masses and broke the ice of the 'Red Scare'; more crucially, by contributing to the formation of a liberal leftist current which favoured co-operation with the KKE, it provided part of the inspiration for the development of the Communist and the entire popular anti-fascist movement. Especially after Venizelos's death and the striking of the republican flag, the refugees' drift to the Left could hardly be contained.[11]

It was probably against this prospect rather than against the fictitious communist 'takeover' that in August 1936 stability came by way of dictatorship. After the death of the caretaker Premier in April, George II, without consulting the party leaders, appointed in his place the retired General Ioannis Metaxas, whose small royalist party commanded seven seats in the Parliament. The majority of the deputies gave him a vote of confidence (or tolerance) and accepted his proposal for a five-month adjournment of the Chamber. On 22 July Sofulis informed the King thathe had reached an agreement with the Populists for the formation of a coalition government, but George II passed it over in silence. Upon the usual pretext – to abort a communist seizure of power – and under the authority of the King, on 4 August 1936 Metaxas suspended a number of key articles of the Constitution and dissolved Parliament.[12] The complicity in the dictatorship of a monarch who owed his throne to a grotesquely falsified plebiscite, and, perhaps more importantly, the failure of the Metaxas regime to destroy the seeds planted in 1935–1936, would cast a formidable shadow on subsequent events.

The Embroilment: Anglo-Greek Relations 1936–1944

In view of several important differences with Nazi Germany and Fascist Italy the Metaxas regime does not qualify as fascist, yet the Greek dictator certainly imitated some of their trappings. In emulation of Hitler's Third Reich, he set his heart upon founding the 'Third Hellenic Civilization' after Ancient Greece and Byzantium. It was a spiritual concept which stood in marked contrast with the economic and social backwardness of an agricultural country heavily dependent on the western industrial centres. The theoretical pundits of the regime were enchanted by Nazi Germany and argued that the enforcement of discipline upon the Greeks, to which the dictatorship aspired, should be made along the lines of the Nazi model. For a start, thousands of communist and bourgeois opponents were thrown into gaol or banished in barren Aegean islands, while even Sophocles's *Antigone* fell victim to state censorship.[13] The soundings of the German *Antikomintern* and the *Gestapo* to the Greek Police for co-operation in the crusade against Bolshevism, and the visits of eminent Nazis – including Joseph Goebbels – to Greece signified the desire for a rapprochement between the two states.

Apart from the ideological sphere, German influence in Greece was also evident in the economic plane. No less than 35.3% of total Greek exports were directed to Germany, and imports from there amounted to 26.2% of the total. The corresponding figures for Anglo-Greek trade were 10% and 13.3% respectively, but Britain's economic foothold in Greece lay in the existence of British companies in crucial sectors of the Greek economy and in her participation in Greece's public debt. Britain was the main creditor, with the British bond-holders' share in the overall Greek public debt amounting to 67.42%.[14]

Britain's attitude towards Greek domestic upheavals in the late 1930s was conditioned by the mounting world crisis. London had rejoiced at the restoration of the profoundly Anglophile George II, who was deemed the cardinal safeguard of British interests in Greece. Metaxas was seen as a lesser man, though useful on account of his willingness to co-operate with Britain. Indeed, the lack of a mass fascist movement left the dictator with the backing of foreign banking capital – predominantly British – and its political representation in the monarchy and the military. Moreover, his awareness of British sea power and the King's predilections had impelled Metaxas to ignore his own ideological leanings and opt for the preservation of the British connection. In 1938 his proposal for an alliance was rejected by a British government reluctant to enter fresh commitments, but in April 1939, a few days after the Italian occupation of Albania, Britain herself offered Greece a guarantee of her territorial integrity if she stood up against a would-be aggressor. With the outbreak of war in September Metaxas pursued a policy of neutrality, but a series of Italian provocations boded ill for the future.

Driven by his aspirations for an independent Mediterranean and Balkan policy for Italy, Mussolini attacked Greece on 28 October 1940. The common cause united the Greeks, who flocked to the colours by the thousands amid a wave of national exaltation. The invasion turned sour for Mussolini as the outnumbered Greek army halted the Italian advance and launched a successful counter-attack deep into Albanian territory. For fear of provoking Hitler, in January 1941 Metaxas declined an offer by Churchill to commit British troops to Greece, but his death at the end of the month and the tightening German grip on the Balkans forced the Greeks to change their minds. A British expeditionary force of 57,000 men was sent to Greece, but neither that nor the Greek army was any match for the Germans.

In order to secure his Balkan flank before the onslaught on the Soviet Union, on 6 April 1941 Hitler invaded Greece. As the British and Greek troops were overrun by the Germans, the Greek government and military were overrun by defeatism. On 18 April Metaxas's successor in the premiership, the banker Alexandros Koryzis, committed suicide and was succeeded by another banker, Emmanuel Tsouderos. Two days later, as the defensive effort was swiftly disintegrating, without government authorization General Tsolakoglou negotiated an armistice. Within days Athens was occupied by the Germans, while George II, Tsouderos's cabinet and the bulk of the British force had fled to Crete with the intention of holding on there. After a massive airborne offensive the island fell to the Germans in late May, and the King, his government and the British and Greek forces withdrew to Egypt. The advent of summer 1941 found Greece under tripartite German, Italian and Bulgarian occupation, with General Tsolakoglou premier of a puppet government in Athens. George II and his government established themselves in London bent on representing the nation.[15]

The Greek-Italian war of 1940–1941 appears as a brief and comparatively positive interlude between the years of dictatorship and the rigours of occupation. The principal aspects of the new regime were exploitation and terror. As the economic and financial resources of the country were put in the hands of the invaders to meet war needs, the already ailing Greek economy plummetted to a point of no return. In the winter of 1941–1942 starvation claimed nearly 100,000 victims, whereas black marketeers were embarking on the process of amassing large fortunes. The setting of plunder and dilapidation was completed by the introduction of harrowing measures which aimed at halting the will to resist. Many Greeks defied the death penalty and assisted stranded British soldiers to flee to the Middle East, and in early May 1941 their unfortunate colleagues who had been captured by the Germans were cheered by the crowds in the centre of Athens. By the end of the same month acts of sabotage were reported from various quarters of the country, yet in these early stages resistance was spontaneous and owed everything to the boldness of a few individuals and groups who felt that the struggle against the Axis had to be kept alive. If that was to evolve from a feeling to a reality engulfing the whole of Greece and assume a form capable of harassing the occupiers effectively, a concrete force was needed to provide the drive.[16]

Although the KKE had survived the repression under Metaxas, the advent of the occupation found most of its leadership in gaol. Many remained there, some escaped, few were released, whilst Zachariadis himself, the Secretary-General, was transferred to Dachau. Even so, in early July 1941 the Sixth Plenum of the Central Committee issued a call for the creation of a national liberation front to fight the occupiers, defend the beleaguered Soviet Union, and form a provisional *all-party* government which would restore democratic liberties and defend Greece 'from any foreign imperialist power'.[17] Throughout the summer negotiations were conducted, but the Populists abhorred any co-operation with the communists, whilst Liberals of all shades regarded organized resistance as untimely or irrational. Thus on 27 September 1941 the KKE, the Agrarian Party (AKE), the small Socialist Party (SKE) and the Union for People's Democracy (ELD) formed the National Liberation Front – EAM – which became the biggest mass movement in Greek history and one of the biggest in occupied Europe. As declared by the signatories, the aims of EAM were the liberation of the country, elections for a constituent assembly, and the protection of the people's right to decide for themselves on their future form of government against 'any reactionary attempt'.[18]

Under the political and organizational aegis of the KKE, the National Liberation Front grew rapidly. Diffuse and amorphous as it may have been, the radicalized republicanism of the 1930s and the hegemonic drive of the KKE combined into a massive popular movement. The claim of its leadership that by October 1944 EAM had 1,500,000 members may be exaggerated, yet no doubt the movement could boast hundreds of thousands of members and an unknown number of unregistered sympathizers.[19] Several EAM functional offshoots provided different sections of the population with specific media for mass participation in the resistance. By far the most important was the National People's Liberation Army – ELAS: a word shrewdly chosen for, when pronounced, it was the very Greek word for Greece (Ellas). The first guerrilla bands took to the mountains in early 1942 under the guidance of Aris Velouchiotis (nom de guerre of Thanasis Klaras), a controversial communist who became the fighting genius of EAM's military wing. From March 1943 ELAS was under a tripartite command structure which consisted of the erstwhile Venizelist Colonel Stefanos Sarafis, one of the key participants in the March 1935 coup, a Political Commissar, and Aris Velouchiotis as the *Kapetanios*, or political and military adviser.[20]

In 1941–1942 several other resistance organizations emerged, including the National Republican Greek League (EDES). Republican and socialist in its persuasion, EDES was nominally headed by General Plastiras – the specialist in republican coups who had exiled himself in France after the abortive one of 1933 – and actually by General Napoleon Zervas. EDES was second only to EAM, but it never reached the mass appeal of the latter.[21] The assertion of authority on the part of EAM/ELAS was often accompanied by ruthlessness, but none the less the movement *did* enjoy mass popular support. Apart from the radicalization process of the previous decade, in the early 1940s the KKE managed to mobilize effectively large segments of the urban and rural population, whilst many Greeks were impressed by the vigour and achievement of EAM's administration in areas under its control. EAM held out the prospect of a different future by putting into practice a system of local self-government and popular justice which met the needs of an overwhelmingly peasant society. It improved communications and educational and health facilities, and even introduced theatrical performances. Women, who had hitherto dwelt on the fringes of Greece's patriarchical society, suddenly found themselves emancipated. Revolutionary sermons against private property were absent from the EAM programme, which was geared to the model of a society of smallholders and producers organized in self-administering units with the full participation of all citizens. It is characteristic that the non-communist EAM leader and Economics Professor Angelos Angelopoulos found the KKE platform – which envisaged a bourgeois democratic regime for postwar Greece, to be followed by a peaceful and democratic approach to socialism – 'in many points very conservative'.[22]

A major reason for the successes of EAM/ELAS was the bankruptcy of George II, his government, and the traditional parties. The latter opposed EAM not so much for fear of a Bolshevik Greece as in despair at the prospect of a mass movement that would lie beyond their grip. Traditional reliance on clientelism and patronage had deprived the old parties of the apparatus needed for mass mobilization, and whatever means they might have had in this respect had evaporated during the forced inertia under Metaxas. Their vote of confidence in him in 1936 had compromised them in the eyes of many Greeks, hence their concern was how to rehabilitate themselves. The Liberals, in particular, were confronted with the same dilemma as experienced in the mid-1930s, between a rapprochement with the KKE or an all-bourgeois alignment with the royalists. Since both big parties considered resistance to be either impossible or unnecessary – and in both cases dangerous – they rebuffed EAM's proposals for co-operation and temporarily united in a republican manifesto calling for a plebiscite on liberation. But their predicament was short-lived. From the second half of 1943 British hostility to EAM held out the prospect of their resurrection – albeit at an onerous price; conversely, their possible alignment with Britain would represent an excellent portent for British aims.[23]

Britain's policy aimed at the restoration of her influence in postwar Greece and the establishment of a friendly regime that would underpin her imperial position by safeguarding sea communications, the routes to India and the oilfields of the Middle East. The principle remained unaltered but the origins of the threat were recast. In May 1944, when it became obvious that the future foe to guard against was the Soviet Union, the War Office warned accordingly:

> Our long term political and military objects are to retain Greece as a British sphere of influence and to prevent Russian domination of Greece which would gravely prejudice our strategic position in the Eastern Mediterranean.[24]

In this light, Winston Churchill and the Foreign Office demonstrated an apostolic zeal in supporting the return of George II. Churchill considered the Greek monarch as the indisputable custodian of Greece's British connection, hence his restoration became the long-term strategic objective with regard to Greece. The two men had established a strong personal relationship during the years of the Republic (1924–1935), when George II had lived in exile in London, and they belonged to the same masonic lodge. Churchill considered the monarchy as a more suitable regime for the Balkans, and in the case of George II he could spice his predilection with a curious personal obligation to him as the head of a state which had valiantly fought on Britain's side in 1940–1941: Greece, in fact, had at that time been Britain's *only* ally.[25]

Yet the British had realized that the King's complicity in the Metaxas dictatorship and the fact that he owed his throne to a patently rigged plebiscite had led to a massive proliferation of republicanism among Greeks. Shortly after the battle of Crete the BBC was flooded by directives from the Foreign Office to propagandize the royal cause. The British fully supported George II and his government under Tsouderos, but in order to render their policy marketable, they put pressure on the Greek government to proclaim the constitutional basis of the monarchy and its own liberal complexion.[26] Dwelling in London and cut off from the realities of occupied Greece, the King was primarily concerned with his immediate return on liberation, whereas his cabinet was preoccupied with postwar territorial claims. Though aware of the weaknesses of the government-in-exile, the British realized that the need to guard the monarchy and conduct effective propaganda required the existence of some government. Tsouderos, a former Liberal deputy, minister, and Governor of the Bank of Greece, was such a dedicated Anglophile that the Foreign Office had favoured him as Metaxas's successor. Following his assumption of the premiership, he professed his loyalty to the King, and in early 1942, under British pressure, he and George II reluctantly promised the restoration of constitutional liberties and ejected from the government those associated with the Metaxas regime. It appeared then that British policy had become marketable.[27]

In Churchill's words, Britain had thus 'definitely established' her relations 'with the lawfully constituted Greek Government headed by the King'. Soon, however, this raised formidable difficulties for her policy towards the Greek Resistance. Until early 1943 British concern focussed on EDES, which, under the nominal leadership of Plastiras, was regarded as the prime menace to the King's cause. Ample information existed about EAM/ELAS, but British policy-makers thought that the National Liberation Front and the Communist Party were two separate things, that the former had managed to contain the latter, and that the KKE had been so gravely depleted by Metaxas that it was incapable of posing a significant threat.[28] In early 1943 this conception appeared to change, as Lieutenant-Colonel E. C. W. Myers and Major C. M. Woodhouse, who led the British sabotage mission *Harling* to Greece, reported more accurate impressions. With the KKE as its dominant component, EAM/ELAS was by far the largest resistance organization, and it was keeping a vigilant eye on Greece's postwar politics; as for the King, there was a widespread demand among Greeks that he should not return unless a plebiscite had decided his fate. Being at odds with official British policy, these reports were ignored in London. However, on 9 March 1943 General Zervas was induced by the British to pledge his support to the King and accept his return even without a plebiscite *if Britain so wished*. From then on the British started to build up the strength of EDES as a counterpoise to EAM/ELAS.[29]

In an attempt to reconcile the republican pursuits of the resistance – for Zervas had concealed his volte-face even from his closest associates – in August 1943 Myers led a guerrilla delegation to Cairo, the new seat of the King and his government. EAM, being by far the largest organization, held four out of the six seats of the delegation, with EDES and Colonel Dimitrios Psarros's National and Social Liberation (EKKA) occupying the other two. The desirable objects – national unity to be evinced in the formation of a broad government including representatives of the Resistance and a common statement on the position of the King – stumbled over the demands put forward by the guerrilla delegates. The first, that the King should not set foot in Greece before a plebiscite, was accepted by the opportunist Tsouderos and his government but met with dogged opposition from the man concerned.

George II sought advice from Churchill and Roosevelt, then at Quebec. Both men – Roosevelt following Churchill's lead despite the advice of the State Department that restoration might even lead to civil war – urged him to defy the demand and stand firm. An attempt by the British to dispose of the guerrilla delegates by shipping them back to Greece was thwarted by the latter's appeal to Tsouderos. The second demand, that the portfolios of War, Justice and the Interior be granted to the guerrilla nominees, who should exercise their duties from within Greece, was instantly turned down by both the King and the government. At that moment the Cairo Mission became a fool's errand, and by mid-September the guerrilla delegates were back in Greece.[30]

EAM was frustrated and embittered by Britain's determination to reinstate the King notwithstanding the wishes of the Greeks. This conviction played its part in the outbreak of hostilities between ELAS and EDES in October 1943. The Germans launched mopping-up operations in western Greece while Zervas had concluded a truce with them. ELAS accused EDES of collaboration – a charge not wholly groundless, though 'co-existence' would be a more accurate term – and attacked it. This miniature civil war, which provided evidence of EAM's determination to dominate the resistance, ended in February 1944 with EDES confined to Epirus and ELAS in control of the greater part of the country. Apart from this military gain for EAM, however, the outstanding political issues remained unresolved.[31]

More ominous than the clash between ELAS and EDES were the new British tactics in the wake of the Cairo Mission. Bent on putting George II back on his throne and anticipating a coup by EAM, in late September 1943 Churchill began preparations for military intervention in Greece in the event of German evacuation. For the time being an attempt would be made to appease republican opinion and contain EAM by political means. A key figure in the pursuit of the latter task was Reginald Leeper, the British ambassador to the Greek government-in-exile. An Australian who had entered the Foreign Office during the First World War, Leeper had formerly served at the British propaganda office (Political Warfare Executive), where his labours had forced Joseph Goebbels to label him as his 'most dangerous opponent in the Foreign Office'. By November 1943 Leeper had amassed a pile of reports from Greece which testified to the unpopularity of the King and pointed out that any attempt to reinstate him would meet with active opposition. The ambassador suggested to his government that it break instantly with EAM, induce George II to proclaim that he would not return to Greece until after the settlement of the constitutional question, and appoint the Archbishop of Athens Damaskinos as Regent. Since this tactical manoeuvre was not intended to forestall the strategic objective but to smooth its way, the British government accepted it. The opposition of the King, however, who felt that a Regency 'might exclude him from Greece for what seemed to him an indefinite period', aborted the scheme.[32]

Following the failure of the opportunity to subvert EAM by eroding its unity from within, Leeper and Tsouderos came up with a new device aimed at the formation of a national government which would include EAM as a minority partner. In the last days of 1943 the bourgeois parties had rebuffed two EAM appeals for a national government, and in January 1944 Tsouderos entered into negotiations with them in order to obtain their support and then haggle with the National Liberation Front from a position of strength. There was a unanimous consensus among the parties regarding the suggestion to appoint Damaskinos as Regent until a plebiscite had solved the constitutional question, but the King and his patron were adamant. When informed of the stance taken by the politicians towards George II, Churchill cabled to Leeper that the monarch could not be discarded 'to suit a momentary surge of appetite among ambitious émigré nonentities', nor could Greece find 'constitutional expression in particular sets of guerrillas, in many cases indistinguishable from banditti'. 'If necessary', Churchill was prepared to 'denounce these elements and tendencies publicly in order to emphasize the love Great Britain has for Greece'.[33]

Negotiations reached a stalemate, and it was the independent initiative of EAM that precipitated events. After its appeals to the political parties had fallen on deaf ears, on 10 March 1944 EAM set up the Political Committee of National Liberation (PEEA) under the much-respected socialist Professor Alexandros Svolos. The tasks of PEEA were the co-ordination and leadership of the struggle for liberation, the administration of the large areas under EAM/ELAS control, and the continuation of the efforts towards the formation of a government of national unity.[34] For Tsouderos and his ministers this represented a challenge which was stepped up in April, when the Greek armed forces stationed in Egypt mutinied, demanding the formation of a national government based on PEEA. In the ensuing crisis Tsouderos was forced to step down, but his successor, Sofoklis Venizelos, son of Eleftherios, proved equally incapable of handling the situation. In the event the mutinies were suppressed after Churchill defied the advice of the British military to refrain from even the threat of force and issued personal orders for firm action. All left-wing and republican elements were purged and nearly half of the 18,500-strong army was put into internment camps. A total of 2,500 men formed the Third Mountain Brigade, a unit of staunch right-wing and monarchist convictions which a few months later was deployed against ELAS. Some of the leaders of the mutiny received capital punishment, but their sentences were commuted in order to avoid ill-feeling.[35]

While the British might thus have furnished the Greek government with a suitably qualified army, the task of bringing EAM/ELAS to heel remained elusive. The opportunity to make a fresh start in this direction was provided by the arrival in Cairo on 15 April 1944 of Georgios Papandreou, the eminent former member of the Liberal Party and, since 1935, leader of the less eminent Republican Party. The newcomer impressed the King and Leeper with his personality, oratorical skills and fresh knowledge of the situation inside Greece, and as he possessed the desirable virtues of republicanism and anti-communism, it was decided that he should replace Venizelos. Once Churchill's approval was obtained, Papandreou overcame the protests of the other Greek politicians at Cairo – who found his eagerness to assume the premiership rather distasteful – and in the last days of April 1944 he was sworn in as head of a government literally 'British made'.[36]

At Papandreou's invitation, delegates of all parties and resistance organizations were summoned to the Lebanon, where a conference would decide on the formation of a government of national unity: EAM would either have to accept its relegation to the status of a minor partner or find itself faced with a united bourgeois front backed by Britain. Even so, Papandreou and the rest of the political leaders derived any authority they might command almost exclusively from British support, whereas EAM could count on its over-whelming political and military strength inside Greece. The Greek Prime Minister and the British wooed the traditional parties, which rallied behind them because they realized that British policy held out the promise of terminating their life on the fringes of Greek politics. The EAM delegates, on the other hand, arrived in the Lebanon with explicit instructions from the KKE leadership – Giorgis Siandos and Yiannis Ioannidis – to demand a temporary settlement of the constitutional question by way of a Regency, and half the ministries of the government-to-be for EAM. Leeper, whose intervention in what he called 'purely a Greek discussion' caused some caustic comments from his US colleague Lincoln MacVeagh, soon found out that the anti-EAM front he had hoped for had come into being. On the eve of the conference all representatives visited him and inquired whether Britain would object to their adoption of a tough line against EAM by denouncing its excesses and demanding the dissolution of ELAS.[37]

During the conference Papandreou's onslaught on EAM forced its delegates onto the defensive. Their demands were never put forth, and on 20 May 1944 they subscribed to the Lebanon Agreement, which, *inter alia*, placed all guerrilla formations under the command of a 'government of national unity', in which EAM was allotted five minor portfolios. As to the King's fate, the Agreement simply stressed the need for order and freedom after liberation, so that the people could decide on the issue and the government they wanted. Leeper himself noted that this clause was worded 'in very general terms' and that any decision in this respect was deftly deferred until after liberation.[38] Yet the Central Committee of EAM was not prepared to write itself off and decided to drive a hard bargain by refusing to take up the ministries allotted to it. After several weeks of haggling, in late July EAM stated its willingness to enter the government on condition that Papandreou was replaced. The latter readily assented provided that he became Vice-Premier and Foreign Minister, for he viewed himself as an 'important national figure' and the single indispensable entity within the Greek political world.[39]

28

His resignation was called off by Churchill, whose minute to Eden revealed the extent of British support for Papandreou against the wishes of EAM:

> We cannot take a man up as we have done with Papandreou and then let him be thrown to the wolves at the first snarlings of the miserable Greek banditti ... Either we support Papandreou, *if necessary by force as we have agreed*, or we disinterest ourselves utterly in Greece.[40] [Emphasis mine]

Subsequently Churchill's determination to resort to arms, if need be, to support Papandreou would be a bitter revelation for EAM. For the time being, in mid-August 1944 EAM cabled to Cairo the names of its ministers. As the KKE explained to its organizations, the decision to join Papandreou's government was prompted by the dilemma between participating as a minority partner or staying out and incurring charges of obstructing national unity. In other words, EAM was 'forced' to join in.[41] This was not enough for Papandreou and the British, who wanted to ensure that in the time-lag between the German withdrawal and the establishment of the government in Athens EAM would not send ELAS marching about in the capital. On 26 September 1944 EAM appended its signature to the Caserta Agreement, whereby ELAS and all other guerrilla forces were placed under the order of the Greek government, which in turn placed them under the order of Lieutenant-General Ronald Scobie, Commander of the British troops which would accompany the government back to Greece. The agreement also stipulated that no action was to be taken in Athens except under direct orders from Scobie, and that the Security Battalions – set up by the collaborationist premier Ioannis Rallis in late 1943 and equipped by the Germans to fight the Resistance – were enemy units.[42]

When liberation came in mid-October 1944, the British and the Greek bourgeois parties had thus managed to contain EAM by granting it a meagre legalization as a lesser partner in the 'government of national unity'. If the principal assets of EAM were its mass popular support and ELAS, there was little the British could do about the former; as for ELAS, however, the Caserta Agreement ensured that the left-wing guerrillas would have to take orders from a British general. The consequences of this would soon become obvious, but if the leadership of EAM had opted for co-operation with their opponents, as suggested by their endorsement of the Lebanon Agreement, failure to agree at Caserta would revive the prospect of denunciation on the grounds of preventing national unity.

The story of EAM supports the thesis that, with the exception of Mao Tse-tung, neither the victors nor the victims of the Second World War anticipated the importance and the scale of the resistance organizations which opposed the Axis. The diversity of these movements makes all generalizations hazardous, but, none the less, two strategies seem to have developed: conservative resistance to restore the former regime, as in the Soviet Union, and revolutionary resistance to take power from an exiled regime, as in Yugoslavia.[43] EAM falls within the larger and diffuse category of European resistance movements which generally accepted coordination by exiled governments in order to obtain allied support and expedite German defeat, but also kept an eye on the postwar politics of their nations. EAM's eye was vigilant, often impatient and at times malevolent, which may in part be attributed to the frustrations of prewar Greek politics; but especially from 1943 onwards, the question was whether EAM would accept that Churchill determine Greece's political and social regime.

Whilst not irrevocably forfeiting any part of its strength, at the Lebanon and Caserta EAM committed itself to a course which curtailed its ability to manoeuvre with minimum peril. While it still relied upon the pillars of mass popular support and ELAS, EAM entered the government and placed its army under the command of a British general. This fact is intriguing and open to multiple explanations. Soviet counsel played its part, as the Soviet Embassy in Cairo made it clear to the EAM delegation that the Lebanon Agreement was a positive development and that the Left should enter the Papandreou government. Then, in late July 1944, a Soviet Military Mission under Lieutenant-Colonel Grigori Popov arrived at the ELAS HQ and, at least with its wary and distrustful attitude, it must have further tempered KKE intransigence. More importantly, however, the KKE found itself under enormous pressure from its partners in EAM to join the government, which was also the desire of the rank-and-file; Svolos, in particular, threatened to resign from the PEEA presidency should the KKE insist on keeping out. Finally, some uncertainty among the communist leadership as to British military intentions must have also played its part in the decision.[44]

Ironically, the Soviet factor entered the picture on invitation by Churchill. Alarmed since spring 1944 by the advance of the Red Army in central and south-eastern Europe, the British Prime Minister approached Stalin with a view to striking an agreement whereby the Soviets would be given a free hand in Romania and in return allow Britain to take the lead in Greek affairs. Stalin made his acceptance of the plan conditional upon the approval of Roosevelt, and the US President was persuaded by Churchill to give his blessing to what he saw as a provisional wartime arrangement of a three-month duration.[45] This was done in July 1944, ten months after Churchill had decided to send British troops to Greece. On 8 August Eden reinforced the case on the grounds that EAM would set up a government which would bring Greece 'under Soviet domination'. On the following day the War Cabinet approved the despatch of 6,000 troops, and Roosevelt and Stalin raised no objections.[46]

Churchill could still find no peace of mind. Overwhelmed by the nightmare that Soviet ambitions might be directed towards spheres he regarded as British, he felt the need for a personal meeting with Stalin. That took place in Moscow in mid-autumn. On the evening of 9 October 1944 the two men concluded the notorious Percentages Agreement on the Balkans, which granted Britain 90% dominance in Greece at the price of an equal percentage for Stalin in Romania. Though Churchill's histrionic account of the story has been successfully de-dramatized and (less successfully) placed in doubt, Stalin's 'tick' on Churchill's 'naughty document' shows that the Kremlin cared little about the prospects of the KKE. For Anglo-Greek relations, the significance of the story lies more in the disclosure of Churchill's determination to have a free hand in securing Greece's location in the British postwar sphere of interest.[47]

The first British troops had landed in the city of Patra, in north-western Peloponnese, one week earlier than the Moscow meeting. There is a general consensus that EAM could have easily seized power during the few days which intervened between the German withdrawal and the advent of the British troops and the Greek government in Athens, and that in such an eventuality 'there would have been little that Churchill could have done about it, whatever his determination to frustrate EAM'.[48] Nine years after its Sixth Congress of 1935, the KKE remained faithful to the Popular Front strategy and relied heavily on its following among the Greek people and the strength of EAM/ELAS as the means whereby to meet eventualities and influence developments at the appropriate moment. As Siandos had explained in August 1943 to General Svetozar Vukmanovič (Tempo), and much to the disappoint-ment of Tito's lieutenant, the KKE had opted for an alliance with the republican and democratic forces of Greek politics in order to prevent the return of George II before the conduct of elections, in which the communists were convinced they would fare extremely well; the KKE's struggle for power would be a political one, deferred until after the polls.[49]

More than the military strength of ELAS, it was this political and moral potential of EAM which ruffled its opponents. If the election of January 1936 was anything to go by, Papandreou's party had secured one seat in the Parliament, and now his government owed its existence and any authority that it might command to British support. A people hugely relieved from the horrors of tripartite occupation granted the British soldiers and the govern-ment an unprecedented welcome, yet an unpleasant potential did exist. The spread and record of EAM had acted as a catalyst to the social and political realignments which had begun in the 1930s, and, as a result, by the end of the occupation the traditional power structures had been rendered obsolete and a collective will for change had emerged. Nowhere was this more vividly manifested than in the different prospects held out to the Greeks by the two rival coalitions: to EAM's dream of a radical transformation of Greek society the old political world had no alternative, no vision for the future; only its own dogged fight for survival, for which it needed no programme except for generous British support. In mid-October 1944 a report by the American Office of Strategic Services (OSS) offered the following appreciation of the EAM identity and the results of British policy:

> The movement created by EAM can only be regarded as a fully-fledged revolution. One cannot conceive the situation otherwise.
>
> The EAM movement dominates. There can be no question of repressing it. The ideology it represents and the interests connected with it are so vital that a compromise (i.e. with the traditional order) is the most that can be hoped for. British political manoeuvring has failed and it can only be said that the populace will no longer tolerate it. England has lost ground and will not be able to regain it in the future.[50]

On liberation EAM granted Papandreou and the British a warm welcome, but Churchill's obsession with George II and London's hostility towards the left-wing resistance had fuelled suspicion. According to KKE sources, in the summer of 1944 the Athens organization of EAM had discovered an operational plan against ELAS, worked out by leading members of the Security Battalions, EDES, and the monarchist organization 'X' of Colonel Grivas.[51] Papandreou and the British troops landed in Greece on 18 October. Three days later the royalists complained to the US Embassy that there was 'a serious situation with EAM in Athens already', and that 'only the British troops are keeping it from developing openly'. The Americans were quick to remark that 'the royalist crowd wants this kind of thing, so that a demand for the King's return as a stabilizing factor may eventuate'.[52] Every party had different priorities of which none answered to the demands of the situation: the Populists wanted to promote the King as the saviour of Greece, whereas the Liberals, convinced that Papandreou's failure was inevitable and in the hope of capitalizing on it, kept aloof from all his efforts.[53] As for the Prime Minister who derived his authority from the British, the task was to establish some of his own. With EAM/ELAS prevailing almost everywhere outside Athens, Papandreou and Leeper wanted to curb communist influence by disbanding ELAS and setting up a national army, thus paving the way for elections.[54]

Negotiations commenced and on 26 October Papandreou stated that ELAS, EDES and the Greek forces of the Middle East would be disbanded. Five days later the liberal daily *Kathimerina Nea* reported that the Third Mountain Brigade, the right-wing unit which had been formed in the wake of the April mutinies, would remain intact; on the same day the Greek Prime Minister asked Scobie to arrange for its immediate despatch from Italy to Athens. Papandreou wanted his government to command some respect, especially in view of the tough demobilization negotiations, but the arrival of the Brigade in Athens on 8 November was seen as provocative even by British officials – let alone EAM. Colonel Woodhouse, who three months earlier had strongly advised against such a step, saw it as 'the most important single factor contributory to the loss of faith by EAM/ ELAS'.[55] Papandreou and the British might have been fearful lest EAM attempted an armed seizure of power, but EAM sustained its own permanent and less ill-grounded fear that its opponents aimed at the restoration of the King and the establishment of a conservative regime. Under these premises, the arrival of the Brigade was seen as the first step towards the implementation of such a policy.

Negotiations reached a stalemate, with EAM demanding the demobilization of the Brigade along with ELAS and Papandreou refusing it. Nevertheless, it seems that the Prime Minister was not against an understanding, for on 20 November 1944 he came to an agreement with the KKE Secretary, Giorgis Siandos, whereby ELAS would be disbanded and the officers and men of the Brigade be granted 'generous leave' to visit their homes.[56] Papandreou had realized that he had to find a peaceful solution, if for no other reason than to raise his personal political stock. Yet he found himself entrapped in that his authority was granted to him by the British and therefore he was bound to be susceptible to their demands. While trying to sort out his differences with EAM, he could not possibly know that two weeks *before* his agreement with Siandos, Churchill had sent the following minute to Eden:

In my opinion, having paid the price we have to Russia for freedom of action in Greece, we should not hesitate to use British troops to support the Royal Hellenic Government under M. Papandreou.

This implies that British troops should certainly intervene to check acts of lawlessness. Surely M. Papandreou can close down EAM newspapers if they call a newspaper strike … I fully anticipate a clash with EAM and we must not shrink from it, provided the ground is well chosen.[57]

Since the agreement of 20 November would not work towards this direction, three days later Eden cabled Leeper his objection to the plan on the grounds that 'generous leave' would be tantamount to disbandment, in which case the KKE might launch a coup against a weakened government. Papandreou conformed, and after he informed EAM that the Mountain Brigade would remain intact, negotiations resumed. The situation had reached its most critical phase. On the morning of 27 November Zervas, who was in Athens for talks with Papandreou and the British, called on Leeper; the British ambassador concurred with the leader of EDES that the Prime Minister should 'show his fist'. Immediately afterwards Zervas held a long meeting with Papandreou and, according to the former's diary, the latter agreed to concede nothing that would weaken the anti-EAM forces.[58]

On the evening of 27 November the Premier accepted a plan put forward by two EAM ministers for the integration of the Brigade and a unit of EDES with an ELAS unit equal in number with the total of the other two, while the rest of the guerrilla forces were to be disbanded. On the following morning Papandreou presented Leeper and Scobie with a draft demobilization decree which made no mention of integration of various units but provided for one ELAS and one EDES unit separate and independent from each other as well as from the Brigade. Thus Papandreou enticed the Greek politicians and the British to believe that his own altered version of 28 November was the initial agreement proposed by EAM on the previous evening. When EAM protested and called again for universal demobilization, the Prime Minister objected and Leeper readily assumed that EAM was breaking its own word.[59]

Papandreou's motives in producing this sleight of hand remain obscure. One interpretation could be that overnight he regretted his major concession to the National Liberation Front, either independently or because he feared London's wrath. Alternatively, he may have hoped to secure British approval for his own version – which was presented as EAM's – and then place the Left in an untenable position. If EAM had accepted it, Papandreou would have got things his way; if not, a unique opportunity would have arisen to denounce it for breaking its own word. The communists were opposed to the separation of units, for the ELAS unit would be outnumbered and might be sent to fight the Germans, leaving EDES and the Brigade in control. But the demand for universal demobilization could not be met, for in many quarters Papandreou was deemed to be soft towards the Left. Zervas recorded in his diary that the British military authorities in Athens charged the Prime Minister with 'timidity and want of will' towards the KKE. So did Churchill, who minuted to Eden on 28 November: 'One begins to ask oneself the question, "Are we getting any good out of this old fool at all?"'.[60]

There is little doubt that Churchill pursued an aggressive and uncompromising policy towards EAM in order to get the chance to deal with it by force. Papandreou might have liked to avoid force, but his dependence on British support deprived him of any independence. Whenever he deviated from the desirable course, Churchill and Eden applied correction, though he did not need much of it. With his sleight of hand on 27–28 November Papandreou had accomplished two seemingly incompatible things: he had assured EAM that its suspicions were not ill-founded and convinced everybody that the blame lay on communist shoulders. Thereafter the rupture drew even closer. On the evening of 30 November General Scobie told Zervas that he was determined to impose order on his own, bringing out British armour to patrol the streets of Athens and trying to avoid the deployment of Greek units. On 1 December the EAM Central Committee called for universal demobilization, whereas Scobie ordered ELAS to demobilize according to Papandreou's plan of 28 November. On 2 December the left-wing ministers resigned from the government and EAM called for a mass demonstration on the following day and a general strike on 4 December. Initially Papandreou granted permission only to withdraw it a few hours later, and the Minister of Supply told Leeper that the Cabinet had unanimously agreed to instruct the Police to prevent the demonstration, if need be by force. But the preparations of EAM had gone so far that it was impossible to notify its followers throughout the city to call it off.[61]

On Sunday 3 December 1944 a huge crowd gathered at Syntagma Square, carrying allied and Greek flags, singing resistance songs and bearing no arms. The Police opened fire and killed fifteen, leaving over a hundred wounded. In confirmation of the statement of the Minister of Supply to Leeper, in 1958 the Chief of the Athens City Police revealed that 'on the basis of the responsible orders which I had had, I responsibly ordered the violent dissolution of the attacking [sic] demonstrators'. As soon as the shooting ceased, the communist Secretary-General of EAM Dimitris Partsalidis proclaimed Papandreou an 'outlaw' and asserted that 'the people will fight for liberty without counting their sacrifices'.[62] Ta Dekemvriana – the December Events – had erupted.

What followed showed that the armed clash, though not inevitable, was desirable from Churchill's point of view. On 4 December Athens reserve units of ELAS attacked police stations but EAM carefully eschewed confrontation with the British troops. Leeper urged London that Papandreou should step down in favour of a new deal, and the Greek Prime Minister duly submitted his resignation. Negotiations started and the octogenarian Liberal leader Sofulis, a choice agreeable to all parties, was prepared to form a new government which would have the support of EAM. But on 5 December Churchill cabled Leeper that 'he should force Papandreou to stand on his duty … Should he resign, he should be locked up till he comes to his senses'. Accordingly, Scobie asked Sofulis to support Papandreou's government, and the Liberal leader agreed on the understanding that the Premier would have to go soon.[63] Then, drawing his inspiration from Arthur Balfour's 'celebrated' telegram to the British authorities in Ireland in the 1880s – 'don't hesitate to shoot' – Churchill sent Scobie the following message:

Do not however hesitate to act as if you were in a conquered city where a local rebellion is in progress … We have to hold and dominate Athens. It would be a great thing for you to succeed in this without bloodshed if possible, but also with bloodshed if necessary.[64]

The British troops came in on the morning of 6 December. In the first days of the battle EAM put forward a number of terms for pacification – Britain to stop interfering in Greek internal affairs, establishment of a Regency, a new government and universal demobilization – but Churchill instructed Scobie 'not to give away for the sake of kindness what has been won or can still be won by our troops'. The British Prime Minister went on to define his aim as follows:

The clear objective is the defeat of EAM. The ending of the fighting is subsidiary to this… Firmness and sobriety are what are needed now, and not eager embraces, while the real quarrel is unsettled.[65]

An EAM appeal for the establishment of an international commission comprising representatives of Britain, France, the Soviet Union and the United States to investigate the causes of the conflict was also rebuffed. ELAS was to fight on its own. When asked by British and Greek officials for his opinion of the KKE's actions, Lt.-Col. Popov, the head of the Soviet Military Mission to Greece, contemptuously shrugged his shoulders and said that the Greek communists had neither asked nor listened to the Soviets.[66]

In the first stages of the battle ELAS was riding high owing to the insufficient numbers of its opponents; Scobie commanded one understrength armoured brigade, one paratroop brigade, the Fourth Indian Division and the Third Greek Mountain Brigade – a total of 15–20,000 men. John Colville, one of Churchill's aides, confided in his diary that 'whatever their vices and their political asininity, the Greeks can certainly fight'; two days earlier the same man had felt that 'the inability of these Levantine bandits to postpone their internecine feuds until Germany is defeated is nauseating'.[67] In 1976 General Leonidas Spais, Assistant Minister of War in Papandreou's government, revealed that the British, 'who were behind us and were pulling the strings', suggested the employment of the collaborationist Security Battalions against ELAS; the General accepted it, thereby provoking EAM's rage.[68] On 11 December Churchill received a report from Alexander and Macmillan, who visited the Greek capital, in which the Field Marshal 'asked for stern measures against the rebels and permission to bomb areas inside Athens'. Even two weeks later, when the tide was turning against ELAS, Alexander told Pierson Dixon, Eden's Principal Private Secretary, that

we could go quicker if we stormed our way through the streets with tanks and "Rotterdamed" whole quarters by air bombardment as the Germans and Russians in a similar situation would probably do. But, apart from other disadvantages of such a policy, the troops would refuse to do it.[69]

Reinforced by more than two full-strength divisions brought in from Italy, the British army put ELAS on the defensive. To counter adverse public opinion throughout the world against British military intervention, but also to investigate the situation on the spot, Churchill and Eden flew to Athens on Christmas Eve 1944. The British Prime Minister at last grasped the feeling against George II and agreed to the appointment of Archbishop Damaskinos – whom he had earlier dismissed as a '"pestilent priest, a survival from the Middle Ages"' – as Regent pending a plebiscite on the constitutional question. There was some difficulty with the King, but after threatening that they would ignore him, Churchill and Eden managed to persuade him to accept the appointment of Damaskinos and to promise that he would not return to Greece unless a free plebiscite had invited him to do so.[70]

The Archbishop took office on 30 December, while on 3 January 1945 a new government was formed without EAM under the impeccably republican General Plastiras. The new Prime Minister was of course equally anti-communist, and in an interview with *The Times* special correspondent he denied any possibility of a negotiated truce and asserted that 'the situation could be put right only by force'.[71] Unable to withstand the counter-offensive of the British troops, ELAS retreated from Athens on the night of 4–5 January 1945. A week later an armistice put an end to an exceptionally ugly battle marked by the atrocities committed by ELAS and the rounding-up of thousands of hostages by both sides. On 12 February an agreement was concluded at the seaside resort of Varkiza, forty kilometres south-east of Athens, to ensure the peaceful and democratic development of postwar Greece.

Nobody had desired a shoot-out except Churchill, who since summer 1943 had been unrestrained in his belligerence not only against EAM but also against all those who dared to question his monarchist predilections. The strategic objective of ensuring that postwar Greece take up its position in the British sphere of influence was to be achieved by way of restoring George II to his throne, a tactical pursuit which drew Churchill into an obsessive intervention in Greek politics. In 1943, when it became clear that along with the republican groundswell in Greece, a powerful left-wing resistance movement was growing from the grassroots, British policy successfully tried to set up a united bourgeois front against EAM/ELAS. For their part, the bourgeois parties had been watching from the fringes the mobilization of the masses by EAM, and in order to regain their prewar status they aligned themselves with Britain. For them, the internal threat of EAM lay not in any KKE designs for a proletarian dictatorship, but in the unity of left-wing parties and their appeal to the people on a vigorously reformist platform: that had already been happening in the EAM-controlled areas, where PEEA had revived old bourgeois legislation and institutions.[72]

In *The Eighteenth Brumaire of Louis Bonaparte* Marx wrote that historical events occur twice – the first time as a tragedy, the second as a farce. The Greek political parties reversed the order. In 1936 they had given their vote of confidence to Metaxas, and the General, together with the King, abolished them. In 1944 they put their trust in Britain, and what followed was a tragedy. Their overwhelming dependence on Britain substantially curtailed their freedom to act independently, Papandreou's case providing the perfect illustration. Though an anti-communist of impeccable credentials, he tried to reach an agreement with EAM over demobilization, which was not Churchill's wish. Papandreou was quick to read the signs of the times and accordingly harden his stance towards the Left.

As for EAM, its intolerance towards other resistance organizations was blown out of proportion to show that the communists were bent on seizing power. Yet in early October 1944 ELAS did not do so, though then it would have been an easy task. Relying on its genuine mass support, EAM had rejected confrontation and opted for infiltration. An ELAS Division commander who tried to alert his men to the likelihood of British intervention was sternly reprimanded by Siandos and Ioannidis, while in November 1944 the KKE instructed its members to co-operate with the Allies and try to attract the middle classes in EAM/ELAS.[73] Then, during *Ta Dekemvriana*, ELAS was manifestly ill-prepared for a protracted clash. It started the battle with insufficient supplies and until 10 December it did not attack British troops unless attacked by them. The first regular ELAS units showed up on the following day, but the total of the experienced regulars never exceeded the 25% of the 16,900 left-wingers who fought in Athens. The bulk of the struggle was carried out by reservists, young men whose average age was seventeen, whereas the cream of ELAS under Stefanos Sarafis and Aris Velouchiotis were sent to Epirus against EDES. No attack was made on British troops stationed in other parts of Greece, nor did the ELAS in Athens attempt to capture points of strategic value, such as airfields and warehouses.[74]

The objective of EAM lay in the sphere of a political compromise with the overthrow of Papandreou and the formation of a new government under the Liberal leader Sofulis, who, it was hoped, might prove more pliant. Since August 1944 the KKE leadership seems to have cherished the objective of bringing Papandreou down should more favourable circumstances occur, and it was determined to prevent any further attempts by its opponents to weaken the position of EAM.[75] Overall, however, the policy of the KKE remained one of national unity, and therefore persistently oblivious of its self-defeating element: that it aimed at co-operation with at least some of the forces which would have to be evicted from Greek politics if the transformation of Greece, as envisaged by EAM, was to come about. At the same time the communists showed that they had learned nothing from the experience of 1935–1936, when their endeavours to forge a republican alliance with the Liberals had been thwarted by the latter's compromise with the King. No wiser, the KKE continued throughout the occupation to woo those political forces which had already furnished proof of their unreliability and hostility towards the communists. In the few exceptions when the opponents of the KKE were pliant, the British stepped in to put things right. Perhaps the most crucial British contribution was that of 4–5 December 1944, when Papandreou's offer to make way for the Liberal leader Sofulis was called off by Churchill, who would not let slip the opportunity to come to blows with EAM.

On 4 December 1944 Professor Svolos of EAM told the US ambassador Lincoln MacVeagh that Papandreou had at first been 'personally in accord' with the communists' views on disbanding the Mountain Brigade, but the British 'wouldn't let him comply'. Svolos added: '"The British must give the

Greeks at least the impression that they are a free people."[76] Four days later MacVeagh attempted to define the cause of the trouble in a letter to his President:

the handling of this fanatically freedom-loving country (which has never taken dictation quietly) as if it were composed of natives under the British Raj, is what is the trouble, and Mr. Churchill's recent prohibition against the Greeks attempting a political solution at this time, if a blunder, is only the latest of a long line of blunders during the entire course of the present war.[77]

The legacy of this policy, along with the exacerbated social, economic and political cleavages which had divided Greeks during the interwar years and the occupation, were to weigh heavily upon subsequent events.

NOTES

1. On Britain and the Empire see: A. Clayton, *The British Empire as a Superpower, 1919–1939* (London: 1986); F.S. Northedge, *The Troubled Giant: Britain Among the Great Powers, 1916–1939* (London: 1966); J. Darwin, *Britain, Egypt and the Middle East* (London: 1981); J. Gallagher, *The Decline, Revival and Fall of the British Empire* (London: 1982); M. Matloff, 'Allied Strategy in Europe, 1939–1945', in P. Paret, ed., *Makers of Modern Strategy: From Machiavelli to the Nuclear Age* (Oxford: 1986), pp.677–702.

2. For the National Schism and the campaign in Asia Minor see: G. Leon, *Greece and the Great Powers, 1914–1917* (Thessaloniki: 1973); M. Llewellyn Smith, *Ionian Vision: Greece in Asia Minor, 1919–1922* (London: 1973); IEE: XV, 15–271.

3. For the events leading to the Republic see IEE: XV, 271–81.

4. For a political, social and economic analysis of the interwar years see: G. Mavrogordatos, *Stillborn Republic: Social Conditions and Party Strategies in Greece, 1922–1936* (Berkeley: 1983).

5. For the political developments from 1932 to 1935 see: IEE: XV, 318–26, 358–72.

6. G. Mavrogordatos, *op.cit.*, pp.334–5, 337–44.

7. *Ibid.*, pp.335–337. On the KKE see D. Sarlis, *I Politiki tou KKE ston agona kata tou monarchofasismou (1929–1936)* 3rd edn. (Athens: 1987).

8. *Ibid.*, pp.246–252; IEE: XV, 282–283; KKE CC, *Syndomi Istoria tou KKE, Schedio, Meros A: 1918–1949* (Athens: 1988), pp.55–7; E. Kofos, *Nationalism and Communism in Macedonia* (Thessaloniki: 1964), pp.68–84; D. Sarlis, *op. cit.*, pp.188–96.

9. KKE CC, *op.cit.*, pp.98–108, 112–17; IEE: XV, 358ff; D. Sarlis, *op.cit.*, pp.270–1, 298, 331–43.

10. G. Mavrogordatos, *op.cit.*, p.346; IEE: XV, 365–74; D. Sarlis, *op.cit.*, pp.346–7, 354–60.

11. G. Mavrogordatos, *op.cit.*, pp.347–8; IEE: XV, 375, 377, 395; D. Sarlis, *op.cit.*, pp.365–9.

12. G. Mavrogordatos, *op.cit.*, p.349; IEE: XV, 374–80; G. Dafnis, *I Ellas Metaxi Dyo Polemon II* (Athens: 1955), 431–2; H. Fleischer, *Stemma ke Svastika: I*

Ellada tis Katochis ke tis Andistasis 1941–1944 I (Athens: 1988), 55–8; D. Sarlis, *op.cit.*, pp.378–81.

13. H. Fleischer, *op.cit.*, pp.59–60. For the ideology of the regime see: IEE: XV, 385–91; N. Mouzelis, 'I Ideologia tis Tetartis Avgoustou', *To Vima* (Athens): 3/8/1986; P. Noutsos, 'Synistoses tis ideologias tou kathestotos tis 4is Avgoustou', in N. Svoronos and H. Fleischer, eds., *Ellada 1936–1944: Diktatoria–Katochi– Andistasi* (Athens: 1989), pp.59–69.

14. IEE: XV,398; R. Meissner, 'I Ethnikososialistiki Germania ke i Ellada kata ti diarkeia tis Metaxikis Diktatorias', in N. Svoronos and H. Fleischer, eds., *op.cit.*, pp.50–8.

15. For a brief account see: H. Fleischer, *op.cit.*, pp.60–77. On Anglo-Greek relations, J. Koliopoulos, *Greece and the British Connection, 1935–1941* (Oxford: 1977). For the war against Germany and Italy, IEE: XV, 411–54.

16. The best general accounts of Greece's history during the Occupation are: H. Fleischer, *op.cit.*, and J.L. Hondros, *Occupation and Resistance: The Greek Agony, 1941–1944* (New York: 1983). For British policy see P. Papastratis, *British Foreign Policy Towards Greece During the Second World War, 1941–1944* (London: 1984). For the economic activities, S.B. Thomadakis, 'Black Market, Inflation and Force: The Social Character of Wealth Transfers in the Occupation Economy of Greece', in J.O. Iatrides, ed., *Greece in the 1940s: A Nation in Crisis* (Hanover and London: 1981), pp.61–80.

17. KKE: E.K., V, no.648: Decision of the 6th Plenum, 1/7/1941.

18. *Ibid.*, no.654: The Formation of EAM. Also P. Papastratis, *op.cit.*, p.122; H. Fleischer, *op.cit.*, pp.145–9; J.L. Hondros, *op.cit.*, pp.110–11.

19. G. Mavrogordatos, *op.cit.*, p.349; N. Svoronos, 'Greek History 1940–1950: The Main Problems', in J.O. Iatrides, ed., *op.cit.*, 1–14; L.S. Stavrianos, 'The Greek National Liberation Front (EAM): A Study in Resistance Organization and Administration', *Journal of Modern History* 24 (1952), 44–54; A. Elefandis, 'EAM: Istoria ke Ideologia. Proypotheseis yia mia epistimoniki theorisi tou EAM', *O Politis* 5 (September 1976), 63–8; L. Baerentzen, 'I Laiki Ypostirixi tou EAM sto telos tis Katochis', *O Mnemon* 9 (1984), 157–73.

20. KKE: E.K., V, no. 657: Decision of the 8th Plenum; C.M. Woodhouse, *Apple of Discord* (London: 1948), p.65; H. Fleischer, *op.cit.*, pp.221–52. An invaluable source for ELAS, first published in Greek in 1946, is S. Sarafis, *ELAS: Greek Resistance Army* (London: 1980).

21. GAK: K 197 (Papers of M.I. Myridakis): the EDES Charter. For EDES and the other resistance organizations see H. Fleischer, *op. cit.*, pp.149ff, 237ff, 371–87.

22. PEEA Archives, pp.156–7, 164: sessions 44 and 45 (27 and 28/7/1944); J.L. Hondros, *op.cit.*, pp.115–22; C.M. Woodhouse, *op.cit.*, pp.146–7; L.S. Stavrianos, *op.cit.*, 44–54.

23. J.A. Petropoulos, 'The Traditional Political Parties of Greece during the Occupation', in J.O. Iatrides, ed., *op. cit.*, pp.27–36; P. Papastratis, *op.cit.*, pp.119–20; *idem*, 'Ta astika kommata ke i exoristi elliniki kyvernisi', in N. Svoronos and H. Fleischer, eds., *op.cit.*, pp.529–40.

24. W.O.201/1598: 'Handling of the Greek Situation',6/5/1944.

25. W.S. Churchill, *The Second World War*, V, *Closing the Ring* (London: 1952), 473, and VI, *Triumph and Tragedy* (London: 1954), 100; T.D. Sfikas, '"The People at the Top Can Do These Things, Which Others Can't Do": Winston Churchill and the Greeks, 1940–45', *Journal of Contemporary History* 26 (1991),

307–32; H. Fleischer, *op.cit.*, p.187. Churchill's obsession with the Greek King is manifest in countless records. A general background analysis in P. Addison, 'The Political Beliefs of Winston Churchill', *Transactions of the Royal Historical Society*, 5th series (1980), 23–47. See also F.O.371/33162 R5766: Draft F.O. Letter to Harry Hopkinson (Cairo), n.d. [September 1942].

26.   F.O.371/29840 R6528: F.O. Minute; F.O.371/29853 R7032 and R7557: F.O. Directives to BBC, 14/7/1941 and 14/8/1941; F.O.371/29854 R9369: F.O. Directive to BBC, 25/10/1941.

27.   H. Fleischer, *op.cit.*, pp.172–84; J. Koliopoulos, *op. cit.*, p.80.

28.   W.S. Churchill, *op.cit.*, V, 481; Ph. Auty and R. Clogg, eds., *British Policy towards Wartime Resistance in Yugoslavia and Greece* (London: 1975), pp.171–3; C.M. Woodhouse, 'The National Liberation Front and the British Connection', in J.O. Iatrides, ed., *op.cit.*, pp.83, 87.

29.   F.O.371/37195 R2266: Copy of Zervas's Telegram,13/3/1943. On the increased British aid to EDES see GAK: K 210 (Papers of M.I. Myridakis): Zervas's Financial Report to the Ministry of War, 19/2/1949. Also: C.M. Woodhouse, 'The National Liberation Front', pp.90–2, 96–7; H. Fleischer, *op.cit.*, pp.391–3.

30.   KKE: E.K., V, Appendix, pp.340–1; GAK: K 163 (Papers of I. Petimezas): 'Report from our [EKKA] delegation in Egypt', n.d.; W.S. Churchill, *op.cit.*, V, 474; B.B. Berle and T.D. Jacobs, eds., *Navigating the Rapids, 1918–1971: From the Papers of Adolf A. Berle* (New York: 1973), p.445.

31.   J.L. Hondros, *op. cit.*, pp.197–9; H. Fleischer, 'Contacts Between German Occupation Authorities and the major Greek Resistance Organizations', in J.O. Iatrides, ed., *op.cit.*, pp.54–5; O.L. Smith, '"The First Round"– Civil War during the Occupation', in D.H. Close, ed., *The Greek Civil War 1943–1950: Studies of Polarization* (London: 1993), pp.58–71.

32.   F.O.371/37194 R1869: Greek Intelligence Summary, 8–14/2/1943; F.O.371/37205: Howard to Brig. Hollis, 21/9/1943; W.S. Churchill, *op.cit.*, V, 475; R. Leeper, *When Greek Meets Greek* (London: 1950), p.35; P. Papastratis, *op.cit.*, pp.144–51. For Leeper's background see W.R. Louis, *The British Empire in the Middle East, 1944–1951* (Oxford: 1984), p.83.

33.   W.S. Churchill, *op.cit.*, V, 481: Churchill to Leeper, 9/4/1944; KKE: E.K.,V, 483; P. Papastratis, *op.cit.*, p.160.

34.   KKE: E.K.,V, no.683: Decision of the 10th Plenum, January 1944; *ibid.*, p.215; Y. Ioannidis, *Anamniseis: Provlimata tis Politikis tou KKE stin Ethniki Andistasi, 1940–1945* (Athens: 1979), pp.208–11.

35.   *Churchill–Roosevelt*, no.379: Churchill to Roosevelt, 11/6/1944; P. Papastratis, *op.cit.*, pp.165–72; A. Kitroeff, 'I vretaniki politiki ke to kinima sti Mesi Anatoli', in N. Svoronos and H. Fleischer, eds., *op.cit.*, pp.541–52.

36.   F.O.371/43730 R6820: Leeper to F.O., 28/4/1944; *ibid.*, R6881: Leeper to F.O., 29/4/1944; R. Leeper, *op.cit.*, p.47.

37.   PEEA Archives, pp.85–8; Y. Ioannidis, *op.cit.*, pp.219–22; S. Sarafis, *op.cit.*, p.289; MVR, pp.512, 521; R. Leeper, *op.cit.*, pp.49–50; F.O.371/43730 R7543: Spears to F.O., 12/5/1944; F.O.371/43731 R7652: Spears to F.O., 13/5/ 1944; *ibid.*, R7677: Spears to F.O., 14/5/1944.

38.   PEEA Archives, pp.103–105, 118–24, 140–51; KKE: E.K., V, Appendix, pp.398–402; S. Sarafis, *op.cit.*, pp. 308–34; R. Leeper, *op.cit.*, pp.53–4; P. Papastratis, *op.cit.*, pp. 177–86.

39.   EAM: LV (I), no.2; V. Georgiou, *I Zoi mou* (Athens: 1992), p.396; P. Papastratis, *op.cit.*, p.195. The internal debates in PEEA in PEEA Archives, pp.96–167.

40. F.O.371/43734 R12782: Churchill to Eden, 6/8/1944; W.S. Churchill, *op.cit.*, VI, 97; EAM: LV (I), no.3.

41. KKE: E.K., V, no. 689: Politburo Statement, 16/8/1944; PEEA Archives, pp.173–7, 180–7, 194–200.

42. KKE: E.K., Appendix, pp.408–10; S. Sarafis, *op.cit.*, pp.382–9; MVR, *op.cit.*, pp.610–14; R. Leeper, *op.cit.*, p.71.

43. J. Shy and T.W. Collier, 'Revolutionary War', in P. Paret, ed., *op.cit.*, pp.832–7.

44. PEEA Archives: pp.140–55; V. Georgiou, *op.cit.*, pp.405, 416–7; Y. Ioannidis, *op.cit.*, pp.248–51, 254–7; L. Baerentzen, 'I afixi tis Sovietikis Stratiotikis Apostolis ton Ioulio tou 1944', in N. Svoronos and H. Fleischer, eds., *op.cit.*, pp.563–97.

45. W.S. Churchill, *op.cit.*, VI, 63–4; *Churchill–Roosevelt* nos 369, 378, 379, 392; *Stalin et al.* I, nos 294, 297; Cordell Hull, *The Memoirs of Cordell Hull* II (London: 1948), pp.1451–5.

46. F.O.371/43715 R12457: Eden Memorandum, 8/8/1944; *Churchill–Roosevelt* no.716, and p.570, n.5; F.O.371/43692 R15193: Clark-Kerr to F.O., 23/9/1944.

47. A documentary record of the meeting of 9/10/1944 in the papers of Lord Inverchapel (Sir Archibald Clark Kerr), F.O.800/298/44/87. According to this draft paper, Stalin 'agreed that Britain should have the first say in Greece'. Churchill's story, in *op.cit.*, VI, 204, has been dismissed by G. Kolko, *The Politics of War* (New York: 1968), pp.141–7, and intelligently scrutinized by P. Tsakaloyannis, 'The Moscow Puzzle', *Journal of Contemporary History* 21 (January 1986), 37–55. The best interpretation is A. Resis, 'The Churchill–Stalin 'Percentages Agreement on the Balkans, Moscow, October 1944', *American Historical Review* 83 (April 1978), 368–87. See also D. Yergin, *Shattered Peace: Origins of the Cold War and the National Security State* (Boston: 1977), p.60.

48. R. Clogg, *A Short History of Modern Greece* 2nd edn. (London: 1986), p.152.

49. D. Lukač, 'I synergasia metaxi ton ethnikon apeleftherotikon kinimaton tis Elladas ke tis Yugoslavias', in N. Svoronos and H. Fleischer, eds., *op.cit.*, pp.483–7; PEEA Archives, pp.156–8; Y. Ioannidis, *op.cit.*, pp.209, 219; V. Georgiou, *op.cit.*, p.431.

50. MVR, p.628: 15/10/1944.

51. *I Ekthesi tou Siandou yia ta Dekemvriana* (Athens: 1986), p.11. The Report was drawn up by the KKE Secretary in early 1945.

52. MVR, p.630: 21/10/1944.

53. *Ibid.*, p.629: 20/10/1944; GAK: K 202 (Papers of M.I. Myridakis): The Diary of General Zervas 1942–1945, p.509.

54. F.O.371/43735 R17175: Leeper to F.O., 24/10/1944; F.O.371/43694 R17645: Leeper to F.O., 31/10/1944; F.O.371/43735 R17678: Leeper to F.O., 31/10/1944; F.O.371/43735 R18697: Leeper to F.O., 21/11/1944 and 22/11/1944, Minutes by Laskey.

55. *Kathimerina Nea* (Athens): 27 and 31/10/1944; W.O.204/8842: Minutes of a meeting between Papandreou and Scobie, 31/10/1944; C.M. Woodhouse, *Apple of Discord*, p.215, n.2; B.Sweet-Escott, *Greece: A Political and Economic Survey, 1939–1945* (London: 1954), p.34; M. Ward, *Greek Assignments: SOE 1943–1948 UNSCOB* (Athens: 1992), p.208.

56. F.O.371/43696 R18941: Leeper to F.O., 20/11/1944.

57. F.O.371/43695 R17961: Churchill to Eden, 7/11/1944.

58. F.O.371/43696 R18941: Eden to Leeper,23/11/1944; F.O.371/ 43735 R19341: Leeper to F.O., 26/11/1944; KKE (es.): E.K., V, no.27/e; GAK: K 202 (Papers of M.I. Myridakis): Zervas Diary, p.506 (27/11/1944); S. Sarafis, *op.cit.*, pp.494–5.

59. KKE (es.): E.K., V, nos 23/a,24/b,27/e; G. Papandreou, *I Apeleftherosis tis Ellados* (Athens: 1948), pp.209–10; W.O. 204/8842: Decision of the Council of Ministers, 27/11/1944; F.O.371/43697 R19718: Leeper to F.O., 30/11/1944; GAK: K202: Zervas Diary, pp.507–8 (29/11/1944); EAM: LV (I), no. 33; R. Leeper, *op.cit.*, pp.97–8.

60. F.O.371/43697 R19672: Churchill to Eden, 28/11/1944; GAK: K 202 Zervas Diary, p.509; Y. Ioannidis, *op.cit.*, pp.330, 332; EAM: LV (I), no. 48.

61. F.O.371/43736 R19864: Leeper to F.O., 2/12/1944; GAK: K202 Zervas Diary, p.508 (30/11/1944); MVR, p.655; W.H. McNeill, *The Greek Dilemma: War and Aftermath* (London:1947), p.137. Professor McNeill was then a US Army officer attached to the US Embassy in Athens.

62. MVR, p.654; *Akropolis* (Athens): 12/12/1958. The best account of the demonstration is L. Baerentzen, 'The Demonstration in Syntagma Square on Sunday the 3rd of December, 1944', *Scandinavian Studies in Modern Greek* 2 (1978), 25–52.

63. MVR, pp.656–7; F.O.371/43736 R19933:Churchill to Leeper, 5/12/1944; EAM: LV (I), no. 64; KKE(es.): E.K., V, no.28; F.O.371/48279 R15585: Political Review of Greek Affairs for 1944, 5/9/1945.

64. W.S. Churchill, *op.cit.*, VI, 252: Churchill to Scobie, 5/12/1944.

65. *Ibid.*, 254: Churchill to Scobie, 8/12/1944; MVR, p.658; KKE (es.): E.K., V, nos 29, 30, 34.

66. KKE(es.): E.K., V, no.30; M. Ward, *op.cit.*, p.213; L. Spais, 'Lathi-Pathi-Taphoi: Dekemvris 1944', *Politika Themata*, no. 125 (4–10/12/1976), 27.

67. J. Colville, *The Fringes of Power: Downing Street Diaries 1939–1955* (London: 1985), p.534 (8 and 10/12/1944).

68. L. Spais, *op.cit.*, 27.

69. P. Dixon, *Double Diploma* (London: 1968), p.125; W.S. Churchill, *op.cit.*, VI, 260; Lord Moran, *Winston Churchill: The Struggle for Survival 1940–1965* (London: 1966), p.213.

70. For the Conference in Athens on 25–28/12/1944 see F.O.800 /414: Papers of Private Secretaries; J. Colville, *op.cit.*, pp.539–46; W.S. Churchill, *op.cit.*, VI, 312, 318–9, 322; A. Eden, *The Eden Memoirs* III, *The Reckoning* (London: 1965), 500; H. Macmillan, *The Blast of War, 1939–1945* (London: 1967), p.625; *Churchill–Roosevelt* no. 493: Churchill to Roosevelt, 30/12/1944.

71. *The Times* (London): 6/1/1945.

72. V. Bouras, 'I Politiki Epitropi Ethnikis Apeleftherosis, Eleftheri Ellada 1944', in N. Svoronos and H. Fleischer, eds., *op.cit.*, p.329.

73. G. Blanas (Kissavos), *Emfylios Polemos 1946–1949: Opos ta Ezisa* (Athens: 1977), p.70; J.O. Iatrides, *Revolt in Athens: The Greek Communist 'Second Round', 1944–1945* (Princeton: 1972), pp.148–70 passim.

74. W.O.170/4048: War Diary, HQ Military Commander, Athens, December 17–December 31, 1944, Intelligence Summary, December 14, 1944; F.O.371/43739 R26412: Leeper to F.O., 10/12/1944.

75. PEEA Archives, pp.194–200: session 56 (24/8/1944).

76. MVR, p.656.

77. *Ibid.*, p.660: MacVeagh's letter to Roosevelt, 8/12/1944.

II The Protectorate: 1945–1946

The Athenians to the Melians

It is a general and necessary law of nature to rule whatever one can.

Thucydides, V : 105

Actiones Vindictam Spirantes: The Varkiza Agreement

After the evacuation of Athens by the ELAS units, the British exerted pressure on the Regent to summon a conference with EAM in order to work out a political settlement. Leeper made it clear that there could be no understanding between the Greek government and 'the hard core of irreconcilable communism that is left of EAM'. In the ambassador's view, the aim of the prospective conference should be the formal cessation of *Ta Dekemvriana* and the creation of conditions for the peaceful evolution of Greek politics. There was, however, an important distinction between pacification and reconciliation: the latter was 'quite unreal', whereas the former meant 'the right political tact to achieve as much disarmament of ELAS as possible' – and that was in Leeper's view the object of the oncoming conference.[1]

For his part, Plastiras stated that his policy would focus on three tasks – the revival of Greece's economic life, the reorganization of the army on a national basis, and the punishment of collaborators.[2] The new Greek Prime Minister selected a Cabinet of conservative centrists, with the notable exception of Ioannis Sofianopoulos, the Foreign Minister. An eminent liberal with leftist tendencies, Sofianopoulos was the leader of the Unified Agrarian Party (AKE) which on 22 July 1936 had entered the KKE-inspired Popular Front. Quite appropriately, at the conference which opened at Varkiza on 2 February 1945 the government delegation was headed by Sofianopoulos; EAM was represented by the Secretary of its Central Committee and member of the KKE Politburo Dimitris Partsalidis, the KKE Secretary Giorgis Siandos, and the leader of the socialist ELD Ilias Tsirimokos.

Ten days of negotiations bore fruit on 12 February 1945, when EAM and the Greek government signed the Varkiza Agreement. Its text and the statements of Siandos and Sofianopoulos were published in the Government Gazette and became a law of the Greek state.[3] Article I stipulated that the Greek government would abolish any illiberal laws, secure the free expression of the citizens' political convictions, and safeguard individual liberties. Article III, by far the most important and controversial, amnestied the political offences perpetrated from 3 December 1944 to the signing of the Agreement, save those common law crimes against life and property which were not absolutely necessary for the commitment of a specific political offence. EAM undertook to free the hostages captured by ELAS during *Ta Dekemvriana* (Art. IV), while all guerrilla armies would surrender their arms and demobilize (Art. VI).

A national army would be set up consisting of professional officers and NCOs, and conscripts – a settlement which allowed for the inclusion of former ELAS guerrillas (Art.V). With Articles VII and VIII the government undertook to purge the Civil Service and the Security Forces of all elements which had served the Metaxas regime or had collaborated with the Occupation authorities. Finally, Article IX stipulated that a plebiscite on the constitutional question should be conducted at the earliest possible date, and certainly within 1945. This would be followed by elections for a Constituent Assembly to draft a new Constitution, and the Allies should be invited to send observers to verify that the people's will would be genuinely expressed.[4] Reactions to the Varkiza Agreement were largely favourable, except for those of the Greek Right and Churchill. The British Prime Minister saw it as a 'mistake' in that the British 'ought to teach the communists a lesson'.[5]

Of the nine articles of the Agreement, two carried obligations for EAM and seven committed the government to specific measures and policies. EAM undertook to release its hostages, demobilize ELAS and surrender its arms. Though it duly fulfilled the first two obligations, it partly failed with regard to the last. On 15 February Yiannis Ioannidis, the Organizational Secretary of the KKE, cabled to all Party Organizations that the basic direction of party policy would be the struggle for democratic liberties and the evolution of the country. Nevertheless, he also instructed them to co-operate with local ELAS *Kapetanioi* in hiding away considerable quantities of arms.[6] Ignorant of the fact that ELAS possessed 70,000 pieces, the British and the Greek government asked for the surrender of 40,000, and ELAS readily handed in 48,973.[7]

The interpretation of the concealment of arms by the KKE suffers by the Cold War overstatement that three days after the signature of the Varkiza Agreement the party started planning a new armed clash, and Ioannidis's understatement that it was simply catering for 'an hour of emergency that could present itself to us'.[8] Certainly the KKE had plenty of reasons to be cautious, but until further records become available, it seems reasonable to conclude that the party had not totally flinched before the prospect of some sort of armed action in some unspecified future. The Cold War overstatement, on the other hand, suffers from four major weaknesses: first, it is anachronistic in that conditions in autumn 1946 – when civil war was slowly unfolding – bore no relationship to the situation in February 1945; secondly, it lacks substantiation from any contemporary source; thirdly, the evidence available to date does not afford an insight into the motives of the KKE in issuing this order; and, lastly, there are sources (to be discussed later) which strongly suggest that in early 1945 the KKE had opted for political struggle rather than armed conflict.

More to the point is an examination of the policy of the Greek government with regard to its obligations as stipulated by the Varkiza Agreement. Laws of the Metaxas regime and the collaborationist governments were not repealed, but rather were used as a legal pretext for the persecution of left-wingers and sympathizers. Legislation dating back to 1917 and 1929, which penalized anyone expressing opinions subversive of public order or likely to 'disturb' the citizens, and which regarded agitation against the existing social system as a criminal offence, remained in full force and were solidly applied against anyone connected with EAM. Thus on 2 April 1945 the Athens Misdemeanours Court sent four citizens to gaol because they had gathered at a house and had been talking about 'matters of the Communist Party'.[9] Freedom of the press existed largely in theory. Though the KKE and EAM dailies appeared regularly in Athens, in the provinces harassment, censorship and terror led to a steady decline in the circulation of left-wing papers. Right-wing bands, often in collaboration with the National Guard and the Security Forces, stormed their offices and expressed their political disagreement by laying waste the premises and assaulting or arresting staff.[10]

In the words of the Assistant Military Attaché at the US Embassy in Athens (and later Professor) W. H. McNeill, 'a rash of self-styled Nationalist organizations grew up within a matter of weeks' after the signature of the Varkiza Agreement and launched an unprecedented persecution against leftist and republican citizens. As early as 22 March 1945, Harold Macmillan admitted that 'a wave of reaction was sweeping the country and now that the Right felt that the Government was firmly installed with British backing, they were out for revenge'.[11] An insight into the formation and aims of such bands is afforded by the unpublished manuscript diary of K. D. Yiannoulis, a former EDES officer, who acted in the district of Arta and helped with his band 'to impose discipline on the communists':

> I remain in Arta with my [EDES] guerrillas who had surrendered their arms until 16 April 1945. During my stay in Arta I quietly organized bands and they broke up the local offices of EAM and spread terror among the cadres of the KKE, without it being apparent that it was I who had given them the orders.[12]

These nationalist bands were assisted by the National Guard, which had been hastily formed during *Ta Dekemvriana* to fight ELAS. Anti-communist and ignorant of the law, most Guardsmen were at best negligent and at worst downright defiant of civil liberty safeguards as promised by Varkiza. The British authorities reported that even 'good Republicans' were 'often beaten up on the pretext that they are communists. Object is to secure return of [the] King through rightist terrorism.' Unless a British Liaison Officer (BLO) was nearby, the Guardsmen acted as 'political partisans', indulging in illegal arrests and condoning, if not participating, in terrorism. Their acts of violence against leftists and republicans were approved and openly applauded by members of the Church and the upper classes. In some cases, and certainly as early as March 1945, they seized arms hidden by ELAS and promptly handed them over to local royalists.[13] Plastiras tried to remind the military authorities and the Gendarmerie, which was often in partnership with the National Guard in such exploits, that they did not belong to any political faction, but no-one took any notice.[14]

The Judiciary, which had served Metaxas and the Occupation authorities, made a mockery of the amnesty provisions. Crimes committed in December

1944 had been partly amnestied, but many leftists found themselves charged for actual or presumed offences perpetrated from 1941 to 1944. The definition of 'crime' embraced the execution of traitors and collaborators, and in some cases the killing of German, Italian and Bulgarian soldiers. Policemen and gendarmes who had joined ELAS faced charges of 'desertion', the collection of taxes for PEEA became 'theft' or 'plunder', and even the participation of civil servants in strikes against the occupiers and their puppets was seen as a punishable offence.[15] The Assistant Public Prosecutor in the Athens Misdemeanours Court, Pavlos Delaportas, noted in his memoir that by March 1945 40,000 were in gaol and 150,000 arrest warrants had been issued:

> Of course only part of the prosecuted were actually perpetrators of crimes, the many were innocent ... All these charges against "invented" defendants, where the plaintiffs knew their innocence, belonged to the same category of lawsuits which Roman Law called lawsuits which breathe vengeance (*Actiones Vindictam Spirantes*).[16]

The anti-EAM/ELAS hysteria reached its peak when arrest warrants were issued against General Sarafis and Aris Velouchiotis on charges of 'moral responsibility', which even Leeper deemed contrary to the spirit of Varkiza.[17] Although these two warrants were never executed, action on thousands of others led to a massive overcrowding of prison population. Decongestion measures did little to ease the situation, as the number of those entering prison exceeded the number of those released.

With regard to the national army, Military Councils were set up to judge on the basis of merit which officers would re-enlist as 'permanent active cadres' (Table A) and which would be kept 'out of service and organic posts' (Table B). The vast majority of officers who had joined ELAS were placed in Table B, whereas officers and cadres of the Security Battalions were largely incorporated in Table A. Judgement on the senior commanders of ELAS was delayed, while within the army monarchist officers formed the League of Young Officers (SAN) with the dual aims of preventing any putsch from the Left and working for the restoration of George II.[18] Former ELAS guerrillas were excluded from the National Guard. Leeper cabled to London that discrimination in this respect was indeed being practised and 'had been rather unfortunately handled', but he went on to justify it: 'By forming a nucleus of Nationalists and then accepting other recruits to fill this framework [the] Government considers that rightful thinking elements will absorb and moderate extremists. In the absence of some such procedure reverse might well be the case.'[19] Similarly, in the Civil Service and the Security Forces the purges were directed against leftists rather than Metaxists and collaborators. Civil servants who had joined 'anti-national organizations' such as EAM and its offshoots were suspended or fired. The academic community and the Church were also cleansed of professors and bishops who belonged to, or sympathized with, EAM.[20]

The treatment of prominent collaborators offers the most revealing insight into the mood of the Greek anti-EAM coalition. Trials opened on 21 February 1945, with twenty-four ex-ministers and officers accused of signing the unauthorized armistice of April 1941, forming a government, collaborating with the Germans, and setting up the Security Battalions. The first prosecution witness, the Liberal Themistoklis Tsatsos, set the tone by arguing that participation in a government under the Germans ought not to be regarded as treason. He justified the Security Battalions as having 'the intention of fighting communism and not of assisting the Germans, and had never, in fact, fought against EDES or EKKA'.[21] The Liberal leader Sofulis, when asked by the Court whether the Occupation governments had betrayed Greece, replied: 'I cannot accept that assumption. I know all the defendants. They are good Greeks. They love their country and I respect them.'[22] Understandably, therefore, in their defence pleas the accused interpreted aggressive attack as their best form of defence. The last collaborationist Premier, Ioannis Rallis, boasted of having modified the German system of indiscriminately rounding-up as hostages communists and nationalists alike, so that only communists were actually arrested. This, Leeper commented, was 'an interesting confession as to the part played by agents of M. Rallis in these later wholesale seizures of hostages, in which Greeks wearing masks used to point out which men should be arrested'.[23] The verdicts, pronounced on 31 May 1945, were deemed scandalously lenient. Colonel Woodhouse perfectly encapsulated the mood of the times as one in which 'Communism seemed a worse crime than collaboration; and collaboration, unlike capital punishment, admitted degrees'.[24]

By summer 1945 Varkiza had become a dead letter. A wave of right-wing repression had spread in most quarters of the country. In Epirus rightist bands were proving themselves adept in 'imposing discipline' on actual or presumed communists; in central Greece and Thessaly, with the tolerance or co-operation of the National Guard, they terrorized and frequently murdered members and sympathizers of EAM; in Macedonia, where EAM had been at its strongest, the Right found less support and thus committed more outrages.[25] The situation in the Peloponnese, historically a monarchist stronghold, was vividly portrayed in a report by Woodhouse, who toured the region in July–August. The case against the Right, which was identified with government authority, was summed up as follows: (i) arrests without warrants were enforced exclusively against leftists, never against collaborators or nationalists; (ii) discrimination was 'fanatically' exercised against the Left by the National Guard and was condoned by most officials; (iii) the government forces were beyond the control of the authorities, with the National Guard being 'far worse than the Gendarmerie in this respect'; and (iv) government forces were arming right-wing civilians to give a hand in breaking up the Left.[26] This state of affairs, labelled the White Terror and interpreted by the KKE as a unilateral civil war, duly alarmed several politicians of the Centre. On 5 June 1945 Sofulis, Tsouderos, Kafandaris (Progressive Liberals), Mylonas (leader of one of the AKE factions), and Plastiras (who had been forced to step down in April) publicly stated that

the terror of the extreme right, which was established throughout the country after the December movement, is expanding daily, and has already

47

acquired such an extent and violence that renders the life of non-royalist citizens intolerable, and prevents any thought about the conduct of a free plebiscite or elections … The terrorist organizations of the extreme right, of which the most important ones had been partly armed by the Germans and collaborated with them in every way, have not only not been disarmed, not only are they not persecuted, but they openly collaborate with the agents of law for the suppression of every democratic wind.[27]

The flagrant violation of the Varkiza Agreement by the Greek state cannot be overstated. The policy of the KKE after February 1945 must be examined against the background of the White Terror, for it is worth remembering that 'the more the state seeks to repress, the greater is the opposition it is likely to engender; and the more opposition it engenders, the greater are the powers it must invoke'.[28] For the time being there is no doubt that within days after the signature of the Agreement the Greek Right went out seeking revenge after four years of EAM/ELAS predominance. The desire for vengeance operated on two levels. On the first, the compromise of the Left rendered the time propitious for all intractable anti-communist elements to avenge the successes (and several excesses) of EAM/ELAS during 1941–1944: as in *Ta Dekemvriana*, old scores now could – or should – be settled.

To define the second level is a more difficult task, for terror and head-hunting were not the only evils facing the Left. The violation of the clauses regarding the amnesty, the purges and the formation of a national army was not perpetrated by monarchist bands, but by the Greek state itself. In this case discrimination aimed to prevent EAM from obtaining a foothold in the state apparatus or uprooting any that might have crept in duringthe Occupation. This is probably as far as the highest echelons of power would go, and there is no evidence to suggest that the lower echelons (the Judiciary, the National Guard and the Security Forces) were acting upon orders. But the latter were Metaxas's appointees, loyal to the King, and therefore in their demonology leftists and republicans were second to none. In the post-Varkiza era, when EAM still commanded political and moral respect among Greeks, the White Terror emerged as a seemingly uncoordinated endeavour of the lower echelons of power to smash that potential.

The militant anti-communism of the state apparatus was bolstered by the less pronounced form practised by the government. Ministers lent a deaf ear to the protests of EAM, while any course designed to observe the Agreement might invoke the abominable charge of fellow-travelling. Prewar anti-communism, wartime envy and December fear had generated hatred against EAM, yet the key aspect of the White Terror was that it was directed against left-wingers and republicans alike. Evidently, it was the desire for the return of the King which provided the common denominator for the deeds of the Judiciary, the military, the Police, the Gendarmerie and the various royalist bands. Certainly it is not irrelevant that as early as October 1945 the US Embassy in Athens reported that the leading Populist (and later minister) Petros Mavromichalis was himself actively involved in financing royalist bands, being in fact the Treasurer of one of them ('X'). His activities were confirmed in the following year by the British Embassy, which added that Mavromichalis had even convinced Crown Prince Paul, brother of George II, to contribute funds to the crusade.[29]

The British attitude vis-à-vis the White Terror cannot be viewed outside the context of the overall British policy towards Greece in the post-Varkiza period. In applauding the Agreement, Leeper had concurred with the KKE Secretary Giorgis Siandos that 'the beaten party' would repose its hopes for the observance of the agreement by the Greek state in Britain. The ambassador – who interpreted Siandos's words to mean that without the guarantee afforded by the British presence in Greece the KKE would never have come to terms with its Greek opponents – was forthright enough to warn his government that the British 'therefore have all the heavier responsibility towards Greece'. This is also what Greeks of all shades understood. Colonel Woodhouse testified to 'a universal belief' that the British were directly responsible for the situation: the Right took the approval of the British authorities for granted, whilst the Left insisted that if the British really wanted to, they could halt the wave of repression within hours.[30] The presence of British Liaison Officers often acted as a deterrent to the National Guard, but they could neither be omnipresent nor deter the nationalist bands. On the other hand, when the Foreign Office made one feeble attempt to intervene, it was brought to book by Churchill. When informed by Leeper that past collaborationism was becoming increasingly fashionable, Sir Orme Sargent, the Under-Secretary of State for Foreign Affairs, cabled the following message to the ambassador:

> Your recent reports suggest that membership of EAM tends to be considered a greater crime than collaboration with the Germans. You should take every opportunity of emphasizing our view that assistance to the enemy is regarded by HM Government as much worse than member-ship of EAM and should be met with prompt and condign punishment. I am by no means satisfied that adequate purge of gendarmerie and other state services has been carried out or is being seriously undertaken.[31]

Sargent's instruction to Leeper was strongly questioned by Churchill, who evidently regretted the end of the fighting with EAM:

> I do not agree at all with your last paragraph. It seems to me that the collaborators in Greece in many cases did the best they could to shelter the Greek population from German oppression. Anyhow they did nothing to stop the entry of liberating forces, nor did they give any support to the EAM designs. The Communists are the main foe, though the punishment of notorious pro-German collaborators, especially if concerned with the betrayal of loyal Greeks, should proceed in a regular and strict manner. There should be no question of increasing the severities against the collaborationists in order to win Communist approval. Their approval is not worth having ... Our policy is the plebiscite within three or four months, and implacable hostility to the Communists whatever their tactics may be.[32]

The staff of the Southern Department of the Foreign Office were taken aback by Churchill's views. William Hayter, the Head of the Department, minuted: 'I should have thought it self-evident that collaboration with Germany was a worse crime than Communism, even in Greece. It seems to me that it could make us look rather foolish if we suggested the contrary to Mr. Leeper'; and D.F. Howard: 'Are we really to tell Mr. Leeper that the Communists are the main foe and should be treated worse than ex-collaborators? It seems to me out of the question.'[33] The Foreign Office painstakingly tried to explain to Churchill that the punishment of collaborators was desirable not in order to win EAM's applause, but to satisfy moderate opinion, avert negative comments engendered by the sluggishness of the Greek authorities in this regard, and thus maintain the balance between Right and Left. Admitting that collaborators were 'on the crest of the wave' and communists 'on the trough', Sargent feared that if the British 'allowed ex-collaborationists of the Right to abuse their position, this might provoke a swing to the Left and make the position of the moderates impossible'.[34] The policy of the Foreign office, therefore, was to bolster up a moderate Centre as a counterpoise to the monarchist Right and EAM.

From Churchill to Bevin, February–November 1945

Britain's handling of Greek affairs since 1941 seemed to have culminated in the armed clash with ELAS in December 1944. Though militarily successful, this policy had done little to underpin the position of the Greek bourgeois parties vis-à-vis the Left. Despite the violence of *Ta Dekemvriana*, EAM still commanded considerable support among Greeks, while the economic catastrophe inflicted upon the country by the war forced more people to turn their eyes on the Left. Plastiras had little idea as to how to tackle the problems of the hugely devaluated currency, the devastated industry, universal unemployment, the Treasury's lack of revenue, and rocketing inflation, whilst his ministers opted for inactivity when they realized that the necessary measures would be immensely unpopular. With relief and reconstruction proceeding very slowly due to lack of planning and central direction, MacVeagh spoke of a 'psychological communism' to which the destitute were prone, and which would provide 'the unscrupulous' – the KKE – with a dangerous weapon.[35]

Georgios Sideris, the Finance Minister in Plastiras's Cabinet, considered the search for British economic aid as his prime duty. The entire government held that since foreign aid was the only remedy, what ministers could do was too little to be worth doing. The notable exception was the highly efficient and experienced Governor of the Bank of Greece Kyriakos Varvaressos, who advocated a programme of rigorous government control of the market.[36] His views, however, incurred the wrath of the financial establishment – industrialists, bankers and economic ministers – who tried to discredit him as a fascist (he had served in the Bank of Greece during the Metaxas regime) or a communist (he had personal links with some left-wing politicians).[37] Indeed, according to the Greek Inland Revenue, there were no fewer than sixteen kinds of business enterprise which since April 1941 had made vast profits; these included public work contractors, construction and salvage businesses, importers, the tobacco, leather, cotton, wine, spirit and olive oil industries, foodstuffs producers, and, of course, the banks.[38] In view of the transparent inequality of life, the economic inactivity of the government exacerbated political divisions and, in the words of the US ambassador, 'fuelled the fires of popular unrest'.[39]

The objectives and tactics of British policy were delineated by Eden, Alexander and Macmillan in a conference held at the Embassy in Athens on 15 February 1945, and were promptly approved by the British government. Though gratified by the dissolution of EAM's 'pretended' authority and the exclusion of the KKE from the government, the British were not prepared to leave Greeks to their own devices. Their intervention would simply 'take on a new form' which, through the structural penetration of the Greek state apparatus, would effectively turn Greece into a British protectorate. The first stage of this policy envisaged the stationing of three British divisions in Greece to supervise the disarmament of the guerrillas, 'guarantee against a fresh rebellion', and mobilize and equip sufficient National Guard battalions to support the Greek administration. Stage two envisaged the reduction of the British forces to one division as a mobile reserve in the event of an emergency, while in the final stage, pushed into some unspecified future, all British troops would be withdrawn, yet 'without endangering the main purpose to which we had set our hand by our intervention in Greek affairs' – notably the neutralization of the leftist challenge. British Missions would advise the Greek authorities on military, police and economic matters, whilst Leeper would be vested with extensive powers to supervise the policies of the Greek government and offer 'guidance' to the heads of the British Missions. The ambassador would be 'something in the nature of a High Commissioner', though 'in deference to Greek susceptibilities he should not bear the title'.[40]

As seen by Nigel Clive, Second Secretary of the Embassy, Leeper would have 'a range of powers and responsibilities more akin to those of a colonial governor than to the head of a normal diplomatic mission'.[41] This policy rested on the premise that the fight against EAM would now shift to the political plane. *Ta Dekemvriana* had reinforced the polarization of Greek politics between the monarchist Right and EAM at the expense of the Centre, which was seen as the only means of isolating the Left and avoiding what Leeper called the 'dangerous, but only temporary addiction to the drug of a right-wing monarchist solution'. In this context the republican anti-communist Plastiras shone as the ideal figurehead Premier; thus at the outset he was vested with British confidence.[42]

But the General had other plans in mind. Convinced that in order to lay a firm grip on power he had to install in the key posts his personal friends and followers and instruct them to see to the observance of law and order, he resorted to clientelism. In this he was unfortunate, for the British soon started to regard his appointees as politically or professionally unsuitable.[43] His decision to resuscitate the Assistant Ministry of Public Order, which had been set up by Metaxas and become synonymous with police brutality, and entrust it to an old friend of his, generated heated controversy. Not only did EAM denounce it as a violation of Varkiza, but even the Interior Minister, to whose Department the new institution would be attached but not subordinated, rose up in protest. Periklis Rallis, who was one of the government signatories of the Agreement, resigned on the grounds that he was prevented from implementing it, and the British, disgruntled with Plastiras's clientelist practices, began to think about his possible removal.[44]

After an unsuccessful attempt to bring him into line, in early March 1945 Macmillan drafted with Leeper an agreement whereby the Greek Prime Minister would have to secure the approval of the British Embassy for the actions of his government.[45] The new scheme did not materialize because the Foreign Office gave it a cold reception on the grounds that such an initiative would increase the appetite of the French and the Soviets to act likewise in their own spheres of influence, and that no Greek government would accept such an agreement. Nevertheless, for the successful application of British policy Sargent recommended that Leeper follow Lord Cromer's example in Egypt in the 1880s. Churchill was persuaded by the Foreign Office and on 7 March he cabled Macmillan that the best course would be to start looking for a suitable replacement and get rid of Plastiras at the earliest convenient moment.[46]

The countdown to the Greek Prime Minister's fall was triggered off by the awareness among British policy-makers that he was not amenable to their demands and therefore could not function under Leeper's 'High-Commission'. The pretext cropped up on 5 April, when a royalist paper published a compromising and defeatist letter written by Plastiras in July 1941. This appeared as the climax of an orchestrated offensive by the Populists, who had been disturbed by the General's republicanism. On the same day Leeper called on the Regent and demanded the resignation of Plastiras on the grounds that 'his stupidity was so dangerous that he must not remain in office any longer'. The real grounds, according to Konstantinos Amandos, Emeritus Professor of History at the University of Athens and Education Minister in Plastiras's government, was the Greek Prime Minister's independent stance and his protestations to Leeper that British pressure annoyed the Greeks' keen sense of freedom. Leeper left it to Damaskinos 'to choose the reason for the change', but 'suggested Voulgaris should take his place'.[47]

On 7 April Plastiras resigned and was succeeded by Leeper's favourite, Admiral Petros Voulgaris, who had demonstrated his anti-communism during the April 1944 mutinies in the Greek Armed Forces. The new Prime Minister selected a Cabinet of centre-right officers and professors, with the exception of Sofianopoulos, who retained the Foreign Ministry. The reason publicly given by the Regent was that the country needed a caretaker government to prepare the elections. The Foreign Office indeed hoped to hold the Admiral in place until the polls, but feared that Plastiras might not 'fade quietly into retirement' but go 'into active opposition'.[48] Meanwhile, the mutual apprehension that further economic deterioration would prejudice the position of the new government prompted Voulgaris to accept Macmillan's plan whereby

British officers and civil servants would be attached to the Greek ministries in Athens and in the administrative centres in the provinces.[49]

The future of the Voulgaris government depended upon its response to the daunting task of economic reconstruction and progress in the preparation for the plebiscite and elections. The prospects seemed promising for the first task when in June Varvaressos entered the Cabinet as Vice-Premier and Minister of Supply. Having secured approval of his reform plans from Churchill and Whitehall, he embarked on a programme of rigorous taxation, control over prices and the processing of imported raw materials, and a drive against gold speculation.[50] The initial success of his reforms came to an end in August, when prices rose again, commodities became scarce and foodstuffs disappeared from the market only to re-emerge in the hands of black marketeers. Varvaressos had anticipated the resistance of industrialists and merchants to his policies, and on 1 September he resigned in the hope that the ensuing chaos would curb the reactions and necessitate his recall.[51] In a radio broadcast two days later, he attacked the economic oligarchy which had subverted his policies to the point of spending millions of drachmae for an organized campaign of opposition and bribery of civil servants and government officials.[52]

Long before the demise of Varvaressos's economic policies, equally acute problems had emerged with regard to the plebiscite and the elections. Realizing that the December violence had played into the hands of the royalists, with remarkable insight Leeper proclaimed himself against an early plebiscite, which according to Varkiza should take place before the end of 1945. In a personal letter to Sargent, on 20 March, he justified his view as follows:

> the early return of the King in the prevailing atmosphere opens up every possible prospect of trouble. Even if the King were himself a man of strong character … I do not see how he could possibly divorce himself from the practices which had brought him back by their vote… The King as soon as he comes back will have poured into his ears every kind of suspicion against the Left and every kind of story against their past and present misdeeds …
> At the same time a violent swing to the Right at any period during the next few months can only lead straight to disaster and the King, with his past associations, would have to be a superman to steer a course between the two extremes in the way that the Regent is now doing.[53]

Once more it was Churchill who stepped in to correct the ambassador's thinking. On 20 April 1945 – just when he was arguing with the Foreign Office about whether in Greece Communism was a worse crime than collaboration[54] – the British Prime Minister sent the ambassador a telling message. Leeper should pursue a policy of getting the plebiscite conducted within three or four months, but as to domestic Greek affairs, he should 'try as much as possible to keep out of the detail of Greek politics'. Churchill even contemplated sending more troops to Greece: 'The progress of the war', he cabled Leeper, 'is not likely to prevent us from giving you the military force the situation requires'.[55] For Churchill the violations of Varkiza were a point of detail, the more so since it was the Left and republicans who suffered from them. Tactical manoeuvres apart, British policy, as ultimately determined by

Churchill, continued to aim at the restoration of the King. In the wake of December 1944, when passions were running high and George II could be marketed as the antidote to EAM, the time seemed propitious for a prompt plebiscite.

Yet there were more obstacles in Churchill's way. In late April the Greek Interior Minister told Leeper that the plebiscite might have to be delayed for five months due to the absence of electoral registers, the dispersal of the population throughout the country, and the need to restore the crippled administrative machine. Leeper added that prevailing conditions would not allow the people a free choice and that the administrative chaos made it highly irresponsible to announce a date for the plebiscite.[56] A setback of far greater importance occurred in early July, when the United States replied to the British invitation to participate in the international supervision of the plebiscite. The new administration under President Truman accepted the invitation but suggested that elections for a Constituent Assembly should precede the plebiscite. Thus, the State Department argued, Greece would promptly acquire a democratically elected and representative government which would first establish itself and then make plans for the solution of the constitutional question.[57] Naturally the suggestion did not go down very well with Churchill, who minuted to the Foreign Office that such a course would run counter to his correspondence with Roosevelt. Moreover, to him it signified a desire 'to deny the Greek people a chance to say whether they will have the monarchy back or not'.[58]

But Churchill's days were numbered. In the British general election of 26 July 1945 the new circumstances of the war years, which resulted in the British people's swing to the Left, and the party's new realism in foreign and domestic policies in the 1930s, gave Labour a comfortable majority with 48% of the vote and 393 seats, against the Conservatives' 39.6% and 210 seats.[59] Greek reactions to Labour's victory varied depending on viewpoint. The KKE daily *Rizospastis* reported it as a major sensation, adorned its front page with photographs of Labour's leaders and congratulated the 'fraternal' papers *Daily Herald* and *Daily Worker*, while the communist Secretary of the EAM Central Committee cabled Attlee his good wishes. The entire Greek Left was animated, whereas the Right lost heart.[60] At the Foreign Office many visualized an apocalyptic future. Alexander Cadogan, the Permanent Under-Secretary, deplored the ingratitude showed towards Churchill at his finest hour. Orme Sargent prognosticated 'a Communist avalanche over Europe, a weak foreign policy, a private revolution at home and the reduction of England to a 2nd-class power'.[61] In the United States the initial sensational and alarmist reaction later gave way to more moderate feelings.[62]

Yet the British Labour governments of 1945–1951 have been described as 'the British variant of "socialism in one country"'.[63] Under the idealist Ramsay MacDonald, after 1922 Labour's foreign policy had been shaped by an emotional and largely pacifist internationalism. That came to an abrupt end in the summer of 1931, when inability to tackle unemployment and industrial stagnation, indecision and intellectual barrenness brought down the Labour government and marked a new era in the party's development. In the 1930s Labour was divided over foreign policy, but pressures towards leftist commitments were invariably rebuffed, so that by the end of the decade both the party and the TUC were under firm centrist or right-wing control. In 1935 Clement Attlee was elected leader of the party as the symbol of moderation, reformism and gradualism, and the entire new leadership illustrated new coherence and realism. In foreign affairs, for instance, this meant the advocacy of rearmament and armed resistance to German aggression in Europe.[64]

In May 1940, when Labour joined Churchill's coalition government, most of its leaders occupied key posts. Attlee became Deputy Prime Minister, while the trade unionist Ernest Bevin became Minister of Labour and supreme director of domestic economic planning. The party's record as a coalition partner was remarkable but internal divisions still existed. The British military intervention in Greece in December 1944 sparked off a crisis in Labour's ranks and led to demands from the left that it should withdraw from the coalition. At the party conference of that month Aneurin Bevan led a vitriolic attack on the government and on Labour's National Executive Committee for their Greek policy. Significantly, it was Bevin who passionately and belligerently supported Churchill's action.[65] This was a fitting prelude to the new Labour government, which was 'remarkably unradical' in its approach to foreign, defence and imperial policy.[66]

Attlee, the new Prime Minister, was uncharismatic, unsentimental and impenetrable, but also an effective pragmatist whose initiatives were often radical and innovative. Ernest Bevin, who took over from Eden at the Foreign Office, was a bluff patriot with an aggressive temperament. He dominated his Department both because he had his own ideas and because he enjoyed Attlee's full confidence. Both were anti-communists (Bevin had showed that even as a trade-union leader), wary and suspicious towards the Soviets, whom Attlee regarded as 'ideological imperialists'.[67] In the new Cabinet the left held only four posts – Education, Food, Fuel and Power, and Health (Aneurin Bevan) – and thus was relatively powerless. Attlee and Bevin controlled the Cabinet, and the Cabinet firmly controlled all levels of the Labour Party, with the result that possible internal dissent would be easily dissipated.[68]

At the Foreign Office civil servants who called for traditionalist policies, such as the maintenance of British imperial power in the Middle East and hostility towards the Soviet Union, soon found out that Attlee and Bevin were in concert. As early as 10 August 1945 Cadogan noted that Bevin had 'sound ideas which we must encourage'. The new Foreign Secretary would work closely with Eden in implementing a bi-partisan foreign policy, with Dixon, his Principal Private Secretary, as the liaison between the two men. Churchill and Attlee 'thought alike' on foreign affairs, and the latter reassured his predecessor that he believed in the continuity of foreign policy on the main lines which the two of them had often discussed.[69]

This continuity was largely founded on the conviction of the entire Labour government – and, in particular, Bevin – that Britain was still a great world power. British policy-makers were to find out that a great-power role was possible, but also that it would be performed under the fear of economic collapse. To fight the war, Britain had sold almost everything she had, including £1,118,000,000 of foreign assets, and had accumulated debts around the world totalling £2,723,000,000. In August 1945 she sat at diplomatic tables as an imperial and world power, but as Sargent remarked, her position in relation to the United States and the Soviet Union resembled that of 'Lepidus in the triumvirate with Mark Anthony and Augustus'. Ominously, British status could only be maintained by US dollars, as shown by the $3.75 billion American loan of December 1945. Nonetheless, since old axioms of foreign policy were fully espoused by the new government, the preservation of British influence in south-eastern Europe and the eastern Mediterranean, and a permanent military and economic involvement in the Middle East, remained sacrosanct objectives.[70] In that context it seemed unlikely that the advent of Labour would initiate a radical break with the past, except perhaps an attempt 'to clothe imperial purposes in suitably moralistic rhetoric'.[71]

Labour's victory added to the confused situation in Athens where, since May, the Liberals and the Left had been clamouring for the formation of a new government; the Populists bitterly opposed this and Eden had insisted on the retention of the Voulgaris Cabinet.[72] On 27 July the Regent summoned Harold Caccia, Minister at the British Embassy, and told him that public opinion in Greece felt that the new situation in London would herald a change of British policy and strengthen the demands for a new government. If he were to resist such pressures his position would become difficult, hence Damaskinos asked Caccia for an 'outward sign' to clarify British policy in Greece.[73] The Labour government responded positively, for it held that the establishment of law and order throughout Greece and the preparations for a plebiscite and elections depended not on the composition of the government in Athens, but on such 'physical facts' as the speed with which the Gendarmerie would take over from the National Guard. The State Department agreed,[74] thus on 1 August Attlee sent the Regent a message of support which did not fail to draw attention to the violations of Varkiza: 'We hope to see the Varkiza Agreement fully carried out, and we are concerned at reports of right-wing excesses in contravention of this Agreement ... It is our earnest hope that law and order may be established ... on a fair and impartial basis, in order that the Greek people may be enabled to express their will as soon as possible.'[75] A week later the Foreign Office instructed Caccia that the Voulgaris Cabinet should remain in power, though certain incompetent ministers might have to be ejected. The Admiral reshuffled his government in what has been described as 'merely cosmetic surgery'.[76]

Meanwhile Leeper, who was on leave in Britain, suggested to Sargent that Damaskinos be invited to London. This would give the Labour government time to study the Greek problem, hold the situation in Athens and enable the Regent to meet the new British ministers and agree with them on a policy likely to steady the position until elections could be held.[77] The suggestion was accepted and the Regent's arrival in London was fixed for 6 September. Bevin was given time to examine the Greek question, and on 11 August he produced a memorandum which argued that: (i) the elections and the plebiscite should be held as soon as possible with the former preceding the latter, though this was a matter for Greek initiative and responsibility; (ii) the present government should be kept in office until the elections, but 'all reasonable steps should be taken to meet justifiable criticisms by the Left-wing parties and to ensure that law and order are maintained on an impartial basis'; (iii) the Regent should be invited to London to assist the British government in working out a satisfactory policy; (iv) Britain should associate the United States in all steps taken with respect to the Greek situation. Bevin justified his recommendations on the grounds that a change in the Greek government might delay the elections and prolong the stationing of British troops in the country. However, the 'most overpowering reason' was that

> we must maintain our position in Greece as part of our Middle East policy, and unless it is asserted and settled it may have a bad effect on the whole of our Middle East position.[78]

More revealing is a Foreign Office document entitled 'Balkan Problems', which illustrates two further aspects in Bevin's reasoning: that until the Greek elections had been held, the British were hampered in pressing for free elections in other Balkan countries; and that since Britain should maintain an adequate military position in Greece, Bevin favoured the installation of two RAF Squadrons there, 'provided that this would be done unostentatiously and would not be misunderstood'.[79]

During the Cabinet discussion of Bevin's memorandum, it was pointed out to him that the Varkiza Agreement was being violated when the officers of the Greek army were recruited from royalist quarters, the government was not giving full effect to the political amnesty, and many leftists were still in gaol awaiting trial for minor offences; these conditions made it all the more important that elections should precede the plebiscite. Bevin replied that he had impressed on the Regent the desirability of giving full effect to the amnesty and that he expected proper safeguards to be taken to meet left-wing criticisms. The Cabinet endorsed the course of action outlined by Bevin,[80] and Caccia was instructed to act accordingly. The British Embassy in Washington informed the State Department of Labour's Greek policy, which Bevin formally defined in the House of Commons on 20 August: Britain would continue to aim at 'the establishment of a stable democratic government in Greece, drawing its strength from the free expression of the people's will.'[81]

In his first *tour d'horizon* Bevin heralded no marked change in British attitude towards Greece precisely because the outlook of the Labour government on Britain's imperial position allowed for no different perception. Just as it had done long before 1945, Greece continued to feature prominently in British policy in the Middle East, for it was maintained that an unfriendly regime in Athens would jeopardize this position in its entirety. On the other hand it was obvious that the new Labour government did not share Churchill's obsession with the restoration of George II and that it showed some verbal sensitivity towards the violations of Varkiza. Yet these modifications were to prove of minor importance. During Damaskinos's stay in London it was decided that the Greek elections should be held as soon as possible in the hope that a government based on the popular will would be able to restore tranquillity in the country; the plebiscite would be held after such conditions had been firmly established.[82] The loud protests of the Greek King were unanimously brushed aside by Bevin and his US and French colleagues, James Byrnes and Georges Bidault, who were also in London for the Council of Foreign Ministers.[83]

Bolstered by the western allies, in late September the Regent returned to Athens with an ambitious plan. In the previous weeks Damaskinos had been veering to the right, and now he proposed to unite all bourgeois parties – even to the extent of a single national ticket – in order to marginalize EAM and secure a 'thoroughly national democratic parliament'. An exasperated Leeper complained to MacVeagh that the Regent had lost touch with conditions in Greece and was developing 'a personal tendency [of] autocracy while allowing growing fear of communism to blind him to the rightist influences in [the] supposedly service government'. Leeper told his US counterpart that he intended to 'apply correction' in the form of pressing Damaskinos to liberalize the Cabinet by removing some ministers and bringing in some well-known liberals.[84] The British ambassador went as far as to speculate on the replacement of Voulgaris by Tsouderos or Varvaressos, but developments were precipitated by the Premier's announcement on 5 October that elections would be held on 20 January 1946. Immediately a major crisis erupted when all parties (save the Populists) threatened to abstain. EAM invoked the persecution of leftists and the falsification of electoral registers; the Liberals and other Centre parties subscribed to these reasons and added that the geography of the country rendered difficult the conduct of elections in winter.[85]

The reasons put forward for abstention were valid. Since September the US Embassy possessed 'positive proof' that electoral booklets – a sort of voter's identity card essential to participation in the polls – 'were being widely duplicated in Athens'; later *The Times* confirmed that people could easily obtain more than one booklet. According to the US Office of Strategic Services, the strong royalist sympathies of nearly all election officials appointed by Voulgaris's government led to the 'flagrantly wide-spread practice' of right-wingers obtaining 'fraudulent duplicate and triplicate booklets'. Some individuals were already known to hold as many as twenty-five booklets each.[86]

The White Terror was in full swing. Bevin had to acknowledge that there were right-wing excesses which he regarded as 'exceptional' and 'gradually decreasing in number' – albeit he admitted that this was difficult to prove.[87] In early October Damaskinos confided to Leeper that 80% of those in gaol for pro-EAM activity were detained on grounds of moral responsibility, a charge that made nonsense of Varkiza. Co-operation between the state apparatus and the monarchist bands flourished to such an extent that 500 gendarmes in the Thessaloniki area – including the heads of all city police stations except for two – were able to join *en masse* the extremist royalist organization X.[88] The third *White Book* of EAM provides numerous documented cases of what it called 'democratic neofascism', and Delaportas's memoir offers a vivid account of the works and days of the Right in the Peloponnese. In the economic sphere, the Director of the Ministry of Supply resigned and revealed that the committee set up by Varvaressos to supervise the distribution of UNRRA supplies existed only on paper: industrialists had no difficulty in obtaining raw materials and other supplies, processing them, and then channelling their production to the black market.[90]

The onslaught against Voulgaris after his announcement of the election date stirred Leeper into action. On 8 October he appealed to London that the political consequences of having a government opposed by both Centre and Left would be grave and that elections under these conditions would be 'a farce'. Voulgaris and his Cabinet had to go and the Regent ought to appoint a new government at once. The Admiral was told to resign and did so on 9 October.[91] The ambassador requested permission to intervene directly towards the establishment of a centre-left government, where 'left' stood not for EAM but for 'men with modern and progressive ideas'. The reply of the Foreign Office disappointed Leeper. Bevin said he was not prepared to run Greece for the Greeks, who should learn how to stand on their own feet. The initiative for a new government would have to be left to Damaskinos.[92] The Regent entrusted the mandate to the Liberal leader Sofulis, who managed to secure the cooperation of republicans and centrists, as well as the support of the Left, but the Populists' dogged opposition blew up his chances.[93] During a prolonged power vacuum, Leeper found himself trapped between London's instructions and the Regent's incessant reference of opinions to him. Eventually on 1 November 1945 Damaskinos nominated Panayiotis Kanellopoulos as the new Prime Minister and the ambassador was notified of it on the following day.[94]

A republican erstwhile professor of Sociology and member of the Greek government-in-exile from 1942 to 1944, Kanellopoulos formed a centre-right Cabinet of academics and experts. As his team was supposed to provide the expertise to tackle the country's problems, and as a new failure might have disastrous consequences, Leeper urged London to support it.[95] Bevin proposed to send to Athens Hector McNeil, his Parliamentary Under-Secretary, with a view to putting to the new Greek government a comprehensive programme for reconstruction. Britain would provide the Greeks with expert advisers attached to the Ministries responsible for the army, finance, railways, roads, distribution and supplies; these advisers would essentially have executive powers. Further assistance would be extended by way of improving Greece's import pro-gramme, strengthening the delivery of supplies by UNRRA, and advising on the issue of a lottery loan. In return the Greeks would have to pledge themselves to several undertakings, including the purge of the army, the issue of a lottery loan, legislation empowering the Greek government to take over industries and institute a system of government retail, and most importantly, fix a date for elections and abide by it.[96] On 6 November, when asked by the British Cabinet whether the projected assistance could restore the position in Greece, Bevin replied that while he could not guarantee its success, 'we could not at this stage withdraw and must make a further effort to get Greece on her feet. This was the best policy he could devise for this purpose.'[97]

Bevin's memorandum testified to a shift of emphasis in British policy. Along with nursing little love for the king, the Labour ministers essentially recognized that Varkiza had become a dead letter, but their sensitivity was to remain largely verbal. Bevin's brand of non-intervention at this stage precluded the exertion of the direct pressure required for stemming the tide of right-wing repression, while economic improvement was seen in London as a panacea for Greece's plight. Nevertheless, the form and manner of application of economic assistance was tantamount to an actual penetration of the Greek state apparatus. The rigour with which this one-sided interventionist policy was to be pursued was exemplified by the downfall of Kanellopoulos. On 14 November the British Embassy presented the Greek Prime Minister with a memorandum specifying the topics to be discussed with Hector McNeil:

> HM Government are willing to send an economic mission upon whom the Greek Government would rely in carrying out the task of economic reconstruction ... So long as the Mission is there, HM Government would expect the Greek Government to assume whatever powers are needed to implement and operate the programme which the Mission devises. Indeed HM Government would be unwilling to despatch such a Mission until an undertaking of this nature had been given by the Greek Government.[98]

Kanellopoulos welcomed the intended despatch of expert advisers but could not accept the suggestion regarding the implementation of their views. Greek sensitivities and the posting of foreigners with executive powers in Greek ministries would prove politically disastrous. Instead of these 'unacceptable' proposals, the Greek government preferred a joint Anglo-American mission of experts who would be attached to their respective Embassies and act in advisory capacity to the Greek Cabinet.[99]

With such views Kanellopoulos would not do either for the British or for the Regent, who considered that reconstruction was impossible without generous British aid. On 17 November Damaskinos told Leeper privately that the economic and financial deterioration urged him to call all parties – including EAM – and inform them that the plebiscite ought to be postponed for three years so that precedence could be given to reconstruction. He then intended to grant Sofulis a mandate to form an all-party government, offering participation to EAM on condition that it condemned the atrocities of *Ta Dekemvriana*. Leeper felt that the plan held some promise but was opposed to the participation of EAM in a government.[100] It is rather unlikely that the Regent was motivated by a sudden impulse to embrace the Left. Frustrated by the political instability, he probably mentioned EAM in order to stir Leeper into action. Even if the scheme was seriously meant, it was unlikely that Leeper would recommend it to London, and even more unlikely that Bevin would endorse it. At any rate, the Foreign Office greeted the Regent's move for a new government with jubilation. William Hayter, the Head of the Southern Department, wrote to Sargent: 'I very much hope you can get this through ... The present Government are figures of fun and nothing included in them is worth anything.'[101]

Kanellopoulos was told to step down, and so he did on 20 November, in line with Plastiras and Voulgaris. Bevin endorsed Damaskinos's suggestion for the postponement of the plebiscite for three years provided that such a decision was incorporated in a wider comprehensive programme towards economic reconstruction. The British Embassy and the Regent developed a working formula whereby the tasks of the goverment-to-be were outlined as reconstruction, elections not later than March 1946 and postponement of the plebiscite till March 1948.[102] George II protested to Bevin that the only remedy to Greek political and economic problems was his return to the country, but Bevin found no difficulty in disposing of the complaint. He explained to his Cabinet colleagues that a would-be return of the King would pose the peril of civil war and concluded that George II 'should not leave this country with a view to returning to Greece'. With Cabinet approval of his line, he sent the King a dismissive letter in which he countered allegations that he intended to prevent the Greeks from deciding about their future.[103]

On 22 November 1945 yet another government came into being in Athens. Themistoklis Sofulis, the octogenarian leader of the Liberal Party, formed a Cabinet of republican centrists recruited from his own party, the Progressives of the veteran Venizelist Georgios Kafandaris, the Agrarians, and the circles of non-party notables. The new formation featured men of expertise and experience: Kafandaris and Tsouderos (the able financier, impeccable Anglophile and former Premier) became Vice-Premiers; Sofianopoulos held the Foreign Ministry and Georgios Kartalis, one of the most outstanding personalities of the non-EAM Resistance, would prove a competent Minister of Supply. Two days later the government was broadened by eight more members, including Nikos Kazandzakis as Minister for Press and Information. The Populists issued a venomous proclamation in which they branded it unconstitutional, dictatorial, the result of a political blackmail perpetrated by foreign agents and 'a tyranny imposed upon the Greek people'. The KKE reacted positively. The Politburo issued a statement to the effect that the new government would enjoy their support, especially in relation to measures aiming at the restoration of law and order, the conduct of free elections and the improvement of the economic situation, provided that industrialists were forced to carry their share of the burden.[104]

The *raison d'être* of the Sofulis government was illustrated in a memoranum addressed by McNeil to Bevin on 10 December. The British emissary had realized that the economic chaos – which, as MacVeagh had already detected, contributed to a 'psychological communism' – and the intransigence of the Right could lead to civil war. The only chance of averting this prospect was to produce 'a body of Centre thought, committed ... to remedy the economic chaos of Greece rather than concentrating on securing party advantage'.[105] On 22 November 1945 it looked as if this objective had been accomplished, for – save the Populist onslaught – Sofulis's government started under ostensibly propitious omens. Yet it was precisely the attitude of the monarchist faction which epitomized several underlying realities. The deplorable conditions of law and order, the violations of Varkiza, the polarization of Greek politics between EAM and the Right, and the latter's clamouring for the restoration of George II, were brushed aside by Bevin in the name of economic reconstruction – the peaceful offensive against leftist appeal. Whether that was the panacea to Greece's problems remained to be seen.

Bevin's axiomatic adherence to the concept of British preponderance in the eastern Mediterranean and the Middle East, and his anti-communism, ensured that the Greek policy of the Labour government would follow in Churchill's footsteps. The message to Leeper in October 1945 that Greece should not be run from London was partly misleading. During the crisis which erupted in the wake of Voulgaris's resignation, Leeper showed his discontent at this message in a private letter to Sargent, where he deduced that the Foreign Office had 'more or less decided that we are not strong enough to see Greece through this mess'.[106] Sargent's reply – also a *private*, and therefore uninhibited, letter – offers a remarkable insight into Bevin's reasoning. Moreover, in as much as official archives are ideologically laden sources, it is an important contribution towards the semantic decipherment of Foreign Office despatches. Arguing that London had a clear conception of British interests in Greece, Sargent epitomized Labour's policy as follows:

I have no doubt that we are physically quite strong enough to establish a Cromerian regime in Greece and to govern that country through a puppet government of our own composing. But whatever Mr. Churchill's personal feelings may have been on this point, can you imagine the Labour Government *consciously* embarking on such a policy? On the contrary, they must inevitably be at pains, while maintaining their Greek commitment, to give it all the trappings of anti-Imperialist non-interventionist respectability. But this does not mean, and has not been interpreted in practice to mean, that we are going to give up the task of seeing Greece through this mess. It only means that the Government are going to explore other and more discreet methods of achieving their object.

There was also a word of sympathy for the ambassador:

I know how exasperating it must have been to you during the recent crisis not to have been allowed to take a hand in the business of Cabinet-making, as you used to do in the good old days.

Sargent summed up by restating Britain's desire 'to encourage the Greeks to think as an independent nation again', which of course did not mean the abandonment of the policy 'of supporting Greece and helping her economic reconstruction'.[107] With these premises shaping the reasoning of the Foreign Office, much depended on the performance of the Sofulis government and *its own* ability to grasp the realities of the Greek situation. Even when seen from the perspective of the KKE, the initiative was in Sofulis's hands, for while trying to articulate a response to the ascendancy of the Right and the White Terror, the communists were following rather than influencing the course of events.

Which Road to Power? The KKE, February–November 1945

The leftward move of the republican masses in the late 1930s, the wartime achievement of EAM and the failures of the other parties had led to such a proliferation of popular support for the KKE that on liberation the party claimed nearly 420,000 members.[108] The corollary of this massive expansion was the emergence of the Greek Communist Party as an heterogeneous mass force encompassing Marxists-Leninists, socialists, petty bourgeois elements and intellectuals brought together by the will to resist the invaders and the vision of a radical break with the prewar past. The Varkiza Agreement and the surrender of arms frustrated many party members and ELAS guerrillas who felt that the latter prospect was, if not abandoned, then postponed to an unforeseeable future. Bitterness and mistrust towards the party leadership set in fast among the rank and file, with the ELAS cadres voicing their feelings openly.[109] But the leaders had decided otherwise and took little heed of such emotions.

The available records on KKE policy from February 1945 onwards must be seen in their proper context with regard to the unleashing and magnitude of the White Terror and the degree of British penetration of Greek politics; otherwise interpretations of the party's gradual transition to militancy would go astray or degenerate into anachronistic value judgements. On the day Varkiza was signed, the KKE Secretary Giorgis Siandos told foreign press correspondents that *Ta Dekemvriana* had been the clash between 'the popular movement of EAM which seeks a new better future' and 'the old world, which regards power in our country as a privilege sent from God, as a situation which never changes'. Siandos pledged that the party would operate within the constitutional framework and argued that although the circumstances necessitated a representative government, the participation of EAM in it would depend on future developments. The confrontation with the British had been an 'unfortunate clash which ended and will be forgotten', whilst the stationing of troops in the country was almost welcomed: 'if the allies decided to maintain English troops here we say that this is in the interest of Greece, for whatever is in the interest of the allies is also in the interest of Greece'.[110]

This was more than lip-service or an attempt to placate the British and the Greek authorities. Ioannidis's telegram to all party organizations on 15 February instructed them to conceal arms but also outlined the tasks ahead: they were to analyse to KKE and EAM/ELAS members the Varkiza Agreement and the reasoning that led to its signature; the Left would focus its struggle on the complete restoration of democratic liberties and on economic development; the unity of the allied war effort should be maintained in the ranks of EAM, and a broad democratic front ought to be established. Significantly, Ioannidis's directive that it would be incorrect to label Plastiras's government 'fascist' indicated that the communists were willing to give the Prime Minister a chance.[111] Yet for many members of EAM/ELAS the post-Varkiza era represented a brusque relegation to the status of passive spectators while the prewar order was being restored. This mood was encapsulated by Markos Vafiadis – member of the KKE Central Committee and *Kapetanios* of the ELAS Group of Macedonian Divisions; henceforth referred to as Markos – who bitterly commented on the difficulties of adjusting to the new 'foreign [British] domination' and co-existing with 'the state agents who [had] willingly entered into the service of the occupiers and faithfully served them!'.[112]

The White Terror augmented the frustration of the Left and led to protests which fell on deaf ears. On 7 March Leeper promised an EAM delegation to call the Greek government's attention to any violations of Varkiza and asked the Left to substantiate its claims.[113] Five days later EAM addressed to the governments of the United States, the Soviet Union, Britain and France a memorandum calling for the formation of a representative government in the spirit of the Yalta Declaration and the despatch of an interallied commission to investigate the situation.[114] Siandos reiterated the same position in an interview with *Rizospastis*, and on 21 March the Macedonian District Committee of EAM submitted to the ambassadors of the Big Four an identical memorandum which portrayed the conditions of the White Terror in the north and called upon the four powers to restore democratic liberties in the country.[115]

Oddly, on that day Roosevelt embarked on a momentous initiative. The US President suggested to Churchill the despatch of a special mission to assist Greece in developing her productive power 'by concerted, non-political action'. Such a mission would consist of Oliver Lyttelton (the British Production Minister), Donald Nelson (Chairman of the US Production Board) and, to Churchill's horror, Anastas Mikoyan (the People's Commissar for Foreign Trade of the USSR). Roosevelt believed that the three experts could achieve swift and positive results, while their presence in Greece 'might have a highly constructive effect on world opinion'.[116] But at the Foreign Office Soviet participation was seen as humiliating at the moment when the Soviets were the masters in Rumania, and impractical, since the Soviet commissioner was thought unlikely to 'behave correctly'. The Foreign Office recommended the acceptance of Roosevelt's proposal without Soviet participation. Churchill approved the recommendation but was exasperated with the Americans' inability to grasp his missionary approach to the Greek question: 'I agree. But – We have had to take all the risk, do all the work, shed all blood and bear all the abuse, including American abuse. Poor old England.'[117] Churchill sent Roosevelt a reply along these lines on 3 April. The President felt that a bilateral mission would be a mistake, for it might appear as a rejection by Britain and the United States of the Yalta decision for tripartite action in Europe's liberated areas, and might even be construed as repudiation by the two western powers of the entire Yalta Agreement.[118] Four days after his reply to Churchill Roosevelt died, silencing a voice eager to placate at least world opinion – if not EAM – about what was happening in Greece.

The frustration of the rank and file, the unfolding of the White Terror, and the official – foreign and domestic – apathy to the protests of the Left placed the KKE in an awkward predicament. In an attempt to restore confidence and analyse party policy since January 1944, the Politburo summoned the Eleventh Plenum of the Central Committee from 5 to 10 April. In his *compte rendu* Siandos reiterated that the struggle of EAM for national liberation had also assumed a 'deeply social content'. Participation in the Lebanon Conference and in the Papandreou government had been necessitated in view both of the common front between the Greek bourgeois parties and Britain and of the desire for peaceful developments. In the key part of his speech, after asserting that *Ta Dekemvriana* had been the people's 'armed resistance against fascism for democracy and the independence of Greece', the KKE leader went on to justify

Varkiza. The stark choice had been between the conclusion of an agreement and the continuation of guerrilla warfare: 'But this war would not be [for] national liberation, it would be a class war.' The KKE leaders feared that the British might confine ELAS to the mountains, 'suppress the movement in the towns' and bring EAM 'in opposition with the entire Greek people':

> The character of that war ... would be the character of a war against the allies. The basis of the struggle would narrow and certainly it would lack the character it had had before the Germans and the Italians left. We would degenerate into a heresy and they could even proscribe us. So we had to choose the lesser of two evils. Hence the Varkiza Agreement is an agreement of necessity, but it is not an unconditional surrender. It is a minimum of liberties for action. It provides a moral [and] legal prop for the anti-fascist struggle. It also provides the advantage to become a case of the masses, of public opinion abroad, and of the allies. For the implementation of Varkiza we can fight from two sides. To make it a case of the masses, but also to make specific laws which safeguard its application.[119]

Unsurprisingly, the outcome of the Eleventh Plenum was a compromise for the benefit of the Politburo. There had been deviations – rightist: the Lebanon and Caserta Agreements; leftist: the conduct of the battle of Athens in December 1944 and the taking of hostages – but the overall party strategy for national unity was justified by the course of events. The Politburo blissfully asserted that this policy had 'mobilized and roused the entire nation in the war for national liberation ... and yielded the great mass communist party of hundreds of thousands of members'.[120]

The critique of the leadership was epitomized in a letter addressed to the Politburo by Markos on 28 May 1945. For the member of the Central Committee of the KKE and former ELAS *Kapetanios*, the root of the trouble lay in the question of power. At the outset of the Occupation the party had not set its heart upon seizing it, and rightly so in the context of those circumstances. Gradually, however, the initial setting became obsolete. The contribution of the KKE in the birth and spread of EAM, the marshalling of hundreds of thousands of Greeks under the EAM flag, the liquidation of state authority and EAM's administrative record, the hostile attitude of the ruling class towards the resistance, the creation of PEEA and the arms of ELAS – all these had ripened the time for the establishment of an EAM government which would pave the way for further decisive developments. Yet the party had not only shrunk from installing such a regime in Athens but had even showed itself unduly fearful of Britain: 'The impression which is left to me', Markos wrote, 'is that since we were faced with the hostile attitude of England, it could not be done otherwise. Translated more clearly, this position flings us into opportunism for it means condemnation of every cause and its success.' The next step in this line of reasoning was an attack on the efforts of the KKE for national unity:

> When the ruling class had repeatedly betrayed the people by establishing the principle of collaboration with the enemy [and] had entirely cut itself off

from the popular masses, we did not have the right to continuously depend the solution of the country's basic problems on the approval of Sofulis etc ... Of course neither discussions and negotiations should stop nor should one exclude a compromise. But a compromise, not subjugation.[121]

In short, the position in which the KKE found itself by late spring 1945 was indeed bizarre. Its Greek and British opponents loathed it for allegedly having tried to seize power by force of arms, whereas its own rank and file and former ELAS commanders assaulted its leaders for not having done so.

Hopes for a breakthrough were reanimated on 29 May, when Nikos Zachariadis, the Secretary-General of the KKE, arrived in Athens. The Moscow-trained, gifted but autocratic Zachariadis had been arrested by the Metaxas regime in September 1936 and kept in solitary confinement until April 1941, when the collapsing Greek authorities handed him over to the *Gestapo*. He was sent to Dachau, where he was kept until he was freed by US troops in May 1945. At the age of forty-two, Zachariadis was considered innocent of recent deeds and misdeeds, a man whose theoretical equipment and organizational skills guaranteed the '"scientific"' analysis of past errors and the steering of the '"future infallible course"' of the party.[122] The other corollary of his absence, notably his estrangement from Greek realities for almost a decade, was lost sight of amidst the exhilaration at his survival and advent.

Zachariadis immediately resumed his duties and took to work. On 1 June a scheduled session of the Politburo decided to propose to EAM for consideration a programme of Popular Democracy (*Laiki Dimokratia*),[123] while the Secretary-General expounded the party's aspirations in an interview with *Rizospastis*. Zachariadis asserted that the KKE had never aimed at seizing power against the people's will and that it would never aspire to a course of action advocated only by 'Trotskyists, anarchists and idiots'. The task ahead was to rally the majority of workers, peasants and the lower-middle classes, who would bring about the bourgeois-democratic transformation of the country.[124]

A few days later the party made a stunning gesture. Aris Velouchiotis, the former *Kapetanios* of the ELAS GHQ, had opposed the policy of integration with the old system and reconciliation with the British and had remained in the mountains. His prophetic insight with regard to the White Terror had come true, yet his ideas annoyed and embarrassed the Politburo. Since the wartime KKE leaders (Siandos and Ioannidis) were in no mood to accept Velouchiotis's criticism, they had already decided at the Eleventh Plenum of April 1945 to excommunicate him. Writing from his Siberian exile in July 1973, only a few days before he committed suicide, Zachariadis admitted that taking the Varkiza Agreement for what it was, namely 'an act of state', and realizing that he could not strike it off without dealing an 'irreparable blow to the movement', he had decided to sacrifice Velouchiotis.[125] On 12 June *Rizospastis* published a condemnation of him on the grounds that his conduct assisted the Right in its onslaught against the Left, and three days later the Politburo expelled him from the party.[126] Denounced by the KKE and hunted down by government forces, Velouchiotis took his own life, with his adjutant following suit. It was a fitting sign of the times that monarchist irregulars chopped the two heads off and hung them from the lamp-post in the central square of Trikala, in Thessaly.[127]

June 15 was a busy day for the Politburo. Apart from Velouchiotis's expulsion, it endorsed a draft programme of Popular Democracy and submitted it to EAM. The EAM Central Committee approved it and published it as a brochure on 23 July. Popular Democracy was defined as a new type of regime embodying the alliance between workers, cultivators, artisans, the intelligentsia and the small and medium bourgeoisie. Private property would not be abolished, and private initiative would be encouraged in order to facilitate patriotic industrialists and businessmen, whose interests should conform to those of the people. After a detailed projection of policies towards a wide range of issues – from unemployment to the position of women and the youth – the Programme concluded with a number of points indicative of the general inclinations of the KKE and EAM: Greece should maintain friendly relations with all four great powers; EAM supported all national territorial claims and demanded frontier rectification at the expense of Bulgaria; and finally, EAM was willing to cooperate with any party which would agree with the 'basic lines' of the Programme.[128]

The coalition of the parties of EAM was the only Greek political organization to present a detailed programme to the people. Whereas the Liberals had no programme whatsoever and the Populists crusaded for rabid anti-communism and the return of the King, EAM and the KKE put forward a set of moderate policies rich in nationalistic overtones and devoid of revolutionary content. More crucially, the publication of this document in July 1945 suggests that the KKE then looked towards peaceful evolution. As Siandos explained to Sarafis, the party anticipated that the people would gradually realize that the government's policies and its submissiveness to London could offer no solution to the country's problems; hence growing popular discontent and the passing of time would outdistance memories of *Ta Dekemvriana* and scale down hostility towards the Left.[129]

Further evidence of the KKE's attitude of patience and expectation lies in Zachariadis's meetings with Leeper and MacVeagh. On 4 June the KKE leader assured the British ambassador that his party would create no difficulties for Anglo-Soviet relations and that it would work towards pacification, free elections and close co-operation with the Big Three. Leeper proclaimed himself satisfied with what he heard.[130] Later in the same month, after a similar meeting with Zachariadis, MacVeagh felt that the KKE 'would seem now to be definitely embarked on a long-term policy of lulling its opponents to sleep by overtly confining itself to politics'. The US ambassador added that if reconstruction proceeded swiftly and there were no delays in the conduct of the elections, Greece 'has little fear in the near future from any renewed direct action initiative on the part of the extreme Left'.[131]

Having identified the real centre of power, Zachariadis directed his benevolent pledges accordingly. On 5 June he published in *Rizospastis* a momentous article on Anglo-Greek relations. These, he asserted, were marred by mutual and deep-rooted mistrust between Britain and the Greek Left. The latter was convinced that London's policy aimed at propping up the reactionary forces in Greece at the expense of EAM, hence the tolerance of the White Terror. Britain was under the strong impression, which Greek reactionaries toiled hard to reinforce, that the regime envisaged by EAM would subvert British strategic interests in the eastern Mediterranean. Yet the Left ought to be fully aware of Greece's location in a vital sea-link of the Empire: if, therefore, the British ceased to interfere in Greek affairs, the Left, conscious of their strategic sensitivities, should reach an understanding with them provided that 'our national honour, independence and integrity are not violated'.[132] This remarkably conciliatory gesture was in line with Zachariadis's promise to Leeper that he would not cause friction between Britain and the Soviet Union over Greece.

The British took no notice, nor were they inclined to do so, but the KKE leader elaborated his views in the Twelfth Plenum of the Central Committee which met from 25 to 27 June. Zachariadis blessed the KKE policy during the Occupation and argued that what had gone wrong was EAM's relations with Britain: EAM had tried to co-operate but its efforts had been subverted by the Greek reaction, which had come to be entrusted by Britain with the protection of her interests. On this basis, he recapitulated on his article of 5 June and postulated his Theory of the Two Poles. As a Balkan-European country, Greece belonged to a pole centred on the Soviet Union, and at the same time, as a Mediterranean country, she belonged to another pole centred on Britain; therefore the correct foreign policy ought to bring these two poles together through a Greek axis firmly rooted in Greek realities.[133] Though simple, no doubt the underlying premise of this thesis was sound, realistic and audacious, for it recognized the vital British interests in the eastern Mediterranean and asserted that the KKE did not in principle object to them. What Zachariadis sought to do was to tackle the exclusive British domination of Greece and allay fears that the regime envisaged by EAM would entail the blindfold alignment of the country to the Soviet Union. The Twelfth Plenum accordingly emphasized that the restoration of friendly relations with London and Moscow, and co-operation with the United States and France, 'must constitute the basic pillar for a democratic foreign policy of Greece'.[134] The initiative for Greek neutrality, postulated by Zachariadis in 1946, had its origins in the Theory of the Two Poles and the political resolution of the Twelfth Plenum.

The new element in KKE policy that emerged from the Twelfth Plenum was the advocacy of 'mass popular self-defence'. As by mid-May 1945 the White Terror had claimed 299 murders and thousands of cases of beatings, arrests and torture,[135] the KKE called upon leftists to defend themselves by way of mass strikes and demonstrations in the towns, groups of unarmed men and women in the villages, and defensive armed actions by former members of ELAS hiding in the mountains; at the outset, however, the self-defence groups were unarmed.[136] The call for mass popular self-defence was issued not only against the background of the White Terror, but also against persistent rumours of a monarchist coup, to be engineered by monarchist organizations within the army and semi-fascist groups outside it.[137] It hardly represented a substantial reversal of policy, for Zachariadis had to use words to stand by the persecuted and placate the party militants who wanted deeds. Thus in early July the KKE spoke of the 'English authorities of political and military occupation', whose inactivity emboldened monarchists desirous of a coup;[138] but that occurred during the last days of Churchill's premiership.

The jubilation at Labour's victory in Britain gave way to frustration when the expectations of the KKE were rebuffed by the new government in London. To avoid participation in the 'comedy' which aimed at 'falsifying the will and the sentiment of the people', on 10 August the KKE withdrew its representatives from the committees revising the electoral registers. Two weeks later Zachariadis told a mass rally in Thessaloniki that Bevin erred when 'he behaved towards Greece like a master towards a colony'. The Left had so far showed self-control and would continue to do so, but once the limits were reached, the ELAS anthem *Embros ELAS yia tin Ellada* (Forward ELAS for Greece) would resound again throughout the country. If Bevin's 'occupation troops' were unable to maintain law and order, they should withdraw; and on account of the White Terror, the KKE leader reiterated the threat of abstention from the elections, which the party had first voiced in mid-June.[140]

Although Zachariadis's speech was branded 'wild and irresponsible' by the Foreign Office,[141] it more closely resembled the highly emotive outburst of a frustrated man who had to articulate a response to the grievances of the persecuted and the party militants. His outburst could also reflect the communists' feelings about the White Terror, their assumptions of British responsibility for it, and the eventual disappointment of the hopes raised by Churchill's electoral defeat. The feeling of frustration among leftists cannot be overemphasized. On signing the Varkiza Agreement the KKE had given concrete signs that it intended to conform to legality; thus it would be of tremendous interest to be able to test the sincerity of its pledges against a background of tranquillity, law and order. Since, however, that was nowhere to be found in Greece in 1945, the evolution of KKE policy must be seen in the context of the White Terror and the extent of British intervention in Greek internal affairs. After all, it was not only the hot-headed who lapsed into emotive outbursts. In June 1945 Sarafis warned Colonel Woodhouse that 'patience has its limits and the Greek people have enough pride and faith in freedom and enough mountains to conduct guerrilla warfare for their ideals, as they have done many times'.[142] Nor were nationalistic outbursts confined to the Left. During his brief tenure as Prime Minister, Kanellopoulos had rejected the vesting of British advisers with executive powers, while Plastiras is said to have once protested to Leeper with the following words: '"after all we are not Savages"'. The high-handed attitude of the British had prompted Professor Amandos to warn Leeper that a prolonged British presence would be seen as a squeeze of Greece's freedom, to which the ambassador angrily retorted that the Greeks must 'not only ask for freedom but also for justice'.[143]

Zachariadis capitalized on slighted nationalist feeling in order to placate die-hards within the KKE, highlight the patriotic fervour of the Left, and, conceivably, awaken some socialist feeling in the hearts of Labour ministers. At any rate, there is more evidence that the Thessaloniki speech fell short of heralding a new line in party policy. At the Seventh Congress of the KKE, held in Athens from 1 to 6 October 1945, the line and actions of the leadership from 1941 to 1945 were blessed.[144] Zachariadis reiterated the essence of his Theory of the Two Poles and called for an understanding with Britain based on the principles of equality, mutual respect, recognition of Greece's sovereign rights, and cessation of British interference in Greek internal affairs. If, however, the British were incapable of halting the White Terror, they should withdraw and a representative government be set up to pursue peaceful developments.[145] Despite some sabre-rattling evident in the proceedings, the Political Resolution of the Congress repeated the threat of abstention from the polls, but a Proclamation to the people suggested that the KKE would change its mind if the White Terror ceased and a general amnesty were granted. The call for mass popular self-defence was reaffirmed, as was the party's aim towards the bourgeois democratic transformation of the country through the Programme of Popular Democracy.[146]

From the Seventh Congress to November 1945 the KKE repeatedly demanded a new government, the suppression of monarchist bands, equality for all citizens, a general amnesty, a genuine compilation of the electoral registers, and rehabilitation of the National Resistance. When Sofulis formed his Liberal Cabinet the Politburo invited the entire democratic spectrum to obey and support it. The KKE would back every measure intended to restore order so that the people could express their will in free elections. It would also support the economic policies of the government provided that 'the exploiters of the people' were forced to undertake their share towards reconstruction.[147]

Were it not for the concealment of arms, there would be little doubt that in the post-Varkiza era the KKE had opted for the pursuit of power through constitutional means. Ioannidis's telegram of 15 February 1945 may cast some doubt on this assumption, but nonetheless it would be a gross anachronism to interpret in the light of that order what happened from summer 1946 onwards. It has to be stressed that whatever the reasons for storing arms, the communists did not start making use of them until a year and a half later. Hence the policy of the KKE must be assessed within the political, social and economic context of 1945 rather than that of 1946. The KKE was a political organization which undoubtedly aimed at power, yet for a considerable period of time the arms remained in store while the party pursued its objectives by means of political and industrial pressure. Had conditions of equality and tranquillity been established, one might speculate whether the KKE would have stuck to its pledges or would have found it more propitious to unearth its arms; and that would be political science fiction. Whatever the ulterior designs of the communists, their initial conciliatory mood gave way to emotional outbursts and threats against the Greek and British governments primarily because the entire Left found itself confronted by the wave of monarchist reaction.

The tension within the Left and the critiques against the KKE leadership were important in so far as they testified to the mood of many former ELAS guerrillas and account for the tougher stand adopted by Zachariadis in late summer 1945. Verbal militancy seems to have been intended as an emollient for the trouble-makers on the left and a stimulus to some pacifying gesture from the British and Greek authorities. The emollient by and large worked, whereas the stimulus did not – for reasons that fell well beyond Zachariadis's responsibility. At least until November 1945 the KKE leaders had plunged themselves into the constitutional arena, though the storing of arms indicates that in the back of their minds there must have been a dim vision of the military as well. Given that there is no evidence that the KKE concealed arms in preparation of civil war, and that in the past four years it had accumulated ample evidence to justify suspicion against the Greek Right and the British, it would seem that Ioannidis's order was largely a precautionary, defensive measure. For the time being the entire Left granted Sofulis its support in the hope that the White Terror would abate and the economic chaos would be tackled. The British apprehension was that a failure of the Liberal leader would lead to a right-wing takeover and virtually to civil war. Since Hector McNeil had also articulated this, the Sofulis experiment assumed over-whelming importance.

The Sofulis Experiment: Restoration of Sovereignty

The government of the eighty-five year-old Sofulis, the last card the British had left to play, was called upon to tackle a wide range of problems including the economic chaos, the state of affairs in the armed forces and the security services, the conditions of law and order, the congestion of prisons, and – most explosive of all – the conduct of elections. On the economic plane, the resignation of Varvaressos had restored the previous policy of apathy. Endeavours towards reconstruction were nowhere to be seen, the peril of rampant inflation was growing, government expenditure far exceeded its revenue, the civil service was totally disrupted, industry and trade were stagnant, and unemployment was widespread. To defeat speculation and restore public confidence Vice-Premier Tsouderos turned to the United States for economic aid, but the Americans were reluctant to put money into Greece until the Greeks themselves did something 'to get their house in order'. By late December 1945 Tsouderos had only secured a $25m loan from the Export-Import Bank, accompanied by the warning that further aid would depend on the effectiveness of the Greek government in dealing with economic stabilization.[148]

American circumspection was in marked contrast to the far more interested British approach to Greek politics. This is a euphemism for a British policy which showed some of the trappings of nineteenth century imperialism. The starting point for this assessment is the qualification, made by John Gallagher and Ronald Robinson, that imperialism does not necessarily have to be directly associated with economic integration, for it often extends beyond areas of primary economic concerns in order to act for their strategic protection. Robinson defined modern imperialism as the process whereby an expanding society gains inordinate influence or control over a weaker society

71

through dollar or gun-boat diplomacy, ideological suasion, conquest and rule, with the object of shaping it in its own interest and image. The key mechanism for the management of the weaker society was the use of local ruling élites as mediators between the expanding power and the indigenous political system, which allowed the expanding society to intervene directly to secure its interests only when the mediating structure broke down or when one ruling élite chose to resist; in the latter case an alternative élite willing to collaborate with the expanding power was installed in office.[149]

British policy in Greece in the 1940s was not founded on considerations of primary economic expansion but on the concept of strategic protection, reinforced by the political and social reality of Greece and the world situation at large. In this pattern the role of mediators was taken up by the traditional parties of Greece, which were lured by what Britain had to offer them in political, diplomatic, military and economic aid. Furthermore, this analogy allows for a parallel to be drawn between the methods used by Britain to control Greek affairs and the pattern whereby imperial policy had been enforced in the Victorian era. Wherever and whenever British supremacy was threatened, the imperial authorities retained full responsibility, or – if they had devolved it – intervened directly to secure their interests. Once a 'responsible' government had been set up, there came a switch to indirect methods of preserving British interests. With regard to colonies, the slackening of formal political bonds enabled Britain to rely on economic dependence and mutual good feeling in order to keep them bound to the metropolis. The pattern of imperial policy involved political action as an aid to commercial supremacy, which in turn strengthened political influence. A central task of imperial policy-makers had been to encourage stable governments as good investment risks or, in weaker and 'unsatisfactory' states, to coerce them into more cooperative attitudes.[150]

In the case of Greece the stage of direct intervention had culminated with Churchill's policy. In the post-Varkiza era the British resorted to the structural penetration of the Greek state apparatus and to indirect methods of control, exercising their prerogative to intervene only when the Greeks were uncooperative. As the scarcity of alternative governments in Athens necessitated support to Sofulis, Bevin offered economic assistance in the hope of establishing the Greek economy on a sound basis. In this he was backed by Hugh Dalton, the Chancellor of the Exchequer, who nevertheless shared American doubts as to whether the Greeks were 'capable of putting their house into order'.[151] Hence the Anglo-Greek Financial and Economic Agreement of 24 January 1946, whereby Greece was offered a £10m credit for stabilizing her currency, waiver of repayment of the £46m she was loaned in 1940–1941, technical assistance by way of a consultative mission on economic, financial and industrial matters and, on invitation by the Greek government, the appointment of British advisers in certain Greek Ministries. In return, the Greek government undertook to set up a Currency Commission (whose composition was arranged by Bevin) and, from the exchange resources of the Bank of Greece, to deposit with the Bank of England £15m from the remaining war credit of £19m, and the new £10m credit.[152]

Although the agreement was not a spectacular affair, it testified to Bevin's preoccupation with restoring the British position in Greece by economic means. This approach grossly overlooked the fact that the White Terror – as ominous a reality as the devastated economy, and yet more pressing – could only be halted by strong political action on the part of those who held power. In late 1945–early 1946 Varkiza remained a dead letter. Two independent reports confirmed that in northern Greece the Left was paying a high price for its predominance during the Occupation. The former deputy D. Andreadis toured the region and submitted to Tsouderos a memorandum on the activities of 'local criminal elements' and collaborators. Geoffrey Hoare, the *News Chronicle* special correspondent, witnessed little terrorism as such but emphasized the injustices against the Left. The favourite pastime of the monarchist X organization was the beating up of 'local "Communists"' – an incredibly elastic term. With the majority of the military and the gendarmerie being staunchly right-wing, redress for the victims or arrest and punishment of the aggressors were unheard of. Discrimination was evinced even in the distribution of UNRRA supplies: not only individual EAM supporters but entire villages of leftist sympathies received very little, usually that which right-wing villages and individuals did not want. In the Peloponnese, according to the military governor of the region, monarchist bands enjoyed even greater liberty; the most active of them had become 'literally the scourge of Laconia and partly of Messinia by plundering, physical assaults, unprovoked murders of old men and women, and its chiefs' easy acquisition of wealth'.[155] In the civil service purges were carried out by monarchists and collaborators, hence large numbers of resistance sympathizers were ousted.[156] The judicial onslaught against the Left had led to a massive proliferation of the prison population, while the number of wanted individuals and those preventively detained exceeded 80,000. A Decongestion Law based on a partial amnesty did little to rectify the situation.[157]

The entire Greek Cabinet was gravely purturbed by the reign of terror in the provinces and by its increasing understanding of the royalist complexion of the army and the security forces. The British, however, undermined their own offspring, for when the Greek War Minister endeavoured to purge the armed forces of collaborators and right-wing extremists, he stumbled over the dogged opposition of Leeper and the British Military Mission. Reporting the incident to London, the ambassador showed that his own prejudices were so powerful that one may speculate as to the extent to which his despatches account for Bevin's distorted view of the Greek situation. On 7 December Leeper cabled to London:

> There is some unrest among officers that the new Government will carry out many changes in appointments in order to ensure that the Republicans are in control. It is felt that such changes, far from neutralizing any Right-wing political tendencies which may be latent in the corps of officers, would only serve to bring back acute political rivalries into an army which is beginning to forget them under the influence of professional zeal stimulated by the work of the British Military Mission. Anxiety in the army

is growing to such an extent that official assurances to it on the part of the Government may soon be imperative.[158]

Leeper and the British Military Mission had espoused the views of right-wing Greek officers that the minister would impair the reorganization of the armed forces. Moreover, the ambassador's own prejudices and the professional parochialism of the BMM staff – which rested in the preoccupation with the establishment of an efficient army notwithstanding its politics – had generated the gross misjudgement that the removal of collaborators and extreme right-wingers amounted to the subjection of the army to republican control and the reintroduction of political rivalries in it. On top of that, Sofulis had his hands tied by an agreement between the Voulgaris government and the BMM/BPM whereby changes in the armed forces had to be approved by the British Missions. The Greek Prime Minister appealed to the advance team of the US contingent of AMFOGE (Allied Mission for Observing the Greek Elections) to exert pressure on the British to allow his government to make five or six changes in the High Command of the gendarmerie and the army,[159] but once more his words fell on deaf ears. The Americans held that the 'apparent hope' of Sofulis's government was to 'maintain power and postpone elections indefinitely or at least until firmly in control [of the] armed forces, gendarmerie and civil services'.[160] As if American backing were not enough, Lieutenant-General William Morgan (Supreme Allied Commander, Mediterranean) urged Sofulis to issue a statement of reassurance to the officers, which the Greek Prime Minister promptly did.[161]

The dissension between the Greek government and the British authorities reached its peak on 20 February 1946, when the Minister of Public Order Stamatis Merkouris resigned after British pressure on Sofulis. Merkouris had side-stepped Sir Charles Wickham, the Head of the British Police Mission, and attempted to bring about changes in the gendarmerie without his permission. The incident is particularly illuminating with regard to the quality of information reaching the Foreign Office from Athens, for the juxtaposition of two pieces of evidence reveals the extent to which the views of British policy-makers were partly based on remarkably biased and short-sighted reports. On 11 February Leeper cabled:

> Gendarmes know that whereas the Right Wing extremists will fight them when driven into a corner but are not fundamentally hostile, Communists are their permanent enemies and are out gunning for them all the time. They also know that they can only cope successfully with the lawbreakers insofar as the population, though being on their side, is ready to supply force, and that for the most part the population is in fact not willing to cooperate against the Right.

The ambassador had convinced himself that Sofulis's government had showed 'a marked political bias in regard to gendarmerie transfers', yet at the same time he admitted that the majority of the force was staunchly right-wing. He spoke to the Greek Prime Minister about the possibility of sacking Merkouris, for 'if purges were effected merely on the score of political leanings, the great majority of the whole gendarmerie force would have to be purged and could not be replaced without a long period of chaos'.[162]

A month after his resignation, in an article in the liberal daily *To Vima*, Merkouris projected an altogether different picture. On his assumption of duties as Minister of Public Order he had realized that the security services 'had deviated from their destination and had become accomplices in the terrorist efforts of the organizations of the Extreme Right'. He attempted to correct the situation but faced 'unprecedented reaction'. The Ministry worked out a plan for the elimination of the monarchist bands operating in Thessaly and Merkouris himself went to Volos to supervise its execution; there the local Gendarmerie Commander told him that the operation would have to be abandoned because the gendarmes refused to move against monarchist bands. As for the Peloponnese, the Minister drew on the confidential reports of the Gendarmerie Chief and asserted that the force had not yet discovered 'the psychological disposition and strength' to implement the law against the Right. Cooperation between the security services and the nationalist organizations continued unabated, for it was impossible even to prosecute the responsible officers at the moment when officers who had overtly collaborated with the occupiers were acquitted almost *en bloc*.

The Police emulated he Gendarmerie in a number of ways: it refused to arrest the perpetrators of 'daily criminal incidents' against leftists even in Athens or to execute warrants against collaborators, whereas citizens were often beaten up in police stations. Merkouris tried his hand but again 'met reaction from all quarters'. In the provincial prisons, which were wardened by the National Guard, right-wingers held on charges of collaboration escaped *en masse*. The arms surrendered by ELAS after Varkiza had been handed over by the National Guard to right-wingers.[163] Merkouris's story was confirmed later by Tsouderos. The Sofulis government tried to eliminate the monarchist bands which 'had been organized in preparation for the March 1946 elections as well as the plebiscite', but Merkouris 'at the last moment faced the opposition of the Army HQ, who refused to co-operate if the rightist bands were to be pursued'.[164]

The White Terror thus becomes the *sine qua non* in the background against which the actions of all sides must be analysed. Occasionally even Bevin had to admit that the state of affairs in Greece was unsatisfactory. On 18 December, while in Moscow, he told Molotov that *Ta Dekemvriana* had been the deed of extremists from both sides, and that now the reprisals against the Left 'were the work of the Greek Government'. When his Soviet counterpart charged that the British were the masters in Greece, Bevin was forced to admit that 'conditions in Greece were the same as in Bulgaria where the Russians were masters'.[165] Even so, at every suitable opportunity the British Foreign Secretary wasted no chance to reiterate what appears to have been his missionary approach to the Greek situation. On 1 January 1946, in an off-the-record talk he told British diplomatic correspondents that he had 'got very irritable over Greece'. The standard of life was far too low and things too unsettled there, so he was trying his 'damnedest to build a sound economy in

Greece upon which the political structure of the country will ultimately rest'. Success in Greece was 'absolutely vital, not only to help herself, but to be a stabilizing factor in the Mediterranean'.[166]

That was only one aspect of the question, for economic aid would enhance Greece's dependence on Britain. Moreover, Anglo-Soviet relations, which had got off to a bad start at the London meeting of the Council of Foreign Ministers in September–October 1945, stayed frigid throughout the remainder of the year.[167] Thus on 17 December the British asserted that the stationing of their troops in Greece was intended as a deterrent to Soviet pressure, or – in the event of Soviet withdrawal from Bulgaria – to the threat of the Bulgarian army itself.[168] Bevin's fears about a clash with the Soviets over Greece were intensified on 21 January 1946, when Andrei Gromyko, Acting Head of the Soviet Delegation to the United Nations, submitted a document to the Security Council charging that the presence of British troops constituted interference with Greece's internal affairs and contributed to tension detrimental to international peace.[169] There followed a lot of falling out between Bevin and Andrei Vyshinsky, the Soviet representative at the United Nations, especially when the latter proposed the despatch of a commission to investigate the situation in Greece; Bevin uttered a patriotic outburst: 'I will have no commission of any kind go to Greece. I am either a decent citizen, and my people are decent citizens, or we aren't.'[170] In the event the matter was declared closed on 6 February, when the Chairman of the Security Council read a summary statement – prepared by the US representative Edward R. Stettinius and accepted by Bevin and Vyshinsky – which acquitted Britain from the Soviet charges but refrained from rebuking the Soviet Union.[171]

The Soviet move was intended to relieve the pressure which had been brought upon Moscow two days earlier, when Iran had protested to the United Nation at the presence of Red Army troops in its northern regions.[172] The evidence in fact points to a very cautious attitude on the part of the Kremlin towards the Greek situation. In early 1945 the minimum objectives of the Soviet Union had been the recovery by the Red Army of the benefits it had secured as a result of the Nazi–Soviet pact and the recognition by the western powers of its right to retain these benefits. By the summer of that year Stalin had achieved far more than this minimum programme, both in Europe and in the Far East. What lay beyond that was not so much a timetable for further expansion but a range of possibilities in Europe, the Mediterranean and the Middle East, which the Kremlin considered and probed without ever committing itself unless circumstances in these areas became favourable to a Soviet involvement. Especially with regard to the British position in the Mediterranean and the Middle East, Stalin had not failed to notice that Britain was an overstretched and declining power, hence likely to abandon some of her commitments. Thus in 1944–1946 the Soviet Union's assumption of diplomatic relations with Egypt, Syria, the Lebanon and Iraq, the pressure upon Iran and Turkey, and the demand from the West of the mandate of former Italian Libya certainly stemmed from the traditional power-politics pursuits of the Tsars, but also signified Stalin's cautious and prudent attempt to advance Soviet influence in the Mediterranean.

Yet there was another factor accounting for the lack of a concrete timetable for further Soviet expansion. The major influence on postwar Soviet foreign policy was the fear that the world-wide expansion of American capitalism would assume an imperialist character and thus strengthen anti-Soviet forces, especially in Europe. To counter this, Stalin decided to mobilize all forces capable of offering unified resistance to American capitalism and extend Soviet power, yet without jeopardizing these forces or unnecessarily provoking the United States. In western Europe communist parties were to cooperate with other 'democratic' and 'anti-fascist' forces, drop revolutionary vocabulary and insurrectional tactics, and cooperate with the West in so far as this did not endanger Soviet security. The underlying aim of this policy was the stabilization of political and economic relations in western and southern Europe within the framework of the existing order, even if this inhibited the development of socialist movements and dashed the hopes of the European resistance fighters for radical social change.[173]

Stalin's attitude towards the Greek Left clearly bears out his cautious and prudent probing of opportunities. Following his 'tick' on Churchill's 'naughty document' on 9 October 1944, during *Ta Dekemvriana* he had refused any assistance to the embattled KKE, while in 1945 his approach to Greece was characterized by circumspection and lack of information. On 8 January 1945 the Soviet government decided to open an embassy in Athens but the arrival of an ambassador was postponed in order not to strengthen the position of the 'reactionary' Greek government. Soon, however, the Soviets admitted that their information on the Greek situation was insufficient, and on 3 January 1946 Admiral Konstantin Rodionov arrived in Athens as the Soviet ambassador. The Kremlin's instructions to Rodionov were to study the policies of the Greek government, the parties of the Left and – especially – of Britain. Significantly, the Soviets had already discerned in Greece a series of indications suggesting a latent internecine strife which might lead to civil war. The embassy staff should be extremely cautious in their behaviour, and Rodionov was specifically instructed to thwart any attempts by the Greek Left to stage friendly demonstrations outside the Soviet embassy, and even denounce such manifestations.[174]

More caution was exhibited by the Soviets when an EAM delegation arrived in Moscow on 15 January 1946. According to British records, after trying in vain for three weeks to meet with Soviet leaders, the delegates departed on 8 February having seen no one more important than a local trade union functionary. They were so irritated with Soviet indifference that they complained to the Greek Embassy in Moscow, and five days later the Foreign Office concluded that the visit 'was not a great success'.[175] The Soviet records tell a different story the essence of which is corroborated by a Greek communist account. On 23 January 1946 an official of the Soviet Foreign Ministry prepared a note on the 'Issues which may be raised during the imminent meeting of the EAM delegates with com. V.M. Molotov'. According to this note, which tallies with the memoirs of the one communist among the delegates, Dimitris Partsalidis, the Soviet counsel was to attract the leaders of those anti-fascist parties and groups now outside EAM; participate in the elections; drop their nationalistic territorial claims against Bulgaria and Albania; and, most importantly, that EAM 'must not be side-tracked by the provocations which will aim at the instigation of an armed clash in the interior of the country, [and] which will justify the retention of the English troops in Greece'.[176]

In Athens and London the Soviet moves were construed otherwise. The squabbles at the United Nations – in essence no more than a bogus internationalization of the Greek situation – offered evidence of the position of the Greek government. Sofulis and his ministers rejoiced over Bevin's grandiose defence of his Greek policy,[177] whereas the Foreign Minister Sofianopoulos was sacked for trying to steer a moderate course between the British and Soviet positions. His fault was to suggest an innocuous compromise statement that the British troops were welcome in Greece until conditions for free elections had been established, and that the restoration of normality in the country was an internal affair which should not be discussed at the United Nations.[178]

Far more important was the impact of the Soviet move upon the British outlook on the Greek question. Fears of an encroachment on the region were kindled and critiques of British policy in Greece were contemptuously dismissed. On 11 February 1946 the Labour MP Konni Zilliacus, a friend and associate of Attlee's, sent the British Prime Minister a note in which he expressed his perturbation over Labour's foreign policy. Especially with regard to the British 'occupation of Greece', the veteran left-winger discerned a continuity of imperial policies:

> In December 1944 Mr. Bevin told the Labour Conference that we had gone into Greece because the British Empire could not abandon its position in the Mediterranean. To put it concretely the Admiralty have insisted from Cairo days onward that we should install a Greek Government that would allow us to build a bigger and better Malta on Greek territory in order to keep the Russians out of the Mediterranean.

This, along with British policy in the Middle East and elsewhere, was 'the traditional language of power politics and these are the traditional aims of British Imperialism since the nineteenth century.'[179]

Attlee dismissed the note as 'based on an astonishing lack of understanding of the facts',[180] but before the end of the year his thinking would undergo a drastic, if temporary, change. According to Hugh Dalton, from early March the Prime Minister started to press on the Chiefs of Staff and the Defence Committee of the Cabinet 'a large view of his own' aiming at 'considerable disengagement from areas where there is a risk of clashing with the Russians. We should pull out, he thinks, from all the Middle East, including Egypt and Greece'.[181] Although this difference of assessment between Attlee and Bevin was to culminate in the end of the year, for the time being it yielded no change in British policy. In a memorandum prepared for the Defence Committee of the Cabinet on 13 March 1946, the Foreign Secretary expounded his overpowering reasons for this:

The Mediterranean is the area through which we bring influence to bear on Southern Europe, the soft underbelly of France, Italy, Yugoslavia, Greece and Turkey. Without our physical presence in the Mediterranean, we should cut little ice with those States which would fall, like Eastern Europe, under the totalitarian yoke. We should also lose our position in the Middle East.

This was the main reason why it was 'essential' that Greece remained 'with us politically'. Furthermore, the very word 'Greece' evoked connotations of liberty and independence, while Bevin was convinced that by protecting the Eastern Mediterranean he was defending social democracy and the British 'way of life'. It was the apostolic approach:

In the European scene ... we are the last bastion of social democracy. It may be said that this now represents our way of life as against the red tooth and claw of American capitalism and the Communist dictatorship of Soviet Russia. Any weakening of our position in the Mediterranean area will, in my view, lead to the end of social democracy there and submit us to a pressure which would make our position untenable.[182]

Bevin's high moral tone could hardly conceal the pursuit of traditional imperial objectives. Within a matter of weeks, and for the following three years, he would have to explain to his party how 'the last bastion of social democracy' could support so profoundly un-socialist a regime as that of Greece. The Foreign Office staff, who did not need to bother their heads about moralizing, encapsulated the position in less refined diction. William Hayter argued that the best possible outcome of the Greek elections would be a left-of-centre coalition strong enough to hold the balance between Left and Right. The worst would be an electoral victory of EAM, 'which would mean the end of British influence in Greece and the rapid conversion of that country into another Yugoslavia'. Irrespective of the outcome of the polls, the Foreign Office feared that the situation in Greece would not be stabilized, therefore the British government had to learn to live with Greek politics, even if that led to a repressive or 'reactionary' regime distasteful to them. As it was impossible to plant a democracy of the British variety in Greece, London's sole aim should be mere independence so that Greece could serve the necessity of a buffer state against Soviet expansion. To that end, Britain would 'bolster up Greece financially' and 'make it plain that we regard her independence as essential to our security'.[183]

The difficulties endemic in such a course prompted Leeper in late February 1946 to suggest to Sargent an astonishing alternative means of keeping Greece 'on our side of the fence'. In the emerging economic and political conditions of the postwar world Greece could not be truly independent, thus to ensure that she would not 'gravitate into Russian orbit', the ambassador proposed that she become a member of the British Commonwealth: 'Objections would no doubt be raised to the incorporation of a very foreign, very Mediterranean element from the other end of Europe in a predominantly Anglo-Saxon group. But ... are we not hoping that before long the utterly foreign peoples of India will enjoy that status?'[184] Leeper was probably unaware that the implicit message in his prescription was a tacit admission that British policy in Greece, as applied since 1943, had failed. The attempts to halt the influence of the Left and bolster (preferably) centrist politicians who would safeguard British interests had been such shambles that twenty-one months after the Lebanon Conference and fourteen months after *Ta Dekemvriana* Leeper was as anxious as ever to keep the country on the British 'side of the fence'.

The Foreign Office was convinced that the policy hitherto pursued was the only tenable one. Hayter commented that Leeper's suggestion was tanta-mount to the incorporation of Greece into the British Empire and the assumption of responsibility for controlling and defending her. Such a scheme would be unworkable for it 'would turn Greece not into a Dominion but into a Crown Colony, which would be much more indefensible internationally and would be quite unacceptable to the Greeks themselves'. Then, the motives of the Greek politicians were regarded as highly suspicious. What they wanted, Hayter added, was that 'they should govern the country themselves and that we should pay for it and defend it'.[185] Christopher Warner of the Southern Department was more sympathetic, primarily because Leeper's idea would be a major step towards the solution of the defence problem: 'We could hardly be criticized for stationing troops in a Dominion'. He had reservations, however, as to the reaction of US and British public opinion to the Dominion solution, and the economic aspect, which was 'the terrible snag in the course we are trying to pursue'.[186] The final blow against Leeper's suggestion was dealt by Hector McNeil, whose minute indicates that temporarily Greece had to be viewed as a sort of colony, unworthy of Dominion status:

> I still think that colonial treatment whether by us or by some trusteeship group is the only method of nursing Greece towards solvency and political stability. "Dominion status" is meantime impossible because, as Mr. Hayter infers, Greece is a backward, extravagant and irresponsible country whose vanities are made greater and whose difflculties are therefore accentuated because for both us and the USSR Greece has strategic importance.[187]

The decision of the Foreign Office to stick to its course raises the question whether British policy-makers had a clear view of the consequences of their policy and whether they were prepared to accept them in the name of keeping Greece on their 'side of the fence'. The issue is properly illustrated in the course towards the elections which, under British pressure, Sofulis had pledged to hold on 31 March 1946. His government had realized the need for their postponement due to the conditions of law and order; the grip of the Right on the army, the security forces and the civil service; and the need to update the electoral registers. Thus on 6 December the Greek Embassy in Washington made an appeal to the State Department. The Americans, inspired by reports that Sofulis wished to cling to power and that all other parties (save EAM) wanted the elections on the above date, rejected it on the grounds that postponement would pose problems for their successful supervision.[188]

On the last day of 1945 Bevin proposed to his Cabinet colleagues that Britain, the United States and France jointly advise the Greek government to make 'a firm and final declaration' that elections would be held on 31 March, and he went on with a plan for their supervision. The projected allied commission would be assembled in Italy 'where, before proceeding to Greece, they would receive a short course of instruction designed to give them the background of the present situation in Greece and to equip them sufficiently to carry out their tasks as observers'.[189] There should be little doubt that what the observers heard in Italy was an account of recent Greek history from the British standpoint. In view of the allied pressure the Regent signed the decree providing for elections on 31 March, but by late February pleas from the Left and Centre for postponement on account of the 'large numbers of bandits and terrorist gangs on the loose' had been reinforced.[190] The persecution of the Left made hopes for fair elections wishful thinking, while it was dubious whether stabilization could be brought about by a predominantly monarchist parliament. The electoral victory of the Right was widely expected as the result of the EAM threat of abstention, the White Terror, and the polarization of Greek politics which had contributed to the emergence of the Populists and EAM as the dominant parties at the expense of the Centre.

Some glimpse of hope appeared in early March, by which time the majority of the Greek Cabinet had come to favour postponement. The justification of the plea was provided by Tsouderos in a letter to Sofulis on 6 March. The Vice-Premier emphasized that the abstention of EAM would produce a parliament which would 'not constitute a real reflection of the country's public opinion' but rather 'an intractable assembly of right-wingers'. Tsouderos showed prophetic insight when he argued that reconstruction 'may even be interrupted by the post-electoral one-sided government because of party obligations'.[191] The implication was that a Populist government would give top priority to the restoration of the King rather than to the economic policy. Under mounting pressure from his Cabinet, on 2 March Sofulis requested from Bevin postponement of the elections, but his appeal stumbled over the latter's pretended ignorance of the actual conditions in Greece. His reply revealed the extent to which the reports of the Athens Embassy were distorted. 'Much surprised' by Sofulis's statement that the armed monarchist bands were reinforced almost by the entire Police and Gendarmerie forces, Bevin held that the Greek Minister of Public Order, in collaboration with Sir Charles Wickham, could ensure that no such cooperation took place. As for the abstention of the Left, that was an insignificant matter: 'I do not think that such an abstention can be any reason for refusing to the people of Greece a chance of electing their Government in accordance with their own free will.'[192]

Bevin's insistence was rooted partly in his conviction that the following of EAM was negligible and partly in his ostensible ignorance, which allowed him to claim that the Greek government and Wickham could co-operate to foil the *esprit de corps* between the army, the security forces and the monarchist bands. Yet as early as 5 December 1945 the British Police Mission had sent the Foreign Office a report which concluded that the Greek Gendarmerie was far from impartial and that the enforcement of the law was not as energetic against the Right as it was against former members of EAM/ELAS. For Bevin, however, postponement would cast a doubt upon British prestige, as it would amount to admitting that conditions did not allow free polls; and that would be a step back from the line that British policy in Greece had always been the right one. Indeed, in early February Bevin had told Leeper that a delay in holding elections might be taken as a sign that the British 'were not yet able to maintain law and order' in Greece.[193] Besides, postponement would prop up the KKE, which was believed to be carrying out the campaign for abstention on orders from the Kremlin in order to sabotage the polls, gain time to build its power, and then strike.[194]

The pressure for postponement became almost unbearable when the chorus of the Greek Left and Centre was joined by *The Times*, seventy Labour MPs who handed Bevin a signed petition, and ten Greek ministers who resigned on 11 March.[195] But for Bevin the solution of the Greek problem had become a choice between two evils. In explaining to the State Department the reasons for his insistence against any delay, he admitted that polls without the Left 'would certainly not be satisfactory' and that if the Right won, Greek political and economic problems 'would be far from being solved'. Yet the disadvantages of holding elections under such circumstances would be far outweighed by the consequences of postponement, which

> would result in a deterioration in the state of law and order and it might even lead to civil war if the Right attempted to take action. It can be safely assumed that a delay of two months would increase rather than diminish the tension between the extreme Right and the extreme Left which is the cause of the present state of insecurity.

He added that on the economic plane postponement 'would almost certainly lead to disaster', since 'no marked progress can be expected until there is an elected Government'.[196] In this spirit, on 20 March Bevin instructed Sir Clifford Norton, Leeper's successor at the Embassy in Athens, that the elections would have to be held on 31 March 1946:

> The right thing for the Greek people, and indeed the duty of the parties and the press, is to use all their power and influence to get an overwhelming poll on March 31st. Greece, for the first time for years, will then express her democratic and independent opinion as to the Government she desires and deserves.[197]

The discrepancy in outlook between these two documents is explicable in terms of the propagandistic nature of the latter, which implied that a democratic and peaceful Greece was on her way to free polls. The juxta-position of the two sources demonstrates that Bevin ignored the details rather than the actual situation in Greece, and also that when he addressed himself to the Americans – that is, when he had to be more candid – he told the whole story, whose end he was not unable to predict. In the aide-mémoire to the State Department the Foreign Secretary recognized that the abstention of the Left would render the elections 'unsatisfactory' and that an elected right-wing government might hardly bother its head about reconstruction. Bevin even spoke of the possibility of the Right attempting to take action in the event of postponement, and the ensuing peril of civil war, which would both be unrealistic unless the Right was firmly in control of the state apparatus and the armed forces. The British Labour government might not have been gratified at the prospect of a repressive royalist administration in Athens, but the alternative of postponement would play in the hands of EAM. Hence the predilection for the first – and lesser – evil, despite the knowledge that the solution of the Greek problem would remain elusive. Warner put it more succinctly: 'We shall be forced in the end to do the best we can with one of the extreme wings ... Obviously the Right in present circumstances.'[198]

On 21 March Sofulis assured the new British ambassador that the elections would take place on the agreed date but cast doubt upon Bevin's contention that conditions of law and order allowed free polls; worse, he predicted that the Right, once it had won, would demand the speedy solution of the constitutional question.[199] Although the latter statement highlighted the probability that the elections would legitimize the clamour of the Right to bring back the King, for the British that was still the lesser evil. Sofulis's warning went unheeded, whilst the last touches in the bogus picture of a tranquil Greece marching towards free and democratic elections were provided by Richard Windle, a Labour Party functionary and chief of the British contingent in AMFOGE: a shrewd choice, as Windle had worked for the electoral organization of the Labour Party at the head of a vigorous cadre of agents and party organizers.[200] On 27 March Windle recommended to Bevin the following answers in case the Foreign Secretary were tackled by the press or the Labour Party:

(i)   Condition of registers and state of law and order must be judged by Greek and not by British standards.

(ii)   Allegation of duplicity of registration and presence of dead voters on the register appears to us at the moment to be exaggerated, though some basis for the allegation exists. To a lesser extent dead voters appear on the register in Britain and other countries.

(iii) There is evidence of disorder in certain districts but this is a country where feuds are prevalent and disorder does not necessarily have a political basis.[201]

Windle's touches were clumsy, but he could not be expected to admit the real extent of the problematic conditions in Greece. Such a recognition would amount to a confession that British policy, advertised as the well-intentioned umpire of civil strife, had yielded very little. Windle therefore conceded that the situation was unsatisfactory, but nevertheless it would do for a place such as Greece. In a statement to the foreign press correspondents three days before the election, Sofulis depicted the country otherwise: as a legacy of dictatorship and occupation, the armed forces, the security services and the state apparatus were in the hands of the extreme Right; state officials generously assisted the armed bands which ruled over the provinces; only monarchist candidates were allowed to tour the countryside and express their views; the elections should have been postponed at least till the autumn of

1946, but 'pressure of international conjecture' necessitated adherence to the last Sunday of March.[202]

Although the Liberal leader had come to power with good intentions, his efforts to redress the balance in the armed forces were subverted by Leeper's bias and the professional parochialism of the British Military and Police Missions. With Bevin pretending ignorance on the matter, the Greek government was effectively denied any real power, unless it is supposed that a government may command power without controlling its army and security forces. Sofulis could not have failed to notice that he was the last moderate and credible card the British had left to play, and yet he opted to remain in office under quite adverse conditions. Certainly he overrated his chances and hoped that even at the eleventh hour he might achieve a postponement, which was seen as the first step towards the restoration of law and order. But that course, too, was a dead end, for the British had made it clear from the outset that he was not to lay his hands on the army and the security forces. It is also probable that he carried on in the hope that the shortness of alternatives might lead many terrorized supporters of EAM to cast their vote for the Liberal Party. In any case, it is certain that he was not fearful of a sizable communist presence in the Chamber: in early February he had rebuffed Damaskinos's scheme for elections on the majority system and nomination of joint candidates by the Populists and the Liberals on the grounds that this would obliterate the differences between the two parties and reduce the contest to communism versus anti-communism, with the latter camp dominated by the royalists.[203]

In this context, the attack of the Left on the government could not have been the greatest nuisance for Sofulis. On 11 December the EAM Central Committee proclaimed that after three weeks in office the government had neither recognized the National Resistance nor tackled the rich, and that the White Terror continued unabated. EAM withdrew its support, insisted on abstention from enrolling in the electoral registers, and demanded its participation in a new government.[204] On 17 December an EAM delegation visiting Britain submitted to Hector McNeil a memorandum arguing that only a government which included EAM would be able to defy right-wing pressures and restore conditions for free elections. The delegation tried to convince the British that the Greek Left acknowledged their interests in the eastern Mediterranean, which could 'be served in the best possible way by an understanding based on equality and mutual respect, both in the political and economic field'. The British took no notice of the offer,[205] but EAM still considered participation in the polls. In mid-January it welcomed the government's promise to verify the registers by instructing its supporters to sign their names.[206] On 7 February its Central Committee handed the Regent and the government a memorandum with the following terms for participation: establishment of a government that would include EAM, an end to the White Terror, a general political amnesty, the purge of the registers, and the removal from the civil service, the army and the security forces of collaborators and members of the Security Battalions.[207] Indicative of the atmosphere in which EAM was trying to secure some concessions was the editorial which appeared on the following day in the monarchist daily *Vradyni*:

It [EAM] will not participate. For it has an interest in not participating. And instructions. But even if it were to participate, the world does not give a penny. It is a minority. The counting will be done by the votes of Abstention. Those who will vote will be Greece. Those who will not vote will be Bulgaria ... But have you ever thought what even ten EAMo-bulgarians will be in the Parliament? Dynamite and treason and national shame.[208]

It was amidst these circumstances, aggravated by the persistent fears of a monarchist coup, that the famous Second Plenum of the KKE Central Committee met from 12 to 15 February 1946 in order to examine the situation and lay out the tasks ahead.[209] The actual decision of the Plenum is the subject of controversy, for the fragmentary evidence hitherto available largely consists of subsequent speeches, interviews and personal reminiscences of KKE leaders; worse, a good deal of them are unduly influenced by the defeat in the civil war and marred by vehement polemics against Zachariadis, whom they blame for a slow drift into armed confrontation without any formal decision or delineation of strategic and tactical objectives.'[210] Yet it seems that there *was* some decision *and* some clear-cut aim. In his memoirs which were published in 1976, the former Central Committee member and ELAS officer Giorgis Blanas (Kissavos), though bitterly critical of Zachariadis, stated unequivocally that at the Second Plenum 'the preparation of armed struggle was orally agreed upon' but, for obvious reasons, it 'was not written down nor signed as a decision even by the Presidium of the Plenum'.[211] In 1981 the member of the Politburo Vasilis Bartziotas revealed that the Second Plenum reached a unanimous decision for some form of armed struggle against the 'unilateral civil war'.[212] The decision has never been published, but it may not have been too far from what Bartziotas – claiming that he draws on his notes from the Plenum – cites as Zachariadis's final *résumé*:

> On our correct thesis (which will be our decision) to reply to violence by violence, we must proceed, gradually and wherever conditions are ripened, from popular self-defence to armed guerrilla groups, and thus to armed opposition to Reaction, with progressive transition to local and nation-wide unification of these groups under a single command, if in the mean-time Reaction rendered increasingly impossible the normal democratic development which the Party and its partners have not for a single moment ceased to fight for.
>
> Primarily the unfolding of armed resistance to the armed terrorism of Reaction represents an additional forceful means of pressure on the opponent for the peaceful, normal evolution, and only in the course of the struggle, if this evolution becomes totally difficult and impossible, the armed struggle will proceed from defence to attack.[213]

In 1956 – destalinization time – Zachariadis was removed as Secretary-General of the KKE and expelled from the Central Committee, and a year later he was expelled from the party. In his speech on that critical moment, when there was nothing he could do to reverse his fate, he adhered to the same thesis. The Second Plenum had opted for the gradual transition to armed resistance, along with 'the policy of reconciliation and unity': 'It was not [a] military plan, we took a political decision.'[214] In the pamphlet *Problems of the Crisis of the KKE*, written by the former KKE leader in 1962 from his Siberian exile, the passage pertinent to the decision of the Second Plenum is worded almost precisely as in the quotation given by Bartziotas.[215] Even in 1973, writing shortly before his suicide, Zachariadis insisted that the Second Plenum was essentially a political reversal of the Varkiza Agreement.[216]

On the basis of the available evidence there should be little doubt that in mid-February 1946 the KKE, facing the White Terror, the deaf ears of the British and the Greek governments, and the prospect of an elected monarchist government, decided upon the gradual build-up of armed resistance in areas where local conditions made it possible. This was a defensive measure aimed at extracting concessions from the government. In 1962 Zachariadis justified the decision for a gradual build-up on the grounds that the KKE did not want – nor did it think that after Varkiza and the surrender of arms it could withstand – an armed clash with the British troops. Besides, it wanted to regain the people's confidence in the ability of the party for military action; but there was also

> the need in the course of such a struggle to persuade progressively as many as possible of the wavering strata of the Centre and Right that the armed confrontation is made inevitable by the armed attack of the Right, which prevents the way to normal democratic evolution.[217]

The defensive objective of the KKE in opting for limited armed struggle in February 1946 would be fully confirmed by subsequent developments. The Second Plenum rather decided to stretch mass popular self-defence to its limits, reserving higher forms of military action for later, should the situation remained unchanged. A timetable and instructions did not come from Zachariadis until late summer 1946, almost six months after the Second Plenum, because the KKE continued to press for postponement of the elections for two months and satisfaction of the EAM terms for pacification.

With the Liberals weakened by the defection of Sofoklis Venizelos, who favoured an understanding with the Populists and tried to steer the party to the Right, Zachariadis tried to woo Sofulis into cooperation. On 7 March he proposed to the Prime Minister a two-month postponement of the polls so that voters could register in the lists and some way could be found to avoid multiple voting; EAM would then be prepared to set up an electoral coalition with Sofulis's Liberals and give them 50% of the seats they might win.[218] Although the proposal held the prospect of strengthening the parliamentary representation of the Liberal rump headed by Sofulis, the Prime Minister did not respond. No doubt he feared the reaction of Bevin and the Populists and abhorred the charge of fellow-travelling, but he also appears to have not as yet given up hopes that he might eventually persuade the British to allow a postponement. Moreover, he probably anticipated that the abstention of EAM, the White Terror, and his conformity to British wishes might increase the number of votes cast for the Liberals.

The Soviet Union advised the KKE to participate in the elections, but the Politburo instructed its representatives in the Central Committee of EAM to ensure that the Left would abstain. On account of the White Terror, the partners of the KKE in the EAM Central Committee – the Agrarian Party (AKE) and some minor socialist groups – *also* favoured abstention, thus even a proposal by Zachariadis for a symbolic participation by way of putting up one candidate in each electoral district was turned down.[219] The matter was not over yet, for the KKE still seemed to desire some sort of participation in the polls, even by proxy. On 20 March, when Zachariadis left to attend the Conference of the Czech Communist Party, Ioannidis (his right-hand man) and Siandos made an interesting proposal to the Left Liberals – a small party of Venizelist origin. They suggested to them to request from the government not a postponement of the elections but an extension of the time-limit for submitting lists of candidates, which expired on midnight of that day; the Left Liberals would then put up their own candidates throughout the country and the entire Left would support them. The two leaders of the Left Liberals visited Sofulis's assistant minister, who showed great interest and promised a prompt reply – albeit one that never came.[220] The Prime Minister had probably realized that he would thus deprive himself of potential leftist votes. For the KKE, on the other hand, in the light of Moscow's pronouncement in favour of participation in the polls, abstention may not have been much more than a negotiating weapon – however misused – since Ioannidis and Siandos could not have made their proposal against the wishes of their master.

The elections were held on 31 March 1946 with the system of proportional representation and under the supervision of the Allied Mission For Observing the Greek Elections (AMFOGE). The Left and some prominent members of Sofulis's government abstained. The number of registered voters was disputed, with the Greek Ministry of the Interior estimating them at 2,211,791, AMFOGE at 1,850,000, and – in either case – an unknown number of false registrations.[221] On the basis of the AMFOGE figures, 1,121,696 voted and 743,000, or 40.3% of the electorate, did not.[222] The Right, which contested the election as the United Camp of the Nationally Minded, received 610,995 votes (55%) and 206 seats in a Parliament of 354; of these, 156 went to the Populist Party. In second place, the National Political Union (EPE), a coalition of the small centre-right parties of Venizelos, Papandreou and Kanellopoulos, mustered 213,721 votes (19.28%) and 68 seats. Sofulis's Liberals came a poor third, with 159,525 votes (14.39%) and 48 seats.[223]

AMFOGE interviewed 1,345 voters and found that only 9.3% (280,000) of valid registrants asserted that they had boycotted the elections; yet, in a gesture of magnanimity towards the Greek Left, it conceded that 'the proportion of qualified voters who abstained for "party" reasons is about 15 per cent, and certainly between 10 and 20 per cent'.[224] These estimates are essentially guesswork, and recent analyses have demonstrated that the AMFOGE Report is laden with highly questionable judgements and conclusions.[225] A few days after the elections ambassador Norton reckoned that the percentage of leftist abstention was 30%, whereas in February his predecessor, Leeper, had estimated that EAM would poll 25–35% and gain 100 seats in a 300-seat Chamber. The Regent had also anticipated 100 EAM deputies, whilst the Central Committee of EAM had calculated that, on account of the White Terror, they would not return more than 100–120 deputies. For his part, Admiral Rodionov, the Soviet ambassador, estimated the strength of EAM at 45–50% of the vote, that of the Right at 30–35%, and that of the Centre at 15–25%.[226] The conclusion of AMFOGE that the elections had been free, fair and representative of the will of the Greeks triumphantly endorsed British policy and cast a blind eye on the White Terror. That was understandable, since the 1,200 observers (mostly Americans) were professional officers, hardly likely to be sympathetic towards EAM. Had there been some who were, Bevin's 'short course of instruction designed to give them the background of the present situation in Greece'[227] must have illuminated them. It has correctly been pointed out, therefore, that the clean bill of health provided to the Greek government by AMFOGE was no more than an attempt to bolster up the international standing of a government entirely subservient to Britain and the United States.[228]

Infinitely more important than the AMFOGE guesswork were the implications of the election results. Bevin might have felt relieved by the legitimization of a Greek government, but his apprehensions for the future would shortly come true. A government emerging from elections conducted after months of intimidation and terror could hardly pacify Greece, and that was known both in London and Athens. The abstention of the Left should have been a warning that the communists, no matter what their intentions in early 1945, had now run out of patience. Their policy had evolved against the background of the White Terror, which, according to the EAM figures, had from 12 February 1945 to 31 March 1946 tolled 1,289 murders, 6,671 cases of injury, 31,632 cases of torture, 509 attempts for murder, 84,931 arrests and 165 rapes.[229] Yet in the light of the polarization of Greek politics between EAM and the Right, the corollary of abstention was that the Populists were granted a comfortable majority to rule the country as they pleased. The British, bent upon maintaining Greece on their 'side of the fence', could rest assured that the legitimate Greek government would not for a moment shrink from that task.

NOTES

1. F.O.371/48247 R936: Leeper to F.O., 12/1/1945; F.O.371/48251 R2291: Leeper to F.O., 27/2/1945.
2. *The Times* (London): 11/1/1945.
3. *Efimeris tis Kyverniseos* vol. I, no. 68 (23/3/1945): pp.235–41.
4. Text of the Varkiza Agreement in KKE: E.K., V, Appendix, pp.411–16; FRUS (1945): VIII, 109–13.
5. Lord Moran, *Winston Churchill: The Struggle for Survival, 1940–1965* (London: 1966), p.234; FRUS (1945): VIII, 114: MacVeagh to Secretary of State, 14/2/1945, and Kirk to Secretary of State, 14/2/1945; EAM: LV (II), p.5; KKE: E.K., V, no.758: Siandos's speech at an EAM conference,

14/2/1945; Sargent Papers: F.O.800/276/GRE/45/3: Leeper to Sargent, 13/2/1945.

6. KKE (es.): E.K., V, no. 760: Ioannidis's telegram to all Party Organizations, 15/2/1945; M. Vafiadis, *Apomnimonevmata* III (Athens: 1985), 90–91; G. Blanas, *O Emfylios Polemos 1946–1949: Opos Ta Ezisa* (Athens: 1976), pp.35–7.

7. S. Sarafis, *ELAS: Greek Resistance Army* (London: 1980), p.525; Y. Ioannidis, *Anamniseis: Provlimata tis Politikis tou KKE stin Ethniki Andistasi 1940–1945* (Athens: 1979), p.371.

8. Y. Ioannidis, *op.cit.*, p.371; G. Kousoulas, *Revolution and Defeat: The Story of the Greek Communist Party* (London:1965), p.271.

9. EAM: LV (II), pp.8ff. The EAM White Books are collections of state documents and newspaper reports from the bourgeois and leftist press. It must be noted that there is no other collection systematically compiled which can cast doubt on EAM's claims; the White Terror is corroborated from a plethora of 'more respectable' sources; even if there are exaggerations, the overall picture is accurate beyond doubt; and it is unlikely that all incidents were recorded, which pays off possible exaggerations.

10. *Ibid.*, pp.15–19; W.H. McNeill, *The Greek Dilemma: War and Aftermath* (London: 1947), p.164.

11. MacVeagh's despatch 1733 (26/10/1945) and Enclosure, ed. by Y. Chouliaras and D. Georgakas, *Journal of the Hellenic Diaspora* 12, no. 1 (Spring 1985), 40; W.H. McNeill, *op.cit.*, p.165; FRUS (1945): VIII, 122: Kirk to Secretary of State, 22/3/1945.

12. GAK: K 116 (F): Precise Extract from the diary of Principal Events, by K.D. Yiannoulis, Officer of EDES, folio for 1942–1945, p.45.

13. GAK: K 210 (Papers of M.I. Myridakis), no.28: Report of P. Aslanidis to the Ministry of War, 8/4/1949; F.O.371/48267R7178: Rapp (Thessaloniki) to Athens, 20/4/1945; F.O.371/48273 R11283: Caccia to F.O., 27/6/1945; DBPO: I, no.309: King (Thessaloniki) to Caccia, 18/7/1945; W.H. McNeill, *op.cit.*, p.163; D. Zafiropoulos, *O Antisymmoriakos Agon* (Athens: 1956), p.80. Zafiropoulos was a senior officer of the Greek army.

14. EAM: LV (II), pp.51–3.

15. *Ibid.*, pp.39–48; S. Sarafis, *Meta ti Varkiza* (Athens:1979), p.24.

16. P. Delaportas, *To Simiomatario enos Pilatou* 2nd edn. (Athens: 1978), pp.87–88. Numerous examples follow.

17. F.O.371/48271 R9478: Leeper to F.O., 7/5/1945.

18. S. Papayiannis, *Apo Evelpis Andartis: Anamniseis enos kommunisti axiomatikou* (Athens: 1991), pp.64–6; EAM: LV(II), pp.27–8, 32–3; GES/DIS, *Istoria tis Organoseos tou Ellinikou Stratou, 1821–1954* (Athens: 1957), p.168.

19. F.O.371/48264 R6325: Leeper to F.O., 5/4/1945.

20. EAM: LV (II), pp.33–8; EAM: LV (I), no.121: EAM Memorandum to the Governments of Britain, the USA, the USSR, France; KKE (es.): E.K., V, no.47; F.O.371/48262 R5617: EAM Memorandum, 12/3/1945.

21. F.O.371/48263 R5857: Leeper to F.O., 19/3/1945; F.O.371/48272 R10144: Leeper to F.O., 5/6/1945.

22. F.O.371/48263 R5857: Leeper to F.O., 19/3/1945.

23. F.O.371/48272 R10144: Leeper to F.O., 5/6/1945.

24. *Loc.cit.*; C.M. Woodhouse, *Apple of Discord* (London: 1948), p.241; EAM: LV (II), pp.48–50.

25. EAM: LV (II), pp.60ff; W.H. McNeill, *op.cit.*, p.166.

26. F.O.371/48279 R14973: 'Situation in the Peloponnese', Report by Woodhouse, 11/8/1945.

27. EAM: LV (II), pp.81–82.

28. R. Miliband, *The State in Capitalist Society* (London: 1973), p.243.

29. MacVeagh's despatch 1733 (26/10/1945) and Enclosure, in *Journal of the Hellenic Diaspora*, *op.cit.*, 37, 42; F.O.371/58703 R12054: Lascelles to F.O., 14/8/1946; N. Clive, *Embeiria stin Ellada, 1943–1948* (Athens: n.d.), p.185.

30. F.O.371/48255 R3053: Leeper to F.O., 12/2/1945; F.O.371/48279 R14973: 'Situation in the Peloponnese', Report by Woodhouse, 11/8/1945.

31. F.O.371/48264 R6325: F.O. to Leeper, 19/4/1945.

32. F.O.371/48267 R7423: Churchill to Sargent, 22/4/1945.

33. F.O.371/48267 R7423: Minutes by Hayter and Howard, 23/4/1945.

34. F.O.371/48267 R7423: Draft Minute to the Prime Minister by Sir Orme Sargent, 24/4/1945.

35. MVR, p.672 (27/2/1945) and p.684: MacVeagh to Kohler, 29/1/1945; *ibid.*, p.669: MacVeagh to Roosevelt, 15/1/1945; F.O.371/48257 R3659: British Embassy to the Greek Government, Aide Mémoire, 15/2/1945; R. Leeper, *When Greek Meets Greek* (London: 1950), p.155.

36. F.O.371/48237 R3109: Leeper to F.O., 13/2/1945; FRUS (1945): VIII, 195–7: MacVeagh to Secretary of State, 26 and 30/1/1945.

37. FRUS (1945): VIII, 205: MacVeagh to Secretary of State, 24/3/1945; F.O.371/48273 R3263: Leeper to F.O., 15/2/1945; F.O.371/48239 R6629: Hill to Waley, 12/4/1945.

38. GAK: Tsouderos Papers, Series C, File 7, I (14): Greek Inland Revenue to Ministry of Finance, 13/10/1944.

39. MVR, p.683: MacVeagh to Kohler, 29/1/1945; R. Leeper, *op.cit.*, p.84.

40. F.O.371/48257 R3559: Discussion on Greece at the British Embassy, Athens, 15/2/1945; *ibid.*, R3669: Meeting held at the British Embassy, Athens, 15/2/1945; F.O.371/48257R3559: Sargent to Macmillan, 1/3/1945; *ibid.*, 'Greece', Memorandum by Eden to War Cabinet, 5/3/1945; F.O.371/48266 R6942: Macmillan to F.O., 18/4/1945; R. Leeper, *op.cit.*, pp.155–7; H. Macmillan, *The Blast of War 1939–1945* (London: 1967), p.662; A. Eden, *The Eden Memoirs*, III, *The Reckoning* (London: 1965), p.520.

41. N. Clive, 'British Policy Alternatives, 1945–1946', in L.Baerentzen, J.O. Iatrides, O.L. Smith, eds., *Studies in the History of the Greek Civil War 1945–1949* (Copenhagen:1987), pp.213–14; *idem, Embeiria*, p.174.

42. N. Clive, *Embeiria*, p.174; *idem*, 'British Policy Alternatives', p.214; FRUS (1945): VIII, 103: Kirk to Secretary of State, 11/1/1945.

43. H. Macmillan, *op.cit.*, p.664; N. Clive, *Embeiria*, p.175.

44. EAM: LV (II), p.8; F.O.371/48257 R3472, R3517, R3564, R3566: Leeper to F.O., 19, 20, 21/2/1945; *The Times* (London): 23/2/1945; N. Clive, 'British Policy Alternatives', p.215; *idem, Embeiria*, p.176; FRUS (1945): VIII, 116, 122: Kirk to Secretary of State, 7, 22/3/1945; *ibid.*, 119: Winant (London) to Secretary of State, 14/3/1945.

45. F.O.371/48259 R4385 and R4386: Macmillan and Leeper to F.O., and Macmillan to Churchill, 5/3/1945; H. Macmillan, *op.cit.*, p.665; N. Clive, 'British Policy Alternatives', p.215; *idem, Embeiria*, p.174.

46. F.O.371/48259 R4385: Athens to F.O., Relations between HMG and the Greek Government, and Minutes by Laskey and Sargent, 5/3/1945; *ibid.*, R4386: Prime Minister to Macmillan, 7/3/1945; N. Clive, *Embeiria*, p.176.

47. F.O.371/48264 R6244: Leeper to F.O.,6/4/1945; K. Amandos, 'Viografika Simiomata', ed. by S.N. Fassoulakis, *Chiaka Chronika* 7 (1975), 77–8.
48. Sargent Papers: F.O.800/276/GRE/45/6: Sargent to Leeper (private letter), 26/4/1945; R. Leeper, *op.cit.*, p.161.
49. F.O.371/48265 R6653: Leeper to F.O., 12/4/1945; H. Macmillan, *op.cit.*, p.668; FRUS (1945): VIII, 211: MacVeagh to Secretary of State, 20/4/1945.
50. F.O.371/48331 R9017: F.O. to Athens, 25/5/1945; To Vima (Athens): 5/6/1945; F.O.371/48272 R10344: Caccia to F.O., 11/6/1945; FRUS (1945): VIII, 222–3: MacVeagh to Byrnes, 4/6/1945; B. Sweet-Escott, *Greece: A Political and Economic Survey, 1939–1953* (London: 1954), p.46.
51. FRUS (1945): VIII, 222–3: MacVeagh to Byrnes, 4/6/1945; F.O.371/48273 R11161: Caccia to F.O.,25/6/1945; R. Leeper, *op.cit.*, pp.174–6; FRUS (1945): VIII, 235: MacVeagh to Byrnes, 3/9/1945; Ch. Hadziiossif, 'Economic Stabilization and Political Unrest: Greece 1944–1947', in L. Baerentzen et al., eds., *op.cit.*, pp.33–4.
52. F.O.371/48280 R15829: Lascelles to F.O., 17/9/1945; F.O.371/48447 R18824: Report on Economic Conditions in Greece covering the period August 16–October 10, 1945; R. Leeper, *op.cit.*, p.177; S. Sarafis, *op.cit.*, p.45.
53. Sargent Papers: F.O.800/276/GRE/45/4: Leeper to Sargent, 20/3/1945.
54. *Supra*, notes 31, 32, 33, 34.
55. F.O.371/48266 R6914: Prime Minister to Leeper, 20/4/1945.
56. F.O.371/48267 R7408: Leeper to F.O., 25/4/1945.
57. FRUS (1945): VIII, 126–128: British Embassy (Washington) to State Department: Aide Mémoire, 16/6/1945; *ibid.*, 132–3: State Department to British Embassy, 5/7/1945.
58. DBPO: I, no. 28: Churchill's Minute to F.O., 7/7/1945.
59. K. Morgan, *The British Labour Governments 1945–1951* (Oxford: 1985), pp.21ff, 41ff.
60. *Rizospastis* (Athens): 27/7/1945; S. Sarafis, *op.cit.*, p.42.
61. D. Dilks, ed., *The Diaries of Sir Alexander Cadogan, 1938–1945* (London: 1971), p.772; P. Dixon, *Double Diploma* (London: 1968), p.166.
62. See F.O.371/44661, F.O.371/44662.
63. K. Morgan, *op.cit.*, p.93.
64. On Labour's 'long march to 1945' see K. Morgan, *op.cit.*, pp.1–44.
65. A. Bullock, *The Life and Times of Ernest Bevin*, II, *Minister of Labour, 1940–1945* (London:1967), pp.340–7; K. Morgan, *op.cit.*, pp.31–2, 235; H. Thomas, *Armed Truce: The Beginnings of the Cold War 1945–46* (London: 1988), p.544.
66. J. Darwin, *Britain and Decolonisation: The Retreat from Empire in the Postwar World* (London: 1988), p.71.
67. *Ibid.*, pp.71–72; K. Morgan, *op.cit.*, pp.47–50, 234–6; H. Thomas, *op.cit.*, pp.293–7; R. Ovendale, ed., *The Foreign Policy of the British Labour Governments, 1945–1951* (Leicester: 1984), p.5; C. Attlee, *As It Happened* (London:1954), p.196. Also: K. Harris, *Attlee* (London: 1982); A.Bullock, *Ernest Bevin: Foreign Secretary 1945–1951* (Oxford: 1985).
68. K. Morgan, *op.cit.*, pp.56–81.
69. D. Dilks, ed., *op.cit.*, p.780; P. Dixon, *op.cit.*, pp.179, 183–4, 195–6, 197–9, 214–15.
70. T.H. Anderson, *Great Britain and the Cold War, 1944–1947* (London: 1981), p.84; R. Ovendale, ed., *op.cit.*, pp.3, 5; J. Darwin, *op.cit.*, pp.65–8; K. Morgan, *op.cit.*, pp.147–51, 235; H. Thomas, *op.cit.*, pp.315–16.

71. J. Darwin, *op.cit.*, p.61.

72. F.O.371/48271 R9518: Leeper to F.O., 28/5/1945; DBPO: I, no.412: Eden to Caccia, 26/7/1945.

73. DBPO: I, no.530: Caccia to Eden, 27/7/1945.

74. *Ibid.*, no.557: Morrison to Bevin, 30/7/1945; F.O.371/48276 R13041: Balfour (Washington) to F.O., 1/8/1945.

75. Bevin Papers: F.O.800/468/GRE/45/1 and DBPO: I, no.505: Attlee to Damaskinos, 1/8/1945.

76. F.O.371/48276 R13166: F.O. to Caccia, 8/8/1945; *ibid.*, R13556: Caccia to F.O., 11/8/1945; H. Richter, *British Intervention in Greece: From Varkiza to Civil War, February 1945 to August 1946* (London: 1986), p.186.

77. DBPO: I, no.592: Leeper to Sargent, 2/8/1945.

78. CAB 129/1/C.P. 45 (107): 'Greece', Memorandum by the Foreign Secretary, 11/8/1945.

79. F.O.371/48276 R13689: 'Balkan Problems', 14/8/1945.

80. CAB 128/1/C.M. 21 (45): 14/8/1945.

81. HC Deb., vol.413, cols.289–291; F.O.371/48277 R13846: F.O. to Caccia, 16/8/1945; FRUS (1945): VIII, 144–5: Balfour (Washington) to Secretary of State, 18/8/1945.

82. FRUS (1945): VIII, 158: Statement by the UK, US and French Governments, 19/9/1945. For Damaskinos's contacts in London see F.O.371/48279 R15302: Bevin to Caccia, 7/9/1945; F.O.371/48280 R16292: Dixon to Sargent, 16/9/1945; FRUS (1945): VIII, 154–5: Winant to Byrnes, 7/9/1945; *ibid.*, 157: Memorandum by Byrnes to Dunn, 13/9/1945.

83. FRUS (1945): VIII, 159: Winant to Byrnes, 19/9/1945; F.O.371/48281 R16589: King of the Hellenes to Bevin, 22/9/1945; FRUS (1945): VIII, 160–1: King of the Hellenes to Byrnes, 22/9/1945; F.O.371/48281 R16589: Bevin to Byrnes, and Bevin to the King of the Hellenes, 29/9/1945; FRUS (1945): VIII, 166–7: Byrnes to the King of the Hellenes, 1/10/1945.

84. FRUS (1945): VIII, 161–4: MacVeagh to Byrnes, 25/9/1945.

85. *Ibid.*, pp.169–71: MacVeagh to Byrnes, 6/10/1945; EAM: LV (III) pp.35–8; GAK: Tsouderos Papers, (E:53): Two documents signed by Sofulis, Tsouderos, Plastiras, Kafandaris, Mylonas: (i) Draft Letter to the Foreign Ministers of Britain, the USA, France; (ii) Letter to the Greek Premier, 29/9/1945; S. Sarafis, *op.cit.*, pp.127–34.

86. MacVeagh's despatch 1622 (2/10/1945) and Enclosure (29/9/1945), in *Journal of the Hellenic Diaspora*, *op.cit.*, 35; FRUS (1945): VIII, 162–4: MacVeagh to Byrnes, 24/9/1945; *The Times* (London): 29/3/1946.

87. Bevin Papers: F.O.800/468/GRE/45/6: Bevin to V. Feather, 6/9/1945.

88. MacVeagh's despatch 1733 (26/10/1945) and Enclosure, in *Journal of the Hellenic Diaspora*, *op.cit.*, 41; F.O.371/48282 R17133: Leeper to F.O., 2/10/1945; *ibid.*, R18502: Leeper to F.O., 2/10/1945.

89. EAM: LV (III), pp.11ff; P. Delaportas, op.cit., pp.109ff.

90. S. Sarafis, *op.cit.*, pp.126–127.

91. F.O.371/48282 R17083 and R17130: Leeper to F.O., 8/10/1945; FRUS (1945): VIII, 172: MacVeagh to Byrnes, 9/10/1945.

92. F.O.371/48282 R17131: Leeper to F.O., 8 and 9/10/1945; FRUS (1945): VIII, 173: MacVeagh to Byrnes, 16/10/1945.

93. F.O.371/48283 R17309: Leeper to F.O., 11/10/1945.

94. FRUS (1945): VIII, 174: MacVeagh to Byrnes, 17/10/1945; *ibid.*, 176–7:

MacVeagh to Byrnes, 2/11/1945; F.O.371/48284 R18581: Leeper to F.O., 2/11/1945.

95. F.O.371/48284 R18698: Leeper to F.O., 3/11/1945; FRUS (1945): VIII, 176–7: MacVeagh to Byrnes, 2/11/1945.

96. CAB 129/4/C.P. (45) 266: 'Greece', Memorandum by the Secretary of State, 3/11/1945.

97. CAB 128/2/C.M. 49 (45): 6/11/1945.

98. F.O.371/48285 R19826: British Embassy, Memorandum to the Greek Prime Minister, 14/11/1945.

99. F.O.371/48285 R19825: Record of a Meeting with Greek Ministers, 15/11/1945; ibid., R19830: Record of a Conversation held at the British Embassy, Athens, 15/11/1945; FRUS (1945): VIII, 270–1: MacVeagh to Byrnes, 17/11/1945.

100. Bevin Papers: F.O.800/468/GRE/45/8: Hayter to Sargent, Enclosure: Leeper to F.O., 17/11/1945.

101. Bevin Papers: F.O.800/468/GRE/45/9: Hayter to Sargent, 17/11/1945.

102. F.O.371/48285 R19555: Bevin to McNeil, 18/11/1945; F.O.371/48286 R20281: Discussion at the Palace of the Regency, 19/11/1945; F.O.371/48287 R20613: Leeper to F.O., 29/11/1945; HC Deb., vol.416, col.773: Bevin, 23/11/1945; FRUS (1945): VIII, 178–9: MacVeagh to Byrnes, 20/11/1945.

103. Bevin Papers: F.O.800/468/GRE/45/10: King of the Hellenes to Bevin, 20/11/1945; CAB 128/2/C.M. 55 (45): 22/11/1945; Bevin Papers: F.O.800/468/GRE/45/11: Bevin to the King of the Hellenes, 22/11/1945.

104. S. Sarafis, op.cit., pp.189–92; Rizospastis (Athens): 23/11/1945; KKE: E.K., VI, no.744: Politburo Resolution, 22/11/1945.

105. F.O.371/48287 R20769: Memorandum by McNeil to Bevin, 10/12/1945.

106. Sargent Papers: F.O.800/276/GRE/45/9: Leeper to Sargent (private letter), 23/10/1945.

107. Sargent Papers: F.O.800/276/GRE/45/10: Sargent to Leeper (private letter), 9/11/1945.

108. KKE(es.) Archives, Avgi (Athens), 6/12/1979: KKE Report to the CPs of the USSR, Yugoslavia and Bulgaria, 12/9/1946; see also Zachariadis's report in I Triti Syndiaskepsi tou KKE, 10–14/10/1950 (Athens: 1988), p.63.

109. M. Vafiadis, op.cit., III, 76, 89; D. Katsis, To Imerologio enos andarti tou DSE 1946–1949 I (Athens: 1990), 62–6; T. Psimmenos, Andartes St' Agrafa (1946–1950): Anamniseis enos Andarti 2nd edn. (Athens: 1985), pp.11–12; P. Nefeloudis, Stis Piges tis Kakodemonias: Ta Vathitera Aitia tis Diaspasis tou KKE, 1918–1968 6th edn. (Athens: 1974), p.256.

110. KKE (es): E.K., V, no.757/f: Siandos's Statements to the foreign press on Varkiza, 12/2/1945.

111. Ibid., V, no.760: Radio-Telegram, 15/2/1945.

112. M. Vafiadis, op.cit., III, 99.

113. R. Leeper, op.cit., p.157.

114. Text in EAM: LV (I), no.121 and F.O.371/48262 R5617.

115. M. Vafiadis, op.cit., III, 96–8; Rizospastis (Athens): 20/3/1945.

116. Churchill–Roosevelt, no.525: Roosevelt to Churchill, 21/3/1945.

117. F.O.371/48264 R6104: Minutes by Hayter, 22/3/1945; Draft Minute to the Prime Minister from the Secretary of State, 31/3/1945; Copy of Prime Minister's Minute, 3/4/1945.

118. Churchill–Roosevelt, no.538: Churchill to Roosevelt, 3/4/1945; no.543:

Roosevelt to Churchill, 8/4/1945.

119. KKE: E.K., V, Appendix, pp.417–32; quotation in p.425.

120. KKE: E.K., V, no. 698; M. Vafiadis, *Apomnimonevmata* V (Athens: 1992), 71–5.

121. Text of the letter in M. Vafiadis, *op.cit.*, III, 110–112; see also *idem*, V, 75–76.

122. P. Nefeloudis, *op.cit.*, p.259; V. Bartziotas, *Exinda Chronia Kommunistis* (Athens: 1986), p.233; V. Bartziotas, *O Agonas tou Dimokratikou Stratou Elladas* 3rd edn. (Athens: 1985), pp.35–6; M. Vafiadis, *op.cit.*, V, 73; V. Georgiou, *I Zoi mou* (Athens: 1992), pp.464, 472. The 'dogmatic Stalinist' Zachariadis is held responsible for most evils that have befallen the Greek Left. Recently the late Professor Nikos Svoronos (the ELAS guerrilla and Marxist historian) described him as 'the only charismatic personality' in the history of the KKE, a man with a competent, if contradictory, mind. See Svoronos's interview in *Synchrona Themata* nos 35–36–37 (December 1988), 52.

123. KKE: E.K., VI, no.702: Politburo Resolutions, 1/6/1945.

124. *Rizospastis* (Athens): 2/6/1945.

125. P. Andaeos, *Nikos Zachariadis: Thytis ke Thyma* 2nd edn.(Athens: 1991), p.502. This book contains Zachariadis's personal papers from his Siberian exile, along with a few documents from the archives of the Soviet Foreign Ministry. See also G. Katsoulis, *Istoria tou Kommunistikou Kommatos Elladas* VI (Athens: 1977), 48(ia)–48(ib). I am indebted to Professor Ole L. Smith for the information that Velouchiotis's excommunication had already been decided by the Eleventh Plenum (personal communication, 23/12/1992).

126. *Rizospastis* (Athens): 12/6/1945; KKE: E.K., VI, no.703: Politburo Resolutions, 15/6/1945.

127. G. Katsoulis, *op.cit.*, VI, 48(ia)–48(ic); P. Nefeloudis, *op.cit.*, pp.266–7.

128. KKE: E.K., VI, no.704 and Appendix, pp.388–95: The Programme of Popular Democracy, 23/7/1945. A summary in English in GAK: Tsouderos Papers, B (9): Bureau of Information for Greek Affairs (London), Political Programme of EAM, 14/1/1946.

129. S. Sarafis, *op.cit.*, p.35.

130. F.O.371/48271 R9722: Leeper to F.O., 5/6/1945.

131. MVR, pp.680–1 (22/6/1945).

132. *Rizospastis* (Athens): 5/6/1945.

133. See Zachariadis's report at the 12th Plenum in [KKE CC], *Deka Chronia Agones, 1935–1945* (Athens: 1945), pp.272–5.

134. KKE: E.K., VI, no.706: Political Resolution of the 12th Plenum, 30/6/1945.

135. EAM: LV (II), pp.72–4.

136. KKE: E.K., VI, no.706: Political Resolution of the 12th Plenum; G. Blanas, *op.cit.*, pp.48ff; D. Votsikas, *I Ipiros Xanazonete t' Armata* (Athens: 1983), p.82; T. Psimmenos, *op.cit.*, pp.30–1; [Y. Zafiris et al., eds.], *O Agonas tou Dimokratikou Stratou sti Samo* (Athens: 1987), pp.16–18; M. Vafiadis, *op.cit.*, III, 115, 119; S.N. Grigoriadis, *Dekemvris-Emfylios Polemos, 1944–1949: Synoptiki Istoria* (Athens: 1984), p.208.

137. MacVeagh's despatch 1733 (26/10/1945), in *Journal of the Hellenic Diaspora*, *op.cit.*, 38; MVR, p.683; KKE: E.K., VI, nos 707, 708: Politburo Statements, 29/6/1945 and 4/7/1945; S. Sarafis, *op.cit.*, pp. 41–2. See also O.L. Smith, 'Self-Defence and Communist Policy, 1945–1947', in L. Baerentzen et al., eds., *op.cit.*, pp.159–77.

138. KKE: E.K., VI, no.708: Politburo Statement, 4/7/1945.

139. *Ibid.*, no.712: Politburo Statement, 10/8/1945.

140. *Rizospastis* (Athens): 25/8/1945; S. Sarafis, *op.cit.*, pp.61–2; KKE: E.K., VI, no.703: Politburo Resolutions, 15/6/1945; FRUS (1945): VIII, 136: MacVeagh to Byrnes, 11/8/1945.
141. F.O.371/48278 R14520: Minutes by Laskey, 31/8/1945.
142. S. Sarafis, *op.cit.*, p.34.
143. *Ibid.*, p.26; K. Amandos, *op.cit.*, 77.
144. Text of Siandos's *compte rendu* in KKE: E.K.,VI, Appendix, pp.396–415; *ibid.*, no.719.
145. *To Evdomo Synedrio tou KKE*, III, *Eisigisi ke Telikos Logos tou Nikou Zachariadi* (Athens: 1945), 21–6; KKE:E.K., VI, no.720: Political Resolution of the 7th Congress, 6/10/1945.
146. KKE: E.K., VI, nos 720 and 721: Political Resolution and Proclamation of the 7th Congress, 6/10/1945.
147. *Ibid.*, nos 738, 740, 742, 744: Politburo Resolutions of 11/10/1945, 18/10/1945, 9/11/1945, 22/11/1945.
148. HC Deb., vol.416, cols.838–9 (Ph. Noel-Baker, 23/11/1945); H.S. Truman, *Memoirs*, I, *Year of Decisions, 1945* (London: 1956), 459–60; FRUS (1945): VIII, 281–3: Greek Embassy (Washington) to State Department, 29/11/1945; *ibid.*, 291–2: Draft Note to Athens, 20/12/1945; GAK: Tsouderos Papers, C (8).
149. J. Gallagher and R. Robinson, 'The Imperialism of FreeTrade', *Economic History Review* 2nd series, 6, no.1 (1953), 6; R. Robinson, 'Non-European foundations of European Imperialism: sketch for a theory of collaboration', in R. Owen and B. Sutcliffe, eds., *Studies in the Theory of Imperialism* (London: 1972), 118–19, 120–4.
150. J. Gallagher and R. Robinson, *op.cit.*, 4–10.
151. CAB 128/5/C.M. 5 (46): 15/1/1946.
152. BSP (House of Commons), 1945–46, vol.XXV, pp.280–282: Bevin letter to Tsouderos, 24/1/1946; GAK: Tsouderos Papers, B (9) no.1; F.O.371/58668 R821: F.O.to Leeper, 20/1/1946.
153. GAK: Tsouderos Papers, E (47): The Situation in Northern Greece, September–November 1945, 3/12/1945.
154. *News Chronicle* (London): 7/1/1946.
155. D. Zafiropoulos, *op.cit.*, p.491.
156. GAK: Tsouderos Papers, B (9): Greek Trade Union News, 15/1/1946; P. Papastratis, 'The Purge of the Greek Civil Service on the Eve of the Civil War', in L.Baerentzen etal., eds., *op.cit.*, pp.41–53.
157. *Eleftheria* (Athens):11/12/1945; Efimeris tis Kyverniseos, vol.I, no.311, 21/12/1945, pp.1566ff; F.O.371/58681 R4702: Norton to F.O., 21/3/1946.
158. F.O.371/48288 R21125: Leeper to F.O., 7/12/1945.
159. FRUS (1945): VIII, 185–6: MacVeagh to Byrnes, 4/12/1945.
160. *Loc.cit.*
161. F.O.371/58667 R155: Leeper to F.O., 21/12/1945.
162. F.O.371/58674 R2233: Leeper to F.O., 11/2/1946.
163. *To Vima* (Athens): 20/3/1946.
164. GAK:Tsouderos Papers, E (49): A Note on the Greek Question (March 1947); *ibid.*, Tsouderos's letter to Henry Wallace, 17/3/1948.
165. DBPO: II, no.300: Bevin–Molotov Conversation, 18/12/1945.
166. Quoted in A. Bullock, *Ernest Bevin: Foreign Secretary 1945–1951* (Oxford: 1985), p.216.
167. See, for instance, the record of a particularly bad-tempered meeting between

Bevin and Molotov, held at the Soviet Embassy in London on 1/10/1945, in F.O.371/50922U9974. In an earlier public session Bevin had compared Molotov to Hitler; even the US Secretary of State James Byrnes protested, and Bevin had to apologize. Records of the London session of the CFM in CAB 133/15 and FRUS (1945): II, 112–555. See also A. Bullock, *op.cit.*, pp.129–37; K. Morgan, *op.cit.*, pp.240–3.

168. DBPO: II, no. 294: Conversation between Byrnes – Bevin – Cadogan – Dixon (Moscow), 17/12/1945.

169. UNO Security Council, *Official Records*, First Year: First Series, Supplement no.1 (London: 1946), Annex 3, pp.73ff.

170. *Ibid.*, pp.78ff; FRUS (1946): VII, 109: Record of a Secret Session during the Meeting of the UN Security Council on 5 February 1946.

171. FRUS (1946): VII, 111–12, Annex; UNO Security Council, *Official Records*, *op.cit.*, 165–173; *Decade of American Foreign Policy, 1941–1949: Basic Documents*, no.137: Consideration of the Greek Problem by the Security Council during the year 1946; CAB 128/5/C.M. 13 (46): 7/2/1946.

172. CAB 128/5/C.M. 7 (46): 22/1/1946; F.O.371/58670 R1147: Sargent to Leeper, 22/1/1946.

173. W. Loth, *The Division of the World, 1941–1955* (London:1988), pp.34–55; A. Bullock, *op.cit.*, pp.6–12, 115–16. The theme of Stalin's 'prudently expansionist' policy is analysed in P.J. Stavrakis, *Moscow and Greek Communism 1944–1949* (Ithaca and London: 1989), pp.1–6, 48–126, 203–15.

174. Soviet Foreign Ministry Archives: On the opening of the Embassy of the USSR in Greece, 8/1/1945; V. Zorin to A. Vyshinsky, 17/1/1945; Zorin to Molotov, 23/1/1945; Greek–Soviet Relations in 1944–1949; all in P. Andaeos, *op.cit.*, pp.430–2, 448–51.

175. F.O.371/58735 R1118: Clark-Kerr to F.O., 23/1/1946; *ibid.*, R2142: Roberts to F.O., 8/2/1946, and Minute by Smyth, 13/2/1946; F.N. Grigoriadis, *Istoria tou Emfyliou Polemou, 1946–1949* (Athens: n.d.), II, p.623.

176. Soviet Foreign Ministry Archives: Greek–Soviet Relations in 1944–1949, in P. Andaeos, op.cit., p.451; D. Partsalidis, *Dipli Apokatastasi tis Ethnikis Andistasis* (Athens:1978), p.199; Partsalidis's interviews in *Tachydromos* no. 25 (1977), *To Vima* (6/1/1980), and *Anti* no.178 (22/5/1981), p.40.

177. Bevin Papers: F.O.800/468/GRE/46/1: Damaskinos to Bevin, 4/2/1946; Lord Halifax to Bevin, 6/2/1946.

178. S. Patatzis, *Ioannis Sofianopoulos: Enas Epanastatis Choris Epanastasi* (Athens: 1961), pp.244ff.

179. Attlee Papers (Bodleian Library, Oxford): Box 31, Folios 166–74: Zilliacus to Attlee, 11/2/1946.

180. Attlee Papers: Box 31, Folio 242: Attlee to Zilliacus, 17/2/1946.

181. H. Dalton, *High Tide and After: Memoirs 1945–1960* (London: 1962), p.105 (9/3/1946).

182. CAB 131/2/DO (46) 40: Memorandum by Bevin, 13/3/1946.

183. F.O.371/58676 R3032: Minute by Hayter, 21/2/1946; F.O.371/58678 R3496: Minute by Hayter, 8/3/1946.

184. F.O.371/58678 R3496: Leeper to Sargent, 27/2/1946.

185. F.O.371/58678 R3496: Minute by Hayter, 8/3/1946.

186. F.O.371/58678 R3496: Minute by Warner, 11/3/1946.

187. F.O.371/58678 R3496: Minute by McNeil, 29/3/1946.

188. FRUS (1945): VIII, 186–187: Greek Embassy (Washington) to State

Department, 6/12/1945; *ibid.*, 192: Byrnes to Greek ambassador (Washington), 11/12/1945; *ibid.*, 185–6, 189–90: MacVeagh to Byrnes, 4 and 8/12/1945.

189. CAB 129/5/C.P. (45) 355: 'Elections in Greece', Memorandum by Bevin, 31/12/1945.

190. FRUS (1946): VII, 99: MacVeagh to Byrnes, 22/1/1946; *ibid.*, 115–16: Gallman (London) Byrnes, 27/2/1946; *ibid.*, 116: Rankin (Athens) to Byrnes, 28/2/1946.

191. *Eleftheria* (Athens): 7/3/1946.

192. FRUS (1946): VII, 117–18: British Embassy to State Department, Text of Message from Bevin to Greek Prime Minister, 7/3/1946; F.O.371/58678 R3462: Message from the Prime Minister of Greece to the Secretary of State for Foreign Affairs, 2/3/1946.

193. F.O.371/48372 R21325: BPM Report, 5/12/1945; F.O.371/58673 R1905: Bevin to Leeper, 8/2/1946.

194. FRUS (1946): VII, 118–19: Rankin to State Department, 8/3/1946.

195. *The Times* (London): 8/3/1946; CAB 128/5/C.M. 23 (46): 11/3/1946; *Rizospastis* (Athens): 12/3/1946.

196. FRUS (1946): VII, 124–5: British Embassy to State Department, Aide-Mémoire, 20/3/1946; Bevin Papers: F.O.800/468/GRE/46/6: F.O.Statement, 'Greek Elections', 20/3/1946.

197. F.O.371/58680 R4527: F.O.to Norton, 20/3/1946.

198. F.O.371/58676 R2713: Minute by Warner, 23/2/1946.

199. F.O.371/58680 R4542: Norton to F.O., 21/3/1946.

200. K. Morgan, *op.cit.*, pp.34, 71.

201. F.O.371/58682 R4891: Norton to F.O., 27/3/1946.

202. F.O.371/58682 R5019: Norton to F.O., 29/3/1946; *The Times* (London): 29/3/1946.

203. F.O.371/58672 R1830: Leeper to F.O., 4/2/1946; F.O.371/58673 R1905: Leeper to F.O., 6/2/1946.

204. *Rizospastis* (Athens): 12/12/1946; KKE: E.K., VI, no.748: Politburo Resolution, 17/1/1946; S. Sarafis, *op.cit.*, pp.210–12.

205. F.O.371/48289 R21484: EAM Delegation, Memorandum, 17/12/1945; Minutes by Laskey, 30/12/1945.

206. KKE: E.K., VI, no.747: Politburo Resolution, 17/1/1946.

207. GAK: Tsouderos Papers E (47): EAM Memorandum, 7/2/1946.

208. *Vradyni* (Athens): 8/2/1946.

209. KKE: E.K., VI, no.750, 15/2/1946.

210. The major advocate of this view is M. Vafiadis, *op.cit.*, III, 120–5, and V, 82–5, 174–83. H. Richter, *op.cit.*, pp.477–95, and 'The Second Plenum of the Central Committee of the KKE and the Decision For Civil War: A Reappraisal' in L. Baerentzen et al., eds., *op.cit.*, pp.179–87, has taken up the criticisms against Zachariadis. Yet the most incisive scrutiny of existing sources can be found in O.L. Smith, 'Self-Defence and Communist Policy, 1945–1947', in L. Baerentzen et al., eds., *op.cit.*, pp.159–77, and mainly in his 'The Problems of the Second Plenum of the Central Committee of the KKE, 1946', *Journal of theHellenic Diaspora* 12, no.2 (1985), 43–62. Smith convincingly argues that the Second Plenum did take a decision.

211. G. Blanas, *op.cit.*, p.72.

212. V. Bartziotas, *O Agonas*, p.27.

213. *Ibid.*, pp.28–30. In his autobiography, *Exinda Chronia*, p.236, Bartziotas cites

what he claims to have been the actual decision of the Second Plenum. In a personal communication (31/1/1990) Ole Smith suggested to me that already when writing his book on the DSE, Bartziotas had access to the decision from his own notes but committed a *faux pas* by publishing what is more or less an unpublished party document.

214. Zachariadis's Speech at the 7th Plenum (1957), in P. Dimitriou, ed., *I Diaspasi tou KKE* I (Athens: 1978), 93.
215. N. Zachariadis, *Provlimata tis Krisis tou KKE* (n.p.:1962), republished as *I Paranomi Brosura tou Nikou Zachariadi* (Athens: 1987), pp.32–3.
216. In P. Andaeos, *op.cit.*, p.502.
217. N. Zachariadis, *op.cit.*, p.33.
218. *Rizospastis* (Athens): 7/3/1946.
219. D. Partsalidis, *op.cit.*, p.196; F.N. Grogoriadis, *op.cit.*, II, 623; Zachariadis's Speech at the 7th Plenum (1957),in P. Dimitriou, ed., *op.cit.* I, 95; N. Zachariadis, *op.cit.*, p.20; *I Triti Syndiaskepsi tou KKE, 10–14/10/1950*, pp.65, 79, 105. See also H. Fleischer, 'The "Third Factor": The Struggle for an Independent Socialist Policy during the Greek Civil War', in L. Baerentzen et al., eds., *op.cit.*, p.197, for an interesting hint that with regard to abstention, 'the socialist part in the decision-making, usually ignored, must actually have been considerable'.
220. F.N. Grigoriadis, *op.cit.*, III, 659ff; S.N. Grigoriadis, *op.cit.*, pp.224–5. Both writers were the sons of Gen. Neokosmos Grigoriadis, one of the two leaders of the Left Liberals.
221. *The Times* (London): 29/3/1946; R. Clogg, *Parties and Elections in Greece: The Search for Legitimacy* (London: 1987), p.18; H. Richter, *op.cit.*, pp.445–6.
222. *Report of the Allied Mission to Observe the Greek Elections* (London: HMSO, 1946), Cmd 6812, pp.28–9.
223. *Loc.cit.*; R. Clogg, *op.cit.*, p.18.
224. *Report of the Allied Mission to Observe the Greek Elections*, p.22.
225. R. Clogg, *op.cit.*, p.20; H. Richter, *op.cit.*, pp.441–56; G. Mavrogordatos, 'From Ballots to Bullets: The 1946 Elections and Plebiscite', in J.O. Iatrides, ed., *op.cit.*, pp.181–94.
226. F.O.371/58684 R5434: Norton to F.O., 6/4/1946; F.O.371/58675 R2628: Leeper to F.O., 19/2/1946; F.O.371/58677R3288: Leeper to F.O., 23/2/1946; F.O.371/58676 R2918: Leeper to F.O., 1/2/1946; F.N. Grigoriadis, *op.cit.*, II, 623; Soviet Foreign Ministry Archives: Greek–Soviet Relations in 1944–1949, in P. Andaeos, *op.cit.*, p.453.
227. CAB 129/5/C.P.(45) 355: 'Elections in Greece', Memorandum by Bevin, 31/12/1945.
228. J. Meynaud, *Oi Politikes Dynameis stin Ellada* (Athens:1966), p.79.
229. F.N. Grigoriadis, *op.cit.*, II, 630. Exactly the same figures are given in KKE: CC, *Syndomi Istoria tou KKE: Schedio, Meros A, 1918–1949* (Athens: 1988), p.244.

III   Changing the Guard: 1946–1947

> To fit in with the change of events, words, too, had
> to change their usual meanings.
>
> Thucydides, III : 82

Bevin and the Populists

Bevin felt that the Greek elections provided an opportune moment for the appointment of a new British ambassador in Athens, something which had been in his mind since late November 1945.[1] Thus in early March 1946 Reginald Leeper, the man who for two years had left a distinct imprint on Greek affairs, was replaced by Sir Clifford Norton, and Anglo-Greek relations entered an ostensibly new era. For the British, the elections of March held the prospect of a partial disentanglement from their Greek burden, as responsibility for Greek domestic affairs was soon to be transferred to the hands of the elected government in Athens. Almost a fortnight before polling day, the Foreign Office had instructed Norton not to emulate his predecessor's control of Greek politics. Henceforth the British government wished the swift and drastic curtailment of its involvement, though it would still enjoy a 'certain influence' on the Greeks, who would continue to rely heavily on London's counsel and aid. Having little confidence in the Populists, Bevin instructed the ambassador to steer their government towards a moderate course. Britain would continue to support Greece, but in return she expected a stable and broad coalition which would press on with the economic agreement of January 1946, maintain constitutional liberties and parliamentary institutions, suppress the armed bands, and refrain from immediately raising the issue of the monarchy. For Bevin the latter was 'very important if Greece is to avoid civil strife'.[2]

As far as can be judged from the royalist press, the Populists had contested the election with no political programme save the restoration of the King and a rumbustious anti-communism. In this context, Bevin's predilection for a broad coalition might scale down right-wing intransigence, but more importantly, unity among all bourgeois parties could politically isolate EAM, reduce the wrangling between monarchists and republicans, and even secure some consensus on reconstruction policy. Anxious to secure the co-operation of the Populists, on 1 April the Foreign Secretary instructed Norton to convey to the Greek political leaders and to the new Parliament a more elaborate version of his wishes. The government-to-be, based on a broad coalition of parliamentary parties, should abide by the Anglo-Greek economic agreement, 'take a progressive view of legislation' and 'put behind them all the troubles that resulted from enemy occupation and civil war'. With the consent of the King and the parties to be represented in the new government, the Regent should be persuaded to carry on because the premature raising of the constitutional question would cause upheaval and impair the work of reconstruction. The same course was to be impressed upon George II by Sir Orme Sargent.[3]

The Populist leadership, however, could hardly wait for the plebiscite; even after Bevin's vague threat that if they pressed on with the matter, full co-operation between the British and the Greek governments would be impossible.[4] According to Norton and the US Chargé d'Affaires Karl Rankin, the Populists, 'somewhat elevated' by their victory, were disposed to hurry on with the plebiscite irrespective of allied opinion. They were convinced that the time was '"now or never"', for they believed that many republicans would vote for the King as an act of refusal to vote along with EAM, whilst, as time went by, the '"inevitable mistakes"' of their government would weaken the royalist cause.[5]

Bevin's desire for a broad coalition government seemed equally hopeless. Sofulis and Papandreou refused to cooperate with the Populists, while Venizelos and Kanellopoulos were put off by their insistence to hold the plebiscite within two months and occupy all key posts in the Cabinet. Echoing his own apprehensions, the Regent cautioned Norton that unless something was done to restrain the Populists, they might 'take the bit between their teeth' and set up a one-party government or even launch a coup. Damaskinos asked the ambassador to impress upon them the hazards of a prompt plebiscite, but despite his promise to do so, Norton said that there were limits to the pressure he could exert on the largest party of an elected government.[6]

The Populists were adamant, but so was Bevin, who remained undeterred by the possibility that his line might prove unacceptable and that the Populists might form a government of their own or even 'refuse to form a government at all'.[7] On 4 April George II, who dwelt at Claridge's, called on the Foreign Secretary and requested a plebiscite not later than September 1946 on the grounds that in the elections the Greeks had condemned Communism and shown their preference for the monarchy, and that a speedy settlement of the constitutional question would create a better climate for economic recovery. In his reply Bevin once more disclosed his mistrust of the Populists, who 'instead of emptying the prisons, would be vengeful and would put more political opponents into prison'. He argued that there were some 6,000 political prisoners in Greece who had not stood trial yet and urged the King to use all his influence in that respect. Yet he ingeniously evaded the plebiscite question, as he wished first to exchange views with his US colleague. The British Foreign Secretary felt that 'our minds would be influenced a good deal by the conduct of this government and by the co-operation exhibited by them on the problem of reconstruction'.[8]

In Athens, meanwhile, the Populists and the National Political Union (EPE) of Papandreou, Kanellopoulos and Venizelos reached a compromise and formed a government under Panayiotis Poulitsas, the President of the Council of the State, pending the election of a leader by the parliamentary Populist Party.[9] The British Embassy, 'distressed at the lack of talent among available candidates for [the] premiership', would have preferred a coalition under Papandreou – the 'best man in sight'.[10] *The Times* was less courteous in its verdict on the victors:

It cannot be said that the new government commands a great deal of confidence. Much cannot be expected of a party which, though it claims to represent Greece, is unable to produce a Prime Minister when required. The three or four Populist leaders who are competitors for the chairmanship of the party are not, moreover, men of proved capacity.[11]

Indeed, problems cropped up very shortly. On 15 April the lack-lustre Konstantinos Tsaldaris, nephew of the prewar Populist leader Panayis Tsaldaris, was elected party chief, but two days later the three EPE leaders resigned from the government. Papandreou, Venizelos and Kanellopoulos were embittered by the Populists' refusal to allot them a proportional share of portfolios, they fell out with their partners over the handling of the plebiscite question, and, significantly, they were uncertain of the ability of the Populist leadership to control its rank and file. Thus on 18 April Tsaldaris was sworn in as both Premier and Foreign Minister of a Populist government whose composition, according to Norton, reflected his predicament: Tsaldaris had to maintain the spirit of cooperation with Britain and, at the same time, meet the desire of his deputies for an early statement in the Parliament on the date of the plebiscite.[12]

The Greek Prime Minister suggested to Norton that a brief postponement of the convocation of Parliament would enable him to reach an agreement with Bevin. The ambassador and the Foreign Secretary found the idea useful, but the royalist press in Athens immediately claimed that the allies 'were showing readiness to consent to the advancement of the plebiscite'.[13] This was not quite so. The State Department argued that the plebiscite should not take place before spring 1947 because a precipitate return of the King would arouse passions and retard the work of reconstruction.[14] The Foreign Office was puzzled by the persistence of the King and the Populists, for the election results had shown that in the event of a plebiscite the Left and the Centre would outvote the monarchists.[15] Norton wrote to Sargent that even among the Right there were people convinced that the immediate return of the King would be a 'mistake' leading to repression, dictatorship and, eventually, civil war. A King, Norton remarked, could hardly retain his throne against an opposition – 'even of 25%' – as active as EAM, unless its press and other public activities 'are tightly muzzled'. That was particularly true of George II, who 'had come to be regarded by many as the symbol of a party'.[16]

By then, however, Bevin had had second thoughts about his own position vis-à-vis the elected Greek rulers, who 'should increasingly and as quickly as possible accept full responsibility for the government of their country'. The Foreign Secretary now held that a protracted constitutional uncertainty would perpetuate the unsettled conditions of Greek political life and prevent the Greek government from focussing on reconstruction. Added to that, insistence on postponement of the plebiscite even until 1947 would raise difficulties with respect to Britain's relations with the Greek King and the 'constitutionally elected government'. The problem was that AMFOGE (in one of the many cases in which it had shot itself in the foot) had left no doubt as to the necessity for a complete recompilation of the electoral registers before Greeks were once more called upon to vote; if Britain acquiesced in the Populists' demand without prior satisfaction of the AMFOGE recommendation, she would lay herself 'open to strong and justifiable criticism'. Bevin was therefore prepared to allow an early plebiscite on condition that the registers were revised under the supervision of an allied mission. At the same time, in order to avoid the probable neglect of the task of reconstruction on the part of the Greek government, Britain would have to require them to bind themselves to implement the economic agreement of January 1946.[17]

Bevin might have had his second thoughts, but the State Department insisted that since the tackling of economic problems was far more important than the settlement of the constitutional issue, the plebiscite should not take place before spring 1947 at the earliest.[18] Then, on 24 April, the Americans became aware of Bevin's changing attitude and sought clarification of the British position.[19] The matter was taken up three days later in a decisive meeting between Bevin and James Byrnes in Paris. The US Secretary of State wanted to press the Soviets to withdraw their armies from Austria, Bulgaria, Rumania and elsewhere, for that would enable allied troops to do likewise. Bevin agreed that Britain should also be in a position to pull out her troops from Greece, though not before the plebiscite; he would thus prefer to have it held in September 1946. His reply to Byrnes's inquiry as to what would happen if the British troops were withdrawn on that date and the plebiscite was held in spring 1947 demonstrated that the Foreign Secretary did have a clear view of the domestic situation in Greece. The Populists, he argued,

> would run the elections [*sic*] and make it impossible for any genuine opposition to the King to be recorded. The result might be an overwhelming majority for the King. A result obtained in this way would not be accepted by many of the Greek people, and might lead quickly to disturbances and a renewal of civil strife.

Byrnes gave in and summed up the common cause to be rigorously pursued:

> it was essential that the Communists should not get into power in Greece. This must be avoided at all costs. He did not mind how it was done. We must keep our eye closely on Greece. He thought that we [British] were in a better position than the US to assess the situation and if we thought that September 1946 was the right date, then the US was quite prepared to accept that.

The decision for an early plebiscite had been taken, yet Bevin could hardly conceal his mistrust of the Populists. He pointed out to Byrnes that since 'a bare majority for the King would be unfortunate', as it would not express the overwhelming will of the Greeks, he preferred to lay down that a majority 'of, say, 60%' would be required if George II was to resume his throne.[20]

After the Paris meeting the prospect of the full restoration of the prewar order in Greece moved from the realms of possibility to those of probability.

Given that the White Terror had commenced soon after the signature of the Varkiza Agreement, and that even Bevin himself was quite sceptical as to the democratic commitment of the Populist Party, his contention that the plebiscite should be brought forward so that the British troops could act as a deterrent to royalist extremism was hardly convincing. Instead, he might have thought that by giving in to the Populists' demand, he would get them to turn to reconstruction, but so far there had been no indications to that effect.

The relations between the West and the Soviet Union in spring 1946 offer a more rewarding field for an inquiry into the motives of Byrnes and Bevin. By February 1946 the unilateral and harsh Soviet conduct in Eastern Europe, the criticisms against what was seen as Byrnes's policy of appeasing the Soviet Union, and the immediate and massive impact of George F. Kennan's Long Telegram – which provided a rationale of Soviet foreign policy as the product of internal influences and therefore not open to persuasion, manipulation or even understanding from the West – brought an end to what President Truman called the 'babying' of the Soviets. The Iranian crisis of February–March 1946 showed that the United States had embarked on a policy of firmness and tough resistance to Soviet demands, and Washington began to draw up plans to check Soviet expansionism.[21]

While Anglo-Soviet relations continued acrimonious over Germany, the Far East, the Middle East, the Mediterranean and Greece, Bevin had already foreseen that the United States and the Soviet Union would soon line up against each other and Britain would have to choose which side to join. In the meantime the repeated assaults of the Soviet press on himself and the British government had compelled the Foreign Secretary to protest to Vyshinsky, whereas Frank Roberts, the British Minister in Moscow, was concerned lest the ideology of the Soviet Union might lead to the modern equivalent of the religious wars which had plagued Europe in the 16th century.[22] In early April Christopher Warner, now Head of the Northern Department of the Foreign Office and member of its newly-formed 'Russia Committee', prepared a paper on 'The Soviet Campaign Against This Country and Our Response to it'. The British should at once organize their defences and 'not stop short of a defensive-offensive policy', for the Soviet Union, he argued, was practising 'vicious power politics' and would 'stick at nothing to obtain her objectives' – save, perhaps, war. On 10 April Bevin sent Attlee an identical assessment of Soviet foreign policy which, according to the Foreign Secretary, was 'based upon militant Communism and Russian chauvinism'.[23]

In such an international context the domestic origins and merits of the Greek case per se were likely to lapse into oblivion and its handling subjected to the requirements of allied foreign policy – a speedy plebiscite, withdrawal of British troops and then pressure on the Soviets to do likewise. As the first skirmishes of the Cold War became more and more frequent, the overwhelming necessity of keeping Greece on the British side of the fence overshadowed every other consideration, even though months earlier the Foreign Office had expressed fears that a swift restoration of the King could lead to civil war. Hence, following Bevin's instructions, on 10 May 1946 Norton informed Tsaldaris that the British government consented to an early plebiscite on condition that the registers were revised and Damaskinos remained as Regent. The ambassador had persuaded Bevin to drop his previous conditions on the grounds that a suggestion on the percentage required for the return of the King would unnecessarily interfere with the constitutional question, and that Tsaldaris's promises to abide by the economic agreement of January would have no practical effect. The Greek Prime Minister was quite happy to accept the British terms.[24]

As the day of the convocation of the Greek Parliament approached, a Populist deputy set the tone by stating that he would call for the arrest, trial and execution of all KKE leaders on charges of 'murders, thefts, high treason, etc.'[25] Half of the monarchist press virulently attacked Communism, the other half extolling the merits of the monarchy. An editorial in the influential *Kathimerini*, entitled 'A Republic is the Ante-Chamber to Communist Dictatorship', invited Greeks to vote for the monarchy because despite its errors, it 'does not fellow-travel … with terror, blood and the enemies of Greece'.[26] Amidst this atmosphere of monarchist intransigence, when the Greek Parliament held its opening session on 13 May 1946 the Regent announced that the plebiscite would be held on 1 September of that year.[27]

The British Cabinet did not debate the issue until a week later. On 20 May Bevin told his colleagues that in view of the session of the Council of Foreign Ministers due in June, he should be in a position to press for withdrawal of all allied armies from occupied countries in south-eastern Europe, including British troops from Greece. The normally uninformative Minutes suggest that the ensuing discussion must have been immensely interesting. One or more Cabinet members expressed the view that an early plebiscite resulting in a narrow majority for the King would generate the belief that his restoration was the consequence of British diplomacy, and violence would then break out afresh. The question was even raised as to whether the British could 'prevail upon the King to renounce his claim to return to Greece'. Partly in a manifestation of wishful thinking, Bevin argued that the evidence available to him – the election results – suggested that a fair plebiscite might well turn out against the King. Overall he was 'satisfied that the balance of advantage lay on the side of holding the plebiscite at an early date'.[28]

As the Populist Party and Bevin cared little about the consequences, the plebiscite was to be duly held on 1 September 1946. The restoration of the monarch who owed his throne to the rigged plebiscite of November 1935, and who had less than a year later co-operated with Metaxas in establishing the General's dictatorship, was bound to stretch the patience of the Left to its limits. If the pursuit of a speedy plebiscite was to be expected of a Greek monarchist faction with no other political programme, for the British it was a substantial retreat from their position of November 1945. Then their awareness of the consequences had prompted them to intervene towards the postponement of the plebiscite until March 1948. Half a year later members of the British Cabinet, including Bevin, continued to fear the outbreak of civil war in Greece, but that seemed to be of minor concern compared with the exigencies of great-power politics.

Bevin's contention that the British troops would be a deterrent to monarchist excesses was both ill-informed and hypocritical. As for his assertions about disentanglement from Greece, these referred only to forms of direct intervention and military presence. On 13 May Norton wrote to Warner: 'I have searched my conscience to see whether there is any alternative to the support of this Right Wing Government ... I am convinced that there is not.'[29] A month later Hayter agreed that 'there is at present no reasonable or obvious possible alternative to a Populist Government ... The King himself, to judge by departmental reports, would be likely to exercise a sensible and moderating influence on the Populist Party if he returned to Greece.'[30] In other words, the British continued to doubt the egalitarian credentials of the Greek ruling party, so much so that they hoped George II might moderate their intransigence. What they failed to grasp was that once in power, the Populists would spare no effort to bring back the King, and that such an eventuality would destroy the patience of the KKE.

The Populists and the Communists

The electoral victory of the Populists came six weeks after the decision of the Second Plenum of the KKE Central Committee for limited armed struggle with a view to a compromise. Although the feasibility of such a goal was a moot point, the decision of the KKE implied that future developments would largely depend upon the Populists' stance towards the Left and *vice versa*. On 20 March 1946 Zachariadis left Athens for Prague to attend the Czech Communist Party Congress, but *en route* to Prague he stopped over in Belgrade, where he met with Josip Broz Tito. The first attempt of the KKE leader to secure pledges of support from the fraternal parties was successful, as Tito wholeheartedly agreed with the aims of the KKE. Then in Prague Zachariadis informed the Czech and Albanian communist leaders and Georgi Dimitrov of the dual strategy of the KKE and received further assurances of moral and material support. The Czechs in particular promised to supply heavy weapons, while Dimitrov emphasized that the conception of a gradual transition to armed struggle was correct. The only communist leaders who are said to have expressed their scepticism with regard to the prospect of the armed struggle in Greece were Maurice Thorez for the French, and Palmiro Togliatti for the Italian Communist Party.[31]

In 1980 the story of Zachariadis's peregrinations was completed by Lefteris Eleftheriou, a KKE cadre who published his recollections from his conversations with Zachariadis in Moscow in 1956. The KKE leader disclosed to him that from Prague he went to Moscow via Belgrade for talks with the Soviet leadership in early April. In a first meeting, Stalin, Molotov and Andrei Zhdanov endorsed the decisions of the KKE, while in a second private meeting with Zachariadis, Stalin urged the Greek party to '"proceed from village to town gradually, in order to avoid an untimely armed intervention of the British, and with the direction of finding a compromise."'[32] No doubt the KKE would have found it very difficult to embark on the policy it had decided in February 1946 without foreign, and particularly Soviet, endorsement. Thus from late February to early April 1946 – that is after the Second Plenum had reached its decision – Zachariadis's line for a gradual build-up of armed action with a view to a compromise was approved by the fraternal parties and, most importantly, by Stalin. Before the end of the year the counsel for the search of a compromise would be repeated, as the Soviets were anxious not to provoke Britain and the United States in an area which had not been designated on their side of the fence.

The Soviet emphasis on a compromise further highlights Moscow's circumspect and prudent approach. Stalin's endorsement of Zachariadis's line does not contradict this evaluation; on the contrary, it indicates that Zachariadis elicited Stalin's support by presenting him with a *fait accompli*. The KKE had disregarded Soviet advice and abstained from the elections, thereby excluding itself from parliamentary politics; the entire Greek Left was the victim of a wholesale persecution which threatened its physical survival; at the Second Plenum of February 1946 the Greek communists had made an independent decision for armed struggle; and subsequently that decision had been approved by the communist parties of Yugoslavia, Bulgaria, Albania and Czechoslovakia. By facing Stalin with these developments, Zachariadis evidently managed to persuade him that the application of military force was the only alternative for the KKE. In this light, Stalin's counsel for a compromise between the KKE and its opponents must be seen as a sign of his unease at the turn of events in Greece and the plans of the KKE.[33]

As for Yugoslavia, which until 1948 proved to be the most generous and stable supporter of the KKE, her motives were certainly short-term and, conceivably, long-term. In the short-term Tito was primarily interested in safeguarding the new communist Yugoslavia from what he perceived as a direct threat emanating from Britain's attempts to expand her influence in the Balkans. Then the Yugoslav leader used to confide to his entourage that his internationalist duty urged him to assist other 'revolutions'. The eminently less noble motive of Yugoslav expansionist designs against Greek Macedonia is regarded a matter of guesswork, though it might have been a long-term prospect for the Yugoslavs. Tito's prime concern remained the protection of the new Yugoslav state.[34]

On 2 April 1946 Zachariadis released a press statement to the effect that the Greek problem could be summed up in the British 'occupation' which prevented the restoration of law and order in the country.[35] Six days later, in a telegram to the governments of the Big Four, all leftist parties rightly asserted that the outcome of the elections had deepened the divisions among Greeks. Britain's 'clumsy' handling of the Greek question would expose her to criticisms and entail fresh international complications. The Left had been embittered by Bevin's statement that the withdrawal of the British troops from Greece would depend on the withdrawal of other allied armies from occupied countries in Europe. Greece, they retorted, was not an enemy country like Germany and her satellites, but a victor and a participant in the common allied struggle, and as such she meant to remain a sovereign and independent state; yet that would remain elusive as long as the stationing of foreign troops and the undisguised interference in her domestic affairs continued.

For the Greek Left, British policy in Greece had failed because it had inspired mistrust even among the Centre and contributed to the ascendancy of the 'monarcho-fascist' faction. To avert further complications, the Left invited Britain either to apply the Yalta Declaration – whereby a 'broad democratic coalition' would create conditions for free and genuine polls – or to refer the matter to the United Nations. In the latter case, the international organization would resolve the matter 'by way of assistance and [a] substantial joint guarantee of all Three Great Powers'. In the eyes of the Greek Left only the above course could deliver an appropriate solution, discharge Britain of any 'understandable misunderstanding' that 'Greek Independence is being sacrificed on the altar of her imperial interests', and spare Greece from the 'agony that her soil is to become a field of recriminations and battle of conflicting allied interests'.[36] With a modicum of hindsight it may be argued that the latter proposal held some prospect of averting the mounting crisis, and that in its early stages the Greek Civil War may be looked upon as a sad story of missed opportunities: in the winter of 1946–1947 not only was consideration given to the possibility of an understanding among the Big Three for the solution of the Greek problem, but also hopes appeared for some palliative action by the United Nations.

After his return to Greece in early April 1946, Zachariadis forcefully advocated self-defence and threatened that if the reign of terror continued the people would have to use the same means.[37] Yet many individuals whom the White Terror had forced to flee to the mountains would not wait for his express instructions. Although until March circulars from the the Politburo forbade the carrying of firearms, some of those hunted down had armed themselves of their own accord. In the summer of 1946 the so-called Bands of Armed Persecuted Democrats (ODEK) sprang up in Thessaly and Macedonia, engaging in clashes with monarchist bands and the Gendarmerie. Some local KKE organizations at first accused ODEK of being 'extremists' and refused to assist them, but many villagers readily offered supplies, as ODEK protected them from the monarchist bands.[38] Already on 10 May the US Chargé d'Affaires in Athens reported to Washington that in some regions there was 'increased disorder' attributable to:

(i) deliberate Communist policy, (ii) boldness of Right extremists following elections, (iii) release of leftists under prison decongestion law and consequent vendetta killings, (iv) reluctance [of] gendarmerie and police to curb Rightists due to their own anti-Communist bias and uncertainty as to Government attitude.[39]

The attitude of the Populist government to the emergence of leftist bands, which was clearly the result of the White Terror,[40] would not remain uncertain for long. On 3 May 1946 the Cabinet decided to set up extra-judicial Public Security Committees which would be empowered to exile to another part of the country any person 'suspected of giving aid to brigands or to fugitives from justice or of any illegal trafficking or of other acts prejudicial to the public order and calm and security of the realm'.[41] The British Embassy promptly warned the Greek Minister of Public Order, Spyros Theotokis, that such a measure would inevitably be regarded abroad as undemocratic, 'and smacking as it did of the evil days of Metaxas, would be a God-send to foreign critics of his Government; and that for the same reason, it might cause H.M.'s Government serious embarrassment'. Theotokis justified it as aimed at those against whom the state could not establish a *prima facie* case according to common law, and promised that it would be applied 'very sparingly'; Norton and Sir Charles Wickham, the head of the British Police Mission, had no doubt that it would be 'exclusively' enforced against communists.[42] The Foreign Office shared the concern of its representatives in Athens and instructed Norton to tell the Greek government that the law should not be promulgated, for it would evoke hostile criticism in Britain and elsewhere and embarrass the British government. Yet Tsaldaris, the Populist leader and Greek Prime Minister, brushed aside any criticisms on the grounds that 'a minority' was 'systematically flouting the law'.[43] While these exchanges were taking place, monarchist bands raided towns and gendarmerie stations in the Peloponnese, in one case shooting three leftist detainees.[44]

Although more legislation was soon to come, the manner in which the Public Security Committees functioned deserves special mention. They were set up in each prefecture and consisted of the president and public prosecutor of the local court of first instance, the prefect and the local police or gendarmerie commander. According to public prosecutor Pavlos Delaportas, the Committees hardly considered whether the person brought before them had indulged in any subversive activities; it sufficed for him or her to be a communist or a 'fellow-traveller' – a term elastic enough to embrace 'centrists, liberals, republicans, socialists, etc.' The process was as follows:

For anybody who had been pointed out or selected for exile, the first stage was a sworn examination of witnesses by the police. The witnesses, usually 8–10, were almost always gendarmes. Their depositions were always as identical as military college or musical band uniforms … There followed some entirely vague and general incidents about the subversive action of the person to be exiled, without any positive or concrete point, and ended with the phrases that the person to be exiled: "happens to be an old and important cadre of the communist party and is highly dangerous for national security". Never was there found in that party even one person to be a novice, newly recruited or apprentice communist. All were always "important and old cadres of the KKE".[45]

Monarchist strongholds such as Gytheion, in the south of the Peloponnese, needed no Public Security Committees because the leftists had already exiled themselves outside the region.[46] Delaportas bitterly commented:

The social problems, which other states solved by huge expenses of billions, were solved hereby spending 0,50 drachmae in each case. Five sheets of paper cost 0,50 dr., the five sheets were cut in half and became ten sheets on which the depositions of the ten witnesses were written, alleging that the person who caused trouble was, "according to fully corroborated informa-tion", an "unrepentant communist and an old cadre of the communist party, therefore highly dangerous for national security".[47]

The Populist government apparently felt that this was not sufficiently drastic. On 6 June Tsaldaris informed Norton that a new draft law 'On Extraordinary Measures Concerning Public Order and Security' was to be put before Parliament that evening. According to the new piece of legislation, persons engaging in activity aimed at the detachment of part of Greek territory from the Greek state, forming or participating in armed bands, and carrying out armed attacks on public authorities, would be punished by death, imprisonment or banishment. Participation in illegal gatherings, strikes in public necessity services and disturbance of the public mind by threatening acts of violence were punishable by imprisonment. In northern Greece Special Courts-Martial would be set up to try offenders against law and order. There would be no right of appeal, bail, postponement of penalties or alternative fines.[48]

The KKE immediately denounced the new draft law as fascist and pointed out that it would lead to civil war, while EAM submitted a memorandum of protest to the ambassadors of the Big Four.[49] The Foreign Office had some misgivings and recommended restraint, but the law was eventually passed by the Greek Parliament on 18 June 1946: it was the notorious Resolution III.[50] The repression which, since the previous year, had been in practice against the Left was legalized, expanded and given an ultra-patriotic tone. Although the KKE had since 1935 dropped its autonomist Macedonian policy and supported Greek territorial claims to the full,[51] Resolution III effectively equated it with the Slavs – who not only were deemed Greece's traditional foes, but also conveniently happened to have communist regimes.[52]

Zachariadis's long-awaited response was in kind. On 16 June 1946 the KKE leader participated in a conference of the party's Macedonia-Thrace Bureau held at Thessaloniki. Evidence of what happened there can be found both in the Foreign Office files and in the memoirs of Greek communists. In a minute dated 2 July, David McCarthy, an official at the Southern Department, summarized 'reliable reports from most secret sources' which 'can of course not be quoted'. According to these reports, Zachariadis

> called for the intensification of activity by [the] KKE against the Anglo-Saxon powers in Greece as part of the international drive against the USA and Britain, the main attack being concentrated for the present on the latter. Within [the] KKE it was necessary to restate party line and to take action against deviationists. The action has taken the customary form, in accordance with Soviet precedents, of violent and concerted denunciations of dissidents in *Rizospastis* … followed by expulsion of those concerned … The dissidents … include a considerable number of party members who are in sympathy with active members of ELAS who advocate extreme action against the Right-wing and to a considerable extent against the British forces.

Internal opposition to Zachariadis existed on account of his 'dictatorial methods' within the party, his absence from Greece in 1940–1945, his reputation as a nominee of Stalin and Dimitrov, his attitude towards personal

109

rivals, and most significantly, 'the responsibility he bears for [the] present policy which is unpopular with certain members of the party, especially members of ELAS who have some influence over the rank and file of the KKE'. Indeed, one of the difficulties confronting Zachariadis was that he had to keep a tight rein on the party militants who were itching for a show-down. But that was neither his policy nor Stalin's wish, thus in the event his line for a dual strategy prevailed:

> the regrouping and preparations of [the] KKE are designed for guerrilla warfare similar to that in Ireland in 1920 rather than the renewal of civil war as waged in 1944, which the more extreme members of ELAS advocate. At present bands are being enlarged and strengthened and in the north are extending their activities to the towns in addition to the country in order to create maximum disorder.[53]

This was a decisive step on the part of Zachariadis to implement the line of the Second Plenum, with the emphasis still being on the gradual build-up of guerrilla activity. According to communist sources, in June 1946 the Macedonia-Thrace Bureau of the KKE held a meeting attended by the Secretary-General. The Bureau proposed the rapid mobilization of 25,000 leftists in the region, but Zachariadis insisted that the number of the guerrillas in Macedonia should not exceed 2,000, to be organized in small and highly mobile bands. The rebuff of the militants' plan was consistent not only with the decision of the Second Plenum, but also with Stalin's counsel to Zachariadis in early April 1946. Besides, this lends credit to the contention of the KKE leader that, in the course of such a struggle, the party had to persuade as many Greeks as possible that 'the armed confrontation is being made inevitable by the armed terrorist onslaught of the Right, which obstructs the way towards [a] normal democratic course'.[54]

Initially, therefore, the limited armed struggle would be of a defensive nature in the hope that the government would be forced into concessions. Even though Zachariadis could have added that the prolongation of the chaotic situation might hopefully bring the Populists down, he could not have possibly embarked upon his hazardous double strategy without endorsement from abroad, especially from Stalin. Apparently he failed to see that if the government showed itself in no mood for concessions, there would hardly be any way out of the escalation of violence; yet a full-scale civil war, breaking out after the dilapidation of the country during the world war and occupation, would be a catastrophe, and that was what Zachariadis at first tried to avoid. That he erred can only be argued with hindsight, since later it would become clear that neither the Populist government nor its foreign patrons were in the mood for a compromise. In 1946 and early 1947 the KKE could have mobilized thousands – for instance: 20–25,000 in Macedonia and Thrace, 25–30,000 from Athens, 10,000 from Thessaly, in Epirus and elsewhere nearly 50% of the army conscripts[55] – but that would have meant a full-scale civil war.

Zachariadis also erred in his belatedly disclosed apology that he wanted to avoid the intervention of the British troops stationed in Greece. The British were anxious not to intervene militarily. Their aim had been the political ostracism of the KKE and its assignment of a peripheral and harmless role in postwar Greek politics – not its military crushing. Bevin had thus succumbed in principle to the pressure for the withdrawal of British troops from Greece, and he was only waiting to secure beyond doubt the objectives which were keeping them there. On 2 July 1946 Hector McNeil minuted that the British forces must not be used, and that the Greek government 'must proceed against Right and Left with determination' – as if the Right was not in the government. Moreover, when Norton likened the situation in northern Greece to that prevailing in Palestine, the comparison was enough to put his superiors in a flutter: the Foreign Office clearly wanted to avoid being trapped in a Greek situation that would degenerate into a second Palestine.[56]

At any rate, legal forms of struggle continued to be the prime means of promoting the demands of the Left. On 29 June *Rizospastis*, which was mild towards Sofulis, published an article by Zachariadis entitled 'So – Are We Heading for Civil War?', in which the KKE leader called for 'reconciliation' and maintained that the party was willing to discuss any measure that would lead to the restoration of normality. On the previous day the Macedonia-Thrace Organization of EAM addressed an appeal to the Foreign Ministers of the Big Four for the restoration of freedom in the country.[57] Throughout June and July *Rizospastis* reported daily cases where the call for reconciliation had materialized at the local level. In many villages in Macedonia and Thessaly monarchists refused to participate in the unilateral civil war and joined hands with leftists; gendarmes and former members of the Security Battalions were trying to arm monarchist villagers against the Left, but the latter often refused; it was even reported that right-wingers appealed to monarchist bands to put an end to the fratricidal strife.[58] This might have been the official party line in Athens, yet in the north the activity of left-wing bands against gendarmerie stations was on the increase. In the wake of the government's legislation more people fled to the mountains for, as Norton reported, leftists and republicans were not prepared to wait patiently in their villages to be summoned by the Public Security Committees or the Special Courts-Martial. Consequently, in Thessaly and Macedonia the condition of law and order was such that not only was a fair plebiscite doubtful, but even the revision of registers could not be accomplished.[59]

On 10 July *Rizospastis* published yet another article by Zachariadis proposing an all-party agreement to restore order and allow the people to resolve the internal question through the plebiscite. The call for reconciliation was addressed even to members of the monarchist organization X, policemen and gendarmes, so that the people could vote freely; then the KKE would recognize whichever result emerged.[60] Two days later a group of X-men attempted to assassinate the Politburo member Miltiadis Porfyrogenis, while EAM requested from the government an all-party conference to find means of putting an end to the White Terror.[61] But these were hard times for reconciliation. On 3 August the US ambassador Lincoln MacVeagh reported to Byrnes that the Populists, having 'embarked on [an] all-out policy [to] root out Communism', were 'making as many enemies as friends on account of growing official tendency (1) to consider all persons Communists unless

Royalists, (2) to protect former Metaxists and collaborators, and (3) to accept armed assistance from disreputable elements professing royalism.' The Populists' 'extremist policy' had not only exasperated the parliamentary opposition, but could even strengthen republican and pro-communist sentiment throughout the country.[62]

Touring northern Greece in July 1946, the Commander of the British Military Mission Major-General Stewart Rawlins witnessed a situation tantamount to a miniature civil war in which the leftist bands had 'their tails up'. Attempts to organize some co-operation between the gendarmerie and the army in dealing with them were inefficient and abortive. Whilst the morale and training of the army thus suffered setbacks, the priorities of the Populist government lay in implying that its policies, and especially the campaign for the restoration of the King, were hand in glove with the wishes of the British. Yet although both parties had the same end – to keep Greece on the British side of the fence – the Populist methods were rather too crude for the British. Rawlins reported that his tour was planned at the instigation of the Defence Minister Petros Mavromichalis – 'who said ... it would create a good impression if we went together!' – but at times acquired such an overly political content that the General felt he was 'an unwilling participant in an Electioneering Campaign': 'In one village I found myself in the middle of a Royalist Youth Rally and felt a bit awkward by being honoured with a personal speech and a faded bouquet!'.[63] As to the failure of the government forces, Daniel Lascelles, the Counsellor of the British Embassy in Athens, commented:

> The Left-wing sympathies of the majority of the population, reinforced in many cases by intimidation of the political minority on the part of the armed bands, deprived these ill-coordinated forces of the local intelligence which is essential in coping with small and highly mobile bands of law-breakers; and for the resulting failure to achieve positive success each "side" openly blamed the other. The all-pervading influence of Deputies interested only in their own constituencies led to the dispersal of military forces in small and often useless detachments.[64]

These difficulties were aggravated by the existence of many leftists in the army. The British Embassy had 'ample evidence from secret sources' that the KKE had infiltrated the army and organized nuclei of leftist soldiers – a fact corroborated from communist records.[65] The recommendation of Rawlins and Lascelles that the army should be subjected to political screening was typical of the British reasoning vis-à-vis the domestic strife in Greece. 'Under existing conditions', the Counsellor argued,

> "screening" might tend to produce an army which was not merely non-Communist, but Right-wing in sentiment. But this tendency can at least be checked by our counsels; and of the two evils there can be no question which is the worse from the point of view of the survival of Greece as an independent State.[66]

This line of reasoning confirms one of the salient elements of British policy towards Greece. When confronted with a choice of two evils, the British invariably opted for the lesser one, even though they were cognizant of the hazards inherent in their choice. The unfortunate results, in so far as they were undesirable, can only be explained by British confidence that their counsels could avert the worst, especially when Right-wing violence had started to receive a similar response from the Left.

Significantly, the Defence Minister Mavromichalis told Rawlins that Thessaly, Macedonia and Thrace were virtually under martial law, but the government would not declare it openly as that would amount to an official admission that conditions were unsuitable for holding the plebiscite. The Populists hoped that they could capitalize on – and escalate – the violence in order to secure the return of the King. As for the KKE, Lascelles was right in arguing that its aim was the postponement of the plebiscite, hence its 'campaign of organized terror', which the government met with 'counter-action designed to conceal the seriousness of the provoking cause'.[67] The plebiscite, therefore, became a key development which could either avert the escalation of violence or precipitate it. Postponement or a republican victory would deprive the KKE of a major propaganda weapon, but if the King were brought back, the complete restoration of the prewar order was bound to stir it into more aggressive action.

Zachariadis's next move was calculated to step up the pressure on the government by implementing the Second Plenum decision for a unified leadership of the leftist bands. In mid-July 1946, one month after the Thessaloniki meeting, the KKE leader gave Markos Vafiadis personal orders to go to Belgrade for consultations with Yiannis Ioannidis and Petros Rousos who, in late August, would establish themselves there as the Politburo Commission. According to Markos, Zachariadis's main orders were that: the existing possibilities should be discussed with the Politburo Commission and acted on accordingly, taking as a basis the already existing leftist armed bands; these bands should be expanded on a purely voluntary basis; army units willing to join the guerrillas should be turned away; action should be confined to striking only 'the armed reaction', avoiding clashes with the army; and, since the KKE action was defensive, there should be no party organizations within the guerrilla units. 'Politically', Markos recalled, 'it was explained that we still hold on to the position of reconciliation and peaceful solution to our internal problem, and that all our action will aim to this end.'[68] Although Markos's evidence says nothing about the numerical strength of the projected guerrilla force, other sources suggest that the KKE leader had probably told him that the prospect for late 1946 (and up to spring 1947) was 20,000 men.[69] Markos himself gave the former ELAS officer and member of the KKE Central Committee Giorgis Blanas (Kissavos) personal orders from Zachariadis to raise a guerrilla army in Thessaly similar in number and strength to the pre-liberation ELAS.[70]

In view of the weakness of the government army and its erosion by the KKE, the question of whether Zachariadis actually ordered the resurrection of nearly half of ELAS is of paramount importance for the grasping of KKE strategy. In Belgrade Markos asked from Ioannidis, the most powerful man in the party after Zachariadis, the mobilization of at least 18–20,000 men until spring 1947. In all probability Ioannidis refused to allow this '"provocation"'. He told Markos that he '"did not understand the policy of the party ... we are not going to resolve our internal problem with weapons, but with a peaceful course"'; the task for Markos was the '"organization of self-defence"' with no more than 3–4,000 men.[71] It seems that with the official party line favouring reconciliation and the unofficial line attaching more importance to defensive armed struggle, Ioannidis was able to skate over the details of mobilization and impress upon Markos a less 'provocative' course of action.[72]

Be that as it may, there was also a crucial detail which can easily be overlooked – the equipment of a substantial force. A memorandum sent by the KKE to the fraternal parties of the Soviet Union, Bulgaria and Yugoslavia in September 1946 stated that the plan was to raise 20,000 men, but there were not enough arms to that end: most of those kept after Varkiza had been hastily concealed, thus the largest part had been discovered by the authorities or broken down; moreover, the KKE was in need of clothing, foodstuffs and medical supplies.[73] Zachariadis had apparently given instructions for the mobilization of 20,000 men in 1946, but *then* the necessary equipment was in short supply.

The important feature of the orders to Markos was that guerilla activity would be directed against 'armed reaction', which meant the monarchist bands and the gendarmerie, rather than the army or the British troops. The KKE memorandum to the fraternal parties reiterated its orientation towards defensive action:

> Against the policy of English imperialism and the monarchy, our party and EAM array the united struggle of all anti-monarchist democratic forces, the mass struggle for economic matters, the slogan of reconciliation combined with the mass popular self-defence, which in recent months has developed into the armed struggle of the guerrilla bands in the mountains.[74]

In its anxiety not to seem too provocative, the KKE publicly dismissed charges that it was resurrecting ELAS, and Zachariadis allowed more than thirty army officers who in the Occupation had emerged as top cadres of ELAS to be exiled by the Populist government.[75] Along with the orders for the co-ordination of guerrilla activity, in the summer and autumn of 1946 the KKE and EAM continued to press for concessions. On 28 July EAM protested to MacVeagh that the attempt of the government to reinstate the King by force was leading to civil war, whereas the Left had been urging in vain for an all-party conference. The US ambassador could offer no more than his admission that the recent measures on law and order were 'largely in [the] hands of unscrupulous reactionaries with restoration aims'.[76] Less generously, Norton advised London that such protests should be dismissed as sheer propaganda, for the communists knew that their terms would be rejected and were only trying to pose as freedom-loving men who had been forced to the mountains in self-defence. Yet at the same time the ambassador himself was reporting to the Foreign Office that the misdeeds of the security forces were driving more and more people to the mountains. As for the EAM call for an all-party conference, Norton thought that it might be 'statesman-like' of Tsaldaris to do this, but he had grave doubts as to whether the Populist deputies would swallow it.[77]

The Greek Prime Minister was willing to make a concession which the Left could not possibly accept: if the KKE stopped the 'insurrection', the government would recommend leniency to the judiciary and might find a way for the participation of EAM in the Parliament without elections, but on the basis of that 9.3% which AMFOGE felt had been the percentage of politically motivated abstention.[78] Yet the crisis was far graver than Tsaldaris's prescription assumed. With the plebiscite due on 1 September, royalist terror and intimidation were booming. Edward Peck, the British Consul-General in Thessaloniki, reported that the Left was 'so strangled by mass arrests that their effective participation seems very doubtful'.[79] Even the parties of the centre-right EPE and the Liberals were intimidated. After a tour in Thessaly, Alastair Matthews, Second Secretary at the British Embassy, reported that moderate republicans were persecuted 'on an extensive scale, with the full cognizance of the authorities and in particular of the Prefects and Right-wing deputies'.[80] Kanellopoulos himself complained to the British Embassy that he was unable to campaign for the republican cause even in his home constituency, whilst his followers feared that if they attended his speeches they would be beaten up by royalist thugs.[81] By early August MacVeagh had come to fear a rerun of the Spanish experience:

> By their policy of continually enlarging their definition of Communism to include all who do not support the restoration of the King, the extremists of the Mavromichalis type now conducting the Government's crusade against Communism are risking the creation here, by confirming the alliance of large numbers of democrats with the extreme left, of the same sort of ideological civil war which has occurred in Spain.[82]

At the same time Lascelles confirmed to London that Mavromichalis, the Populist Minister of Defence, was actively involved in financing monarchist bands and had even persuaded Crown Prince Paul, brother of George II, to contribute funds to the crusade.[83]

With the plebiscite emerging as the last opportunity to avert an even deeper schism among Greeks, Zachariadis proclaimed that the KKE would participate because it 'adhered to normality'. Yet for reasons exemplified in an article by Plastiras in *Kathimerina Nea* on 26 May 1946, a united republican front proved elusive. To prevent the restoration of the King and civil war, for which he blamed directly the Populists and indirectly the British, the life-long champion of uncompromising republicanism called for a 'national Republican Coalition' in which, however, 'the leadership of the KKE had no place at all. An unbridgeable chasm separates us on the national question.' Plastiras's thinking was common currency among the leaders of the Centre. When Sofianopoulos, the former Foreign Minister, made a similar appeal to them, they refused to co-operate because, devoid as they were of 'self-confidence and political courage', they feared lest they be branded as leftists.[84] The liberal daily *Eleftheria* wondered, 'Is it worth sacrificing the future of Greece for the sake of an institution and an individual which are universally bankrupt?'.[85] For the Populists it certainly was.

According to the report of the AMFOGE Chiefs Richard Windle and Leland Morris, in the plebiscite of 1 September 1946 the King mustered 1,166,665 votes against 174,411 for a republic and 346,913 blank – almost 69% of the total. Windle and Morris had misgivings about the existence of conditions necessary for a fair plebiscite, but they patched them up in an impressionistic fashion:

> There is no doubt in our minds that the party representing the government view exercised undue influence in securing votes in support of the return of the King, but without that influence we are satisfied that a majority of votes for the King's return *could* have been obtained.[86] [Emphasis mine]

In a confidential supplementary report submitted on 13 September, the two chiefs were even more doubtful as to the fairness of the plebiscite, but still felt that even a small royalist majority could have been obtained under any circumstances.[87] This was a godsend for the Foreign Office. The Southern Department opined with relief that once AMFOGE had found that the plebiscite returns were 'broadly in accordance' with the wishes of the majority of the Greeks, Britain could not allow her policy towards the new regime 'to be influenced by the fact that the result of the plebiscite unduly exaggerates the amount of support for the King'. Both the Foreign Office and the Americans wanted the report to remain confidential – Ralph Selby of the Southern Department noted that 'the less said about the report the better' – but Bevin regarded the matter serious enough to require communication to Tsaldaris and the King.[88]

The British Foreign Secretary and Hugh Dalton were 'very sorry that the King had won the plebiscite', as they would have preferred a republic. Bevin sent a message to George II through Buckingham Palace to impress upon him to behave constitutionally, 'or he would soon come to grief'. '"Kings are pretty cheap these days"', he confided to the Chancellor.[89] The pessimistic outlook and wishful attempts to exorcize their fears were common even amongst those Britons who were better acquainted with Greek realities. In a private letter to one of his Greek wartime associates, Colonel Woodhouse expressed his concern at the swift and complete restoration of the prewar order. 'The only solace' he could find was the hope that 'the quickest remedy for the royalists might be the arrival and presence of the King, as no doubt the quickest remedy for the communists would be the valuable assets of a Russian occupation'.[90]

George II returned to Athens on 28 September 1946. The Greek monarch with the unconstitutional and dictatorial past was not Greek and looked down upon his subjects. The American journalist Cyrus Sulzberger wrote of him that 'if he were not a King, he would be the kind of fellow people call upon at the last minute to fill up a party or a celebrated gossip columnist in the American press ... Every time I talk to him, he impresses me as an amiable idiot without any feeling for Greece, its people and politics.'[91] To Pierson Dixon he seemed a man who 'really doesn't understand big issues or big conceptions'. The King's last words to him about the Greek politicians and their failings were: '"Perhaps I shouldn't say it, but they are a b——— lot."'[92]

Nevertheless, the 'b——— lot' were quite willing to welcome him. The EPE leaders, all republican, expressed their readiness to work and serve under George II, whilst Sofulis told Norton that he would accept even a royalist dictatorship if that guaranteed Greece against the Slavs and the KKE.[93]

George II would not resume his throne with any intentions for reconciliation. On 14 September he had handed Bevin a memorandum on the policies he envisaged. His main objective was to unite all non-communist politicians, isolate the KKE and thereby consolidate parliamentary democracy; then he would endeavour to improve the organization of the struggle against the guerrillas; with regard to any appeasement of the Left, he only envisaged measures such as limited pardon, provided they were introduced gradually;[94] not much in the way of pacification, but still the course towards a conflagration was not irreversible.

Missed Opportunities: August 1946–January 1947

In early June 1946 Tsaldaris made public his intention to visit London and Paris in order to promote Greece's territorial claims against Bulgaria and Albania. In Norton's judgement, the Greek Prime Minister wanted to emulate the previous governments in their frequent contacts with British statesmen and thereby attract some attention to himself. The ambassador encouraged him to proceed with his trip in the hope that this would improve his image as a national leader. Though 'a decent and well-meaning man', Tsaldaris was devoid of personal charm and needed some boost to his prestige if he were to keep control over the 'wilder elements' of his party.[95] Soon it also turned out that the Greek Prime Minister wanted to visit Washington to discuss economic matters with US officials. The State Department, sceptical after Greek 'inertia' towards reconstruction, jibed that Americans would wonder whether the Populist government, oblivious of its problems at home, was 'on junket'.[96]

On 2 and 4 July Tsaldaris met with Bevin in Paris and handed him a memorandum on the reconstruction of Greece. When the document was forwarded to the Foreign Office, the clerks were staggered by the request for foreign aid to the amount of $6bn (£1.5bn) for the reconstruction of the Greek economy over a period of five years. Tsaldaris hinted that such assistance could be forthcoming from the United States, but he could not have known that the Americans considered the figure of $6bn to be 'not within the realm of possibilities'.[97] In London, where he met with Attlee, Dalton and Foreign Office officials, Tsaldaris stressed Greece's economic needs and inquired whether the British would object to his approaching the Americans for aid. Dalton was delighted, especially when Tsaldaris revealed details of a report from the Greek Embassy in Washington suggesting that the United States was preparing to grant massive economic assistance to Greece.[98]

The Foreign Office was less sanguine. McNeil argued that the Greeks could not continue to live from hand to mouth and that they should work out a long-term reconstruction plan; Tsaldaris was 'vague and unintelligent' on this point. Then the Labour government was increasingly concerned and embarrassed by the conditions of law and order in Greece. In London Tsaldaris saw the Parliamentary Committee of the Labour Party, who gave him 'a bad time'; most of the questions addressed to him were hostile, and his replies were 'a bit confused'. The Foreign Office cautioned him against 'excessive zeal which might be difficult to defend in the House of Commons and give Greece's enemies material for propaganda about discrimination and despotic behaviour'. Strong objections were also raised to the Greek government's practice of arming civilians against leftist bands, while Sargent criticized Resolution III and requested its moderate enforcement. Tsaldaris confined himself to a promise that he would not apply it to the KKE leaders.[99]

The preoccupation of the Greek Prime Minister was to secure foreign aid and enhance his country territorially. On 12 July he inquired at the US Embassy in London whether he could send a team of experts to Washington to discuss the possibility of a loan. The chilly reply from Dean Acheson, the Acting Secretary of State, was that the Greek Embassy in Washington had misconstrued US intentions: there could be no loan, primarily because the Greek government had yet to use the £25m credit of December 1945 and had thus far shown itself unable to make effective use of funds.[100]

Then came the collapse of Tsaldaris's dream to become the architect of a greater Greece. London and Washington held that Greek territorial claims against Albania and Bulgaria were ethnically and strategically unjustifiable and could even lead to Albanian, Bulgarian and Yugoslav counter-claims against Greek Epirus, Macedonia and Thrace. If Tsaldaris's attempt to rally support from Bevin and Byrnes was logical, his plea to Molotov was no doubt an imprudent move. On 4 July 1946 he met the Soviet Foreign Minister in Paris and sought his support for the Greek claims, only to hear an unusually mild reply from Molotov that Greece should focus on her domestic troubles and refrain from making territorial demands on her Balkan neighbours. For different reasons, Bevin and Byrnes were in tacit agreement with this line. Britain and the United States would have preferred to see the Greek claims completely dropped, but the Foreign Office counselled that by doing so they would incur the ire of the majority of the Greek people. The western powers should not thereby lay the blame on themselves but throw it on the Soviets' lap. The Foreign Office reckoned that since the Kremlin would surely veto the Greek claims against the Albanian and Bulgarian comrades, the wisest course would be to make it clear to the Greeks that Britain and the United States could not back them, and then let them proceed with their case till they stumbled upon the Soviet opposition. The incrimination would thus be directed against Moscow.[101] Empty-handed and with his prestige withering away, Tsaldaris returned to Greece on 23 July. The British had found him 'not a bad old thing but rather a muddle-head', while in Athens the liberal and leftist press dismissed him as an inept oaf struggling to keep afloat in the ocean of international diplomacy. Norton had to come to his rescue by way of public commendations of his performance and the 'good results of his trip'.[102]

Yet, even though Tsaldaris had secured little for his country and even less for himself, some hope appeared for an inquiry into the intrinsic causes of the Greek question. From 26 April to 9 May 1946 three Labour MPs (Norman

Dodds, Leslie Solley and Stanley Tiffany) had toured the country and produced a lengthy report which, after a recital of cases of terror and repression, concluded that Greece was 'rapidly becoming a fascist state': 'Under the façade of democracy, there exists a unilateral civil war, the war of the extreme Right against all democratic elements who dare to disagree with the government.'[103] Incensed, the Greek government officially invited a British Parliamentary Delegation to come to Greece and investigate existing conditions. In July McNeil told Tsaldaris that he would arrange for a Delegation of five Labour, two Conservative and one Liberal or Independent MPs to visit the country in mid-August.[104]

The British Parliamentary Delegation arrived in Greece on 16 August 1946 and remained until 24 August, holding meetings with all sorts of politicians, party leaders and officials, and visiting prisons, hospitals, factories and various public institutions. In the end they were satisfied that they had been able to form 'a fair impression' of conditions in the country and endeavoured 'to state their views as clearly and objectively as possible'. This they did, for their report constitutes a largely accurate portrayal of Greece on the verge of civil war. The British delegates witnessed a 'very distressing' political atmosphere, with extremists on both sides engaging in acts of violence and terrorism:

> Although the feelings of hatred, fear, revenge and discontent resulting from the events of December 1944 have by no means died away, it is clear that acts of violence by both sides have considerably increased since the advent of the present Government.

In several parts of Macedonia and Thessaly a miniature civil war between leftist bands and the Gendarmerie was well under way. Although these bands received aid 'from the other side of the frontier', it would be erroneous to attribute their activities to 'foreign inspiration' alone:

> There is evidence that amongst these bands are many Left-wing supporters who have fled to the mountains to escape terrorism exercised by the extreme Right. On the other hand, many Right-wing partisans have been shot by the Left, and this has given rise to acts of retaliation and revenge.

In Thessaly the authorities tolerated, and made no attempt to suppress, the right-wing bands. These operated 'with the utmost audacity' and their mission was not always the crusade against Communism:

> Although it is claimed in certain quarters that their object is to prevent the spread of Communism, the fact is that they never engage the Communist bands in battle but devote themselves to terrorizing the villages and exacting blackmail from anyone rich enough to pay it. In the area south of Pharsala, we were told, the Right Wing bandit leader levies a toll of one percent upon the production of the district. Although it is unlawful to bear arms, this law is only enforced against members of the Left. In certain districts in Thessaly the Government are supplying arms to their civilian supporters.

In the Peloponnese, being unable to verify the charges and counter-charges, the Delegation could only say

(1)   That the charges made by the Left were far more numerous and detailed (names and dates given in many cases) than the counter-charges made by the Right which, on the whole, were vague.

(2)   That as the Right appeared to be in a large majority and had behind them the coercive powers of the Security Committees and the Gendarmerie, they had far more opportunities of intimidating the Left than the Left had of intimidating the Right. The Delegation are of the opinion that these opportunities have not been entirely neglected.

The Public Security Committees had so far deported some 1,000 persons, including members of EAM local committees, editorial staffs of leftist papers, and women – some with children. The death penalties imposed by the Courts-Martial were 'frequently carried out within a week of the sentence'.

The Delegation felt that the plebiscite would go the Populists' way due to 'a great fear of communism' and the conviction that social stability would thus be restored. But there was also 'the almost universal belief, fostered to some extent by Right-wing propaganda, that the British Government desired such a result, and that a vote against the King would be a vote for Russia against Britain and for Balkan aggression against Greek integrity'. At any rate, the Populist government 'intended to take few chances in the matter' and utilized all available means for monarchist propaganda. The Opposition was handi-capped, with Liberal deputies complaining that monarchist bands prevented them from visiting their constituencies. A former Liberal minister feared that he would be shot if he dared to go outside Athens. Though the Delegation had little doubt as to the result of the plebiscite, they stated that the Populist practices 'may have had the effect of deepening the resentment with which sections of the community regard the Government'.

Greek perceptions of Anglo-Greek relations were an embarrassment to the British MPs. The degree of British responsibility was manifested in 'a wide-spread belief – not confined to the extreme left – that everything the Greek Government does is in accordance with British wishes'; then there was 'an almost helpless reliance on Britain to help Greece out of all her financial and economic difficulties'. The Greek politicians had 'got so much into the habit of looking to Britain to put their economy on its feet, that they have almost lost sight of the imperative need of doing their utmost themselves to put their house in order'. The MPs interviewed Greek officials on any detailed plans for reconstruction, but no such plans were produced or, indeed, existed. The black market was booming while a tiny class of 'Tax-Free Rich' lived in clover:

There is a small class of wealthy people chiefly residing in and around Athens. Members of these families, to which many of the leading politicians belong, live in great luxury. They have gold pounds at their disposal … and so are indifferent to the high cost of living, and as there is no Income Tax in the British sense they live practically tax-free.

The Delegation concluded that unless a policy of moderation and recon-ciliation was followed, Greece would fall into ruin. To avoid this, their report made nineteen specific recommendations: they proposed, *inter alia*, that 'the opportunity given by the return of the King should be used to initiate an entirely new policy in and towards Greece'; they also proposed the formation of an all-party government, 'with the possible exception of the extreme Left'; a general amnesty, or at least 'a generous policy of Clemency towards political offenders'; the establishment of law and order and the restoration of constitutional liberties; the repeal of the special security decrees and the release of persons deported for political reasons; the improvement of conditions in prisons; elections 'after a certain defined period' on an up-to-date register; and, finally, that 'subject to considerations of strategy and high policy the British troops should be withdrawn at an early date'.[105]

The report was couched in cautious terms, as befitted British MPs officially invited by the Greek government. Nevertheless, it essentially confirmed the picture of a repressive, doggedly anti-communist administration bent upon curbing the political and moral potential of EAM and securing the return of the King at all costs. In addition to that, and irrespective of what the British liked to think, many Greeks were convinced that their government would only act at the behest of London; this was both the result of Populist propaganda and the corollary of British involvement in Greek affairs since the war years.

For the KKE, on the other hand, the presence of the Delegation in Greece was yet another opportunity to publicize its thesis on Anglo-Greek relations. In an address to the MPs through *Rizospastis* on 21 August, Zachariadis charged that the civil strife was fomented and exacerbated by the government measures. But civil war was not the only means of resolving the Greek question. The alternative was 'popular reconciliation' and the 'free popular verdict'. The KKE was willing to work to this end, but it would not give in to coercion. The British should either abandon Greece to her own devices or change their policy so as to meet the KKE's demand for an 'equal, democratic, and based on mutual respect, Anglo-Greek friendship'.[106] It is of great importance that when the report of the Delegation was published, EAM and the KKE gave it a warm welcome and proclaimed their readiness to accept its recommendations as a basis for an all-party agreement and a new deal.[107] But no-one would listen, and yet another opportunity to put the intentions of the KKE to the test was lost.

The report was heartily welcomed also by the Centre. For the Right, however, it was a misfire. Its press charged that such 'partial and misinformed' suggestions from abroad trespassed on Greece's independence.[108] In an official protest to Seymour Cocks, the veteran of the Union of Democratic Control and leader of the Delegation, Tsaldaris absolved his faction of any blame:

While particular stress is laid on the prevailing conditions in Greece, no attempt whatsoever has been made to investigate into the original causes which account for them. Should such an inquiry be conducted in the dim days of the enemy occupation and the afterward period, it might have led to the conclusion that it would not be in conformity with justice to lay the responsibility on Greek shoulders.[109]

The British records do not afford an insight into the reception of the report by the Labour government. McNeil circulated it in the Cabinet along with a memorandum of his own, dated 2 December 1946. The Minister of State described the report as 'a considerable achievement' but took great liberty in drawing his colleagues' attention to those findings which seemed to vindicate British policy: that the King 'would in any event have secured a majority', the 'warm tributes' paid by the MPs to the work of the British Missions, and 'the integrity of the Greek judiciary'. McNeil concurred with many of the recommendations, yet eschewed any initiative:

> The extent to which it will be possible to give full effect to the majority of them depends both on the ability of the Greek Government to put its house in order and on the measure of economic and administrative assistance which HM Government, in spite of our own strained resources, can make available to Greece, or can persuade the United States to supply, in the critical year ahead.[110]

The Minister of State made no mention of the political recommendations for a new policy 'in and towards Greece', a broader or all-party government, an amnesty, the restoration of constitutional liberties and the repeal of repressive legislation, which would have hardly cost anything in economic terms. Whether he convinced the Cabinet or, indeed, whether the report was discussed at all, will remain elusive, as nothing is recorded in the Minutes. Its official endorsement would have given rise to doubts as to the soundness of British policy in Greece, whereas any attempt to impress its recommendations upon the Populists would have contravened Bevin's policy of 'non-intervention'. Whether a different attitude would have pacified Greece is a moot point, but it is fair to say that of the three parties involved, only the Greek Left showed readiness to negotiate a compromise based on the recommendations of a British Parliamentary Delegation officially invited by the Greek government and sanctioned by the British. The absence of any response from the other side represented a missed opportunity to test the sincerity of the KKE and possibly prevent the slow but steady drift to civil war.

The second opportunity emanated from the KKE and was equally important, both on account of its content and because it demonstrated that, in 1946 at least, the party did not want an all-out clash with its opponents. In late August 1946 Yiannis Ioannidis and Petros Rousos established themselves in Belgrade as the KKE's liaison with the fraternal parties. On 29 August Zachariadis cabled Dimitrov that Ioannidis carried a memorandum on the Greek situation and requested that he be allowed to go to Moscow.[111] In the memorandum the KKE promulgated a bold proposal:

> Since the English do not show any intention of abandoning Greece, and the Greek monarcho-fascist government serves them in everything and presents to the Greek people the maintenance of English troops in Greece as a guarantee against the danger of an attack by her Northern Democratic neighbours, and especially by the Slavs, we submit for your consideration whether it is also in the interest of the USSR and the Democratic countries to proclaim Greece a neutral country under the guarantee of the great powers.[112]

In a second telegram to Dimitrov on 30 August Zachariadis explained that this should be done under the responsibility of the United Nations. Ioannidis did not go to Moscow because the Soviet Communist Party sent a representative to collect the memorandum. On 10 November he cabled Zachariadis that Dimitrov had agreed with the proposal but the Kremlin kept silent.[113] According to all indications the Soviets were not enthusiastic. On 21 November Ioannidis cabled to a Bulgarian official:

> Regarding the question which was raised as to the neutrality of Greece under the guarantee of the great powers, com[rade] Zachariadis told us that he received an adverse reply from M[oscow]. Having in mind the discussion with com[rade] Grandfather [Dimitrov], we would request com[rade] Grandfather, on his own part, to ask for the opinion of the comrades from M[oscow] and to announce it to us.[114]

But there was more silence from the Kremlin, as on the last day of 1946 Zachariadis reminded Ioannidis that 'we have had no reply on neutrality yet'.[115]

What caused Zachariadis to complain was the absence of an *official* reply from Moscow. Yet, without knowing it, he had received Stalin's pronouncement. According to the files of the Soviet Foreign Ministry, on 29 July 1946 the Soviet ambassador in Athens reported to Moscow that Zachariadis had sought, through the TASS correspondent, the view of the Soviet government on the proposal for Greek neutrality. For the KKE leader this concept involved the true independence of Greece, which would not belong to any sphere of influence, nor have foreign troops or military bases on her soil. Most significantly, Zachariadis added that this proposal presupposed that all Great Powers would guarantee Greek security. The Soviet ambassador sought Moscow's permission to convey to Zachariadis his 'personal view'; this *was approved by Stalin* and conveyed to Zachariadis by the TASS correspondent not as Moscow's reply but as the 'personal opinion' of the Soviet ambassador in Athens. The prospect of an independent and neutral Greece, rid of all foreign military presence, was welcomed, but the security guarantee was meaningless, as it implied that the threat emanated from the Balkan communist states – a proposition which the Kremlin was in no way prepared to accept.[116]

It is clear from Stalin's reply that the acceptance of the proposal for neutrality could at worst be of no harm to Soviet interests, whilst, at the unlikely best, it would see the British off Greece. However, the rebuff of the call for guarantees was against the interests of the KKE because it undermined the credibility of the whole scheme. Since the KKE leader wanted to allay the nationalists' fears that Greece's northern borders were threatened, without this ingredient his proposal could easily be seen either as idle rhetoric or an impudent slogan to get the British out.

Nonetheless, despite the adverse reply from Moscow, the KKE and EAM would later publicize the concept of Greek neutrality under the auspices of the United Nations. At this stage it was promulgated at a time when the KKE maintained that 'the further development of the struggle would depend not only on the domestic, but also on the international conditions'.[117] Although, in view of British and American determination to retain Greece in their own side of the fence, Zachariadis's proposal might appear somewhat quixotic, it certainly indicates that the KKE was not contemplating a full-scale civil war. Nor was it entirely estranged from reality. In December 1946 some consideration was given to the possibility of a three-power understanding on Greece, and two months later some Foreign Office clerks would momentarily toy with the idea of solving the issue by way of a United Nations trusteeship.

Meanwhile, on 26 October 1946 Markos established in the mountains of northern Greece the Guerrillas' General Headquarters, and shortly afterwards the leftist bands were named Democratic Army of Greece (DSE), with General Markos as Commander-in-Chief. The KKE still tried to avoid a full breach with legality and pretended it had nothing to do with the DSE. *Rizospastis* did not mention its existence until mid-November, when it reprinted an article by the *Daily Worker* correspondent Betty Bartlett.[118] MacVeagh, who on this occasion felt he had deciphered a cryptic message, reported that the 'well calculated' choice of the word 'Democratic' (which in Greek also means 'Republican') was reminiscent of the IRA and would 'appeal to anti-British sentiment particularly in the US'; apart from that, the ambassador was right in sensing that the only change would be in the propaganda plane.[119] The KKE requested from the fraternal parties aid to raise 20,000 guerrillas, but the reply confirmed that at this stage the armed struggle was only an additional means of pressure on the government. On 10 November Ioannidis cabled Zachariadis that the view of Dimitrov and 'of those above' – that is, of Moscow – was as follows:

FIRST: Winter period and international situation make it imperative that the armed movement does not assume great proportions.
SECOND: The main task must be the mass political struggle of the people and the preservation of even the smallest legal possibilities, so that the link of the party with the masses is maintained.
THIRD: To preserve party cadres and not to expose them to the dangers of their extermination.
  We [the KKE] stressed that the party line concurs with [the] recommendations.[120]

While the Soviet Union was cautious not to provoke the West over Greece, in London some influential people had misgivings about the wisdom of assisting the small but embattled ally. In June 1946 the British Cabinet had decided to pay for the maintenance of a 100,000-strong Greek army only up to the end of that year, as Dalton insisted against a more permanent commitment favoured by Bevin.[121] When the news came in about the Thessaloniki meeting of the KKE on 16 June, the Foreign Office, in its anxiety to avoid an entanglement similar to that in Palestine, called for the recognition of the proper function of the Greek army and the definition of the nature and aims of Britain's assistance to Greece. In an astonishingly blunt statement of intent, on 20 July William Hayter minuted that the time had come 'to grasp this nettle and make up our minds that the Greek army are our mercenaries'.[122] By September, the intensification of guerrilla activity prompted the Greek government to request the increase of its armed forces by 30,000 men, to be armed, clad and equipped by Britain. Norton seconded the request,[123] but in London there was frustration and dissent.

The British Chiefs of Staff reasoned that if Greece fell to the KKE, the entire British strategic position in the Mediterranean and the Middle East would change to the advantage of the Soviet Union; thus they counselled Bevin to retain the troops in Greece throughout 1947 and to finance, train and equip the Greek army until the emergency was over.[124] Dalton, on the other hand, asserted that Greece was a bad investment for Britain's limited postwar resources, and Bevin was forced to admit that the situation was exacerbated by the inability of the Greeks to work out a reconstruction programme.[125] By late November the Foreign Secretary had come to feel 'a temporary revulsion against all things Greek', which the news that the Americans were working on 'a new policy' towards Greece did little to alleviate.[126] The best exponent of the frustration was McNeil. On 29 November 1946 he wrote to Sargent that despite all that Britain had done for Greece since 1945, the situation had deteriorated and the KKE was now 'exerting an apparently increasing influence'. The answer to the Greek problem was not further military aid but substantial economic reconstruction, for which funds could only be forth-coming from the United States. Hence, before deciding to continue bearing the 'political stigma' of occupying Greece for another year, Britain should find out whether the Americans were prepared to lend a hand; if not, Britain could do no more to improve the Greek chaos, in which case it might be better to abandon Greece and defend her Mediterranean position from Cyprus.[127]

At the same time several dissenters within the Labour Party and the TUC voiced a strong dissatisfaction with their government's foreign policy. Some prominent party members sent Attlee a private letter which *The Times* described as 'both a dissentient declaration of faith and a survey of foreign policy after the manner of Mr. Henry Wallace'.[128] The government faced a serious challenge on 18 November, when the House of Commons debated a foreign affairs amendment to the address. Signed by fifty-eight Labour MPs, not all of whom belonged to the leftist fringe of the party, the amendment called for a British socialist alternative to the United States and the Soviet Union. Richard Crossman moved it by attacking the government's 'drift into the American camp' and warning that anti-communism 'is as destructive of true democracy and of Socialism as is Communism'; the Labour MP called upon the 'British Socialist Government ... to show the world that it was not faced with the bleak and blank alternative of American free enterprise or Russian Communism, but that there is a better way of living ... which could be squeezed out by the struggle of those two great Powers'.[129] Greece received one passing reference as a country whose people had 'danced in the streets when the Labour Government came into power', only to be subsequently frustrated by Britain's lining up with the United States.[130] Bevin came under fire for a foreign policy which enjoyed full Conservative support, but Attlee backed his Foreign Secretary. The government eventually defeated the amendment by 353 votes to none, but sixty to seventy Labour MPs abstained and some 120 in all were unaccounted for.[131]

It may well have been this challenge which prompted Attlee to undertake a major initiative towards a drastic re-evaluation of British foreign and defence policy. Anglo-Soviet relations, but also British policy towards Greece, were at the core of his argument. On 1 December 1946 the Prime Minister wrote to Bevin:

> I think that we have got to consider our commitments very carefully lest we try to do more than we can. In particular, I am rather worried about Greece. The COS are suggesting that we must keep our forces there for at least another year. I cannot contemplate the financial and economic burden with equanimity... Meanwhile we have to accept a very great deal of criticism. I feel that we are backing a very lame horse.

Attlee regarded the Middle East as 'only an outpost position' and believed that the British military tended to overrate the strategic importance of communication lines. He was 'beginning to doubt whether the Greek game is worth the candle' because Greece, Turkey, Iran and Iraq were too weak to become together an effective barrier against the Soviet Union; and more significantly, Britain did not command the resources to make them so. The Prime Minister's alternative was a bold one:

> If it were possible to reach an agreement with Russia that we should disinterest ourselves as far as possible in them, so that they became a neutral zone, it would be much to our advantage. Of course it is difficult to tell how far Russian policy is dictated by expansionism and how far by fear of attack by the USA and ourselves. Fantastic as it is, it may very well be the real grounds of Russian policy.

Attlee was even dubious about US policy towards Britain:

> There is a tendency in America to regard us as an outpost, but an outpost that they will not have to defend. I am disturbed by the signs of America trying to make a safety zone round herself while leaving us and Europe in No Man's land. While I think that we should try to find out what the Americans are prepared to do, we should be careful not to commit ourselves.[132]

With Bevin absent in New York, on 2 December 1946 Attlee summoned McNeil and told him that he was 'particularly sore' about the fact that even if the United States offered Greece economic aid, Britain would still have to shoulder the political animus of occupying that country. He therefore intended to raise the whole question of Anglo-Greek relations in the Cabinet, and Bevin should not enter into any fresh commitment until the Americans agreed to 'take up their load'.[133] McNeil communicated Attlee's views to Bevin on 4 December. The Cabinet would await his return to discuss the question, but in the meantime it would be useful if he could informally obtain 'some more definite indication as to what the Americans propose to do for Greece and Turkey'. The Minister of State warned his master that there was growing impatience in London:

I think I should tell you that, in my opinion, the whole question of our policy towards Greece and Turkey is in the melting pot, and that there is a very great reluctance here to contemplate a continuation of our military, financial and political commitments in Greece.[134]

Bevin was surprised and shocked. It would be useless for him, he wrote to McNeil, to raise the question of Greece and Turkey with Byrnes pending a reconsideration of British policy in these quarters. But had it not always been a fundamental assumption that those two countries were essential to Britain's political and strategic position in the world? 'Am I to understand that we may now abandon this position? I really do not know where I stand.'[135]

The lively debate foreshadowed by these exchanges was further animated by Tsaldaris, who at that time came up with an idea of his own directly involving the Big Three. In December the Greek Prime Minister was in New York to launch in person before the UN Security Council Greece's complaint against her northern neighbours for assisting the guerrillas of the Democratic Army. On 6 December he told Bevin that in view of the likely Soviet veto, he did not have much confidence in the ability of the Security Council to resolve the problem. He suggested therefore that Britain, the United States and the Soviet Union might examine the situation outside the Security Council and 'fix up a direct solution' in whose wake the Soviets would 'call off their satellites' from Greece. In return, Tsaldaris said, his government would make some concessions to its northern neighbours, and he went as far as to seek Bevin's advice on whether he should see Molotov. At first Bevin had no objection, but as shortly afterwards he decided that it might be better to see his Soviet counterpart himself, he asked Tsaldaris to postpone the discussion of the Greek complaint at the Security Council.[136] On the same evening Bevin saw Molotov and told him that he wished Britain and the Soviet Union did not squabble over Greece. If the Soviet Foreign Minister would talk to Tsaldaris, the way could be paved for a meeting between Bevin, Byrnes and Molotov to discuss the Greek question as a whole. Molotov agreed that the causes of friction between the Soviet Union and Britain should be removed, and requested time to think the matter over, which Bevin interpreted to mean consultations with the Kremlin.[137]

Although the records are unclear as to whether Bevin's willingness to embrace Tsaldaris's suggestion was influenced by McNeil's message, an opportunity had emerged for a direct understanding at the highest level, which could resolve some of the difficulties awaiting Bevin in London. Yet almost overnight the Foreign Secretary had second thoughts about the outcome of a meeting with his US and Soviet colleagues, as he recalled the failure of similar attempts to settle the situation in Rumania in January 1946. Moreover, he was outraged by Tsaldaris's clandestine manoeuvres to rally support for the cession of Cyprus to Greece. Overcome by distrust for the Greek Prime Minister, Bevin thought it better not to bring him together with Molotov; he jibed that 'it was impossible to deal with M. Tsaldaris if instead of sticking to his essential tasks, he was always introducing fresh considerations, designed for his own political prestige at home ... It was time that the Greeks produced a statesman instead of a lot of politicians.'[138]

On 9 December the Soviet Foreign Minister proclaimed himself worried over the Greek situation and in favour of a meeting with Bevin and Byrnes, but he did not wish to see the 'weak and incompetent' Tsaldaris who 'did not command a following among the Greek people'. Bevin at once sought to consult with Byrnes, only to hear from the American that there should be no such meeting and that Tsaldaris should put his case before the Security Council. With a slight touch of disappointment, on 10 December Bevin instructed Dixon to inform the Soviets that the idea of a three-power conference on Greece would have to be abandoned.[139]

Although this was by no means the end of Bevin's troubles, it did look like yet another missed opportunity. At the Southern Department of the Foreign Office McCarthy regretted that little effort had been made 'to reach some accommodation about Greece between the "Big Three"'.[140] By that time the Soviets, who were certainly interested in a compromise, had been informed by their ambassador in Athens of the KKE proposal for the solution of the Greek question by way of neutrality and a three-power guarantee, which was not entirely irrelevant to the suggestion made by Tsaldaris to Molotov via Bevin. With some pressure from the Kremlin Zachariadis might have been persuaded to be more patient, while the fact that the proposal was put by Tsaldaris indicates that some restraint could be forthcoming from the Greek government, too. Bevin, on the other hand, was quick to overcome his initial shock at McNeil's message, and with the unwitting support of Tsaldaris's unfortunate diplomatic manoeuvres over Cyprus, he retreated to his earlier position. Given the attitude of the United States towards the Soviet Union and the degree of British dependence on co-operation with – and assistance from – Washington, Byrnes's opposition to a meeting of the three Foreign Ministers was probably the main reason for this retreat. Any anxiety which Tsaldaris, Bevin and Molotov may have had to discuss the Greek question was neither fervent nor shared by the US Secretary of State. The days when James Byrnes was 'babying' the Soviets had long been over.

In the meantime, while Tsaldaris's idea was foundering, Dixon prepared a note for a reply to Attlee's letter. Though the Foreign Secretary apparently did not use it,[141] there is no reason to doubt that Dixon voiced his master's views. The note held that the rendering of the countries over which Britain and the Soviet Union squabbled (Greece, Turkey, Afghanistan, Iran, Iraq) into a neutral zone would not be 'practical politics'. A neutral zone there would mean 'the loss of the British position in Egypt and Arabia as well', and would 'bring Russia to the Congo and the Victoria Falls'. Since the Mediterranean was no longer of use to Britain as a communications route in war, the interest in retaining the British position there was 'to keep others out', for in the event of a Soviet encroachment in the region, 'we should lose our influence in Italy, France and North Africa'. Finally, there was the need for defences: 'In an atomic age we cannot afford to dispense with a first line of defence. Even if a neutral zone was feasible, can we risk having no first line of defence between Central Africa and Russia?'[142]

The debate seemed likely to gather new momentum on 11 December 1946, when the British Chiefs of Staff went back on their decision of the previous month and recommended the speedy withdrawal of all British troops from Greece. The reversal was prompted by the alarming report of Field-Marshal Montgomery, who, after a brief visit to Athens, held that if the Greek army failed to crush the DSE by spring 1947, 'then that would be the end of Greece and the Country will go under'.[143] The COS concluded that irrespective of the outcome of the struggle, the retention of British troops would be meaningless: if the guerrillas were defeated, British troops would be otiose, whereas if the reverse happened, they would have to be withdrawn hastily in order to avoid a possible entanglement in hostilities. They suggested, therefore, that the Cabinet should consider whether to provide the Greek government with the arms and money needed for victory and whether to continue to finance its army beyond March 1947.[144]

By the last days of 1946 there were evident signs from Attlee, the Treasury and the military that British policy in Greece might have to change. The Foreign Office felt some unease but its determination to stand firm did not abate. In an undated memorandum Michael Williams, Acting Head of the Southern Department, admitted that opposition to Bevin within the Cabinet was anticipated on the following grounds: a British Labour government could not possibly support a regime which conducted itself as did that of the Populists; the continuation of British assistance to Greece would be detrimental to the already strained Anglo-Soviet relations; and, after all, Greece's strategic importance was not paramount. Williams accepted that there was some grain of truth in these claims but reckoned that the disadvantages of relinquishing Greece would be far more grievous. If British support for the Populist government ceased, Greece would fall to the communists, with the result that the will of the Iranians and the Turks to resist Soviet pressure would weaken; Britain's interests in the Persian Gulf and her commercial undertakings in the Middle East would be in jeopardy; the consequences for the state of affairs in the western Mediterranean, especially in Italy, would be undesirable. If Greece were sold to the KKE, Britain's world image as a champion of social democracy would be damaged and Anglo-American relations would be at risk. Williams claimed that the United States would interpret this as 'the beginnings of a new Munich' and come to view the British as 'doubtful supporters of the principle of national independence and integrity'. That would be most unfortunate at the moment when Britain had to rely on American goodwill on a number of fields.[145]

Yet the difficulties confronting the Foreign Office were greater than those implied in Williams's confident memorandum. Exasperated by the inefficiency of the Populists, the Southern Department momentarily toyed with the idea of Norton intervening towards the formation of a government including Sofulis and possibly EAM, which would reach a new Varkiza Agreement. This faint-hearted suggestion was swiftly abandoned as soon as Norton counselled against it. The major obstacle to such a solution, according to the ambassador, lay in the relations between the Populists and Sofulis's Liberals. As the elected majority, the former would be unwilling to relegate themselves in the projected Cabinet, since Sofulis would probably demand the premiership for himself. The King would also have to be persuaded to accept such a solution, and even if he did, the bulk of Populist deputies might not. Added to these doubts, Norton was uncertain as to whether Sofulis would invite EAM in a government. The probable outcome would be the continuation of guerrilla activity while Sofulis was be trying his hand at some sort of appeasement; but the government should first establish itself in a position of strength and then enter into any negotiations with the Left. Norton summed up that British intervention in favour of Sofulis might benefit the KKE and would certainly be 'incompatible with [the] normal principles of Parliamentary majority rule to [the] realization of which our policy has hitherto been directed'.[146]

The Foreign Office was convinced. McNeil minuted that the British 'should not have any part in Cabinet-making at this stage and at no stage have any part in urging the King to be otherwise than a constitutional monarch'. Since the Foreign Secretary 'had often expressed himself against Cabinet-making in Greece', the matter was left to rest on this premise until Bevin's return from New York. By then the British government might have decided to terminate all aid to Greece, in which case the British would have little right to press their views on the Greeks and even less interest in what might happen to them.[147] It was an ironic coincidence, however, that at the same time *Rizospastis* was putting out feelers on the Liberals and asserting that Sofulis could still offer his services to the nation.[148]

Even so, Bevin's troubles were anything but over. On 5 January 1947 Attlee sent him a memorandum which represented a sharp break with long-standing notions of British strategy and foreign policy. The Prime Minister took as his starting point the conclusions of the Chiefs of Staff and the Imperial Defence College on Near Eastern Policy. According to them, the Soviet Union, the only possible future enemy, could be deterred from attacking Britain only by the threat of counter-attack. In the wake of the Second World War air-power had assumed cardinal importance for the defence of Britain, for if she found herself at war with Moscow without her strategic positions in the Middle East, she would lose vital air bases for the sort of action which alone could decrease the threat of attack on the British Isles. By contrast, if Britain retained her air bases in the Middle East, she could strike at the Soviet industrial heartland in the Ukraine and at the oil supplies in the Caucasus. The importance of the Middle East, therefore, lay no more in safeguarding imperial communication lines but in defending Britain herself, hence British influence and troops in the region should be maintained. The support of several states, which this policy necessitated,[149] was a source of acute concern for Attlee:

> Greece appears to be hopelessly divided. In the other countries there is a small class of poverty-stricken landworkers at the bottom. Their governments are essentially reactionary. They afford excellent soil for the sowing of communist seed. Our position is, therefore, made very difficult before the world and our own people. We shall constantly appear to be supporting vested interests and reaction against reform and revolution in the interests of the poor. We have already that difficulty in Greece. The same position is likely to arise in all these other countries.

Attlee suggested that unless Britain was convinced that the Kremlin was 'irrevocably committed to a policy of world domination', she should, before committing herself to a confrontation strategy, 'seek to come to an agreement with the USSR after consideration with Stalin of all our points of conflict'. The Prime Minister contemplated an Anglo-Soviet understanding – for instance by way of convincing the Soviet Union that Britain had no offensive intentions against her, settling the Dardanelles question according to principles applicable to all international waterways, and even reaching an agreement on oil rights in Iran.[150]

Bevin replied on 9 January 1947. Prior to that he had summoned a meeting with top Foreign Office officials, where the idea prevailed that 'even if Russian world domination can be discounted bear will not certainly resist pushing paw into soft places'.[151] The Foreign Secretary dismissed Attlee's arguments on both political and military grounds but focussed on the former: 'You point out that the Middle Eastern countries are a fertile ground for communism. This is indeed the case, and this makes it all the more certain that if we leave the Middle East, the Russians will move in.' Then came the favourite historical parallel. Negotiations with Stalin and a possible withdrawal from the Middle East 'would be Munich over again, only on a world scale, with Greece, Turkey and Persia as the first victims in place of Czechoslovakia.' Withdrawal would, moreover, mar Anglo-American relations:

The effects on our relations with the USA would be disastrous. We are to a large extent dependent on them economically, and without their help we cannot maintain the standard of life of our people. We are hardly less dependent upon them militarily. With great labour, we have at least succeeded in persuading them that their strategic interests are involved in the maintenance of our position in the Middle East. If we now withdraw at this moment, I should expect them to write us off entirely.

Bevin was in no hurry for negotiations with Stalin until Britain had acquired a position of strength:

Your proposal would involve leading from weakness. Our economic and military position is as bad as it will ever be. When we have consolidated our economy, when the economic revival of Europe which you mentioned has made progress, when it has become finally clear to the Russians that they cannot drive a wedge between the Americans and ourselves, we shall be in a position to negotiate with Stalin from strength. There is no hurry.[152]

The records suggest that Attlee was not entirely – or, at least, immediately – convinced, but also that he did not pursue his thesis further. On the same day (9 January 1947) the two men held a meeting with the Defence Secretary Albert Alexander; Bevin then dictated a note to Dixon to the effect that no further withdrawal of troops would take place and that his overall policy would continue. Attlee confined himself to the reservation that, in his judgement, British defence plans did not require the continuation of the present policy in the Middle East. Nevertheless, within a few weeks he would irrevocably abandon his position and become as fervent a custodian of British policy in the region as Bevin himself.[153] The initiative of the British Prime Minister hardly emanated from a desire to repudiate British world power. His letter to Bevin on 1 December 1946 manifests that he was alarmed by the prospect of the United States lapsing into isolationism and Britain being drawn into confrontation with the Soviet Union in the Middle East as well as in Europe. If in the event he dropped his argument, it was because of pressure from Bevin and the Service Chiefs. The Foreign Secretary and his staff were determined to entrench British preponderance in that region, whereas Field-Marshal Montgomery, in his capacity as Commander of the Imperial General Staff, told Attlee that he and the other two Service Chiefs would resign if the Prime Minister insisted.[154]

Given that for Bevin the preservation of the British position in the Middle East was a sacrosanct axiom, his exchange with Attlee revealed the extent to which he was anxious to secure American goodwill. Britain's economic and military dependence on the United States made it imperative that she displayed the utmost resoluteness in standing firm towards what was seen as Soviet expansionism. Attlee had no doubts about the need for America's helping hand but disagreed with Bevin as to whether this should be secured whatever the short-term costs. The Greek situation entered the picture on precisely this point because it had become a source of acute embarrassment for the Labour government. Attlee implicitly argued that Britain could not pose as the last bastion of social democracy and at the same time support the Populist regime in Athens, therefore alternative means should be found to underpin British security. Yet Bevin and the Foreign Office, having few scruples about the moral capital to be sacrificed in the process, supported the Populist government which was seen as the only alternative to a communist Greece.

For the Labour government and the Foreign Office, Anglo-Greek relations were hardly decided on the basis of what was actually happening inside Greece. Even after 1945 British policy-makers adhered to the thesis dating back to the times of Cromwell and William III, and which had become standard policy since the Younger Pitt and Palmerston, that British preponderance in the Middle East was vital to the security of Britain's world position.[155] Developments inside Greece played an important part in the tactical aspect of British policy there, but they could have no influence upon this fundamental strategic consideration. John Gallagher has remarked that a state which operates a world system cannot isolate any single individual situation and examine it on its own merits, for 'every possible solution squeezes the trigger of another problem' and 'every strategic case modulates into another'.[156] For London that was the guiding principle of Anglo-Greek relations, while at the other end the Populists were happy to comply, since the objective was essentially the same. It would seem then that none of those missed opportunities to put an end to the violence in Greece in August 1946–January 1947 was either genuine or promising. Yet in this judgement the tendency to see what one seeks is all too evident; and as 'the tyranny of knowing what came next' makes it difficult to insulate the account of what is transpiring from the knowledge of what is to transpire later, it is necessary to remember that if historical experience is anything to go by, the outcome will betray all expectations and falsify all predictions.[157]

Throughout the latter part of 1946 Bevin's tactical objective of isolating the KKE by way of a coalition government in Athens remained elusive. The embarrassment caused by the repressive domestic policies of the Populists gave force to his case, but at the same time these very policies strained relations between the Greek government and the Opposition, thereby obstructing the formation of a coalition. Several Populists were persistently agitating for the repeal of the Varkiza Agreement of February 1945, the arrest of the KKE leaders and the formation of a voluntary auxiliary police force, whereas Sofulis protested that Resolution III would introduce a police regime. In a typical incident, on 24 June 1946 the entire Opposition walked out of the Chamber when a monarchist deputy lectured on the historical merits of dictatorship and lauded the deeds of the royalist bands and the security forces.[158] Nevertheless, statements that they were willing to serve under the King, made by the EPE leaders and Sofulis on the morrow of the plebiscite, showed that the Opposition was not at loggerheads with the government over the strategic goal of holding the Left at bay; it was the Populists' crude tactics which generated resentment.

Hopes that the gap might be bridged arose on 24 August, when the Ukrainian delegate to the United Nations, Dimitri Manuilsky, protested before the Security Council at the policies of the Greek government and the stationing of British troops in the country. The matter withered away ingloriously after some academic debates reflecting the broader divisions between the great powers,[159] yet it certainly highlighted the case for bourgeois unity. Tsaldaris insisted that a coalition would be feasible only if the other party leaders agreed to serve under the Populists. In early October Norton encouraged the King to pursue this objective in order to isolate the Left and restrain right-wing terrorists who, by 'confusing Republicans with Communists', forced law-abiding citizens to flee to the mountains.[160] MacVeagh seconded his British colleague by urging the monarch to bring unity among 'all nationally-minded Greeks' under the leadership of the Crown. The new government would have to relinquish some unsavoury practices such as the imprisonment or deportation as hostages of the wives and children of leftist guerrillas. MacVeagh was convinced that with a policy of tolerance and justice 'at least 70% of the existing banditry in Greece would disappear'. As to the need for a broad government, one obvious difficulty was Sofulis, who was holding out for the premiership.[161] On the question of the domestic policies which had become an international embarrassment for Britain and the United States, the obstacle lay in Populist perceptions of Greece's relations with the allies. The Greek government perceived itself to be in a vantage ground which allowed it to dictate terms. On 14 October MacVeagh noted:

> It is commonly thought here that Britain and the US must infallibly support Greece, no matter what line she follows internally. My British colleague was actually told this to his face by the Greeks when trying to moderate Royalist extremism on a number of occasions.[162]

However embarrassing, such perceptions did not sway MacVeagh and Norton from impressing on Tsaldaris the need for a broader government. On 25 October the Prime Minister invited the Opposition to enter his Cabinet but negotiations broke down after EPE and the Liberals demanded his removal from the premiership.[163] The King's efforts proved equally abortive. On 26 October George II complained to Cyrus Sulzberger 'of the stupidity of the Greek politicians': 'He says that they all have the same program, but one does not like the moustache on another's face, and another does not like the necktie that the fourth wears, and they never seem able to get together.'[164] Sofulis would not enter the government 'if either Tsaldaris or someone outside Parliament were Premier', which was another way of saying that he wanted to be Premier himself. Though the centre-right EPE of Papandreou, Venizelos and Kanellopoulos were willing to co-operate, negotiations broke down within hours because Tsaldaris wanted his party to retain the portfolios of Foreign Affairs, Defence and Co-ordination.[165]

The brawl was carried into Parliament. Venizelos charged that Tsaldaris invited them to join in the application of Populist policies which offered no guarantee of success, whereas the latter retorted that the Opposition wanted to topple the government or force it to concede bankruptcy.[166] The King was right in arguing that all bourgeois parties had the same programme: in the absence of specific policies, the common ground amongst them was the desire to suppress the Left and appeal to the allies for generous economic assistance. Norton, who had come to regard the Greeks as 'extremists by nature', admitted that although the Opposition had plenty to find fault with in the domain of law and order, only Sofulis advocated 'a full appeasement policy'. The ambassador voiced his own bewilderment by quoting the King: 'Greek politics indeed make one feel, as the King recently remarked, like Alice in Wonderland.'[167]

By distancing himself from many of the crude Populist measures, Sofulis had come under criticism from the Right. At the same time he cautiously refrained from spelling out the detailed appeasement policies he envisaged towards the KKE in the hope that he would avoid being seen as the Greek Alexander Kerensky.[168] The British, however, would not wait, for the domestic situation in Greece was an ever-increasing embarrassment. Lenient sentences for collaborators were in sharp contrast with the heavy sentences passed on leftists; according to the British Police Mission there were 2,532 persons in exile, while the number of those in transit camps or detained pending their sentence was unknown; conditions in camps were 'deplorable', and so was the practice of imprisoning or deporting as hostages the wives and children of 'fugitives'. Norton's formal protests to Tsaldaris came to no avail.[169] While this strengthened the case for a broad government in which the Centre might curb Populist extremism, the overwhelming reason that spurred the British and the Americans into action was yet another re-emergence of the Greek question at the United Nations. On 3 December 1946 the Greek government charged Yugoslavia, Albania and Bulgaria with assisting the guerrillas of the Democratic Army, fomenting civil war and acting against Greece's territorial integrity. On 19 December the Security Council unanimously accepted a US proposal for the despatch of a Commission to investigate the Greek allegations on the spot.[170]

In view of the visit of the UN Commission to Greece, some of the ugliest aspects of the Populist regime had to be papered over. Sir Oliver Harvey of the British contingent at the United Nations told his Greek colleague Athanasios Agnidis that Greece should 'put her own house in order as far as possible'; in particular, a broad coalition should be established and the number of deportees be drastically reduced. To Harvey's inquiry as to the obstacle to a coalition, Agnidis replied that it was Tsaldaris himself, 'because other Greek politicians were not prepared to serve under a man of whose intelligence they did not think highly. M. Tsaldaris, on the other hand, was under the influence of his masterful and ambitious wife, and did not wish to stand down.'[171] The State Department, which shared the British concern, instructed MacVeagh to take joint action with Norton towards the establishment of a coalition government before the advent of the UN Commission.[172]

But the task still remained a daunting one. Norton was 'disgusted' when 'a leader of the Right-Centre', speaking of Tsaldaris, said: '"We haven't killed him yet, but he is seriously wounded."' The ambassador appealed to Bevin that it would be wrong if the British tried to 'impose' their own standards and methods on the 'mercurial and semi-Oriental' Greeks: 'Even at its best Greece will afford a happy hunting ground for those who seek evidence of muddle, incompetence, evasion, corruption, political persecution and lack of planning and control. So long as Greece remains truly democratic those things will exist in greater or lesser degree.' Norton considered that in Greece there would always be political crises and vendettas, and that his duty was therefore 'to prevent these from growing into civil war leading to a dictatorship of the Right or of the Left'.[173]

In Athens a new round of negotiations commenced in early January 1947. Tsaldaris told Norton that if the UN Commission found his government at fault, he would be prepared to hold fresh elections, adding that he was 'toying' with the idea of making such an announcement and that the KKE should meanwhile order a ceasefire.[174] On 8 January the Foreign Office instructed Norton to press for the immediate broadening of the government, an extended amnesty, the suppression of right-wing bands and the modification of deportation policy – which amounted to little more than cosmetic surgery on a repressive regime. When it came to more promising measures the British were anxious to uphold the tenet that their Greek policy had been correct. The Foreign Office dismissed Tsaldaris's idea for new polls on the grounds that it would cause more unrest, split the Populist ranks and lead to demands for a new AMFOGE. The overwhelming reason, however, was that new elections would cast doubt on those of 31 March 1946. When consulted by Norton, MacVeagh agreed that this would weaken the authority of the present government.[175]

On 10 January Tsaldaris assured Norton that his desire to broaden the government stumbled over Sofulis's demand to become Prime Minister and apply a policy of appeasement. The British Embassy reckoned that the ambition of the Liberal leader was to head a government which would grant a general amnesty, bring about changes in the army and the security forces and hold new elections as soon as possible.[176] Negotiations broke down by 15 January, and five days later Sofulis made a vague statement on appeasement. He spoke about cleansing Greek politics 'from the psychosis, hatred and passion which lead to political ideals being confused with brute force and crime',[177] which was more than enough to anger the increasingly interested Americans. George Marshall, the successor of Byrnes at the State Department, wondered whether the old man had 'made his position vis-à-vis the Communists clear'. If not, 'he should do so since it would manifestly be unfair to call upon the Greek people to support [a] leader who has not the courage to take steps to isolate the Communists and Communist-contaminated groups'.[178]

Sofulis would not budge. On 24 January 1947 a new government was sworn in without the Liberals. Dimitrios Maximos, a seventy-three years old, long-retired Populist and ex-Governor of the Bank of Greece, assumed the premiership, but the Populist leader Tsaldaris remained the strong man as Vice-Premier and Foreign Minister. The coalition consisted largely of the Populists and EPE, with the addition of Napoleon Zervas, the former leader of EDES who had entered Parliament as the champion of intractable anti-communism. The British feared – correctly, as it soon turned out – that this 'regrettable' appointment would 'expose the new Government to adverse criticism from the start'.[179] The Left, which would have favoured a Cabinet dominated by Sofulis, scorned the Maximos government as the 'Disaster Coalition' and 'The Bazaar', while commending the Liberal leader for his absence from such a 'governmental "gathering"'. Everybody else was relieved. The King depicted to Norton his efforts to broaden the government as trying 'to control a lot of jumping fleas', adding that the new scheme 'merited a pat on the back' from London. The British ambassador, who liked the 'intelligent and moderate' Maximos, agreed.[180]

The objective of uniting all bourgeois parties into a solid anti-communist front was only partially accomplished. Bevin was irritated by the tendency of the Greeks 'to play politics a little too much in a critical period like this',[181] but allied pressure, the imminent advent of the UN Commission, the spreading of DSE activity, and Sofulis's obduracy eventually brought them together. The latter opted to preserve the Liberals as a credible alternative between the Populists and the KKE, while his party felt genuine resentment against the government legislation which forced many non-communists to the mountains.[182] Also, if an appeasement policy applied by a Liberal government bore fruits, the entire credit would go to Sofulis's party and reinforce its role in future Greek politics.

Following British pressure, on 27 January 1947 Maximos announced an amnesty and the suspension of deportations of women and children.[183] This was not a breakthrough, for even the British Embassy admitted that the guerrillas had 'some ground for distrust of [the] amnesty offer quite apart from their general distrust of those to whom it falls to implement it'.[184] Napoleon Zervas, the Minister of Public Order, illustrated what the British feared when he declared in Parliament that 'in Greece all Greeks are right-wingers in the sense that all left-wingers are not Greeks' – a statement

136

followed by loud protests from the Liberals.[185] More telling was the reply of Giorgos Yiannoulis, a cultured lawyer and officer of the Democratic Army, to the invitation by the War Minister Filippos Dragoumis to accept a personal guarantee for his safety and freedom and descend from the mountains. Yiannoulis, who before the war had been Dragoumis's secretary, recalled that in 1935 his boss had told him that 'in Greece there is no-one more incompetent, more immoral, a more negative personality than George II'. Yiannoulis then recalled that in his pre-election speech in 1946 Dragoumis had declared that 'there is no other saviour than George II': 'Then I lost all confidence in you... We will surrender our arms before a state in which EAM participates.'[186]

The Maximos government had to come to grips with a disconcerting military situation and the prospect of imminent economic collapse. The first sketchy operations against the leftist bands in the north, which had begun in May 1946, had been thwarted by the guerrillas' hit-and-run tactics and excellent intelligence network. The attacks of large DSE bands on remote gendarmerie and army stations, followed by immediate withdrawal, were facilitated by the fragmentation of the army into numerous small units, each one guarding the constituencies of individual deputies.[187] In the winter of 1946–1947 the Democratic Army consolidated its hold on a continuous belt in western and central Macedonia and launched operations in Thrace, Thessaly, central Greece and even in the Peloponnese. By January 1947 there were 14,800 guerrillas led by experienced former ELAS cadres.[188]

The government army, trained by the British Military Mission for regular warfare, was inexperienced and ill-equipped for counter-guerrilla mountain operations. The government and the British were further alarmed by the existence of a large number of leftist sympathizers among the conscripts. From September 1946, after several instances of leftist soldiers deserting to the guerrillas when attacked by them, a process of segregation was adopted by way of establishing non-combatant units of unarmed leftist conscripts.[189] The situation in the higher echelons of the army was equally disturbing. Morale among commanding officers was rapidly dwindling because few of them were sanguine about the outcome of the struggle. On 18 February 1947 the King summoned Norton and MacVeagh to request reinforcement with new recruits and additional equipment to revive morale, otherwise he feared 'serious [and] widespread breakdown of discipline'.[190]

In the economic plane the situation was even more depressing. Apart from the massive deficits in the budget and the balance of payments, the increasing demand for military and relief expenditures made substantial economies virtually impossible. UNRRA supplies had practically ceased, whilst the position of the working classes seemed irredeemable as commodities were left piling up in the warehouses of Piraeus harbour. The plan of the British Economic Mission to set up consumer co-operatives for the distribution of goods had been obstructed by merchants and the Ministry of Supply, hence in the markets essential foodstuffs were becoming increasingly scarce amidst higher prices.[191] A Greek Economic Mission had visited the United States in

August 1946 and submitted to the State Department and the Export-Import Bank a 'poorly conceived and inadequate' memorandum requesting a loan of $175m. Influenced 'by Greek slowness and inefficiency' in utilizing the already existing $25m loan, the Americans merely promised that they would send to Greece an economic mission to investigate conditions.[192]

Under the pretext of launching the Greek complaint at the Security Council, Tsaldaris had spent most of December 1946 in the United States trying to achieve something that would restore his withering prestige at home.[193] Despite MacVeagh's warnings to the State Department that without foreign aid Greece would financially collapse, Tsaldaris's 'lack of precision' and the 'complete absence of any well-prepared data to substantiate [his] exaggerated demands' made a dismal impression upon the US government. The American fears that the Greeks would waste any assistance granted to them turned to indignation when the Prime Minister 'became eloquent' on territorial claims. Dean Acheson 'quite lost patience with him and told him what sort of statesmanship it was that frittered away its time and energy on territorial claims, when not only northern Greece but all Greece was headed hell-for-leather toward total destruction'.[194] Convinced that Tsaldaris was seeking foreign aid for his own political prestige, the State Department was enraged when he blatantly admitted that the complaint to the Security Council had been a pretext. The only official promise made was that a US economic mission would visit Greece, but on 28 December 1946 Acheson confidentially informed MacVeagh that the State Department was already preparing a programme for relief aid.[195]

This was a turning point in the growing American concern. By summer 1946 only Greece, Turkey and Iran – the northern tier – stood between the Soviet Union and the oilfields of the Middle East and the Persian Gulf, whose importance had been prodigiously enhanced after 1945. The United States and Britain came to be solidly convinced that their difficulties in Greece were due to the schemings of the Kremlin. Soviet pressure on Iran and Turkey and the unravelling of civil strife in Greece were construed as evidence that the Soviets aimed at breaking through the northern tier and dominating the eastern Mediterranean. Reckoning that the weakening of Britain and France might prompt the peoples of the region to turn to the Soviet Union for the solution of their social and economic problems, the Division of Near Eastern and African Affairs of the State Department recommended to President Truman that the United States step in to win the Near East for the western world.[196] By mid-October 1946 the British had learned 'under strictest injunctions to complete secrecy' that the Americans were working on a 'new policy' towards Greece. Acheson explained to MacVeagh that the increasing tension along Greece's northern frontier had led to a re-evaluation of American thinking on the premise that Greek independence was vital to the security of the United States; Washington was consequently prepared to take appropriate measures to support the political and territorial integrity of that country.[197]

What the Americans contemplated at that stage was diplomatic support, some grants and economic advice rather than blanket satisfaction of Tsaldaris's requests. An economic mission was scheduled to visit Athens in January 1947 to study the Greek economy, recommend to the Greek government steps for the effective utilization of domestic resources, and inquire into the extent of foreign aid needed.[198] Although both the Americans and the British were irritated by Tsaldaris's demagogy in Athens that he soon expected American aid,[199] the preparedness of the United States to come to the rescue of the Greek government was irreversible. On 17 February 1947 Paul Porter, the head of the US economic mission, transmitted to Washington his bleak preliminary impressions. The Greek state was virtually bankrupt, since it spent more than 50% of the national income on non-productive purposes; the budget deficit was vast, inflation was rampant, and the Greeks were overcome by a sense of national helplessness manifested in the conviction that the country should be taken care of by her rich allies. Having no confidence in the ability of the Greeks to administer the extensive reforms needed, Porter recommended that any aid offered should be subject to 'day to day guidance' by US personnel:

> There is really no State here in the Western concept. Rather we have a loose hierarchy of individualistic politicians, some worse than others, who are so preoccupied with their own struggle for power that they have no time, even assuming capacity, to develop economic policy. While I have no actual proof of venality in high places, the discussions current in journalistic and commercial circles claim that there exists a high degree of corruption. The civil service is a depressing farce.[200]

Later, in September 1947, Porter would claim that behind the Greek government there was 'a small mercantile and banking cabal ... determined above all to protect its financial prerogatives, at whatever expense to the economic health of the country'.[201] On 3 March 1947 the American official drafted a telegram to Truman but apparently never sent it. Porter, a '"new-deal" liberal', begged the President to make US aid to Greece conditional upon an armistice: 'You are aware of [the] complete reactionary nature of [the] present Government ... but one must work with them as I have to understand how incredibly weak, stupid, and venal they really are.' The United States, he argued, could only through the search for a peaceful solution offer to the Greek people 'something more than bloodshed and tyranny'.[202] To the British Porter said that he did not like the idea of US aid coinciding with the beginning of large-scale military operations against the guerrillas, hence he favoured their suspension in order to avoid America's association with a 'blood bath' in Greece. MacVeagh was shocked. He tried to convince him that as the problem was much wider, the United States should 'stop Russia', and then urged the State Department to keep Porter quiet in the future, perhaps by offering him a regular government job. The US ambassador told Norton that although 'after long exhortation on American policy [he] can temporarily get him on the right lines, Porter repeatedly slips back into the young New Dealer attitude that the Greeks are hopelessly corrupt, inefficient and divided.'[203] Nevertheless both Porter and MacVeagh had urged Washington to step in fast to prevent Greece's collapse, and the Truman administration was prepared to heed the warning.[204] The impetuosity of its response, however, was precipitated by the communication of decisions which had already been made in London.

Since July 1946 the British had made it clear to Tsaldaris that their exchange position would not permit any further loans. By September the Labour government, and especially Hugh Dalton, had come to view Greece as a poor investment for Britain's stretched postwar resources. Bevin himself admitted that the situation had been exacerbated by the Greeks' inability to 'put out a reconstruction programme to rally the people and isolate the Communists'.[205] In his anxiety to cut payments for the armed forces – mainly those stationed overseas – on 20 January 1947 Dalton sent Attlee a sharp 'Note on a Difference of Opinion'. The Chancellor of the Exchequer complained that some of his Cabinet colleagues seemed unaware of the gravity of Britain's economic and financial predicament and of the measures necessary to avoid a 'first-class economic and political disaster'. Being at loggerheads with Albert Alexander over the reduction in the size of the armed forces, Dalton particularly resented the fact that the Cabinet had backed the Defence Secretary and warned Attlee that he could not carry on indefinitely if his views 'were to continue to be brushed aside as of no account'. The British government, he urged, should come to see national defence 'not only against the more distant possibility of armed aggression, but also against the far more immediate risk of economic and financial overstrain and collapse'.[206]

Five days later Bevin prepared a memorandum proposing the increase of the Greek army as recommended by the Chiefs of Staff and the reduction of the British forces in the country to one Brigade of four Battalions, to be withdrawn when the Red Army evacuated Bulgaria. Britain should provide the Greek army with the desperately needed additional equipment on condition that the Greeks met the extra cost (some £2m) up to 31 March. As to the long-term economic position, the current British commitment expired on that date, and since the United States had indicated its interest in Greece, Bevin proposed to discuss with Washington the question of the cost of the Greek armed forces with a view to sharing it. It would also be essential to ascertain the specific American proposals and the extent of economic and military assistance they would be prepared to offer Greece over a period of three years.[207] The Cabinet invited Bevin to arrange for a committee of officials representing the Foreign Office, the Treasury and the Ministry of Defence in order to consider (i) the financial implications of granting assistance to the Greek government to enable its army to undertake operations against the DSE, and (ii) what proposals should be put to the Americans about the long-term economic, financial and military aid to Greece.[208] On 30 January 1947 the Foreign Office notified the US Chargé d'Affaires in London of these decisions.[209]

From Athens Norton emphatically reported on the precariousness of the situation, urging speedy and drastic action. The very real danger of economic collapse would lead to political collapse in Athens, and 'hence through a period of civil war and great suffering to the incorporation [of Greece] in the Soviet system of buffer police states controlled by Communist minorities and dependent on Moscow for economic aid'.[210] On 11 February Dalton sought from Attlee a flat decision to terminate all aid to Greece, which since the end of the war had received – almost to no avail – £39m from the British coffers.

If the Labour government wanted to avert economic disaster at home, they should embark on the 'most ruthless economy in overseas expenditure'. The Chancellor 'would begin at once by cutting off the Greeks'.[211] Two days later he wrote to Bevin that Britain should not enter into any fresh commitments, as she would find it difficult 'to feed, clothe and employ' the British people themselves: 'We must ... face the issue squarely and tell both the Greeks and the Americans where we stand.' Bevin thought that Dalton's views were justified, especially since the Greeks themselves would not help. The policy of supporting Greece would be untenable unless the United States or some international financial institution agreed to shoulder the main financial burden.[212] On the morning of 18 February the two men decided to send a strong telegram to the Americans asking them what they were going to do, and another one telling the Greeks that Britain would discontinue her assistance.[213]

On the following day Bevin instructed Lord Inverchapel, the British ambassador in Washington, to submit to the State Department a memorandum on the Greek situation. The country was on the verge of collapse and her military needs were heavy if she was to defend herself against the guerrillas. The British had done their utmost, but as from now on it would be impossible to provide any further aid, it was imperative that the United States take a prompt decision as to what assistance it could make available to Greece.[214] Meanwhile Norton cabled London a strong plea that no communication should be made to the Greeks, for the ensuing panic and possible breakdown might render US aid worthless. The Foreign Office heeded the advice,[215] and on 21 February 1947 the British Embassy handed the State Department two separate memoranda on Greece and Turkey along the lines suggested to Inverchapel by Bevin.[216]

In Washington the urgent tone of the British memoranda sparked off a round of top-level discussions among Departments, Congressional leaders and President Truman. The State Department asked the British government to continue its assistance to Greece on an emergency basis until US aid became available. The British agreed to loan the Greeks £2m for the maintenance of their army until June 1947, but their request to have the loan reimbursed by the Americans or by Greece out of US funds was flatly rejected by the State Department. The Americans sought confirmation of their assumption that Britain would fully co-operate in supporting the political independence and territorial integrity of Greece; the British offered it, adding, however, that they would withdraw their troops in the summer of 1947. Attlee indicated that he would accept Acheson's appeal for the retention of the British Missions in Greece.[217] The State Department dictated to the Greek Chargé d'Affaires in Washington the text of the Greek request for US aid,[218] and on 12 March 1947 President Truman asked Congress to authorize assistance to Greece and Turkey amounting to $400m until 30 June 1948; he also requested the despatch of US civilian and military personnel to these countries to assist in the task of reconstruction and supervise the utilization of aid. In the case of Greece, the US government would endeavour through primarily economic aid to render the country self-supporting and help her 'to build an economy in which a healthy democracy can flourish'. In more general terms, the President let the world know that the policy of the United States of America must be 'to support free peoples who are resisting attempted subjugation by armed minorities or outside pressure'.[219]

The Truman administration had already embarked on an intense public relations campaign to convince the American people of the need to intervene in Greece. Apocalyptic terms were used to warn against Soviet advances, and during the ensuing Congressional hearings MacVeagh presented a grotesquely distorted picture of the Greek situation. After trivializing the achievements of '"the so-called resistance movement"', the ambassador claimed that the Varkiza Agreement had been a victory for the KKE and that the Democratic Army was only after looting. He even paraphrased the name of their commander Markos into 'Markov' and assured Congressmen that 'Markov' had frequently been in gaol for various crimes.[220] Despite criticism and delays, on 22 May 1947 the Bill for aid to Greece and Turkey became Law, and on 20 June MacVeagh and Tsaldaris signed the US-Greek Agreement regulating the American assistance to Greece. The United States was vested with considerable control over Greek affairs through the supervision of US aid by the American Mission for Aid to Greece (AMAG), which had the right to remove Greek officials and effect changes in the composition of the Greek government.[221] Following Porter's recommendations, American experts with executive powers were appointed in Greek Ministries to prevent the misuse or waste of US dollars by corrupt and inefficient Greek politicians.[222]

On 15 March President Truman received messages of gratitude from Prime Minister Maximos and Sofulis, who asserted that the American aid would be devoted 'to the purpose of constructive rehabilitation and the cause of peace and freedom'.[223] In Athens the right-wing press was elated. The tone was set by the editor of *Kathimerini* in an editorial incongruously entitled 'Independence': 'There is no question of Independence. There is only one question: that of the Boss. Our Boss is one, or rather, two: America and England.'[224] The liberal press gave a more qualified response in that the American offer would prevent an immediate collapse, but also render Greece an 'instrument' of US foreign policy and deprive her of the right to choose her own policy according to her own interests at a later stage.[225] In a defiant article in *Rizospastis* on 14 March, Zachariadis proclaimed that its bitterness and frustration notwithstanding, the Left would keep up the struggle: 'If the North Americans envied Scobie's glory, they may come to Greece to gain it. It is one of the "glories" which bring death and annihilate morally those who gain them.'[226] Despite the equivocal and debilitating Soviet reply, in order to dispel fears that a withdrawal of the British troops would be followed by the invasion of foreign communist hordes, the KKE, EAM and the Democratic Army called once more for Greek neutrality within the framework of the United Nations.[227]

The global conflict between Communism and the Western states enunciated by the Truman Doctrine later prompted Dalton to reflect that 'my little push for small economy in Whitehall had released world forces far more powerful than I ever guessed'.[228] It was an apposite remark, for Greece had indeed become the microcosm of the differences between the West and the Soviet Union, and for the Americans, the testing ground of their resolve to protect the principle of self-determination. In the long-term the response of the Truman administration to the internal conflict in Greece became the pivotal point in the development of a global strategy designed to combat communist expansion. A recent analysis has demonstrated convincingly that Greece was the first battlefield of a 'new kind of war' which involved the use of guerrilla warfare, propaganda, war in the shadows, terror tactics and victory based on outlasting the enemy. The legacy of the Truman Doctrine was to be a lasting one, and twenty years later, in the mid-1960s, President Lyndon Johnson would still refer to Greece as the model for America's growing involvement in Vietnam.[229]

Yet Greece was also the country where one of the least appealing aspects of the Truman Doctrine was first evinced. This was the policy of support to authoritarian and repressive right-wing regimes in the name of freedom, soon to be repeated in several cases – most notably in South Korea and Indo-China. The origins of this policy are to be found in the diagnosis of Soviet expansionism as the cause of the civil war in Greece, which urged the United States to pick up the torch of defending 'democracy' as construed by the Populist Party and the monarchist irregulars. In this the Truman administration received the helping hand of the British, whose reactions indicated that they would emulate the Americans in cynically interpreting the Greek situation as exemplifying the struggle of democratic majorities against totalitarian minorities. The Foreign Office welcomed the Presidential declaration, with the exception of Gladwyn Jebb, the Assistant Under-Secretary, who deemed it a hasty, ambiguous, 'badly-thought and impetuous gesture' seeking to incite anti-Communist opposition within Communist states. Christopher Warner and Sir John Balfour, the British Minister in Washington, discarded such views and emphasized the need for American resoluteness after the vacillations towards totalitarianism in the run-up to 1939. McNeil told Jebb that he was 'overpitching his case', while Attlee and Bevin welcomed the President's Message.[230]

On 6 March Lord Inverchapel cabled the Foreign Office that the British 'can be gratified with the manner in which [the Truman] administration has set about assuming the task with which they have been confronted … and have girded themselves to tackle Congress'.[231] Evidence that the British were careful not to jeopardize American initiatives lies in Norton's important contribution to the Greek government's acceptance of the US-drafted request for aid. When Tsaldaris sought the ambassador's advice on the 'fateful' provision for American advisers with executive powers, the latter replied that in view of Greece's 'desperate' position and Britain's inability to cope with it, the Greeks should 'make no difficulties'. Tsaldaris returned with the suggestion of accepting the US terms 'for a period of years', but Norton insisted that the Greek Prime Minister 'would be ill-advised to quibble'.[232]

Britain's own economic and financial setbacks in early 1947 account substantially but not wholly for the reasons which prompted the aide-mémoire to the State Department. Dalton had long before voiced his objections to pouring sterling into Greece, but with the Cabinet dominated by Attlee and Bevin, the Chancellor's view did not command attention until Bevin himself came round. Britain was spending more than she could afford on the Greeks, while the Greeks themselves would not bother their heads about tackling their problems. For Dalton the huge injections of funds which alone could avert Greece's economic collapse were unavailable from Britain's strained resources, the danger of civil war was ever-present, and the Populist regime was 'not one about which the Labour Government can feel any enthusiasm'.[233]

Such considerations would have to be reconciled with the tenet that Greece was a strategic stronghold. When Attlee suggested withdrawal from the Middle East, including Greece, Bevin made it clear that he regarded the British position in the region an indispensable asset. That he eventually gave way only to the extent of discontinuing aid to Greece may in part be attributed to the rapid deterioration of domestic conditions there and his 'revulsion against all things Greek'. Yet it also seems that Greece's ranking in the long list of British foreign policy priorities came under reconsideration. Dixon conceded that the Mediterranean was not important as a line of communications and that the British were there in order 'to keep others out'. The *real* British interest was perceived as laying in the Middle East proper rather than in its northern tier. If the United States could be dragged into sustaining the Mediterranean position, the long-term British strategic interests in the Middle East would be adequately safeguarded. The Truman Doctrine met this expectation and, at the same time, relieved the Labour government of an economic incubus.

Henceforth Britain was free to direct her energies predominantly towards the Middle East. Yet she would not forget – nor would the Americans let her forget – Greece. The Labour government was still heavily involved, and would thus take a great interest, in the weakest country guarding the northern tier of the British Empire in the Middle East. From March 1947 onwards Britain and the United States would be riding 'in double harness'.[234] In assuming a leading role in global affairs, the Americans made it abundantly clear that they relied on British co-operation. On 20 March 1947 the British Cabinet accepted Washington's request for the retention of the British Military Mission in Greece because a refusal might make it difficult for the administration to secure Congressional agreement for economic aid to that country. Bevin told Marshall that his government had agreed to Acheson's proposal that Britain should carry the financial burden in Greece from 31 March 1947 until the enforcement of the Congressional decision, and that he had already committed £18m to that purpose.[235] The US representatives in Greece would be 'most anxious' to secure the cooperation of their British colleagues.[236] As for the Greek government, the 'sincerely pro-British' Tsaldaris was aware that he was 'disliked by the Americans' and would pledge that 'his first loyalty was still to Great Britain'.[237] Contrary to common assumptions, the story of Anglo-Greek relations from March 1947 to the end of the Greek Civil War shows that the ties between London and Athens were anything but looser after the enunciation of the Truman Doctrine. In his annual report for 1947 Norton reflected:

The Greek Government still wished for British interest and support, and HM Government still retained both troops in Greece and three Service missions and a police mission ... The US Government made it clear that they had no desire to exclude Britain from Greece.[238]

NOTES

1. Bevin Papers: F.O.800/468/GRE/45/13: Bevin to Leeper, 30/11/1945.
2. F.O.371/58679 R3748: F.O. to Norton, 13/3/1946.
3. F.O.371/58682 R5025: Bevin to Norton, 1/4/1946.
4. F.O.371/58683 R5170: Norton to F.O., 2/4/1946; Bevin to Norton, 3/4/1946; *ibid.*, R5246: Norton to F.O., 3/4/1946.
5. F.O.371/58688 R6576: Norton to F.O., 20/4/1946; FRUS (1946): VII, 128–30: Rankin to Byrnes, 2/4/1946.
6. F.O.371/58683 R5123: Norton to F.O., 2/4/1946; *ibid.*, R5240: Norton to F.O., 3/4/1946; *ibid.*, R5276: Norton to F.O., 3/4/1946; *The Times* (London): 3/4/1946; FRUS (1946): VII, 128–30: Rankin to Byrnes, 2/4/1946.
7. F.O.371/58683 R5247: F.O. to Norton, 4/4/1946.
8. Bevin Papers: F.O.800/468/GRE/46/7: Bevin to Norton, 4/4/1946, and Enclosure: George II to Bevin, 4/4/1946.
9. F.O.371/58684 R5321: Norton to F.O., 4/4/1946; *ibid.*, R6576: Norton to F.O., 20/4/1946; *The Times* (London): 5/4/1946.
10. FRUS (1946): VII, 128–30: Rankin to Byrnes, 2/4/1946.
11. *The Times* (London): 6/4/1946.
12. F.O.371/58688 R6785: Norton to Bevin, 26/4/1946.
13. F.O.371/58687 R6081: Norton to F.O., 19/4/1946; F.O. 371/58688 R6785: Norton to Bevin, 26/4/1946.
14. FRUS (1946): VII, 131–2: Byrnes to Rankin, 5/4/1946.
15. *Ibid.*, 134–5: Winant (London) to Byrnes, 10/4/1946.
16. F.O.371/58688 R6516: Norton to Sargent, 15/4/1946.
17. FRUS (1946): VII, 137–9: British Embassy to State Department, Paraphrase of telegram from F.O. to C.V. Norton, 15/4/1946; F.O.371/58687 R6081: Draft Reply by Bevin, n.d.
18. FRUS (1946): VII, 144–5: Byrnes to Rankin, 18/4/1946.
19. *Ibid.*, 146: Acheson to Rankin, 24/4/1946; F.O.371/58687 R6302: Lord Halifax (Washington) to F.O., 24/4/1946.
20. F.O.371/58687 R6382: UK Delegation (Paris) to F.O., 27/4/1946; FRUS (1946): VII, 148–9: Memorandum of Conversation between Byrnes and Bevin (Paris), 27/4/1946.
21. H.S. Truman, *Memoirs*, II, *Year of Decisions* (New York: 1955), 551–2; FRUS (1946): I, 1160–5: Memorandum by Joint COS, Basis for the Formulation of a US Military Policy, 27/3/1946; *ibid.*, 1165–6: Joint COS to the Secretary of State, Foreign Policy of the US, 29/3/1946; *ibid.*, 1167–71: Memorandum by Matthews to State-War-Navy Coordinating Committee, 1/4/1946. Text of the Long Telegram (Kennan to Byrnes, 22/2/1946) in FRUS (1946): VI, 696–706. See also W. Loth, *The Division of the World 1941–1955* (London: 1988), pp.85–8, 97–8, 106–14; J.L. Gaddis, *The Long Peace: Inquiries into the History of the Cold War* (New York: 1987), pp.29–40; *idem*, *Strategies of Containment: A Critical Appraisal of Post-war American National Security Policy* (New York: 1982), pp.13–22.

22.   Bevin Papers: F.O.800/478/MIS/45/14: The Foreign Situation, Memoran-
       dum by Bevin, 8/11/1945; F.O.371/56780 N1471: Bevin to F.O., 31/1/1946;
       F.O.371/56763 N4065: Roberts (Moscow) to F.O., 14/3/1946.

23.   F.O.371/58632 N6344: F.O. Paper by Warner, 'The Soviet Campaign Against
       This Country and our Response to it', 10/4/1946; F.O.371/56885 N5169:
       Minutes of the First Meeting of the Russia Committee held on April 2, 1946;
       Bevin Papers: F.O.800/501/SU/46/15: Bevin to Attlee, 10/4/1946.

24.   F.O.371/58688 R6575: Norton to F.O., 30/4/1946; *ibid.*, R6733: Norton to
       F.O., 3/5/1946; F.O.371/58690 R7099: Norton to F.O., 10/5/1946.

25.   *Ta Nea* (Athens): 4/5/1946.

26.   *Kathimerini* (Athens): 12/5/1946 and 30/4/1946; *Embros* (Athens): 4/5/1946;
       Vradyni (Athens): 2/5/1946.

27.   EPSV, 126 (13/5–20/6/1946) (Athens: 1946), pp.2–3; F.O. 371/58690 R7194:
       Norton to F.O., 13/5/1946.

28.   CAB 128/5/C.M. 50 (46): 20/5/1946.

29.   F.O.371/58694 R8479: Norton to Warner, 13/5/1946.

30.   F.O.371/58696 R9040: Minute by Hayter, 24/6/1946.

31.   See Zachariadis's speech at the 7th Plenum (1957), in P. Dimitriou, ed., *I
       Diaspasi tou KKE* I (Athens: 1978), 94; also G. Vonditsos-Gousias, *Oi Aities yia
       tis Ittes, ti Diaspasi tou KKE ke tis Ellinikis Aristeras* II (Athens: 1977), 151, 250;
       L. Eleftheriou, *Synomilies me ton Niko Zachariadi* (Athens: 1986), pp.34–5, and
       Zachariadis's open letter to the Greek people (1968), in *ibid.*, p.115. For the
       scepticism of Thorez and Togliatti see D. Partsalidis *Dipli Apokatastasi tis
       Ethnikis Andistasis* (Athens: 1978), p.199.

32.   L. Eleftheriou, *op.cit.*, p.35. Eleftheriou first revealed his secret in *Avgi*
       (Athens): 27, 29 and 30/1/1980.

33.   A similar interpretation in P.J. Stavrakis, *Moscow and Greek Communism 1944–
       1949* (Ithaca and London:1989), p.110.

34.   E. Barker, 'The Yugoslavs and the Greek Civil War of 1946–1949', in L.
       Baerentzen, J.O. Iatrides, O.L. Smith, eds., *Studies in the History of the Greek Civil
       War 1945–1949* (Copenhagen: 1987), pp.301–2. See also E. Kofos, *The Impact of
       the Macedonian Question on Civil Conflict in Greece (1943–1949)* (Athens: 1989).

35.   *Rizospastis* (Athens): 3/4/1946.

36.   KKE: E.K., VI, Appendix, pp.434–6: Telegram of the Parties of the Left to the
       Four Powers, 8/4/1946.

37.   *Rizospastis* (Athens): 16/4/1946.

38.   M. Vafiadis, 'Omilia pano sto proto thema tis Imerisias Diataxis', *Neos Kosmos*
       no.4–5 (April–May 1957), 52; *idem, Apomnimonevmata* III (Athens: 1985), 115,
       119, V (Athens: 1992), 90–1, 93; D. Katsis, *To Imerologio enos Andarti tou DSE
       1946–49* I (Athens: 1990), 71–3; G. Blanas, *Emfylios Polemos 1946–1949: Opos
       ta Ezisa* (Athens: 1976), p.61; Kikitsas, interview in *Avgi* (Athens): 3 and
       5/2/1980; M. Tsantis, interview in *Avgi* (Athens): 10/2/1980.

39.   FRUS (1946): VII, 159–60: Rankin to Byrnes, 10/5/1946.

40.   GAK: Tsouderos Papers, E (49): A Note on the Greek Question, March 1947,
       and Tsouderos's letter to Henry Wallace, 17/3/1948; F. Smothers, W.H.
       McNeill, E.D. McNeill, *Report on the Greeks: Findings of a Twentieth Century
       Fund team which surveyed conditions in Greece in 1947* (New York: 1948), pp.153,
       169, 182–3; P. Delaportas, *To Simiomatario enos Pilatou* 2nd edn. (Athens:
       1978), p.106.

41.   F.O.371/58838 R6783: Norton to F.O., 4/5/1946.

42. F.O.371/58838 R6795: Norton to F.O., 4/5/1946.

43. F.O.371/58838 R6795: F.O. to Norton, 11/5/1946; *ibid.*, R7552 Norton to Tsaldaris, 14/5/1946; *ibid.*, R7661: Memorandum by the Greek Foreign Minister to British Embassy, 20/5/1946; *ibid.*, R8062: Tsaldaris to Norton, 22/5/1946.

44. F.O.371/58691 R7411: Norton to F.O., 16/5/1946; F.O.371/58692 R7667: Norton to F.O., 21/5/1946.

45. P. Delaportas, *op.cit.*, pp.243–4.

46. *Ibid.*, p.245.

47. *Ibid.*, p.247.

48. F.O.371/58838 R8579: Norton to F.O., 6/6/1946.

49. KKE: E.K., VI, no.760: Politburo Resolution, 7/6/1946; *Rizospastis* (Athens): 12/6/1946; F.O.371/58838 R8781: Norton to F.O., 10/6/1946; *ibid.*, R9378: Norton to F.O., 12/6/1946.

50. EPSV: 126 (13/5/–20/6/1946), 242–3; F.O.371/58838 R8579: Norton to F.O., 16/6/1946; *ibid.*, R9160: Norton to F.O., 18/6/1946; *ibid.*, R9380: Norton to F.O., 20/6/1946; F.O. 371/58698 R9905: Norton to F.O., 19/6/1946.

51. *Rizospastis* (Athens): 2/6/1945; [KKE CC], *Deka Chronia Agones 1935–1945* (Athens: 1945), pp.252ff.

52. N. Alivizatos, 'The "Emergency" Regime and Civil Liberties 1947–1950', in J. O. Iatrides, ed., *Greece in the 1940s: A Nation in Crisis* (Hanover and London: 1981), pp.220–8.

53. F.O.371/58698 R10399: Minute by McCarthy, 2/7/1946. In the same file a memorandum by Hayter entitled 'Law and Order in Greece' (24/7/1946) stated: 'It has been reported from a pretty good secret source that at a special meeting of the Greek Communist Party (KKE) [at] Salonika on June 16 it was decided to issue instructions for the Party to be ready for active guerrilla operations to begin at the end of July.'

54. N. Zachariadis, *Provlimata tis Krisis tou KKE* (n.p.: 1962), reprinted as *I Paranomi Brosoura tou Nikou Zachariadi* (Athens: 1987), p.33. For the communist accounts which support the essence of McCarthy's minute see: M. Vafiadis, 'Omilia', 52 and *Apomnimonevmata* III, 126, V, 103–104, 192; L. Stringos, 'Omilia', *Neos Kosmos* no.4–5 (April–May 1957), 86; G. Blanas, *op.cit.*, pp.74–5; G. Vonditsos-Gousias, *op.cit.* I, 135–8; V. Bartziotas, *Exinda Cronia Kommunistis* (Athens: 1986), pp.247–8.

55. M. Vafiadis, 'Omilia', 50, *Apomnimonevmata* III, 126, V, 103; P. Mavromatis, 'Omilia', *Neos Kosmos* no.4–5 (April–May 1957), 102; V. Bartziotas, *O Agonas tou Dimokratikou Stratou Elladas* 3rd edn. (Athens: 1985), pp.28, 31; *idem*, *Exinda Chronia*, pp.245, 257; Kikitsas, interview in *Avgi* (Athens): 3/2/1980; M. Tsantis, *Avgi* (Athens): 10/2/1980; G. Vonditsos-Gousias, *op.cit.* I, 135–6; D. Votsikas, *I Ipiros Xanazonete t' Armata, 1946–1949: Dimokratikos Stratos Elladas* (Athens: 1983), pp.83–4.

56. F.O.371/58698 R10399: Law and Order in Greece, Memorandum by Hayter, 24/7/1946; Minutes by Warner (24/7/1946), McCarthy (15/7/1946), McNeil (2/7/1946).

57. *Rizospastis* (Athens): 29/6/1946, 25 and 27/7/1946; F.O.371/58698 R10091: Norton to F.O., 28/6/1946.

58. *Rizospastis* (Athens): 6, 21, 22, 25, 29, 30/6/1946; 1, 2, 5, 8, 9, 10, 11, 12, 13, 17, 18, 19, 23/7/1946.

59. F.O.371/58698 R9950: Norton to F.O., 29/6/1946.

60. *Rizospastis* (Athens): 10/7/1946.

61. KKE: E.K., VI, no.761: Politburo Statement, 12/7/1946; *Rizospastis* (Athens): 13 and 18/7/1946.

62. FRUS (1946): VII, 186–7: MacVeagh to Byrnes, 3/8/1946.

63. F.O.371/58881 R11888: Report of Tour by Commander BMM(G), 21/7/1946.

64. F.O.371/58881 R11888: Lascelles to Bevin, 2/8/1946.

65. F.O.371/58881 R11888: Lascelles to Bevin, 2/8/1946; DSE Archives, *Eleftherotypia* (Athens): 10/3/1986: Biographical Report of Ilias Apoultsis.

66. F.O.371/58881 R11888: Lascelles to Bevin, 2/8/1946.

67. F.O.371/58881 R11888: Lascelles to Bevin, 2/8/1946.

68. M. Vafiadis, 'Omilia', 52–53; *idem, Apomnimonevmata*, V, 91.

69. KKE (es.) Archives, *Avgi* (Athens): 6/12/1979: KKE Memorandum to the CPs of USSR, Yugoslavia, Bulgaria, 12/9/1946; G.Blanas, *op.cit.*, p.75; *idem*, interview in *Eleftherotypia* (Athens): 22/2/1980; K. Koliyiannis's speech in *I Triti Syndiaskepsi tou KKE, 10–14/10/1950* (Athens: 1988), p.166; G. Vonditsos-Gousias, *op.cit.* I, 290; Zachariadis's speech at the 7th Plenum (1957), in P. Dimitriou, ed., *op. cit.* I, 95.

70. G. Blanas, *op.cit.*, p.75; *idem*, interview in *Eleftherotypia* (Athens): 22/2/1980.

71. M. Vafiadis, 'Omilia', 53; *idem, Apomnimonevmata* V, 99–101; *idem*, interview in *Eleftherotypia* (Athens): 19/2/1980; G. Blanas, *op.cit.*, pp.94, 202.

72. See O.L. Smith, 'A Turning Point in the Greek Civil War, 1945–1949: The Meeting between Zachariadis and Markos, July 1946', *Scandinavian Studies in Modern Greek* 3 (1979), 35–47.

73. KKE (es.) Archives, *Avgi* (Athens): 6/12/1979: KKE Memorandum to the CPs of the USSR, Yugoslavia, Bulgaria, 12/9/1946; M. Vafiadis, *Apomnimonevmata* V, 131, 134.

74. KKE (es.) Archives, *Avgi* (Athens): 6/12/1979: KKE Memorandum to the CPs of the USSR, Yugoslavia, Bulgaria, 12/9/1946.

75. KKE: E.K., VI, no.762: Politburo Statement, 11/9/1946; *Rizospastis* (Athens): 17 and 20/9/1946; S. Papayiannis, *Apo Evelpis Andartis: Anamniseis enos kommunisti axiomatikou* (Athens: 1991), p.66; *Avgi* (Athens): interviews with Kikitsas (3 and 5/2/1980), Makridis (2 and 4/3/1980), Tsantis (10/2/1980).

76. MVR, p.696.

77. F.O.371/58700 R10703: Norton to F.O., 18/7/1946; *ibid.*, R10776: Norton to F.O., 18/7/1946; *ibid.*, R10946: Norton to F.O., 23/7/1946; F.O.371/58698 R9950: Norton to F.O., 29/7/1946.

78. *Estia* (Athens): 27/7/1946.

79. F.O.371/58751 R12833: Weekly Report by Peck, 10–16/8/1946.

80. F.O.371/58704 R12612: Lascelles to F.O., 24/8/1946; F.O.371/58751 R12443: Weekly Report by Peck, 3–8/8/1946.

81. F.O.371/58702 R11969: Lascelles to F.O., 13/8/1946; MVR, pp.696–7: tel. 1132, 28/8/1946.

82. MVR, p.698: despatch 3010, 10/8/1946.

83. F.O.371/58703 R12054: Lascelles to F.O., 14/8/1946; N. Clive, *Embeiria stin Ellada* (1943–1948) (Athens: n.d.), p.185.

84. S. Patatzis, *Ioannis Sofianopoulos: Enas Epanastatis Choris Epanastasi* (Athens: 1961), pp.203–4: Sofianopoulos's letter to M. Embeirikos, 8/8/1946; *Kathimerina Nea* (Athens): 26/5/1946; *Rizospastis* (Athens): 6/7/1946.

85. *Eleftheria* (Athens): 29/8/1946.

86. AMFOGE Report (7/9/1946) in F.O.371/58708 R13798 and FRUS (1946): VII, 204–7.

148

87. F.O.371/58710 R15035: AMFOGE Supplementary Report, 13/9/1946.
88. F.O.371/58710 R15035: F.O. Minute, 19/9/1946; Selby to U.K. Delegation to Paris, 12/10/1946; Minute by Dixon,15/10/1946; Minute by Bevin, n.d. On the plebiscite see also R. Clogg, *Parties and Elections in Greece: The Search for Legitimacy* (London: 1987), pp.205–6.
89. H. Dalton, *High Tide and After: Memoirs 1945–1960* (London: 1962), p.156.
90. GAK: K 163 (Papers of I. Petimezas), file '1943–1953: Documents': letter from Woodhouse to Petimezas, 9/9/1946.
91. C. Sulzberger, *A Long Row of Candles: Memoirs and Diaries (1934–1954)* (London: 1969), pp.257–8.
92. P. Dixon, *Double Diploma* (London:1968), p.228: diary entry for 26/9/1946. On George II's contempt for his subjects, see H. Fleischer, *Stemma ke Svastika: I Ellada tis Katochis ke tis Andistasis, 1941–1944* I (Athens: 1988), 58–9, and Fleischer's preface in N. Svoronos and H. Fleischer, eds., *I Ellada 1936–1944: Diktatoria–Katochi–Andistasi* (Athens: 1989), pp.xiv–xv.
93. F.O.371/58707 R13459: Norton to F.O., 2/9/1946.
94. F.O.371/58709 R14079: Memorandum by the King to Bevin, 13/9/1946; Bevin to Norton, 17/9/1946.
95. F.O.371/58905 R8253: Norton to F.O., 7/6/1946; ibid., R9798: Norton to F.O., 1/7/1946.
96. FRUS (1946): VII, 169–70: Acheson to Rankin, 13 and 14/6/1946.
97. F.O.371/58698 R9897: Bevin (Paris) to F.O.,2/7/1946; F.O. 371/58730 R10330: Minutes of a Conference between Tsaldaris and Bevin, 2/7/1946; Bevin to McNeil, 4/7/1946; *ibid.*, R10375: Memorandum by Tsaldaris, 3/7/1946; FRUS (1946): VII, 177–8: Memorandum of a Conversation between Byrnes and Tsaldaris (Paris), 5/7/1946; *ibid.*, 177, n.28: Byrnes to State Department, 8/7/1946.
98. F.O.371/58906 R10729: Minutes of a Conference between Attlee and Tsaldaris, 10/7/1946; Minutes of a Conference between Dalton and Tsaldaris, 10/7/1946; S. Xydis, *Greece and the Great Powers, 1944–47: Prelude to the Truman Doctrine* (Thessaloniki: 1963), pp.257–8.
99. F.O.371/58698 R10234: F.O. Minute, 8–11/7/1946; *ibid.*, R10392: F.O. Minute, 12/7/1946; F.O. 371/58906 R10651: Hayter to Norton, 19/7/1946.
100. FRUS (1946): VII, 180–1: Harriman to Byrnes, 12/7/1946; *ibid.*, 181–2: Acheson to Harriman, 13/7/1946.
101. F.O.371/58886 R6032: Halifax (Washington) to F.O., 17/4/1946; F.O. to Washington, 26/4/1946; F.O.371/58906 R10729: Communiqué on the visit of the Greek Prime Minister in London, 17/7/1946; Soviet Foreign Ministry Archives: Greek-Soviet Relations 1944–1949, in P. Andaeos, *Nikos Zachariadis: Thytis ke Thyma* 2nd edn. (Athens: 1991), p.453.
102. F.O.371/58906 R10651: Hayter to Norton,19/7/1946; *ibid.*, R10890: Norton to F.O., 22/7/1946; *ibid.*, R11166: Norton to F.O., 27/7/1946.
103. N. Dodds, L. Solley, S. Tiffany, *Tragedy in Greece* (London: League for Democracy in Greece, 1946), p.61.
104. F.O.371/58698 R10234: F.O. Minute, 8–11/7/1946; HC Deb., vol. 426, col. 260 (Philip Noel-Baker, 1/8/1946).
105. F.O.371/67017 R2822: Report of the British Parliamentary Delegation to Greece (August 1946), 10/10/1946. Also in CAB 129/15/C.P. (46) 447.
106. *Rizospastis* (Athens): 21/8/1946.
107. *Rizospastis* (Athens): 3, 16 and 30/11/1946, 17/12/1946; F.O.371/67017 R399:

Norton to F.O., 9/1/1947.

108. F.O.371/67017 R399: Norton to F.O., 9/1/1947.

109. F.O.371/67017 R835: Tsaldaris to Seymour Cocks, 8/1/1947.

110. CAB 129/15/C.P.(46) 447: Memorandum by McNeil, 2/12/1946.

111. KKE (es.) Archives, *Avgi* (Athens): 2/12/1979: Zachariadis's telegram to Dimitrov, 29/8/1946.

112. *Ibid.*, KKE Memorandum to the fraternal parties, 29/8/1946.

113. *Ibid.*, Zachariadis's telegram to Dimitrov, 30/8/1946; Ioannidis to Zachariadis, 10/11/1946.

114. *Ibid.*, Ioannidis to Chervenkov, 21/11/1946.

115. *Ibid.*, Zachariadis to Ioannidis, 31/12/1946.

116. Soviet Foreign Ministry Archives: Greek-Soviet Relations 1944–1949, in P. Andaeos, *op.cit.*, pp.453–4.

117. KKE (es.) Archives, *Avgi* (Athens): 5/12/1979: KKE Memorandum to the CPs of the USSR, Yugoslavia and Bulgaria, 12/9/1946.

118. M. Vafiadis, *Apomnimonevmata* V, 135–7; *Rizospastis* (Athens): 16/11/1946.

119. FRUS (1946): VII, 268: MacVeagh to Secretary of State, 23/11/1946.

120. KKE (es.) Archives, *Avgi* (Athens): 2/12/1979: Ioannidis to Zachariadis, 10/11/1946.

121. CAB 129/10/C.P. (46) 213: Bevin's Memorandum, 'Greece', 30/5/1946; CAB 128/5/C.M. 54 (46), 3/6/1946. The initial arrangement on the Greek army in W.O. 202/892: File BMM 51/5/G, June 1945.

122. F.O.371/58701 R11542: Minute by Hayter, 20/7/1946.

123. F.O.371/58851 R14368: Norton to F.O., 25/9/1946; *ibid.*, R14730: Norton to F.O., 4/10/1946.

124. F.O.371/58714 R16360: Report by Joint Planning Staff, 6/11/1946. The COS adopted the Report on 13/11/1946.

125. F.O.371/58708 R13858: Minute by Bevin, 17/9/1946; H. Dalton, *op.cit.*, p.171.

126. F.O.371/58890 R17285: Warner to F.O., 25/11/1946; F.O. 371/58710 R14984: Minute by Selby, 16/10/1946; F.O.371/59712 R15733: Minute by Warner, 20/10/1946.

127. F.O.371/58716 R17463: Memorandum by McNeil to Sargent, 29/11/1946.

128. *The Times* (London): 18/11/1946.

129. HC Deb., vol.430, cols.529, 530.

130. *Ibid.*, col.531.

131. For the whole debate see *ibid.*, cols.525–94; *The Times* (London): 18 and 19/11/1946.

132. Bevin Papers: F.O.800/475/ME/46/22: Attlee's letter to Bevin, 1/12/1946.

133. F.O.371/58659 R17594: Minute by McNeil, 2/12/1946.

134. Bevin Papers: F.O. 800/468/GRE/46/39: McNeil to Bevin, 4/12/1946.

135. Bevin Papers: F.O. 800/468/GRE/46/40: Bevin to McNeil, 5/12/1946.

136. F.O.371/58891 R17677: Bevin to F.O., 6/12/1946; F.O.371/58892 R18531: Interview between the Secretary of State and M. Tsaldaris on December 6th, 1946.

137. F.O.371/58891 R17689: Bevin to F.O., 7/12/1946.

138. F.O.371/58892 R18531: Interview between the Secretary of State and M. Agnidis on December 7th; F.O.371/58891 R18129: Warner to Williams, 11/12/1946.

139. F.O.371/58891 R18129: Record of Conversation between the Secretary of State and M. Molotov on Monday 9th December 1946; Minutes of Conference between Bevin and Byrnes, 9/12/1946; Note by Dixon, 10/12/1946.

140. F.O.371/58891 R18129: Minute by McCarthy, 19/12/1946.
141. A. Bullock, *Ernest Bevin: Foreign Secretary 1945–1951* (Oxford: 1985), p.340.
142. Bevin Papers: F.O.800/475/ME/46/24: Note by Dixon, 9/12/1946.
143. F.O.371/58716 R17687: Montgomery to COS, 2/12/1946.
144. F.O.371/58718 R18419: Minutes of COS, 11/12/1946.
145. F.O.371/66996 R532: Memorandum by Williams, n.d. See also F.O.371/ 58659 R18501: Draft Brief for the Foreign Secretary, by M.S. Williams, 26/12/1946.
146. F.O.371/58717 R17830: Minute by Williams, 12/12/1946; *ibid.*, R18152: Minute by Williams, 24/12/1946; F.O. to Norton, 25/12/1946; *ibid.*, R17830: Norton to F.O., 2 8/12/1946; F.O.371/58715 R17200: Norton to F.O., 27/11/1946.
147. F.O.371/58717 R17830: Minutes by Williams (12/12/1946), Warner (15/12/1946), McNeil (17/12/1946).
148. *Rizospastis* (Athens): 20/12/1946.
149. Bevin Papers: F.O.800/502/SU/47/2: Near Eastern Policy, Broad Conclusions of the Chiefs of Staff and of the Imperial Defence College, 5/1/1947. See also CAB 131/4/D.O. (47) 23: Memorandum by the COS, 7/3/1947; Lord Montgomery, *The Memoirs of Field-Marshal The Viscount Montgomery of Allamein* (London: 1958), pp.435–6.
150. Bevin Papers: F.O.800/476/ME/47/1: Attlee to Bevin, Near Eastern Policy, 5/1/1947.
151. Bevin Papers: F.O. 800/476/ME/47/2: Note by Dixon, 5/1/1947.
152. Bevin Papers: F.O.800/476/ME/47/4: Bevin to Attlee, 9/1/1947.
153. Bevin Papers: F.O.800/476/ME/47/5: Note by Dixon, 9/1/1947; A. Bullock, *op.cit.*, p.354; J. Darwin, *Britain and Decolonisation: The Retreat from Empire in the Post-War World* (London: 1988), p.77.
154. Lord Montgomery, *op.cit.*, p.436.
155. J.Gallagher, *The Decline,Revival and Fall of the British Empire* (London: 1982), pp.149–50.
156. *Ibid.*, p.128.
157. J.L. Gaddis, *The Long Peace*, p.21; G. Barraclough, *An Introduction to Contemporary History* (London: 1967), p.42.
158. F.O.371/58698 R9905: Norton to F.O., 19/6/1946; *ibid.*, R10223: Norton to F.O., 8/7/1946; EPSV (1946):127 (21/6–31/7/1946), 301–2.
159. UNO, *Official Records of the Security Council*, 1st Year, 2nd Series, Supplement no.5, p.149; FRUS (1946): VII, 197–200: Clayton to Johnson, 5/9/1946; *ibid.*, 202–4: Clayton to Johnson, 7/9/1946; *ibid.*, 207–8: Memorandum of Conversation between Cadogan and Johnson, 8/9/1946; *ibid.*, 220–1: Johnson to Byrnes, 19/9/1946; UNO, *op.cit.*, nos 4–16, pp.33–422 *passim*.
160. F.O.371/58711 R15177: Norton to F.O., 10/10/1946; FRUS (1946): VII, 224: MacVeagh to Byrnes, 24/9/1946.
161. FRUS (1946): VII, 233–5: MacVeagh to Byrnes, 11/10/1946.
162. MVR, pp.703–5: MacVeagh to Cannon, 14/10/1946.
163. F.O.371/58712 R15607: Norton to F.O., 24/10/1946; *ibid.*, R15713: Norton to F.O., 26/10/1946; F.O.371/58714 R16408: Weekly Report by Norton, 27/10– 2/11/1946.
164. C. Sulzberger, *op.cit.*, p.301.
165. F.O.371/58713 R16018: Norton to F.O., 2/11/1946; *ibid.*, R16021: Norton to F.O., 3/11/1946.

166. EPSV (1946): 128 (1/10/1946–27/2/1947), pp.656–67 (6/11/1946).

167. F.O.371/67007 R16571: Norton to Attlee, 9/11/1946; F.O. 371/58710 R14870: Norton to Bevin, 2/10/1946.

168. EPSV (1946): 128, p.724; *Rizospastis* (Athens): 13/12/1946.

169. F.O.371/67075 R339, R488, R1101: British Consulate-General (Thessaloniki) to Athens, 1/1/1947, 11/12/1946, 1–15/1/1947; *ibid.*, R1719: Norton to F.O., 5/2/1947; F.O.371/58941 R17739: Norton to Warner, 3/12/1946; FRUS (1946): VII, 261–2: MacVeagh to Byrnes, 5/11/1946.

170. F.O.371/58891 R18181: Letter from the Acting Chairman of the Delegation of Greece to the Secretary-General, 3/12/1946, and enclosed Memorandum.

171. F.O.371/66994 R33: Interview between Harvey and Agnidis, 28/12/1946.

172. F.O.371/66994 R77: Inverchapel to F.O., 1/1/1947.

173. F.O.371/66994 R143: Norton to Bevin, 28/12/1946.

174. F.O.371/66994 R113: Norton to F.O., 2/1/1947.

175. F.O.371/66994 R113: Norton to F.O., 8/1/1947; F.O.371/66995 R460: Norton to F.O., 11/1/1947.

176. F.O.371/66995 R460: Norton to F.O., 10/1/1947; F.O.371/66996 R517: Lascelles to Bevin, 13/1/1947.

177. F.O.371/66997 R856: Lascelles to Bevin, 20/1/1947.

178. FRUS (1947): V, 9–11: Marshall to Athens, 21/1/1947.

179. F.O.371/66997 R1029: Lascelles to F.O., 23/1/1947; *ibid.*, R1094: Lascelles to F.O., 24/1/1947; *ibid.*, R1032: Lascelles to F.O., 24/1/1947; F.O.371/72240 R2576: Norton to Bevin, 18/2/1948, Annual report for 1947.

180. *Rizospastis* (Athens): 24, 25 and 29/1/1947; F.O.371/66997 R1138: Lascelles to F.O., 25/1/1947; F.O.371/66998 R1514: Norton to F.O., 3/2/1947; *ibid.*, R1515: Norton to F.O., 3/2/1947.

181. HC Deb., vol.427, col. 1498 (22/10/1946).

182. EPSV (1946–47): 128 (1/10/1946–27/2/1947), pp.931–3: statements by the Liberal deputy leader Konstantinos Rendis, 23/1/1947.

183. F.O.371/66998 R1190: Lascelles to F.O., 27/1/1947; *ibid.*, R1246: Lascelles to F.O., 28/1/1947; F.O.371/66999 R1613: Lascelles to F.O., 30/1/1947; F.O.371/66994 R185: F.O. to Dominions, 29/1/1947; EPSV (1946–1947): 128, pp.936–9.

184. EPSV (1946–47): 128, pp.941, 1012–20; F.O.371/66999 R1809: Norton to Bevin, 5/2/1947; *ibid.*,R1660: Norton to F.O., 5/2/1947; *ibid.*, R1676: Norton to F.O., 5/2/1947; F.O.371/66998 R1218: Lascelles to F.O., 28/1/1947.

185. EPSV (1946–1947): 128, p.1008.

186. DSE Archives, *Eleftherotypia* (Athens), 21/4/1986: Open Letter from Yiannoulis to Dragoumis, 27/1/1947.

187. GES/DIS, *O Ellinikos Stratos kata ton Antisymmoriakon agona (1946–1949): To Proton Etos tou Antisymmoriakou agonos, 1946* (Athens: 1971), pp.65–6; Th. Tsakalotos, *Saranda Chronia Stratiotis tis Ellados* II (Athens:1960), 51; D. Zafiropoulos, *O Antisymmoriakos Agon* (Athens: 1956), p.66

188. F.O.371/67075 R3419: British Vice-Consulate (Kavala) to HM Consul-General (Thessaloniki), 7/3/1947; F.O.371/72240 R2576: Norton to Bevin, 18/2/1948, Annual report for 1947; M. Vafiadis, *Apomnimonevmata* V, 162.

189. GES/DIS, *op.cit.*, p.61, 63; Th. Tsakalotos, *op.cit.* II, 47; D. Zafiropoulos, *op.cit.*, pp.178, 183, 187; F.O.371/58851 R13458: Norton to F.O., 9/9/1946; *ibid.*, R13488: Norton to F.O., 27/9/1946; F.O.371/58698 R10197: Norton to F.O., 9/7/1946; F.O.371/58851 R13981: Land Forces (Greece) to W.O., 16/9/1946.

190. D. Zafiropoulos, *op.cit.*, pp.201–2: Report of B Army Corps (no.251), 15/2/1947; FRUS (1947): V, 27–8: MacVeagh to Marshall, 19/2/1947.

191. F.O.371/58852 R18476: Clark to F.O., 27/12/1946; F.O.371/72240 R2576: Norton to Bevin, 18/2/1948: Annual Report for 1947.

192. FRUS (1946): VII, 190–1: Acheson to MacVeagh, 14/8/1946; *ibid.*, 201–2: Acheson to MacVeagh, 7/9/1946.

193. *Ibid.*, 263–4: MacVeagh to Byrnes, 13/11/1946; F.O.371/58891 R17508: Norton to F.O., 3/12/1946.

194. FRUS (1946): VII, 282–283: MacVeagh to Byrnes, 14 and 16/12/1946; *ibid.*, 286–8: Byrnes to MacVeagh, 3/1/1947; J. Jones, *The Fifteen Weeks (February 21–June 5, 1947)* (New York: 1955), p.75; D. Acheson, *Present at the Creation* (New York: 1969), p.199.

195. F.O.371/58718 R18543: Inverchapel to F.O., 28/12/1946; FRUS (1946): VII, 285–286: Acheson to MacVeagh, 28/12/1946.

196. Documentation in FRUS (1946):VII. See also L.S. Wittner, *American Intervention in Greece, 1943–1949* (New York: 1982), pp.36–69; H. Jones, '*A New Kind of War*': *America's Global Strategy and the Truman Doctrine in Greece* (New York: 1989), pp.17–35; W. Loth, *op.cit.*, pp.134–42.

197. F.O.371/58710 R14984: Minute by Selby, 16/10/1946; F.O. 371/58712 R15733: Minute by Warner, 20/10/1946; F.O.371/58658 R15570: F.O. to Washington, 24/10/1946; FRUS (1946): VII, 235–7: Acheson to MacVeagh, 15/10/1946.

198. FRUS (1946): VII, 240–245: Memorandum by the Office of Near Eastern and African Affairs, 21/10/1946; *ibid.*, 257: Byrnes to MacVeagh, 31/10/1946; *ibid.*, 278: Acheson to MacVeagh, 11/12/1946.

199. F.O.371/66994 R78: F.O. Minute, 3/1/1947; FRUS (1947): V, 1–2 Memorandum of Conversation between Byrnes and Inverchapel, 4/1/1947.

200. FRUS (1947): V, 20: Porter to Clayton, 17/2/1947.

201. P. Porter, 'Wanted: A Miracle in Greece', *Collier's* no. 120 (20/9/1947), 14–15, 106–7.

202. In Porter Papers (Truman Library), quoted by L.S. Wittner, *op.cit.*, p.69.

203. F.O.371/67034 R3055: Norton to F.O., 6/3/1947; L.S. Wittner, *op.cit.*, p.69.

204. FRUS (1947): V, 16–17: MacVeagh to Marshall, 11/2/1947; *ibid.*, 28–9: MacVeagh to Marshall, 20/2/1947; *ibid.*, 29–31: Acheson to Marshall, 21/2/1947.

205. CAB 128/6/C.M. 66 (46): 8/7/1946; F.O. 371/58698 R10235: F.O. Minute, 8–11/7/1946; F.O.371/58708 R13858: Minute by Bevin, 17/9/1946.

206. Attlee Papers (Bodleian Library, Oxford): Box 49, Folios 86–91: Dalton to Attlee, 20/1/1947; H. Dalton, *op.cit.*, pp.193, 197.

207. CAB 129/16/C.P. (47) 34: Memorandum by Bevin, Policy Towards Greece and Turkey, 25/1/1947.

208. CAB 128/9/C.M. 14 (47): 30/1/1947.

209. FRUS (1947): V, 13–14: Gallman to Marshall, 31/1/1947.

210. F.O.371/67032 R1900: Norton to F.O., 5/2/1947.

211. F.O.371/67032 R2443: Memorandum by Dalton to Attlee, 11/2/1947.

212. F.O.371/67032 R2440: Dalton to Bevin, 13/2/1947; Bevin to Dalton, 15/2/1947; *ibid.*, R2443: Minute by Bevin, n.d.

213. Bevin Papers: F.O.800/468/GRE/47/2: Memorandum by Bevin, 18/2/1947; F.O.371/67032 R2442: Minute by Bevin, 18/2/1947.

214. F.O.371/67033 R2969: Bevin to Inverchapel, 19/2/1947.

215. F.O.371/67032 R2629: Minutes by Williams and Sargent, 22/2/1947; F.O.371/72240 R2576: Norton to Bevin, 18/2/1948, Annual Report for 1947.

216. FRUS (1947): V, 32–37: British Embassy to State Department, 21/2/1947; F.O.371/67032 R1900: F.O. to Washington, 21/2/1947.

217. FRUS (1947): V, 72: State Department to British Embassy, 1/3/1947; *ibid.*, 79–81, and F.O.371/67034 R3190: British Embassy to State Department, 4/3/1947; *ibid.*, 105: Memorandum of Conversation between Acheson and Inverchapel, 8/3/1947; *ibid.*, 116–17: Memorandum of Conversation between Acheson and Inverchapel, 14/3/1947; *ibid.*, 123–4: Gallman to Secretary of State, 17/3/1947.

218. F.O.371/67034 R2999: Minute by Sargent, 3/3/1947.

219. *Public Papers of the US Presidents: H.S. Truman* III (Washington: 1963), no.56: Special Message to the Congress on Greece and Turkey: The Truman Doctrine, March 12, 1947.

220. L.S. Wittner, *op.cit.*, pp.86–7. For the campaign to rally public support for the Truman Doctrine and the reactions to it see *ibid.*, pp.70–102.

221. *Public Papers of the US Presidents: H.S. Truman* III, no. 107; EPSV (1947): 130, pp.1421–2 (20/6/1947); *A Decade of American Foreign Policy: Basic Documents, 1941–49* (New York: 1950; reprinted: 1968), no.297; FRUS (1947): V, 215–16: Memorandum by Villard, 9/7/1946; *ibid.*, 219–24: Marshall to Griswold, 11/7/1947; *ibid.*, 279–80: Griswold to Marshall, 5/8/1947; *ibid.*, 378–80: Griswold to Marshall, 24/10/1947.

222. F.O.371/67119 R5211: Washington to F.O., 11/4/1947; F.O. 371/67102 R10370: Final Report of the British Economic Mission to Greece, 10/7/1947.

223. *Public Papers of the US Presidents: H.S. Truman* III, no. 57: Statement by the President Concerning Greek Reaction to His Message. March 15, 1947.

224. *Kathimerini* (Athens): 16/3/1947; *Vradyni* (Athens): 13/3/1947.

225. *To Vima* (Athens): 14/3/1947.

226. *Rizospastis* (Athens): 14/3/1947. See also O.L. Smith, 'KKE Reactions to the Truman Doctrine', *Journal of Modern Hellenism* 5 (1988), 1–8.

227. *Rizospastis* (Athens): 23 and 28/3/1947.

228. H. Dalton, *op.cit.*, p.209.

229. On the concept of the 'new kind of war' see H. Jones, *op.cit.*, pp.3–16, 36–62, 123–39, 214–36.

230. F.O.371/65782A UN2001: Memorandum by Jebb, 19/3/1947; McNeil to Jebb, 19/3/1947; Minutes by Warner (25/3/1947) and Balfour (19/4/1947); Lord Gladwyn, *The Memoirs of Lord Gladwyn* (London: 1972), pp.200–202.

231. F.O.371/67034 R3038: Inverchapel to F.O., 6/3/1947.

232. F.O.371/67001 R2810: Norton to F.O., 1/3/1947.

233. F.O.371/67032 R2443: Dalton to Attlee, 21/2/1947.

234. N. Clive, 'British Policy Alternatives', in L. Baerentzen et al., eds., *op.cit.*, p.223.

235. CAB 128/9/C.M. 30 (47): 20/3/1947; FRUS (1947): V, 128–9: Memorandum of Conversation between Bevin and Marshall, Moscow, 22/3/1947.

236. Sargent Papers: F.O.800/276/GRE/47/1: Norton to Sargent, Personal, 7/3/1947.

237. F.O.371/67003 R6476: Norton to F.O., 8/5/1947; F.O.371/67145 R11452: Bevin (Paris) to F.O., 2/7/1947.

238. F.O.371/72240 R2576: Norton to Bevin, 18/2/1948: Annual Report for 1947.

IV Riding in 'Double Harness': 1947

The Melians to the Athenians

We see that you have come prepared to judge the
arguments yourselves ... If we surrender, then all
our hope is lost at once, whereas, so long as we
remain in action, there is still a hope that we may
yet stand upright ... We put our trust ... in the
help of men – that is of the Spartans.

Thucydides, V : 86, 102, 112

The United Nations Investigate: January–June 1947

The United Nations Commission arrived in Greece in January 1947 to
investigate the charges levelled by the Greek government against Yugoslavia,
Bulgaria and Albania for assisting the guerrillas of the Democratic Army. In
this context, the manipulation of its work by Britain and the United States was
instrumental in substituting the dogma of Soviet expansionism for the
overwhelmingly domestic origins of the Greek Civil War. For the Left, the
rekindling of its hopes for a peaceful settlement was evinced in Markos's order
to all units of the Democratic Army to facilitate the work of the Commission
and prepare memoranda on local conditions.[1] Yet to the US, British and
Greek governments the United Nations investigation afforded an opportunity
to forge evidence of Soviet designs and present the guerrillas as mercenaries of
foreign powers. The British stance towards the Commission would be crucial,
as the Foreign Office had since 1945 hoped that the United Nations
Organization could be used to inflate Britain's dwindling world power.[2] Such
aspirations ran counter to Attlee's pledge in November 1946, during the
debate on the foreign affairs amendment, that the Labour government was
anxious to co-operate with the Soviet Union and supported the UNO 'in the
interests of peace ... [and] prosperity for the whole ... of the world'.[3] In either
case, the aspirations of the Foreign Office and Attlee's professions would
have to be reconciled with the axiom that British policy in Greece had always
been sound.

On the eve of the Commission's arrival the KKE appealed in vain for the
participation of EAM in the government and the conduct of free elections.[4]
The Foreign Office continued to regard the Populists as 'somewhat reactionary by western standards', but the Embassy in Athens was sceptical about
the possibility of appeasing the communists. The Counsellor Daniel Lascelles
maintained that the aims of the KKE were totally incompatible with those of
all other Greek parties. Then, even if a compromise were achieved and the

guerrillas laid down their arms, no Greek government could guarantee their safety against reprisals, since the anti-communism of the army, the security forces and the provincial bureaucracy lay beyond the grip of any administration. A 'perfectly fair deal' with the KKE had to be ruled out, and the best that was to be expected of the Maximos government was that it might drive a wedge between the moderate Left and the communist die-hards and impose its authority on the latter by force.[5]

Zachariadis's cautious welcome of the UN Commission fell in a void. The Secretary-General of the KKE proclaimed that 'with the minimum objectivity and impartiality', its verdict would vindicate the Left, and along with the report of the British Parliamentary Delegation of August 1946, could assist towards a peaceful settlement.[6] His hope, however, rested on the premise that Greece's domestic situation fell within the Commission's terms of reference. This was to prove a major source of friction among its members. A more practical offer emerged on 19 January 1947, when the Central Committee of EAM proposed a truce during the presence of the Commission.[7] The British Embassy grasped the significant timing of the gesture. While negotiations were under way for a broader government, the truce offer appeared as a way out of the impasse, thus threatening to diminish the solidarity of the Populists and confirm Sofulis's faith in a peaceful solution. Lascelles, who was in favour of Tsaldaris's accepting it or at least exploring it further, voiced the British scepticism as to whether the government could ensure full respect for a truce:

> While Left-wing bands can, I think, be adequately controlled by [the] KKE because their fate depends on its backing, no single responsible authority controls Right-wing bands. Nor can these be entirely suppressed by force since the instruments of force at the State's disposal are for the most part strongly in sympathy with them.[8]

MacVeagh was less generous. The US ambassador justified his outright dismissal of the truce offer on the grounds that a positive response would prejudice the position of the Greek government; after all, he added, the DSE was no rebel army but 'merely criminals whom it is the duty of the state to suppress as such'.[9] Tsaldaris, determined to do nothing that might weaken the state in its struggle to impose its authority, rebuffed the offer as a sign of weakness on the part of the KKE.[10]

The UN Commission held its first meeting in Athens on 30 January 1947. Its eleven members represented Britain, the United States, the Soviet Union, France, China, Belgium, Syria, Poland, Colombia, Australia and Brazil. The familiar Richard Windle stood for Britain, while the US representative Mark Ethridge had been head of the delegation of American observers sent to Bulgaria and Rumania in 1945 to report on Soviet policies there. The Yugoslav and Bulgarian liaisons set the tone by insisting that since the Greek regime was responsible for the situation in the Balkans, the Commission should primarily inquire into conditions in Athens and southern Greece. EAM stepped up its anti-British propaganda by assuming responsibility for the appearance on the night of 30 January of the words 'The British Must Go' displayed in electric lights on the Acropolis.[11] The first source of friction occurred on 2 February, when the Secretariat of the Commission encouraged an urgent request from EAM for the suspension of death sentences. Ethridge 'unfortunately' supported it, thus incurring British charges that he tended to adopt 'the newspaper man's approach to the problem'.[12]

The appeal for the postponement of executions enraged the Greek government, but Marshall cabled MacVeagh that the Greeks should comply until the completion of the inquiry, otherwise world opinion would focus on the executions of political prisoners rather than on the border incidents.[13] On 9 February, following an appeal by the UN Secretary-General, the Greek government grudgingly gave in. Norton was dismayed, insisting that the task of the Commission was not to meddle in the 'Greek internal quarrel' in a manner prejudicial to the legitimate Greek government, but to investigate the charges of foreign intervention. With remarkable consistency, when the Greek authorities refused to permit an EAM rally in Athens the ambassador assured London that EAM planned to provoke incidents in the hope that the government's inevitable use of force would gravely embarrass it in the eyes of the Commission.[14]

For the private session of 10 February the Secretariat of the Commission had included in the agenda the question whether to consider an EAM communication regarding the proposed truce. Though Windle and Ethridge managed to remove it, the Foreign Office had already been ruffled by the 'improper activities' and 'bias' of the Secretariat and began to contemplate the possibility of changes in its personnel.[15] The British were convinced that the propaganda of EAM enjoyed the support of 'the Commission's Secretariat, whose head, a Norwegian, was too much in the hands of his principal assistant, a Polish Jew, and of his press officer, a Canadian national possibly of Russian origin.'[16] Norton was adamant that the 'insincere' truce offer, which implied that the 'rebels' were an 'entity' entitled to treatment 'on equal terms', aimed at putting the Greek government in an unfavourable light before the Commission; moreover, since immunity from private retribution was 'more than the best disposed government could guarantee', the Commission would find itself 'in deep waters' if it embarked on such an intermediary role. Accordingly, the ambassador submitted to London that it would be 'ill-advised' to suggest to the Greeks that a truce was feasible.[17]

The Southern Department of the Foreign Office had two good reasons for taking a less inflexible attitude. In mid-February 1947 the assumption of economic responsibility for Greece by the Americans had yet to be fully confirmed, while the British feared that the circumstances might force them to modify their Greek policy. Williams and Selby agreed that nothing should be done to eliminate the possibility of the Commission fulfilling an inter-mediary role, especially in the event that the United States was not prepared to 'take it on'. The British feared that the guerrillas might not be taken by force, in which case there should be an alternative means of restoring peace in Greece. If the Greek government had the necessary forces to suppress them, the idea of a truce was 'inappropriate'; but it might be better to reach a kind of *modus vivendi* with the guerrillas while it still had some forces rather than wait until the collapse of the army after the stoppage of British aid. Unaware of the

American preparedness to pick up the torch, Williams proposed to discuss with Norton the idea of a political settlement before entering into any discussions with Washington.[18]

In an attempt to find 'less sure but cheaper' means 'of maintaining Greek independence', the Southern Department asked Norton whether Greece might be placed under some United Nations trusteeship which would assume control of her economy and guarantee the inviolability of her frontier. The UN Department of the Foreign Office questioned the idea as impracticable, whilst Norton dismissed it as politically unfeasible. Unoriginally but consistently, the ambassador reasoned that since the quarrels among the Commission's members had already started, any UN body charged with the supervision of Greek domestic affairs would inevitably disintegrate into antagonistic factions based on rival ideologies.[19] This was enough to sway the Foreign Office, which, after all, had not been overwhelmed by a sudden bout of benevolence. It was a provisional inquiry into means of halting the advance of the KKE by diplomacy, prompted by the fear that the United States might decline to provide the money to do so by force of arms. Fortunately for the Foreign Office, the Truman Doctrine made any further inquiries superfluous.

In Athens, following an appeal by EAM, the Commission had decided to hear from its Central Committee and the Confederation of Trade Unions. This was a partial victory for Windle and Ethridge, as many other leftist organizations which had requested a hearing had been turned down. The difference of opinion as to the object of the inquiry was transparent. Norton found it best 'to hear EAM at once and get it over, while the Communist Trades Union Executive can probably be disposed of quickly as having little to say relevant to the inquiry'.[20] The Left insisted that the root of the evil lay at home. According to Michalis Kyrkos, leader of the EAM partner Democratic Radical Party, an EAM delegation sought Sofulis's opinion. The Liberal leader reportedly urged them to appear before the Commission with yet another onslaught on Tsaldaris: ' "Gentlemen, we shall not make Tsaldaris's case the case of Greece!" '.[21]

On 17 February 1947, speaking before the Commission on behalf of the Central Committee of EAM, Kyrkos put forward the KKE's familiar terms for pacification: Greek neutrality under the United Nations; withdrawal of the British troops; the participation of EAM in the government; cessation of hostilities; a general political amnesty; and dissolution of the Parliament and speedy elections. Interestingly enough, Zachariadis's proposal for neutrality was also there, though without any mention of guarantees for Greece's borders. This was the result of Soviet disapproval, already conveyed to the KKE leader in the previous year and now repeated on 5 February 1947, when he called on the Soviet ambassador in Athens to inform him of the EAM intention to reiterate his appeal.[22] Even more indicative of the disposition of the KKE was Zachariadis's statement that on the basis of prior agreement on the restoration of order and the conduct of free elections, the Left was prepared to entrust Sofulis with the 'leadership' and the 'initiative' for the solution of the Greek political problem.[23]

With Sofulis holding himself aloof from the communists, it was Venizelos who showed how far the other side could go. On 24 February Norton reported that the Vice-Premier sounded Windle and Ethridge on a pacification plan whereby the Democratic Army would lay down its arms to the Commission, with new polls following under the auspices of the latter. Although there was little common ground between the KKE terms and this scheme, the reasons for which Norton and Windle dismissed Venizelos's plan as impracticable betrayed a poor understanding of Greek realities. First, they feared that if charged with the task of dealing with the Greek question as a whole, the Commission would split into ideologically rival groups; then the guerrillas might surrender a small part of their arms, with the remainder concealed for future use; the inability of any government to halt the deeds of right-wing bands would enable the Left to charge the government with 'bad faith'; and the above problems could not be resolved even by new elections – a task for which the UN Commission was neither 'coherent' nor 'technically qualified'. In truth, however, the difficulty with Venizelos's scheme lay more in its similarity to the the Varkiza experience, which prompted the KKE's refusal to surrender its arms to a government that would not include EAM. Unable to grasp this, Norton confined himself to a jibe at Venizelos: 'It may be wondered how any responsible member of the present Government could seriously espouse such a scheme. I do not profess to know why M. Venizelos should do so; but unworkable and fantastic schemes are a feature of Greek political life.'[24]

Events were set to take their course in the battlefield when Norton's views were endorsed by Whitehall. In early March the British Cabinet decided that the campaign against the Democratic Army, scheduled to commence in April 1947, should be 'successfully carried through' as the 'necessary preliminary' to the restoration of order in Greece. The UN Commission was an 'unsuitable body' to indulge in mediatory activities, and Windle was instructed 'to confine them to the strict letter of their terms of reference'.[25] Even so, contacts among Greeks would resume, but this time under the inauspicious shadow of the Truman Doctrine.

Meanwhile the Commission moved to Thessaloniki to examine the situation in the north. There it found itself confronted with a row over whether to see Markos. The request of the DSE Commander was supported by the Labour MP George Thomas, who had spent a week with the guerrillas. Thomas did so much to the chagrin of the British Embassy (which noted that 'this irresponsible escapade did great harm to British prestige'), and the Greek government, which claimed that 'Markos should be examined in Yugoslav territory if at all'.[26] Despite Windle's dogged opposition, the Commission decided to send a team to meet Markos. Windle's only victory was the curious concession that if he failed to show up, no-one else would be interviewed.[27] The team set out from Thessaloniki on 12 March and two days later reached the village of Kastanofyto, twenty kilometres from the Greek-Albanian frontier, where Markos was expected to appear by 16 March. As he did not, at 7.30 a.m. that morning the team took the road back to Thessaloniki.[28] Although deliberate army operations may have impeded Markos, the main obstacle was the long distance between the meeting-point (arranged by the team) and his headquarters. Influenced by the propaganda that the guerrillas were marauding bandits from across the border and that their leaders were stationed on foreign soil, the UN investigators insisted on meeting Markos very near the Greek-Albanian frontier. Yet in an attempt to counter these slanders, towards the end of 1946 Markos had moved the General Headquarters of the Democratic Army right at the centre of Greece, in southern Thessaly. To have met there, he claimed, would have exposed the fallacy upon which the charges against his guerrillas were based.[29]

The Soviet and Polish members did not join the team but met Markos nearer to his Headquarters on 20 March. Two days later they returned to Thessaloniki with a long memorandum 'On the Causes of the Civil War and Our Opinion for its Cessation', addressed by the DSE GHQ to the Commission.[30] It was a memorable document, not for the familiar terms it proposed but because it featured an orderly record of the unravelling of the White Terror in the wake of the Varkiza Agreement. Classified according to regional DSE HQs, towns and villages, the memorandum is a detailed inventory of torture, terror, imprisonment and assassination of thousands of citizens, with full names, locations and descriptions of the sufferings provided. The eloquence of the total numbers – 1,059 murders, 9,809 cases of torture, 10,397 people imprisoned, 2,426 deported, 211 rapes – is only augmented by the fact that they refer to no more than one third of the prefectures of the Greek State.[31]

In early April 1947 the Commission moved to Geneva to draft its report, while the Security Council established a Subsidiary Group in Thessaloniki with identical terms of reference.[32] In Geneva the rift between communist and non-communist members of the Commission deepened. On 18 April the Soviet and Polish members requested the translation and circulation of the DSE memorandum. Windle's objection was brushed aside and it was decided by seven votes to four that the document should be translated and circulated. The Foreign Office was exasperated, for this appeared 'to give Markos and his organization a status which we have been concerned to deny them'. Another source of irritation was the attitude of Mark Ethridge, less dogmatic than Windle's and therefore 'most disappointing'. London asked Windle whether the American was likely to compromise on any important point in the report, so that the Foreign Office could take up the matter with Washington.[33]

Further complications arose when Windle complained at the emergence in the Commission of a '"centre bloc"'. This was championed by the Frenchman M. Daux, who held that the report should draw no conclusions, for it ought to avoid laying the blame on Albania, Yugoslavia and Bulgaria. The Foreign Office instructed its ambassador in Paris to 'persuade the French Government not to let their desire to sponsor satisfactory compromises override their judgement', and to order Daux to drop his 'manouevres'.[34] The State Department concurred with the British position that Daux's recommendations for an amnesty and new polls amounted to intervention in Greek domestic affairs and acceptance of the Soviet argument that the frontier troubles emanated from the internal situation in Greece.[35]

Then it was Ethridge's turn to show why the British had taken a dislike to him. On 2 May he circulated his draft recommendations which included an amnesty for guerrillas and political prisoners to be internationally supervised by a body set up by the Security Council.[36] The face value of this recommendation was insignificant. *Rizospastis* called it a 'diplomatic manoeuvre' because a general amnesty could only be the first measure to be taken by a government which would come after an understanding and a guarantee of Greek neutrality. None the less, the KKE daily swiftly picked up the point that the proposal implicitly recognized the domestic causes of the conflict.[37] Elsewhere the reaction to Ethridge's proposal was unanimously hostile. The State Department felt that a recommendation for an amnesty should not appear in the final report,[38] while Tsaldaris told Norton that he had 'no great faith' in a general amnesty because the DSE 'were acting under orders' from Moscow.[39]

The British were enraged. Norton charged that the Americans had 'got off to a bad start in Greece owing almost entirely to Mr. Ethridge's folly' – 'an absolute gift to the extreme Left'. Although according to the British ambassador the ideal solution would be a political one, in practice only a combination of political and military measures could work: 'Political appeasement ultimately depends on orders received by the Communist Party from the top. We have no (repeat no) indication that there is any softening there.'[40] In its anxiety to ensure that Ethridge's proposal would not be used as an indictment of the Greek government, the Foreign Office stated that Britain would welcome an amnesty 'consistent with the maintenance and improve-ment of public security'. Yet such a proposal should have no place in the Commission's report, thus Windle was instructed to secure its withdrawal or modification.[41]

The British eventually accepted a compromise worked out by the State Department. The Greeks should announce that they were considering a new amnesty so that the report could 'take note of it with satisfaction', but there would be no international supervision, as that would invite the participation of the Soviets or their friends. The Greek government should itself invite some other country not open to charges of partisanship to carry out this task. However, there was one qualification: the Greeks could make any renewed offers of amnesty dependent upon satisfactory steps being taken to seal the frontier against further incursions of guerrillas.[42] On 20 May the Greek government did this,[43] but the northern frontier was not sealed.

The Commission signed its report on 23 May 1947. The Soviet and Polish members rejected it, while their Colombian and Belgian colleagues appended their signatures with the reservation that since the Commission had a conciliatory role to perform, it should not itself pronounce a judgement on the extent of the northern neighbours' responsibility. Daux abstained for the same reason and because he doubted the wisdom of inquiring into particular events without extensive probing into the history of the Balkans since 1940. The report diagnosed that Yugoslavia and, to a lesser extent, Albania and Bulgaria, provided the guerrillas of the Democratic Army with refuge and material and moral support. The Yugoslav and Bulgarian governments were fomenting separatist movements in Macedonia, but it was also true that in the wake of the Varkiza Agreement of February 1945 more than

161

25,000 Greek citizens, many of them of Slavo-Macedonian origin, had fled to Yugoslavia and Bulgaria owing to discriminatory treatment on the part of the Greek state.

The Commission felt that Greece's domestic situation could not be ignored. The persecution of minorities and opposition groups since early 1945 had forced thousands to take to the mountains or seek refuge across the frontier, where they formed groups actively opposed to the Greek regime. Yugoslav, Bulgarian and Albanian responsibilities notwithstanding, the policies of the Greek government and the disturbed conditions within the country were factors which helped to explain – and thus bore an indirect relation to – the situation along Greece's northern border. Yet these matters fell outside the Commission's terms of reference, hence the recommendations dealt with the differences between Greece and her Balkan neighbours.[44]

The story at the Security Council was predictable. The consideration of the report commenced on 27 June 1947 with the lead in American hands. When successive Soviet vetoes prevented the adoption of US resolutions embodying the Commission's recommendations, the Americans referred the matter to the General Assembly. On 21 October 1947 the General Assembly adopted a US resolution calling Yugoslavia, Albania and Bulgaria to stop aiding the DSE, and established the United Nations Special Committee on the Balkans (UNSCOB) to observe their compliance with the recommendations.[45]

The work of the UN Commission in Greece affords a good insight into how in its early days the role of the United Nations was undermined by the exigencies of the Cold War. In the wake of the Truman Doctrine, when it was imperative to give every possible support to the policy of moral and material opposition to Communism, the Americans ensured that the activities of the United Nations in Greece fell in line with, and essentially complemented, their intervention in that country. If that was to be expected of the Truman administration, the British for their part looked more Catholic than the Pope. Even Mark Ethridge grasped that Greek domestic affairs had to be taken into account, whereas Windle typified the British concern to justify their own policy, apportion blame exclusively on the northern neighbours, and avoid an indictment of the Greek government. The British attitude was determined by the conviction that behind the KKE lay Stalin. In typical fashion, on 19 June 1947 Bevin told the House of Commons that

in Greece, we all know – why disguise it? – that with the lift of the finger the civil war would stop tomorrow … If the tip were given – if only the tip were given – that it had to stop, then Greece could settle down, and carry out her own political settlement without interference. I am as certain of it as I am of standing here.[46]

Bevin's exuberant oversimplification that the Greek communists were puppets of the Kremlin contrasted sharply with two crucial facts: the KKE's defiance of the Soviet advice to participate in the elections of March 1946 and its paternity of the decision to embark on guerrilla warfare, which was only subsequently endorsed by Stalin, Dimitrov and Tito. It was the growing propensity for discerning Soviet designs at every corner, and the concern to protect the tenet that their policy in Greece had been correct, which accounted for the British refusal to recognize the predominantly domestic causes of the Greek question. Accordingly, the Foreign Office regarded the UN Commission as an unsuitable body for mediatory activities and was annoyed when some of its members took a less dogmatic attitude.

Perhaps unwittingly, however, when the British rejected the EAM truce offer they implicitly conceded a fundamental cause of the civil strife in Greece. They argued that a compromise would be unworkable in the face of the anti-communism of the army, the security forces and the provincial bureaucracy, but these had been features of Greek politics long before mid-1947. The admission that the right-wing bands would be reluctant to contribute to an understanding came belatedly, for these bands had also been operative long before mid-1947. In view of their attitude towards the White Terror since 1945, it is astonishing that two years later the British felt so few inhibitions in admitting the potential for – and tacitly the extent of – right-wing repression. But now there was no harm in doing so, since they maintained that the Soviets were to blame for the entire situation. Hence they decided that the guerrillas should be dealt with by the Greek army. In considering alternatives, in June 1947 Norton ruled out both a direct understanding with the Kremlin and the despatch of US troops to Greece; instead he proposed action by the United Nations to prevent or curb the volume of foreign assistance to the Democratic Army.[47] Pending that, the ambassador subscribed to the American line for the conduct of military operations

> combined with the encouragement of the Greek government to hold out a
> somewhat vague olive branch.[48]

By and large it was in this direction that events would unfold in the next three years. One difference was that the olive branches would be held out mostly by the Greek Left. Another was that they were not all that vague.

Military Operations and Olive Branches (I)

Britain's conduct in the UN Commission offered ample evidence of her sustained interest and involvement in Greece in the wake of the Truman Doctrine. Besides, even had the Labour government wished to retain a low profile or dissociate itself, the escalation towards full-scale civil war and the emergence of surreptitious overtures for a political settlement made that impossible. In 1947 both the KKE and the Greek government hardened their stance and marched to the battlefield, while secretly wooing each other with an eye on a compromise. The British would be watching as closely and anxiously as ever.

From January to April 1947 the KKE continued to call for Greek neutrality, an understanding based on the proposals of the British Parliamentary Delegation of August 1946 and an 'objective' report by the UN Commission, the participation of EAM in the government, and free polls.[49] What *Rizospastis* could not have mentioned is that in mid-February the Politburo decided that while still trying to take full advantage of all legal

163

possibilities, priority should be given to the armed struggle. The only mention of this decision is found in a memorandum dated 13 May 1947 and addressed by Zachariadis to Stalin,[50] but soon the KKE leader embarked on a course which testified to a change in party tactics. In January he appealed to Stalin for economic aid, and by early February the first instalment was on its way; even the British Communist Party offered the symbolic sum of £100.[51] By early spring the KKE seemed confident that substantial quantities of military equipment were forthcoming from the fraternal states. In an article in *Rizospastis* on 4 April Zachariadis hinted that the party would toughen its stance because the intransigence of the government left no other option but a 'dynamic confrontation'.[52]

On the government side the hardened attitude was evinced in further purges of actual or presumed leftists from the civil service and Populist agitation for action against the KKE leaders. The zestful activity and 'unduly severe' sentences meted out by the Courts Martial had 'disconcerted' the Foreign Office, which contemplated a joint Anglo-American recommendation to Athens.[53] Repression intensified in late February, when, contrary to British wishes, Zervas once more took over as Minister of Public Order. The number of death sentences decreed in January–March (34) tripled in April–May (100), while on 4 March Zervas issued personal orders for the arrest and deportation of 550 people from the Athens area suspected of assisting the Democratic Army.[54]

British embarrassment and unease increased when it became fashionable to demonstrate severed heads of guerrillas in the squares of towns and monarchist bands levied their own taxes from local villages.[55] In spring 1947 the Greek authorities indicated that the former ELAS Commander Stefanos Sarafis, deported since September 1946, would be brought to trial for collaboration. British opinion recalled that 'the tradition of shooting Generals is well established in Greece', and the Embassy in Athens regarded the specific charge 'ridiculous'. The Greek Justice Ministry grasped the nonsensical nature of its aspiration and indicated that the trial would be dropped.[56] Finally, a motion by some Populist deputies to ban the KKE was aborted by Norton and MacVeagh for fear of the impact of such a step on world opinion.[57]

More evidence of the government's hardened attitude lay in the launching of the first large-scale campaign against the guerrillas. The Democratic Army had by June increased its ranks to nearly 20,000, but Zachariadis appealed to Moscow that arms were needed to equip the volunteers.[58] The gradualist approach to the armed struggle meant that the party masses remained in the towns to pursue legal activities, hence the DSE consisted mainly of peasants. Yet it was probably the shortage of equipment which accounts for the fact that at least until March 1947 even in the villages most men had not as yet been recruited. According to Mrs. Fothergill-Payne, a member of the UN Commission team which tried to contact Markos, this was 'very noticeable'. On the other hand, she was surprised to see many young girls in the DSE ranks:

> When asked why they were in the army they replied that their mothers were serving in other units and their fathers and brothers were either exiled

or in prison so that there was nothing left for them to do but join the army. The average age of these girls was eighteen ... The majority of them said they did not like fighting; all admitted they had killed men in order to get their uniforms and weapons, and said they would have to continue fighting until Greece was rid of foreigners.

Mrs. Fothergill-Payne added incredulously: 'The idea was apparently to impress upon us that they were all Greek nationalists who did not want to see their frontiers changed.'[59]

Those men and women would not be available for too long, as the government embarked on two measures which would have far-reaching repercussions for the Democratic Army. In February 1947 the Chief of the Greek General Staff recommended the establishment of three camps for leftist conscripts, suspect men and women, and prisoners. According to General Zafiropoulos, from 1947 to 1950 Makronisos, by far the most gruesome of the three, accommodated some 1,100 reservist officers and 27,700 conscripts who could not be counted upon to perform 'the duty to the Nation'.[60] Then, on 16 February, *Rizospastis* reported that the Prefect and Gendarmerie Commander of the district of Veroia ordered the evacuation of three villages because, according to the KKE daily, their inhabitants were 'democrats'. By August 1947 the British Embassy spoke of 'at least 200,000 refugees, some thousands of whom had been obliged to leave their villages by the Government forces in order to deny supplies to the rebels' and 'prevent them from assisting the bandits'. This economically disastrous policy caused widespread bitterness and despondency but succeeded in depriving the KKE of much-needed manpower.[61]

The first large-scale operations against the Democratic Army, planned as a result of Field-Marshal Montgomery's visit to Athens in December 1946, commenced in April 1947. The British Commander of the Imperial General Staff was one of the prime movers of the offensive, as he had 'expressed the strong view that all available Greek armed forces should at once be set to the task of stamping out the bandits in Northern Greece'.[62] Moving from central Greece to the north, the army tried to encircle and eliminate regional guerrilla units, but with little success. The mobile DSE formations, assisted by their excellent intelligence networks, avoided the encircling drives, pursued diversionary operations, and managed to threaten the towns of Konitsa and Ioannina. By late August 1947 the fatigue of the troops and the need to divert units to central Greece to counter regional DSE activity forced the government to abandon the main operation against the guerrillas' stronghold on Mount Grammos.[63] The abortive outcome of the campaign, the Anglo-American representations for some leniency towards leftists, and Ethridge's recommendation for an amnesty undermined the morale of the army and led to impatient appeals from the Greek government to be allowed to take tougher measures.[64]

If the campaign against the DSE in April 1947 showed that the government was to escalate the civil strife into a fully-fledged confrontation, at the same time Zachariadis steered the KKE towards civil war. In the wake of the mid-

February decision that priority should be given to the armed struggle, he set out to define the strategy of the Democratic Army and adjust its tactics. On 17 April 1947 he instructed Markos that in order to 'liberate Greece from foreign occupation and monarchofascism', the DSE should be transformed into a regular army and prepare for positional warfare aimed at the establishment of a free area on the mountains and in districts of political and economic importance. The DSE should work out a competent plan and solve its manpower problems so as to build up an experienced force which would carry out a surprise attack and occupy Thessaloniki.[65]

It was a calculated risk prompted by the frustration of Zachariadis's dual strategy. The lack of response to the KKE offers for pacification meant that the defensive armed struggle aiming at a compromise had reached a dead end. From then on the only alternative to capitulation was the escalation of violence and the creation of the second *fait accompli* – after that of early 1946 – in the hope that the Soviet Union would grant the necessary wholesale assistance. Yet for Stalin the desirable objective of reducing British influence in the eastern Mediterranean was not one to be pursued at the cost of risking a clash with the West and jeopardizing Soviet gains in eastern Europe. No doubt the prospect of a powerful KKE gradually advancing itself to a position of power in a perpetually unstable Greek state was attractive, but an all-out insurrection would hardly serve the prime concern of Soviet foreign policy.[66] Had he wished to bring Greece into the Soviet orbit, Stalin would already have furnished the KKE with the essentials; but as he had failed to do this, Zachariadis took a calculated risk. The thrust towards full-scale civil war would create the second *fait accompli* and present Stalin with the stark dilemma – either to turn his back on the KKE, risking its physical extermination and the loss of any foothold in Greece, or to endorse the KKE militancy and then proceed in such a manner as to prevent it from sparking off a wider conflagration. The unfolding of events suggests that he opted for the latter, whilst simultaneously trying to achieve a political settlement of the Greek conflict.

Until the end of April 1947 Zachariadis dwelled in Athens as leader of the legally functioning KKE. It was a further indication of its disposition that until then the party had declined to take an official position towards the Democratic Army, and that *Rizospastis* reported its activities as those of armed persecuted citizens. This, Zachariadis argued most implausibly, was in order not to vindicate the allegations of the British and the Greek governments that the armed struggle was organized and directed by the KKE.[67] However, on 21 April 1947 the KKE leader crossed the border and met with Tito to inform him of the reorientation of party policy and the requirements for its success; the DSE should reach a ceiling of 50,000, while in the towns of the areas to be attacked armed insurrections must be organized from within.[68]

Since the real mine of the desired aid was the Soviet Union, in May Zachariadis went to Moscow to take up the matter with Stalin, Molotov and Zhdanov. The evidence available strongly suggests that there the KKE leader secured promises of substantial military and political support. In a memorandum to Stalin, dated 13 May 1947, Zachariadis mentioned the decision for priority to the armed struggle and repeated his terms for pacification: a new government including EAM, a general amnesty, a truce, free polls, and a guarantee of Greek neutrality under United Nations auspices. In all probability, the new tactics were endorsed by Stalin, for on 4 June Ioannidis cabled the Politburo section in Athens: 'In recent weeks Cuckoo [Zachariadis] met with Grandfather [Stalin] and our issues were effectively discussed. From the results of these talks we must be entirely satisfied.'[69] Nineteen years later, in 1966, Zachariadis himself hinted that the Soviet leadership had endorsed his plans and promised him ample support. In denouncing Otto Kuusinen – the Comintern veteran and member of the CPSU Politburo who had presided over his demotion in 1956–1957 on a number of charges including the 'adventurous' and 'opportunistic' policy of 1946–1949 – he wrote:

Also on the question of the armed struggle [of] 1946–49 Kuusinen demonstrates the same political immorality, for he knows very well what was discussed and decided in Moscow in June 1947 in the Politburo of the CPSU in the presence of Stalin etc. (plus [Mikhail] Suslov).[70]

The very least to be derived from the evidence is that Stalin raised no objections to the KKE plans and that Zachariadis left Moscow with the impression that he could go ahead. Thus in early June he returned to Belgrade, from where he sent a reminder to the Soviets that the KKE needed urgent material assistance. He also informed them that the Politburo member Miltiadis Porfyrogenis would soon go to Moscow.[71]

Meanwhile in Athens there were indications that each side entertained some qualms about the escalation of violence, for once more feelers were being put out about a compromise. After indirect contacts between Venizelos's party and the KKE, on 20–22 April 1947 the Prime Minister Maximos requested a formal note with the terms of the Left. The Athens section of the Politburo suspected the government of trying to present the KKE as intransigent and justify further repressive measures. From Belgrade Ioannidis cabled that 'there is no reason today to retreat from [the] basic preconditions we put for [the] clear-up of [the] situation'.[72] However, on 24 April EAM submitted to Maximos the memorandum the Premier had asked for. The prerequisite for a peaceful settlement was the ending of foreign intervention, which Britain and the United States justified by way of an imaginary threat to Greek independence. To allay such fears EAM reiterated the proposal for Greek neutrality, accompanied by guarantees for her integrity and independence; once the 'national interests' had thus been secured, the question would become 'purely political' and could be settled by negotiations among Greeks.[73]

In this memorandum, to which no official reaction is recorded, the KKE adhered to its long-standing terms. These made sense as a guarantee for the observance of a would-be new Varkiza Agreement, and as the only means of eliminating the Anglo-American presence, which for the Left was one of the main causes of the conflict. The motivation of Maximos and Venizelos is less clear. The Prime Minister appears to have put out feelers on EAM even before mid-March, but the Truman Doctrine must have put an end to his ability or will to manoeuvre.[74] Being less hot-headed than the Populists, Maximos and

Venizelos may have felt some curiosity as to whether and how a settlement could be achieved. Whatever their reaction to the EAM terms, the task of selling any package to the Populists, the British and the Americans remained a grim one. The cynical interpretation that the government aimed to distract the attention of the Left from the military campaign which had just started cannot be documented; besides, the fact that Venizelos was to pursue his efforts in May suggests that some opponents of the KKE were persistently inquisitive.

The attention of the British was drawn to the possibility of a compromise in early May, when the EAM Macedonia-Thrace Bureau publicly appealed for a 'special conference' to find 'drastic remedies' which would bring the civil war to an end. The Foreign Office considered the appeal 'well-drafted' and 'reasonable' but could not overcome its mistrust of the KKE. McCarthy minuted that 'knowing the policy of those who run EAM we cannot attach any reliance to it, and I do not think, unless EAM lay down their arms, that we could advise the Greek Government to act on it'. Selby dismissed it as 'another EAM propaganda stunt'.[75] The Foreign Office clerks acted in accordance with the decision of their government that since the defeat of the guerrillas was the 'necessary preliminary' to the restoration of order, the military operations should be 'successfully carried through'. The matter was not taken higher because Britain and the United States insisted on military operations accompanied by a 'somewhat vague olive branch' from the Greek government.[76]

Venizelos came back with something more than this. In mid-May he proposed to EAM the surrender of arms by the Democratic Army under the supervision of the United Nations, the dismissal of Zervas from the Cabinet and elections held by a government possibly headed by Plastiras and perhaps including members of EAM. Ioannidis replied that prior to any understanding with the KKE, EAM must join the government.[77] Whatever his motivation, Venizelos could not have predicted that the US Secretary of State George Marshall would soon instruct Dwight Griswold, the head of the American Mission for Aid to Greece, that the Greek government should be drawn from parties of the Right, Centre and Left, 'but not so far to the left that they are disposed to make concessions to, or deals with, the Communists'.[78]

At the same time the question arose whether the KKE would support a government under Sofulis. One stumbling block was the experience of Sofulis's premiership in 1945–1946, when despite his good intentions, the Liberal leader had failed to curb the White Terror. Another obstacle cropped up on 20 June 1947, when the Foreign Minister Tsaldaris and MacVeagh signed the agreement which allowed the United States to control Greek affairs through supervising the utilization of aid. Ioannidis cabled to the Athens section of the Politburo that for the KKE it was 'unthinkable' even to tolerate a government which accepted this agreement, and that 'after last year's lesson with the Sofulis experiment, today we are not allowed such tests'. The KKE still drew a distinction between the Right and the Liberals but demanded the participation of EAM in the government: 'what actually matters', Ioannidis emphasized, 'is not the words but the actions', and this distinction 'cannot have the meaning of any tolerance towards the Centre'.[79]

Adherence to its long-standing terms had led nowhere, thus the KKE had already resolved to push matters to a head. After Zachariadis's contacts with Stalin in May, the Politburo member Miltiadis Porfyrogenis apparently visited Moscow in June. The purpose of his visit is unknown, but he must have discussed the content of a speech he would deliver at the French Communist Party Conference at Strasbourg. There, on 27 June 1947, Porfyrogenis announced that in view of 'the intransigence of reaction', the KKE would set up a 'Free Greece with its own Government' unless the other side yielded to its terms.[80] No doubt the Soviet Union must have been forewarned of this declaration, and its endorsement would be consistent with its acquiescence in Zachariadis's novel military plans. Evidently, Stalin once more found it expedient to consent to a KKE policy which Zachariadis sought to present as a *fait accompli*, or else risk the defeat of the Democratic Army and the elimination of all communist prospects in Greece.

Whereas it was the KKE leader who formulated aggressive policies, Stalin's consent was hardly in contradiction with his overall strategic concern to consolidate gains in eastern Europe whilst avoiding a conflagration with the West. Although the Soviets had minimal control over the primary conception of KKE policy, they were nonetheless able to supervise its enforcement in such a way as to conform to Soviet interests. First, the success of the KKE plans relied on massive military assistance which only the Soviet Union could furnish; in this case – as in the Spanish Civil War, when Soviet aid to the Republic was principally calculated to prolong resistance – Stalin could ensure that aid to the KKE aimed simply at keeping it afloat. Secondly, as long as the Democratic Army remained undefeated, both the Kremlin and the KKE could attempt overtures for a political settlement that would preserve some communist influence in Greece.

The Greek government responded to the Strasbourg Speech with a wave of arrests. Starting on 9 July, 13,751 persons were rounded up in the Athens–Piraeus area and deported on the pretext that the KKE had planned an armed insurrection for 10 July. The arrests were carried out so incompetently that, according to the US Embassy, even 'persons of known anti-communist views were taken into custody'.[81] The matter was raised at the British Cabinet, where McNeil misinformed his colleagues that there had been no prior consultations between London, Washington and Athens, and overpitched his case that the recent DSE activity 'gave some colour' to the allegations that a KKE plan existed.[82] The Foreign Office and the Embassy regretted the arrests, which dealt little damage to the KKE but a good deal to Greece's international image, and made relevant representations which led to the release of 1,500 persons. Yet there remained 17,000 deportees and 17,890 prisoners (of whom only 61% were convicted), whereas the Special Courts Martial had already stepped up the severity of sentences.[83]

Measuring reactions to the Strasbourg Speech, MacVeagh noted that Sofulis alone had attacked the government and the Right 'for things having come to such a pass'.[84] It was probably for this stance that the Liberal leader and the former Prime Minister Emmanuel Tsouderos were singled out as the recipients of a peace initiative which represented a decisive drive on the part of the KKE to reach a compromise before implementing its new policy. The prelude to these contacts was the personal overture of the non-communist EAM notable Michalis Kyrkos, who in late June–early July 1947 indirectly approached Sofulis and urged him to undertake an initiative. The latter accepted the appeal, met with Maximos and then with the King. George II had died on 1 April 1947, but his brother and successor King Paul proved equally impervious. A reportedly shaken Sofulis related to Kyrkos the words of the new monarch:

> Mr. President, I fully share your views and those of the Prime Minister. Unfortunately, we can do nothing. It is too late! The Americans have entered too deeply into the Greek question and they will never accept a solution which can be accepted by the others as well. They consider this a defeat for themselves.[85]

The essence of Kyrkos's account is corroborated by other sources. It is certain that the intermediary between him and Sofulis (the powerful editor of *To Vima*, Dimitrios Lambrakis) favoured negotiations with the KKE; that the Americans were opposed to any concessions to, or dealings with, the KKE and wanted to see the Greek business through so as to make a point to the Soviets; and that Sofulis did meet with Maximos and King Paul.[86] At any rate, Kyrkos's testimony is important in so far as it highlights the overwhelming American presence, which threatened to thwart Greek initiatives, and suggests that Sofulis might have been receptive to appeals.

The more interesting story is the following one. On 8 July 1947 the British Embassy in Athens reported that the KKE had been approaching Sofulis seeking to come to terms with him upon the formation of a new government. On 12 July a KKE emissary submitted verbally to a representative of Sofulis the following terms: dissolution of Parliament, formation of a '"pure centre"' government under Sofulis and including Plastiras and Tsouderos, but not any KKE or leftist figure; such a government would come to an agreement with the KKE on the basis of previous public statements made by Sofulis and Tsouderos – appeasement, a general amnesty, guarantees of security for those who would surrender, and a promise of new elections on revised registers as soon as possible; in return the KKE would 'call off' the war; this agreement to be guaranteed by the United Nations or '"allied factors"'.[87]

According to the US records, before 7 July Sofulis had sought MacVeagh's advice. The Liberal leader assured him of his anti-KKE sentiments but felt that some reply was needed in order to avoid the charge that he opposed a settlement. MacVeagh's response bordered on cynicism. The US ambassador and his government had 'no intention of intervening in Greek internal politics', but he was convinced that the 'EAM manoeuvre cannot be considered apart from [the] general Communist campaign against Greece's independence and territorial integrity'. Hence he suggested that Sofulis refer the matter to Maximos so that the 'patriotic heads ... get together to decide on [a] common attitude against [the] enemies of Greece'.[88]

US records have it that Sofulis and Maximos agreed that the only concession to the Democratic Army could be an internationally supervised amnesty after it had surrendered its arms. They had no clue whether the KKE would accept this, but Sofulis urged that the opportunity be seized 'to "unmask" them definitely'.[89] Ever holding out for the premiership, Sofulis was too clever to commit the fatal error of presenting himself to the Americans as anything but mulishly hostile to the KKE. But from a personal viewpoint the specific terms were tempting in that the eighty-seven-year-old Liberal could become head of a government which might just manage to end the civil war. This may well be the reason why the British records cast him in a different light and tend to corroborate Kyrkos's account. The document which mentions the contacts between the KKE and Sofulis and the communists' terms reveals the following:

> In reporting the above information obtained from secret sources, the British Embassy in Athens adds that, according to further secret information which they have obtained, they learn that M. Sofulis, who saw the King on 11 July, was most unfavourably impressed by his failure to understand the present political situation or to grasp its seriousness. The Embassy point out that this is likely to make M. Sofulis *more receptive* than before to [the] KKE's approach.[90] [Emphasis mine]

The hint is very broad that despite what he told MacVeagh and Maximos, Sofulis was not as hostile to the offer as the US records imply. The British document suggests that initially he had been receptive, and that is why he sought an audience with the King. What was actually said there is not known, but from Sofulis's reaction it is clear that he inquired into the possibility of a royal initiative to install him as Prime Minister in an attempt to pacify the country, and that King Paul ruled this out on account of the anticipated reactions of the Populists and the Americans. This hypothesis is substantially confirmed from a secret source which reported to the US Embassy that Sofulis had insisted on assuming the premiership and that the King had refused to embark on a political initiative 'without the advice and consent of responsible Ministers'.[91]

At this point a second intermediary entered the picture. On 13 July 1947 the British Embassy received a message from Tsouderos, who had also been approached by the KKE. The former Prime Minister had been given a copy of the memorandum which EAM had submitted to Maximos in April, and without informing the Americans, he now sought British advice. Patrick D'Arcy Reilly, the new Counsellor of the Embassy, replied that he would have to inform his US colleagues so that the two governments could consult each other. On the following day Reilly saw MacVeagh, who again dismissed the KKE offer. Anxious to ensure that the issue would not drive a wedge between the United States and Britain, the US ambassador recommended consultations between London and Washington.[92]

On 16 July 1947 the British Embassy in Washington received a cable from Bevin instructing them to enter into urgent talks with the State Department. The Foreign Secretary had given the issue some thought. He pointed out that since no advice could be offered to Tsouderos behind the back of the Greek government, Tsouderos should be told that the proper course was to inform Maximos. Bevin was in no doubt as to the 'dangerous nature' of the KKE offer, but in order to make this clear to Sofulis and Tsouderos and ascertain their reactions, he wanted the British and US ambassadors to raise a few queries with them. Was there any reason to believe that the King would be prepared to evict the government and dissolve Parliament, or that this would be tolerated by the Army and the Gendarmerie? Then, was it not likely that a general amnesty would give rise to reprisals? Was there any reason to believe that even after the revision of the registers the Centre would obtain a parliamentary majority? Besides, Bevin could not see how a guarantee either by the United Nations or by the allies could be implemented in the event of the KKE's failing to call off the guerrilla activity. Finally, either guarantee 'would open the way to Soviet interference in the internal affairs of Greece'.[93]

Marshall's reply, on 18 July, left no room for further deliberations. Though the US Secretary of State saw no harm in putting Bevin's queries to the two Greeks, he preferred

> to inform them more bluntly that [the] KKE proposals though fair sounding are regarded by the US Government as insincere and dangerous and that in their view, the hand of the Communists would be strengthened and future attempts to obtain positive action through [the] UN would be weakened if proposals were given serious consideration.

MacVeagh was instructed to convey the message to the British and to Sofulis and Tsouderos.[94] This was unnecessary in the case of Sofulis, who on 18–19 July had taken 'an extreme anti-communist line' and grasped 'the overriding necessity of standing together against Communism'. MacVeagh was delighted and found it needless to issue a warning to the Liberal leader.[95] Having read the sign of the times, Sofulis had probably decided that in view of the omnipotent American presence, a conciliatory mood towards the KKE would mar his chances of some day resuming the premiership.

Tsouderos thought differently. EAM had approached the two men separately, and while Sofulis had turned to the Americans, the Anglophile Tsouderos had sought British advice. MacVeagh correctly suspected that Tsouderos, backed by the powerful editor of *To Vima*, tried to obtain British blessing independently and in advance, before attempting to persuade Sofulis to embrace the communist terms. According to the US ambassador, Lambrakis and Tsouderos hoped that the KKE could be used by the Liberals to defeat the government and then be controlled by political means.[96] The Lambrakis–Tsouderos connection certainly existed, and Tsouderos's Papers afford an insight into the reason why the KKE chose to woo the former Prime Minister. In April 1947 Tsouderos had published in *To Vima* five articles arguing that the Left drew its strength from the social and economic despair of the masses and the persecutions by the post-Varkiza state. His prescription envisaged a government without the royalists and the communists, which would launch a bloodless offensive against the latter by way of economic reconstruction, jobs for the unemployed, social security for working people, and improved standards of living and education. The crux of this programme rested on the dissolution of the Parliament, and this could be brought about only through allied pressure on King Paul.[97]

The scheme sounded fair and was not far removed from the KKE proposals. However, it essentially amounted to a repeat of the Sofulis experiment of 1945–1946, which had been superseded by the course and gravity of events. Apart from the mundane difficulties – such as ensuring the impartiality of the authorities – Tsouderos failed to take into account two fundamental considerations; that the Americans were hostile to a compromise, and that, if adopted, this solution would be a blow to British prestige, for it would cast doubt on their Greek policy since 1945 and make it difficult for the United States to justify its takeover.

Yet, as it transpired from his reply to Bevin's queries, Tsouderos was confident. On 19 July he told Reilly that he counted on strong Anglo-American pressure on the King to dissolve Parliament; once Paul had consented, the country would accept it. The polls would probably return a Populist majority, but the Centre would be strong enough to hold the balance between Right and Left, while 'the presence of the latter in the Chamber would be a big gain'. He envisaged neither an agreement between a new government and the KKE nor a new Varkiza; instead, on receipt of an authoritative statement from the KKE, the Democratic Army would have to call a truce; then Britain and the United States would urge the King to dissolve Parliament and install a Centre government which would declare an amnesty and grant the DSE thirty days within which to lay down its arms. Tsouderos even hinted that an understanding between the West and Stalin about Greece would be possible. Reilly regarded the KKE offer as a 'smoke screen' and replied that London was not prepared to bring pressure on the King or to act independently of the Americans, whose attitude was unequivocal. Tsouderos went away hoping that the communists would fail to produce acceptable terms in black and white.[98]

The Foreign Office was concerned lest Tsouderos should pursue talks with the KKE, in which case he might not be 'clever enough to beat them at their own game'. Reilly was to tell him to inform Maximos of the KKE proposals.[99] On 22 July Reilly reported that Sofulis had met Tsouderos and reiterated his determination to abstain from any government unless as Premier of one of his own choosing. Sofulis wished to preserve himself as the only important figure capable of presenting an alternative programme, hence he insisted 'on the exclusion of the Populists from any such Government'. On that day the KKE was expected to deliver its written terms, in which case Sofulis and Tsouderos would discuss what further steps to take and seek again Reilly's advice.[100]

Being more flexible than the Americans, the British deemed Sofulis's stance as 'sensible', for if he participated in a coalition he would 'undoubtedly forfeit a great deal of the strength of his present intermediary situation'. But they were also pragmatists, and they grasped the irrationality of forming a government without the Populists, who occupied nearly two-thirds of the Parliament. Even so, they wanted Reilly to get hold of a written text with the KKE terms. Warner, Wallinger and Balfour agreed that 'until we have actually studied the terms of these proposals, I do not see that we can give Mr. Reilly any advice further to that already given to him'.[101]

For the British and Tsouderos the matter ended when the KKE failed to produce a formal note. For the Americans the *a priori* rebuff of the offer was subsequently facilitated by one contradiction. The KKE told Sofulis that it wanted a pure centre government, whereas the memorandum to Tsouderos demanded the inclusion of EAM. An even greater disparity occurred on 17 July, when the DSE radio called for the participation of EAM in the government and then said that it considered necessary the creation of its own government.[102] In this case, as the military campaign was in full swing, Markos may have simply wanted to bolster the morale of his guerrillas. One of the thrusts of KKE policy in 1946–1947 was to make repeated offers for a settlement, which was consistent with the Soviet desire to preserve communist influence in Greece by way of a negotiated solution rather than a military victory of the Democratic Army.

For the KKE the matter ended in the wake of the mass arrests of 9 July. Eight days later, in a report to the Soviet Communist Party, the Politburo member Petros Rousos asserted that the government had thereby blocked the way for further contacts, and that its blatant refusal to negotiate left the KKE with no other option but the armed struggle. The manoeuvres of the politicians of the Centre were construed by the communists as window-dressing, if not deliberate fraud; they were particularly enraged by Sofulis, who on the eve of the arrests 'was obliquely promising to EAM that he would come into contact with the government to discuss the possibility of a compromise solution'. The overtures of July 1947 thus emerge as a turning point in the history of the Greek Civil War. Especially for the KKE, they were something of a last temptation before the implementation of the Strasbourg declaration. After their frustration, the communists would go their own way.[103]

Interestingly enough, the British were more inquisitive and less high-handed than the Americans. Unlike the State Department, Bevin and the Foreign Office had the experience to know that a Centre government in Greece in 1947 was not tantamount to the Bolshevization of the country. More importantly, there is evidence that the Labour government continued to be haunted by its reserves about Greece and was conscious of the unpopularity of the Greek commitment in the Labour Party. In its annual report for 1947 the Embassy in Athens explicitly maintained that these reserves were reinforced by back-bench criticism in the House of Commons, and that the Labour government was further embarrassed by the openly anti-communist and anti-Soviet line of US policy in Greece. The Americans had sensed this, and in May Acheson had asked the Embassy in London whether Bevin's thinking was influenced by criticism from the back benches. It was a valid assessment on the part of the Truman administration that the British Foreign Secretary was indeed sensitive to domestic critics, but this would affect the outward implementation rather than the fundamentals of his policy towards the Soviet Union.[104] Bevin's inquisitiveness and comparative flexibility towards the KKE overtures of July 1947 came to confirm this evaluation.

In Athens Tsouderos did not happen to meet Maximos so as to inform him of the KKE overture. On 30 July 1947 Reilly reported that the matter 'looks as if it might be dead', and three weeks later that it was 'entirely dead'.

Tsouderos had ceased to attach any importance to it, and in early September the issue was reported 'buried'.[105] By then the British and US governments were already preoccupied with a major controversy which threatened to unsettle their relations with regard to Greece.

Bevin, Marshall, the Troops, and the Balfour Memorandum

Apart from the 1,100 officers, men and administrative staff of the British Military Mission, in 1947 the Labour government retained 5,000 British troops in Greece as a symbolic gesture that Britain would stand up against any foreign encroachment.[106] What made up for the lack of evidence for such a threat was the mood of the late 1940s, when few things seemed incredible; thus in March 1947 Britain had assured the United States that she would continue to cooperate in advancing Greece's political and territorial integrity. Although the British intended to withdraw their troops in the summer of that year, the fundamental premise of their reasoning remained to deny Stalin any foothold in and beyond the *cordon sanitaire* represented by Greece, Turkey and Iran.[107]

Considering the determination with which this policy had been pursued, it came as a surprise when on 28 July 1947 Bevin instructed the Chiefs of Staff to study and report on the possibility of the complete withdrawal of the British combat forces from Greece by 30 September 1947. The reasons given by the Foreign Secretary were that the troops were not strong enough to meet aggression, that their presence generated 'many political difficulties' at home, and that they had little strategic value.[108] Two days later the Embassy in Washington was instructed to inform the State Department that the British government had decided the immediate withdrawal of its troops from Greece 'on financial and manpower reasons', which were irrelevant to those given to the Chiefs of Staff. Simultaneously, the Embassy in Athens was notified to say nothing to the Greeks.[109]

Even the Foreign Office was taken aback by this decision. The Southern Department viewed it 'with frank alarm' on account of the psychological effect it would have on the Greeks, while Sargent feared that Britain would be seen as lacking confidence in victory against the Greek guerrillas. As to the reasons given, the Permanent Under-Secretary argued that despite Britain's convertibility crisis, the dollars saved by this withdrawal represented such an infinitesimal fraction of the adverse dollar balance that 'no foreigner will ever believe that we have decided on withdrawal at this moment for purely *financial* reasons'.[110] Nevertheless, on 30 July Sir John Balfour, the Minister at the Embassy in Washington, officially communicated the decision to the Americans.[111]

The State Department informally cautioned that the announcement should be made in such a way as to indicate no change in Anglo-American policy. Balfour cabled London that the Americans were 'distressed' and had pointed out that if the withdrawal had been decided on financial and manpower reasons alone, Britain could withdraw a corresponding number of troops from another theatre.[112] Balfour himself was uneasy. He warned London that the

Truman administration might view the British decision as 'a desperate eleventh-hour abandonment of our international responsibilities'. The 'growing impression' in Washington that Britain could be 'permanently written off as an important world power capable of sharing with the USA the burdens of world leadership', might deprive her of the advantages she possessed over other nations in seeking American assistance. 'In sum', Balfour concluded his exhortation, 'we should do our best to inspire confidence that, come what it may, we shall remain America's best bet as we have proved ourselves to be in the darkest days of the war.'[113]

On 1 August came the official US reaction by way of a strong personal message from Marshall to Bevin. The American Secretary of State felt that 'such abrupt action' rendered cooperation 'unnecessarily difficult', but he was 'still more disturbed' at its possible implications for future British policy. As the reasons offered for the withdrawal of the troops were incomprehensible, the State Department feared that this was the first step of a series of British actions stemming from new policies which were unknown to Washington. Marshall scarcely veiled a threat that if such new policies had been adopted in London, the United States might reconsider its economic commitments in Europe and re-examine its strategic position, 'because US foreign policy had been ... predicated upon British willingness to contribute to [the] maintenance of stability in Europe'. The US government would also face difficulties in filling the gap after the British troops had pulled out.[114] MacVeagh enhanced these apprehensions when he cabled that the 'astonishingly ill-timed' and 'little short of catastrophic' British decision should be postponed until 'other possible security measures equally valid' were taken. If the British deterrent against 'possible Slavic irruption' was withdrawn and not replaced by US troops, the Americans '"might as well pack up and go home"'.[115]

On 2 August Bevin assured the US ambassador in London that there had been no change in British policy and inquired as to how long the Americans wished the troops to remain in Greece. In the next few days Bevin and Sargent told the ambassador that no withdrawal would take place without full consultations with Washington, but on 20 August Bevin insisted that the withdrawal must be completed by autumn 1947.[116] The Americans, who suspected that British policy was conditioned by domestic political considerations, were angered. In a US Cabinet meeting on 8 August, the Secretary of State for Commerce Averell Harriman noted that leftist elements in the Labour Party were calling for a reduction of British military strength, the withdrawal from Greece, and a more vigorous nationalization of British industry: 'It is a serious question whether we should underwrite the stability of a government whose objectives seem to be moving further to the Left as they lose the support of even moderate Liberals.'[117] Marshall was more forthright:

our thorn-pulling operations on the British lion continue to be beset by her stubborn insistence on avoiding the garden path to wander in the thicket of purely local Labour Party misadventures. They are far too casual or freehanded in passing the buck of the international dilemma to [the] US with little or no consideration for the harmful results.[118]

Bevin adhered to his decision on several grounds. Not only had he informed the Americans long before that the troops would be withdrawn, but his domestic position would become untenable if a single British soldier were killed in Greece and trouble between the Soviet Union and Britain were thereby precipitated; moreover, since US policy in the Middle East was unknown to him, he proposed talks aiming at an understanding on the region.[119] Drawing on the views of the Joint Chiefs of Staff, Marshall countered that the presence of British troops in Greece was symbolic of western resolve to ensure her independence. In the event of a withdrawal, the Democratic Army would be strengthened by 'sizable forces from outside', the country would go red and apocalyptic developments would follow. The chances of retaining Italy, Turkey and Iran oriented towards the West would suffer a formidable setback. Access to the oilfields of the Middle East, essential to the economic welfare and military potential of both the United States and Britain, would be jeopardized. In sum, British withdrawal from Greece would result in a marked deterioration in the overall strategic position in the Mediterranean and would break the common Anglo-American front against Communism.[120]

Bevin remained unswayed. On 12 September he proposed the immediate withdrawal of one battalion, with the remaining three staying until the withdrawal of the Red Army from Bulgaria on 15 December 1947. Marshall reluctantly agreed provided that the future of the three battalions would be subject to review in the forthcoming Pentagon Talks.[121] Though Greece was not on the agenda, the Americans then made it clear that they regarded the retention of British troops as essential to the prevention of Greece's collapse. They indicated that they were willing to co-operate in the Middle East, but it would be on Greece that the British would have to prove their sincerity.[122]

During the Pentagon Talks the British offered a glimpse of another possibility which may have prompted the decision of 28 July. On 17 October the Defence Secretary Albert Alexander minuted to the Chiefs of Staff that a forthright message should be sent to Marshall with a view to eliciting American intentions:

As things are, we are constantly pressed to retain in Greece a few soldiers who, if trouble were to break out from beyond the frontiers, could only retreat, thus placing HM Government in an ignominious position. What we want to know frankly is whether the US intend themselves to undertake the military responsibilities which are the necessary counterpart of their political and economic responsibilities towards Greece.

On 19 October Attlee and Bevin decided to approach Marshall on these lines. Although apparently they never did,[123] the implication that the British were aiming at the despatch of US troops to Greece is reinforced by what was said in a meeting between Bevin and Tsaldaris a few days later. When the Greek Foreign Minister inquired about the American attitude in the event of the establishment of a KKE 'government', Bevin replied that Washington 'might perhaps put troops into Greece and ... that the US could not save the world with dollars alone'.[124]

Precisely how and when Bevin gave in to the American pressure is not clear. On 21 November 1947 he told the Chiefs of Staff that Washington insisted on the retention of the British troops in Greece as a test case of British co-operation. He conceded that

> there were many political difficulties, but if the presence of a token British force was an effective contribution to the maintenance of Greek morale, he did not wish to increase the task of the US, Greek and British Governments in creating stability in Greece by insisting upon the withdrawal of our forces.[125]

The impression is that Bevin's *volte-face* had occurred at some earlier point, but the records are inconclusive. At any rate, the matter ended there and the last British troops did not leave Greece until early 1950.

The exaggerated American reaction to the British note of 30 July is understandable. In its first steps towards a global policy of containing Communism, the United States was banking on full British support. The withdrawal of 5,000 British soldiers from Greece might not have jeopardized the survival of the West, as the Americans implied, but it would have affected adversely the morale of the Greek government and bolstered the KKE. Bevin's motives for this venturesome decision are less clear, not least of all because of the striking discrepancy between the reasons given to the Chiefs of Staff and the manifestly untenable ones cabled to Washington. Financial considerations failed to convince even the Foreign Office clerks, while there was very little to justify the need for manpower; the 5,000 troops in Greece were a drop in the ocean of the 1,500,000-strong armed forces which Britain maintained in 1947. Two inferences seem plausible. Bevin may have thought that financial and manpower reasons would be more easily digestible for the Americans; and that the decision for withdrawal might have been intended as an important bargaining counter in the overall framework of Anglo-American relations; it was a curious coincidence, after all, that the issue cropped up amidst preliminary discussions for the Marshall Plan and the Brussels Pact.

The one source that hints at the most acceptable explanation is Alexander's minute, which suggests that there was a snag in Anglo-American relations with regard to Greece. By mid-August Bevin was emphatically discontented with the United States over the division of responsibility:

> The Secretary of State feels that we must now realize that America has taken on from us responsibility in Greece. Having done this she must also take on the responsibility of providing manpower to carry out her obligations ... At present they do not want to use a man overseas but to protect their interests by use of dollars. We must disabuse them of any idea of using us to man their outposts overseas and we shall bring them up against this by removing our troops from Greece. At the present moment, though we do not have sufficient troops to do anything in Greece if trouble blows up, they are sufficient to allow the Americans to feel that they can still evade their responsibilities.[126]

Bevin wanted the despatch of US troops to Greece because that would have substantially discharged Britain of her Greek burden and allowed her to concentrate on her primary concerns in the Middle East. But the US government would not send troops for neither could it obtain Congressional approval nor did it want to take such a 'disturbing and provocative' step. In the Pentagon Talks of October–November 1947 the Americans endorsed British aims in the Middle East and supported Britain as the predominant regional power. Though these talks marginally dealt with Greece, Bevin made it clear that her independence was vital to Anglo-American security: if the northern tier of the Middle East were infested and the main area fell, that 'would virtually mean the end of England as a power'.[127] Yet Bevin clearly resented Washington's policy of trying to save the world by US dollars and British soldiers, and thought that he could make his point by threatening to withdraw the troops from Greece. At the same time he used the issue as a bargaining counter to achieve some other goal as well, probably a firm US undertaking to underwrite the British position in the Middle East.

This interpretation should allow some room for the 'political difficulties' invoked by Bevin. Although the Foreign Office records do not prove that these amounted to a major motive, in 1947 there was a wider unhappiness within the Labour Party at the direction of its foreign policy. It was argued in various quarters of the party that Labour's diplomacy ought to be committed to world-wide reconciliation rather than being constantly applauded by Churchill and Eden.[128] Critiques of Bevin's Greek policy came not only from the thinly populated Marxist fringe of the Parliamentary Party, but even from the wider membership and the TUC. In April 1947 fifteen non-communist Labour MPs formed the *Keep Left* group which urged the government to stop acting as America's lieutenant in the struggle against Communism and revert to socialist policies, especially abroad. Their main thrust was the call for a foreign policy independent of the United States and the Soviet Union and supportive of democratic, socialist and nationalist movements in Greece, the Middle East and Indonesia. In May 1947 the group published a pamphlet demanding, *inter alia*, a timetable for the withdrawal of the British troops from Greece, Palestine and Egypt. 'In Greece', they charged, Britain had been 'gradually pushed into the position of supporting reactionary and semi-fascist forces'. Their demand was: 'No Truck with Churchill – Kill the Tory idea of bolstering up the British Empire with American dollars and fighting America's battle with British soldiers.'[129]

Significantly, Bevin's own feelings about the division of Anglo-American responsibility in Greece echoed this criticism. Others, like the veteran propagandist of the Union of Democratic Control Leonard Woolf, pointed out that since Washington intended to use its economic aid to Europe for political ends, the recipients found themselves committed to the side of America in its struggle against the Soviet Union. In the case of Greece, Spain and the Persian oil Britain should follow a policy which ought to be supported by the Kremlin and opposed by the Americans.[130] In the annual TUC Conference of September 1947 Bevin faced a hostile resolution on troop reductions which gave considerable attention to Greece; also at that time prominent Labour members openly criticized Attlee's leadership for lack of commitment to socialist principles, especially in domestic policies, and tried to get Bevin to assume the premiership himself.[131]

Throughout 1945–1947 leftist disapproval had failed to sway Bevin's determination to retain Greece on the western side of the fence. Nevertheless, the long-standing misgivings which the Labour government entertained about its unpopular Greek commitment were reinforced by the manner in which the Truman Doctrine was applied in Greece. In the Annual Report for 1947, compiled for the Embassy in Athens by Patrick D'Arcy Reilly, the Counsellor reflected:

> More generally, the strongly anti-communist and anti-Soviet line given to the US policy in Greece was embarrassing to HM Government, who were then under fire from Parliamentary critics of their attitude to the US and Soviet Governments. It would, indeed, at this period have suited HM Government very well to have been able to withdraw from Greece entirely.[132]

Whatever the measure of Bevin's embarrassment by the particulars of US policy in Greece, the domestic political difficulties may well have played some part in prompting his decision of 28 July 1947. The overwhelming reason, however, seems to have been his resentment at having to bear the military onus of this policy alone. The withdrawal of the British troops from Greece became the leverage whereby the Americans could be forced to grasp the nettle. Bevin did not succeed in that, but it was certainly a bigger gain that at the same time the United States hastened to underwrite the British position in the Middle East.

While Bevin did not contemplate relinquishing British interests in Greece, some Foreign Office officials proved too enterprising in seeking remedies for the Greek question. In September 1947, while Bevin's dispute with Marshall was raging, Geoffrey Wallinger, the new Head of the Southern Department, instructed David Balfour '"to sketch out a possible compromise policy" for Greece'. Except for the date, there is nothing to link this initiative with the issue of the troops. Balfour hinted that what prompted it was the failure of the summer offensive: 'the present trouble … is hardly likely to die out of its own accord, and since the attempt to deal with it by force is not meeting with much success and may lead to disaster, it is worth considering what form a peaceful political solution might possibly take.'

For Balfour, the object of a compromise would be to offer the KKE such concessions as would induce it to stop fighting and settle down to normal political activity; therefore a compromise worth attempting would have to be a thorough one, brought about by common agreement of the leaders on both sides. Balfour offered this remarkable prescription: (i) a truce, the cessation of hostilities, the suspension of arrests, trials, deportations, dismissals and executions, and the liberation of all those detained or exiled by the Public Security Committees; (ii) the dissolution of the Parliament in order to remove power from the Right-wing majority and make possible the appointment of a new government which could negotiate with the KKE; (iii) the formation of a government capable of negotiating with the KKE: men like Tsaldaris, Zervas and Papandreou would have to be excluded, whilst the likes of Tsouderos and Sofianopoulos should be brought in; (iv) the negotiation of a compromise agreement, including the disarmament of the guerrillas, acceptance by the KKE of the King and the Anglo-American Missions, minimum admission of EAM and the KKE in the Cabinet (Ministries of Supply, National Economy and, perhaps, Interior), a broad amnesty, the repeal of repressive legislation, and guarantees of impartial administration and equal opportunities for leftists in the public services; (v) the settlement of Trade Union issues; (vi) a thorough revision of the electoral registers; and (vii) new elections with proportional representation.

Balfour admitted that his scheme left out 'an all-important factor' – 'the policy of Moscow, of the Comintern, [and] of Greece's neighbours'; he realized, however, that 'by coming to an agreement with the leaders of [the] KKE, a Greek Government would in fact be making ... a tacit agreement with the larger forces supporting [the] KKE'. In the short-term there appeared to be a more difficult problem – how to persuade the Populist-dominated government to embark on negotiations for a truce and lay the foundations for its own dismissal:

> The answer under present circumstances can only be: Anglo-American pressure – direct pressure exerted with the utmost determination and consistency on an unwilling King, Government and Chamber. In other circumstances it might perhaps come about under a different form of pressure: the pressure of impending defeat, of panic and despair. But in that case it would no doubt be too late. Greek and international communism would be in no mood for compromise and would look forward to dictating their own terms.[133]

The memorandum was put into 'cold storage' without a copy being sent to Norton. Wallinger minuted that any attempt to put such a policy into effect then would be dangerous, for in case of failure the impact on Greek morale would be disastrous; magnanimity could be shown after a major victory of the government army. But the main reason why the scheme was cast aside was the British perception of Soviet involvement in the Greek Civil War. In June 1948 Wallinger wrote to Norton that though 'well-thought', Balfour's proposals had been 'unworkable so long as it is Soviet policy towards Greece and not the activities of the rebels themselves which is the determining element in the conflict.'[134]

This premise was in harmony with Bevin's thinking. After the failure of the Moscow Council of Foreign Ministers in March–April 1947 to settle the disputes between the West and the Soviet Union, the British Foreign Secretary had come to interpret Soviet policy as proof that Stalin had 'gone back to original Lenin idea' of the revolution.[135] The unfolding Cold War had now completely obscured the domestic origins of the Greek Civil War, and what was foreign endorsement of a Greek decision was perceived as a foreign *diktat* faithfully executed by the local puppets. Even so, it is difficult to explain why this memorandum was commissioned, unless it is assumed that in autumn

1947 the Foreign Office staff had so little to do that they indulged in speculative diplomatic exercises. The Greek question might not have had any of the apocalyptic qualities attached to it by the Americans, but nonetheless it was too serious to offer itself for such treatment. No doubt the memorandum was produced not because some clerks momentarily lapsed into frivolity, but because there was some reason.

This reason is nowhere to be found in the records. The document implies that the abortive campaign, which had ended in August, and the successful challenge of the Democratic Army had triggered off some danger signal in London. The British were not particularly confident about the effectiveness of US policy in Greece and wanted to avoid a military disaster which would lead to a settlement on the KKE terms. To avert this, either US troops would have to be committed – a tactical aim which had been one of Bevin's motives in threatening to withdraw the British troops – or a settlement should be attempted while the Greek government still retained the advantage.

By September 1947 it was clear that the Americans would not commit any troops. What remained was the alternative of probing into the chances of a compromise, and in this respect Balfour did remarkably well. The terms he put down came very close to the demands of the KKE, though it is a moot point whether the latter would have embraced provisions such as the acceptance of the Anglo-American Missions and the King. The Soviets might exercise some pressure to that end, but things never came to such a pass. Instead, as in so many other instances since 1945, nothing was done to put the sincerity of the KKE to the test.

The most striking feature in Balfour's memorandum (and in Wallinger's despatch to Norton nine months later) is the implicit assumption that the United States would agree to such a compromise. Although in July 1947 the Americans had made it clear that there would be no concessions to (or dealings with) the KKE, neither Balfour nor Wallinger seemed to realize that Washington would be unlikely to embrace the scheme and exert pressure on the Greeks to implement it; on the contrary, Wallinger was adamant that the stumbling block was Soviet policy. The absence in both Balfour's memorandum and Wallinger's despatch of any reference to the likelihood of US hostility towards the plan may be accounted for in terms of a momentary lapse into inadvertence or a change in Foreign Office thinking. The former is more than doubtful, the latter less so, but save the chronological coincidence, there is still little to relate this initiative to Bevin's row with Marshall. Despite the intriguing indifference to US reaction, there is no evidence to suggest that the Foreign Office cherished the transient idea of trying its hand alone. A more pertinent interpretation, which may also be linked to the dispute between Bevin and Marshall, is that the British had reservations about the effectiveness of American policy in Greece, and that these were enhanced after the abortive outcome of the summer military offensive against the Democratic Army. If so, it was a sad thing that the scheme was put into cold storage on account of the erroneously surmised Soviet designs.

Christmas Eve, 1947

Even before the elections of March 1946 Bevin had tried to secure a Centre-Right coalition in Athens in order to isolate politically the KKE. Although shortly after the polls the Populists' unsavoury domestic policies became a constant source of embarrassment for the Labour government, its earnest exhortations for a coalition stumbled over Sofulis's refusal to share power with them. The Liberal leader often held the Populists partly to blame for the drift into civil war, and this may well have been the reason why he was put on the receiving end of the KKE overtures of July 1947. His intermediary position and flirtation with the KKE alarmed the Americans, who wanted a government that would make no concessions to the communists.[136] In public Britain and the United States blamed the Soviet Union for the Greek Civil War, but in private both conceded that the situation was due to internal as well as external factors.

The State Department admitted that the repressive policy of the previous Populist government had played a substantial part in leading to the present confrontation. By encouraging and arming rightist extremists, it had exacerbated the state of turmoil and subscribed to violence and repression, while on the economic plane there had been no programme except to allow a few people to make huge profits and evade taxation. The perpetuation of these policies would lead to the failure of the US Aid Programme, hence it was imperative to set up a coalition government under an anti-communist personality enjoying the confidence of most Greeks.[137] Tsaldaris, however, who as Vice-Premier and Foreign Minister remained the strong man in Athens, was unaware of this indictment and had steered a different course. Banking on the parliamentary majority of his party, and apparently exasperated with Maximos's and Venizelos's overtures to the Left, he agitated for a pure Populist administration.

On his way to New York for the Security Council deliberations, Tsaldaris met with Bevin in Paris on 1 July. Fully conscious of the Americans' dislike for him, he professed that 'his first loyalty was still to Great Britain' and tried to elicit Bevin's support for a '"homogeneous"' government. In public Bevin may have been impervious to leftist critiques of his Greek policy, but in private he would have preferred not to provide his critics with more ammunition. He told Tsaldaris that a right-wing government would be undesirable in Washington and pose difficulties for the British government at home.[138] Tsaldaris went on to the United States, where again the suspicion prevailed that the aim of his visit was to extract something that would improve his own position in Greece. The US government remained deaf to his entreaties and impressed upon him the need for a broader cabinet.[139]

A frustrated Tsaldaris returned to London and on 18 August met with Sargent. He appealed to the Permanent Under-Secretary of the Foreign Office that instead of the strong government required under the circumstances, and which could come only from the party with the largest parliamentary majority, he found himself in the 'invidious' position of being member of a coalition. Sargent's efforts to change his mind, either by referring to the critical circumstances or to Churchill's example in 1940, came to no avail: 'M. Tsaldaris refused to be convinced and I would not be surprised if, when he gets back to Athens, he will try to reconstruct the Government on a purely party basis by expelling all the Ministers who represent the minority parties.'[140]

In Athens the stage was set for a new government, albeit not on Tsaldaris's terms. Maximos indicated to Dwight Griswold, Head of the American Mission for Aid to Greece, that changes could be made to polish Greece's image at home and abroad and achieve unity among the politicians. Griswold agreed that changes were needed; Zervas, for instance, would have to be evicted for 'he is making more communists than he is eliminating'. MacVeagh concurred, but there was dissent between the two American officials as to how the changes should be effected. The ambassador counselled that the initiative should be left to the Greeks, whereas Griswold claimed that 'we do not need to be affected by a fear that we will be accused of "interfering"'.[141] The crisis erupted on 21 August, when Venizelos, Papandreou and Kanellopoulos demanded changes in the government, including the eviction of Zervas and the undertaking of new efforts to secure the co-operation of Sofulis. Tsaldaris rejected these demands and on 23 August the three leaders of the National Political Union resigned, with Maximos following suit. On the same day King Paul gave the Populist leader an unconditional mandate.[142]

The State Department decreed that the new government should not give the impression that there was 'a slackening in [the] determination ... to restore law and order' or a hesitancy which would strengthen the morale of the communists.[143] To Tsaldaris's proposal for a Populist–Liberal coalition on equal terms, Sofulis replied with demands which would have put it under Liberal control. MacVeagh and Griswold tried to get Sofulis to accept a compromise but his obduracy brought the negotiations to a deadlock.[144] Following the rebuff of his appeals to the other parties, on 26 August Tsaldaris stated that he would form a purely right-wing cabinet. Griswold retorted that this would be 'inadmissible', and under more American pressure Tsaldaris agreed to serve under a neutral Prime Minister. Talks had nearly delivered a new Maximos government when once more they broke down; Tsaldaris had demanded that the Foreign Minister – that is, he himself – should not be subject to the Prime Minister's control, whilst more bickering involved the portfolios of War and Public Order, with Zervas still claiming the latter.[145]

On 29 August Tsaldaris put an end to the negotiations by announcing the formation of a Populist government. Reactions ranged from regret to indignation, yet some government, even if temporary, had to be formed to quell the anxiety of the army, whose morale was being sapped by the political muddle.[146] During the crisis the British Embassy kept a low profile, partly because Bevin opposed direct intervention in cabinet-making, but mainly because the Americans had no scruples about doing the job themselves. The Embassy praised MacVeagh for his refusal to impose any particular solution and criticized Griswold, who had 'been out of his depth in the difficult waters of Greek politics, into which he has plunged with perhaps too much alacrity'. The head of AMAG went as far as to make threats of economic sanctions, which showed 'the danger of political intervention by someone with his special authority but no local knowledge'.[147]

The *coup de grâce* to the US intervention was the despatch to Athens in the last days of August of Loy Henderson, Director of the Office of Near Eastern and African Affairs of the State Department.[148] The US government possessed a formidable weapon for bringing the Greek politicians into line, and Henderson put it to good use. He told Sofulis and Tsaldaris separately that if they did not co-operate in a coalition, each would be individually responsible for the stoppage of American aid. The two Greeks were furious but had no choice. On 4 September they reached an agreement whereby a coalition government would be set up with Sofulis as Premier and Tsaldaris as Vice-Premier and Foreign Minister. In the event a new Cabinet of ten Liberals and fourteen Populists was sworn in on 7 September 1947.[149]

At the age of eighty-seven Sofulis became Prime Minister again, albeit at a price even higher than in November 1945. Then he had been installed by the British as the last resort before civil strife, only to find that his freedom of action was held in leash by the British themselves. In September 1947 he would have no freedom of action whatsoever except for the pursuit of the civil war to the bitter end. The British Embassy reported that Henderson, who had come to Athens because the United States 'had at last decided to impose a solution', soon got 'up to the neck in this wasps' nest'.[150] His task was not only to bring Tsaldaris and Sofulis together but also to ensure that the latter was qualified for the post, as since January 1947 Marshall had been suspicious of the Liberal leader and by August MacVeagh had come to consider him 'a possible Kerensky'.[151] For that reason on 4 September 1947 Sofulis submitted to Henderson a note which profusely underlined the anti-communist credentials of the Liberals and specified the measures he envisaged: he would grant an amnesty to those surrendering their arms, but the prisoners and deportees would have to wait until the rebellion had come to 'a complete end out of its own accord'; and he would offer security of life and political freedom to all those 'who would return to the bosom of the Greek Family'. Adding that these measures were to be internationally supervised, Sofulis offered as a 'guarantee of faithful and sincere application' his own personality, which symbolized the policy of 'pacification and democratic equality'.[152]

In this manner the Americans ensured that the new Greek Prime Minister would make no concessions to the KKE. The British, on the other hand, were immediately alert to the quibbling nature of the achievement. Balfour noted that the Populist majority in the new Cabinet was in itself sufficient to disperse any hopes of appeasement. It would not, for instance, be easy to convince the Left that the allocation of the Interior Ministry to the mentor and financier of monarchist bands Petros Mavromichalis – whom the British regarded a 'second Zervas, only probably worse' – was a gesture of mollification. Balfour was right in asserting that Sofulis had done

what he always used to say he would not do: apply his "appeasement" policy in the company of ministerial colleagues compromised in his eyes and in the eyes of the KKE by their partiality and their indiscriminate use of "dynamic" methods.[153]

Rizospastis was equally right in pointing out that Sofulis was a prisoner capable of doing nothing, for behind him lay the Populists and above him the Americans.[154] To illustrate the point, on 6 September, even before the government was sworn in, the top Anglo-American officials in Greece agreed that the Prime Minister was to make no changes in the army command; should he insist, he would have to be brought into line by the threat of holding up supplies. Tsaldaris happily concurred.[155]

If for the two Greeks cooperation was a necessary evil, for Britain and the United States the Populist-Liberal coalition was a timely achievement. The national anti-communist front had at last been established and the KKE was isolated. The possibility of Sofulis emerging as a Greek Kerensky was eliminated, for the new Prime Minister was now hardly in a position even to think of a compromise. The two parties could be used as levers on each other, with the Liberals acting as a brake on the unsavoury policies of the Populists and the latter preventing the Liberals from further flirtations with the Left. The arrangement perfectly suited the Populists who, since realizing that they were not allowed to rule on their own, had been trying to prevent Sofulis from posing as the symbol of appeasement by bringing him into the government.

On 8 September 1947 Sofulis presented Parliament with a programme identical with the note to Henderson. The Liberal Justice Minister Christos Ladas had the 'sad privilege' of tabling the draft amnesty law, 'the last, sincere and honest gesture of the State'. The law, which did not apply to deportees and prisoners, offered an amnesty to those willing to surrender their arms within thirty days; those who had not 'directly taken part in the revolt' would be amnestied only if they lent a hand with its suppression by supplying the authorities with information.[156] Norton reported that members of right-wing bands were also included in the amnesty, and that those who would surrender would be set free although they were wanted for offences not included in it. The Populists were in fact against any amnesty, and when a Liberal deputy dared to speak of a general one he suffered an onslaught even by Papandreou.[157]

The discrepancy in the law is explained by the mood of the Parliament and the Populist majority in the government. Participants in the 'rebel movement' were offered an amnesty, whereas those not directly implicated would have to turn over information. The Foreign Office pointed out that this might 'provide a peg on which the Communists and their supporters would hang a propaganda line suggesting an amnesty for "sneaks and betrayers"'.[158] Clearly, since any 'appeasement' policy would have to conform to the wishes of the State Department and the Populists, Sofulis's offer aimed at weakening the guerrilla movement from within. Ladas assured the Parliament that it was a 'sad privilege' to table the draft law, whilst his leader confirmed that his mollifying intentions were superficial. On 12 September he told Norton that his reference to an international supervision of the amnesty was 'partly window-dressing and partly by way of assurance that the government would do its best to protect those who gave themselves up'. The Greek Prime Minister had an original idea:

> Sofulis thought that two thirds of the rebels were reluctant to go on with the fight. His problem was where to put them. Could not the British Dominions offer to take them? I [Norton] said that this seemed to me unlikely.[159]

186

Even so, the formation of the Sofulis-Tsaldaris coalition was a major development. On 9 September *Pravda* commented that the Democratic Army had four good reasons to ignore the amnesty: it was a 'trap' for it did not include the thousands of political prisoners; the Left still remembered the Varkiza Agreement and the White Terror; the presence of the Liberals in the government was not a guarantee, as the Populist majority could dispose of them whenever they wished; and Sofulis's entrance into a government featuring Tsaldaris demonstrated that he was incapable of resisting American pressure.[160] In an editorial entitled 'The Birth of a Monster', *Rizospastis* wondered how long the United States could maintain the discipline in a government whose members loathed each other and which was set to follow a policy of 'Super-Dynamic Appeasement'. The DSE radio broadcast a personal attack on Sofulis and rebuffed the amnesty. According to the British Embassy, its effect was 'negligible', as of the 10,261 who surrendered 6,372 were right-wingers.[161]

This was no surprise. Zachariadis's April directives to Markos and the Strasbourg declaration signified that the KKE had set itself on a different course. The abortive attempts towards a compromise in May–July 1947 and the incorporation of Sofulis into a Populist-dominated Cabinet, which meant that the Liberal leader would no longer be available for overtures, could only have underpinned the adherence to that course. Throughout August *Rizospastis* propagated the EAM terms for pacification – Greek neutrality and the inclusion of EAM in the government – but on 5 August Ioannidis instructed Markos to secure a free area for the seat of the future KKE government; its establishment, however, did not depend on the existence of such a free area.[162]

At the same time it seems that the KKE started to receive foreign material assistance. On 7 August Ioannidis cabled Markos that the party 'has at its disposal great quantities of material, which, however, you are not able to receive.' The material was sufficient 'to more than completely double the strength of the DSE'.[163] Five days later Zachariadis wrote to Tito that despite difficulties in transport, the party had secured the needed supplies, that the political and military conditions were ripe for the creation of a KKE government, and that the Democratic Army would soon secure a permanent free area.[164] On 1 September 1947 Zachariadis wrote to Zhdanov to thank him for the despatch of material and financial assistance and request additional equipment including 60 cannons, 2,000 anti-tank weapons, clothing for 15,000 men, 3–4 lorries, 20 wirelesses, and money.[165]

The arrival of supplies had inspired the KKE with optimism, whilst the frustration of the peace overtures added to its determination. Yet the initiatives for a compromise were to continue throughout the civil war. Though by late summer 1947 the KKE was disillusioned with the politicians in Athens, it continued to cherish expectations of an intermediary role by the United Nations. On 5 September the DSE radio announced that the DSE General Headquarters was sending a memorandum to the General Assembly describing the situation in Greece and offering to send a delegation to expound the views of the Greek guerrillas. The Foreign Office cabled the Permanent UK

Representative at the United Nations that such proposals should be turned down.[166] The DSE memorandum reiterated that the responsibility for the civil war lay with the Anglo-American intervention and called for the participation of EAM in the government and an end to foreign interference in Greek domestic affairs. A new soothing element was the request for the despatch of a UN Commission to supervise a 'democratic settlement'; the aggressive element was that the Democratic Army did not recognize the 'reactionary minority government' of Athens and sought permission to send a delegation to the General Assembly.[167] The memorandum was not circulated but only published in the list of private communications received by the UN Secretary-General.[168]

To refute the charges that the Greek leftists had '"sold themselves to foreigners and become stooges of the Slavs"', and that they wanted '"to take power by force"', Markos sent a letter to *The Times*, which the London paper published on 10 September 1947. The former charge, Markos argued, collapsed in the face of all those who fought in the DSE ranks, were imprisoned, deported and faced the firing squad. The second charge should be discarded in the light of the KKE terms for the participation of EAM in the government, a general amnesty and elections without foreign interference. Concluding with the request to send a representative to put the DSE case before the General Assembly,[169] the letter was intended to drum up the support of British and world opinion for it. But the United Nations would not even circulate the memorandum.

By September 1947, when the chance of a compromise had vanished, and with foreign aid on its way, what remained for the KKE was the formalization of Zachariadis's April directives and the preparations for setting up a government. These issues were addressed in the Third Plenum of the Central Committee, which met in two sessions: one in Yugoslavia on 11–12 September, where six members (including Zachariadis, Ioannidis and Markos) and four senior DSE commanders took the decisions, and one in Athens on 27 September, when these were discussed and approved by the Central Committee members who could be found in the capital. The Third Plenum decided that conditions were ripe for the creation of a free area with its own government, and that the party should give priority to the political and military plane in order to rally the required force. The DSE, then numbering 24,000 men and women in 55–60 battalions, should by spring 1948 be transformed into a regular army organized in brigades and increase its size to 55–60,000. The Third Plenum thus belatedly decided to mobilize the party masses and approved the operational plan *Limnes* [Lakes] for the creation of a free area in the north, with Thessaloniki as its centre.[170]

On 27 September the Central Committee members in Athens endorsed the decisions, but for several days *Rizospastis* did not publish anything, apparently because of disagreements among the EAM partners.[171] On 8 October the KKE daily published a Statement which, though vague, could not fail to act as a provocative warning: the KKE approved the speech made by Porfyrogenis at Strasbourg, it would intensify its military campaign, and called every one to support the Democratic Army and organize the 'popular struggle' in the towns.[172] When a week later *Rizospastis* published an appeal by Markos – 'Everybody in Arms' – the government decided that it had had enough with the leftist press. On 21 October 1947 the Parliament passed a Resolution banning all papers and journals which supported or fomented the 'rebellion'.[173]

The Statement of 8 October and the Resolution of the Third Plenum asserted that the KKE would continue its efforts for a compromise on the basis of the EAM proposals; in other words, the KKE would demand the participation of EAM in the Athens government while preparing to set up its own in the north. This curious decision may be explained in terms of the KKE's position in summer 1947. Once there was little hope of an acceptable compromise, the communists could either capitulate on the government's terms or move towards a head-on collision. This might have also been seen as a means of self-formalization for the KKE, its army and its struggle, an attempt to place itself centre-stage; and if coupled by some recognition by the communist states, the demoralizing effect this would have in Athens would be enormous. Yet the available sources hint that despite the promises, the recognition of a 'free Greece' was not a foregone conclusion. Zachariadis himself believed that this would happen if the Democratic Army managed to occupy a town to seat the government. On 20 September he wrote to Tito asking for mediation to 'all other parties' to provide material as well as moral support in the form of formal recognition of 'democratic Greece'.[174]

In a letter to the Politburo section in Athens on 18 September 1947, Zachariadis tried to justify his decision to leave the capital as follows:

> The situation makes it necessary to mobilize to the mountains as many forces as we can. It would be a mistake if we wavered on this point ... I think that the circumspection we had six months ago does not stand today. Nor should we be influenced by friendly advice and opinions, no matter how valuable they may be, for it is we who have the responsibility for our line and action in Greece and it is we who must decide.[175]

The KKE evidently received 'friendly advice and opinions' which were critical of its new plans. These came from its partners in EAM, who are known to have been 'benumbed', 'demoralized' and lacking confidence in victory.[176] It is also known, however, that some foreign communist parties had reservations about the prospects of the KKE struggle. The French and the Italian communists had already expressed their scepticism in early 1946; in the autumn of that year Harry Politt for the British Communist Party had told the London and Paris correspondents of *Rizospastis* that the KKE should 'not be carried away by enthusiasm' and warned them of 'the traps laid by imperialism'. Then in spring 1947 Porfyrogenis had sought the view of the French Communist Party with regard to the decision to set up a provisional government. Jacques Duclos adopted an attitude detached enough to suggest strong reservations, if not disapproval.[177]

Yet what mattered was not the opinion of the French, Italian or British Communist Parties, but that of the Soviet Union. The KKE announced its intention to set up a 'free Greece' with its own government after Porfyrogenis had apparently visited Moscow in June 1947. If so, he must have discussed the content of the speech he would make at Strasbourg, and the Soviets must have raised no doubts about the policy of the KKE. Once more the Greek communists acted independently and then, *after* the decision had been made, they sought Stalin's opinion and support. This establishes a considerable degree of independence in KKE policy-making, but at the same time it emphatically demonstrates that the implementation of policy was contingent on Stalin's whims. In the pile of promises and hints from Moscow there was also evidence of Soviet reserves about supporting the Greek communists. A strong indication that the KKE lay in the periphery of Soviet foreign policy interests emerged in late September 1947 at the founding meeting of the Cominform in Poland; the KKE was not invited in Szklarska Poreba, its struggle was not mentioned, and when the Yugoslav delegates tried to initiate some discussion of it they were silenced by Andrei Zhdanov.[178]

In practical terms the success of the KKE plans rested on realizing the aspiration to raise a force of 55–60,000 men. In this respect the government policy of mass evacuation of rural areas proved opportune. By November 1947 the number of evacuees was estimated at 310,000. Unlike those who had fled voluntarily, the majority wanted to return to their villages, where the risks were preferable to the miseries of refugee life. Next to the economic implications of mass evacuation, Griswold pointed out the political dangers. As the army transported the evacuees to safe areas and thereafter assumed no further responsibility, the latter felt 'abandoned' by the government and were 'subject to communist propaganda'.[179] Yet the need to prevent the expansion of the Democratic Army far outweighed the suffering of those people and the effect on the Greek economy. Not only would the American aid soon start to tilt the balance towards the government, but the KKE had disclosed its aims in June and thus given its opponents enough time to take appropriate measures. In the event these delivered the goods, for when the communists tried to build an army of 60,000, very few recruits were available.

While the last weeks of 1947 rolled on with each side bracing itself for the realization of its aims, the overall state of the country remained depressing. Economic problems were as formidable as ever, for a very large share of the budget was diverted to military and police functions, whilst an equally large share of Greece's manpower was engaged in civil war activities. Though it had prevented an immediate collapse, the American involvement had disappointed hopes that by the end of the year growing prosperity would weaken the guerrilla movement.[180] Another source of concern for the British and the Americans was the precarious coalition between the Populists and the Liberals. Each party felt that it had been forced into a government dominated by the other: the Populists were mindful of their parliamentary majority, whereas the Liberals were acutely aware they had sacrificed the asset of being the only alternative.

Even though the KKE challenge had brought down the fences between the two parties, one problem emerged as a result of the Populists' all-embracing definition of Communism. By December 1947 the strains on the coalition had become so severe that the Americans had to warn Tsaldaris of the adverse effect a new crisis would have on the extension of aid. Convinced that the activities of certain Liberal Ministers were driving the country 'on the path of Kerenskyism', the Vice-Premier and Foreign Minister threatened that unless Sofulis denounced them, co-operation would become impossible and he would either have to form a Populist government or retire from politics. The black sheep was the Justice Minister Konstantinos Rendis, who had allegedly released thousands of deportees without Tsaldaris's knowledge, had appointed in his ministry all 'communist' civil servants previously sacked for 'communist' activities, had called ELAS a 'national army', and had even had the temerity to accuse the Right of extremism. It is highly debatable whether Rendis had indulged in such activities, which, according to Tsaldaris, aimed at dislocating the regime and leading to Communism. The British records confirm that Rendis was open to attack simply for making appointments and transfers in the security forces on party grounds. At any rate, the Americans made strong representations to both leaders that the coalition should be maintained.[181]

On the military plane, the British Military Mission warned in October that the situation was as precarious as ever, mainly because the guerrillas' will to fight had not been broken. The British regarded military victory as 'an essential prerequisite' to a political settlement and economic recovery, hence they urged that the offensive against the Democratic Army should resume with 'renewed vigour'.[182] They had embraced Tsaldaris's request for the increase of the government army, but the Americans, who would have to meet the cost, were far less enthusiastic; the Greeks, Truman wrote, 'wanted equipment, advisers, money to expand their army, and would have given all our aid to the military if we had let them do it'.[183]

In September 1947 the marked deterioration engendered fears in the US Embassy that the whole of Thrace would have to be '"written off"' unless arms were issued to the local peasants and the army launched an attack under US military supervision. On 15 September Griswold urged Washington to sanction the increase of the Greek army and request from the British, who already had troops in Greece, to furnish operational advice; if they declined, the US government should despatch 125–200 American officers to do the job.[184] Indicating that it would accept the proposals, the State Department sent Major-General S.J. Chamberlin to Greece as a special representative of the US Chief of Staff to survey the situation and counsel accordingly. On 3 November 1947, on the advice of Chamberlin and the National Security Council, President Truman approved the despatch to Greece of a US advisory and planning group which would furnish the Greek armed forces with operational advice. The Joint US Military Advisory and Planning Group (JUSMAPG) arrived in Athens in December 1947 and started to function in the first weeks of 1948.[185]

Bevin was unwilling to take up the task envisaged by Griswold. The British Military Mission dealt with the organization and training of the government army and offered no advice on specific operations. What it did, according to its Deputy-Commander Brigadier C.D. Steel, was 'to discuss and advise on tactical methods to be employed, organization of forces, technique of Command and Staff work required for operations generally against the bandits'.[186] In other words, the BMM did assist the Greek military, whereas the British troops had a 'static role' and would not get entangled in battles unless attacked or their security was threatened.[187] For fear of his domestic critics, Bevin was anxious not to appear too deeply involved in the Greek quagmire. His concern for this was strongly reaffirmed when King Paul requested to be accompanied by the BMM Commander Major-General Stewart Rawlins in a visit to troops in the north. Norton advised that the request be granted, but the Foreign Office found it 'embarrassing'. Bevin had recently rebuffed a proposal put forward by the Embassy in Athens and backed by the British Chiefs of Staff, that BMM members should not be debarred from joining Greek army formations used in operations so long as they did not run any risk of becoming themselves involved in these operations. The Foreign Office instructed Norton to accept the request provided that King Paul visited rear positions and that it was made clear that Rawlins escorted him as his guest and not in his capacity as military adviser.[188]

An incident more embarrassing for the Labour government occurred on 10 November, when the *Daily Mirror* published reports about decapitations of guerrillas and other atrocities perpetrated by the government forces, and embellished its front page with pertinent photographic evidence. The issue was raised at the House of Commons, where some MPs inquired whether Britain should withdraw her Missions from Greece. According to George Thomas, the MP whose pro-DSE activity in February–March had incensed the Embassy in Athens, the Greek Minister of Public Order had stated that it was 'a Greek custom to bring back these heads when rewards are claimed'. The embarrassment prompted the Foreign Office to draw the Greek government's attention to these 'ugly reports' and to instruct its Embassy in Washington to do likewise with the US administration.[189]

Somewhat more serious was the British reaction to the establishment of JUSMAPG. The British military appeared uncertain as to the position of their own Missions, and feeling that the Americans might be planning to take over their functions, they informally suggested that these might be reduced or withdrawn from Greece. Washington insisted on the maintenance of the British Missions not only because they performed an important task, but also because there would be no conflict of functions since British policy ruled out the furnishing of military advice to the Greek army by British officers. The Americans were still suspicious of the British, especially as the dispute between Marshall and Bevin was just then withering away, and wanted 'to check any British disposition to use new American activities as [an] excuse for curtailment [of] British activities'.[190]

In Athens the British Embassy and the BMM were anxious to continue their cooperation with AMAG, and both parties suggested the integration of the two Military Missions.[191] For the State Department any such agreement should preserve the dominant role of the US staff and their freedom to advise the Greeks independently in case the American and British military disagreed. The Labour government, on the other hand, was mindful of its parliamentary critics. Bevin and Albert Alexander assured the US ambassador in London that there was no question of withdrawing the Missions, but their integration would have to be ruled out because of the trouble it would cause in the House of Commons.[192] The matter was neatly settled in January 1948, when it was decided that the US Army Group would provide advice on supply, operational and logistical matters, and the BMM would see to the organization and training of the Greek army.[193] Interestingly enough, some Greek officers felt that the American decision to advise them on operational matters had a double sting: against the Greek military, who were supposedly responsible for the perpetuation of the war, and against the BMM Commander for his failure to take appropriate organizational measures and 'his pressing interference in the conduct of operations'.[194]

In this manner Britain and the United States were propping up the Greek forces for better performances in the battlefield. The KKE, on the other hand, saw in the last weeks of 1947 that the implementation of the decisions of the Third Plenum was lagging behind. Two letters from Zachariadis to a certain Soviet official named Baranov on 6 October and 10 November disclose that the volume of foreign material aid to the Democratic Army was insufficient and agonizingly slow in arriving.[195] On 2 December the KKE leadership was annoyed to notice that the recruitment targets had not been met, and that consequently the DSE GHQ still had no strategic reserves to implement the *Limnes* Plan. The regional headquarters were ordered to reach their recruitment targets by February 1948, and despite the obvious setbacks, the KKE decided that a 'government' should be set up in the regions of 'free Greece' by the end of the year.[196] On 11 December Markos and Ioannidis cabled to the Politburo section in Athens proposing the participation of some EAM cadres in the forthcoming government. The reply was that the latter agreed but it was impossible to organize their escape to the mountains. Others chose to quibble. When sounded out by the communists, Ilias Tsirimokos, one of the KKE's wartime partners in EAM and now leader of the small socialist party SK-ELD, first vacillated, then accepted and eventually refused to take part in the KKE government.[197]

On Christmas Eve 1947 the DSE radio announced the formation of the *Provisional Democratic Government of Free Greece* (PDK). It consisted of eight KKE cadres, with Markos as 'Premier' and 'War Minister'. The objectives of the PDK included the liberation of the country from 'the yoke of the foreign imperialists and their instruments', the nationalization of heavy industry, banks and foreign assets, and the pursuit of a foreign policy 'within the context and aims' of the United Nations.[198] A government must have its seat, and this the Democratic Army tried to secure on the night of 24–25 December, when a large force launched a major offensive on Konitsa, a few kilometres from the Greek-Albanian frontier. The battle of Konitsa, the first attempt of the DSE in positional warfare, was bitterly fought by both sides until the last day of 1947. Then the garrison of the town was heavily reinforced and the attackers found themselves outnumbered. On 4 January 1948 the DSE retreated without having secured a seat for its government.[199]

The establishment of the Provisional Democratic Government set the KKE irrevocably on the path of civil war. By September 1947 the party was faced with three options: to capitulate on its opponents' terms, to continue the hit-and-run tactics, or to push matters to a head. Zachariadis opted for the latter because the first option was out of the question and the second could at best aim at a compromise through the unbearable disruption of normal life. Yet the United States was not in a mood for a compromise, while the influx of aid would soon tilt the balance towards the government. Despite his earlier optimistic estimates, by the end of the year Zachariadis must have realized that time was not on his side and that the KKE needed a military success before what he called 'the objective correlation of forces' slipped further to its disadvantage. The third option would then present all interested parties with a *fait accompli*: for the Greek government and its patrons it would be the last straw, but for the KKE it could turn out as a means of securing a greater commitment from its principal ideological ally. The Greek communists probably deemed this the only way they could redress the balance and seek a solution from a vantage point.

In treading on the path of civil war from the latter part of 1947 onwards, Zachariadis took a gamble. That he did so was because of the shortage of alternatives, which he made up for by trying to elicit promises of support from Moscow. No doubt he received them, but the success of his plans depended upon whether these promises were sincere. If Markos is to be believed, the KKE leader himself does not appear to have been wholly convinced that this was the case, hence his habit to accompany his appeals with *fait accomplis*. According to the DSE commander, just a few days before the offensive on Konitsa Markos asked him whether there were any chances for the recognition of the Provisional Democratic Government:

> Zachariadis said that we will take Konitsa, we will set up the Government and *possibly* [pithanon] we will be recognized.[200] [Emphasis mine]

The degree of confidence professed in this assessment must be juxtaposed with the certitudes prevailing in Athens, London and Washington.

NOTES

1. M. Vafiadis, *Apomnimonevmata* V (Athens: 1992), 347, 364.
2. DBP0: I, no.102: Memorandum by Sargent, 11/7/1945.
3. HC Deb., vol.430, cols.577–83; *The Times* (London): 19/11/1946.
4. *Rizospastis* (Athens): 22 and 23/1/1947, 6/2/1947.
5. F.O.371/66995 R420: Minute by Selby, 9/1/1947; F.O.371/66997 R1138: Lascelles to F.O., 25/1/1947.
6. *Rizospastis* (Athens): 12/2/1947.
7. *Rizospastis* (Athens): 19/1/1947.
8. F.O.371/66997 R858: Lascelles to F.O., 20/1/1947.
9. F.O.371/66997 R924: Lascelles to F.O., 21/1/1947.
10. EPSV: 128 (1/10/1946–27/2/1947), p.928 (23/1/1947).
11. F.O.371/66999 R1809: Norton to Bevin, 5/2/1947; *Rizospastis* (Athens): 31/1/1947.
12. F.O.371/72240 R2576: Norton to Bevin, 18/2/1948: Annual Report for 1947; F.O.371/67062 R2096: Peck (Thessaloniki) to Athens, 5/2/1947.

13. FRUS (1947): V, 817–18: MacVeagh to Marshall, 7/2/1947; *ibid.*, 818–20: Marshall to MacVeagh, 8/2/1947; F.O.371/66999 R1850: Norton to F.O., 10/2/1947.

14. F.O.371/66999 R1791: Permanent UK Delegation to UNO (New York) to F.O., 9/2/1947; *ibid.*, R1869: Norton to F.O., 10/2/1947; F.O.371/72240 R2576: Norton to Bevin, 18/2/1948: Annual Report for 1947; F.O.371/66999 R1753: Norton to F.O., 6/2/1947; *ibid.*, R1801: Norton to F.O., 10/2/1947.

15. F.O.371/67062 R1972: Windle to F.O., 10 and 16/2/1947.

16. F.O.371/72240 R2576: Norton to Bevin, 18/2/1948: Annual Report for 1947.

17. F.O.371/67000 R1975: Norton to F.O., 12/2/1947.

18. F.O.371/67000 R1975: Minutes by Selby (17/2/1947) and Williams, (19/2/1947).

19. F.O.371/67013 R1591: Minutes by Selby (12/2/1947), Williams (13/2/1947), Warner (15/2/1947); F.O.371/67062 R2548: Norton to F.O., 24/2/1947.

20. F.O.371/67062 R2091: Norton to F.O., 14/2/1947.

21. KKE (es.) Archives: *Avgi* (Athens) 20/1/1980: Extracts from the unpublished memoirs of Michalis Kyrkos.

22. *Loc.cit.*; *Rizospastis* (Athens): 18/2/1947; Soviet Foreign Ministry Archives: Greek–Soviet Relations 1944–1949, in P. Andaeos, *Nikos Zachariadis: Thytis ke Thyma* 2nd edn. (Athens: 1991), pp.457–8.

23. *Rizospastis* (Athens): 1/3/1947.

24. F.O.371/67062 R2548: Norton to F.O., 24/2/1947.

25. F.O.371/67000 R2733: Minute by Warner, 5/3/1947.

26. *Rizospastis* (Athens): 19/2/1947; M. Vafiadis, *op.cit.* V, 156–7, 347–8; F.O.371/67062 R2550: Norton to F.O., 24/2/1947; *ibid.*, R2896: Norton to F.O., 27/2/1947; *ibid.*, R2945: Tsaldaris to Norton, 22/2/1947; F.O.371/67063 R3062: Norton to F.O., 7/3/1947; F.O.371/72240 R2576: Norton to Bevin, 18/2/1948: Annual Report for 1947.

27. F.O.371/67063 R3266: Windle to F.O., 11/3/1947; F.O.371/72240 R2576: Norton to Bevin, 18/2/1948: Annual Report for 1947; *Rizospastis* (Athens): 26/2/1947.

28. F.O.371/67064 R3656: Windle to F.O., 18/3/1947; *ibid.*, R4206: Report by Mrs Fothergill-Payne, 20/3/1947.

29. KKE: E.K., VI, Appendix, pp.437–9: Statement of DSEGHQ, 23/3/1947; *Rizospastis* (Athens): 15/5/1947; M. Vafiadis, *op.cit.* V, 137–8, 143, 219–20, 348–51; D. Katsis, *To Imerologio enos Andarti tou DSE 1946–49* I (Athens: 1990), 339–43.

30. M. Vafiadis, *op.cit.* V, 351–6; F.O.371/67064 R4206: Report by Mrs Fothergill-Payne, 20/3/1947; F.O.371/72240 R2576: Norton to Bevin, 18/2/1948: Annual Report for 1947. The DSE Memorandum has recently been published in Greek as *Etsi Archise o Emfylios: I Tromokratia meta ti Varkiza. To Ypomnima tou DSE ston OIE* (Athens: 1987).

31. *Etsi Archise o Emfylios*, p.395.

32. FRUS (1947): V, 816–17: Ethridge to Marshall, 3/2/1947; *ibid.*, 821–3: Marshall to Ethridge, 20/2/1947; *ibid.*, 829–30: Acheson to Ethridge, 1/4/1947; *ibid.*, 835–6: Austin to Marshall, 16/4/1947; F.O.371/67064 R4162: Norton to F.O., 26/3/1947; F.O.371/72240 R2576: Norton to Bevin, 18/2/1948: Annual Report for 1947.

33. F.O.371/67065 R5291: Windle (Geneva) to F.O., 18/4/1947; F.O. to Windle, 23/4/1947.

34. F.O.371/67065 R5556: Windle (Geneva) to F.O., 24/4/1947; F.O. to Paris, 26/4/1947.
35. F.O.371/67066 R5742: Inverchapel to F.O., 29/4/1947; FRUS (1947): V, 837–8: Marshall to Ethridge, 1/5/1947.
36. F.O.371/67066 R6129: Draft Recommendations of US Delegation (Geneva), 2/5/1947.
37. *Rizospastis* (Athens): 8 and 11/5/1947.
38. FRUS (1947): V, 840: Marshall to Ethridge, 3/5/1947; *ibid.*, 840–3: Marshall to Ethridge, 7/5/1947; F.O.371/67003 R6226: F.O. to UK Delegation (Geneva), 10/5/1947.
39. F.O.371/67003 R6226: Norton to F.O., 8/5/1947.
40. F.O.371/67067 R6345: Norton to F.O., 10/5/1947.
41. F.O.371/67003 R6226: F.O. to UK Delegation (Geneva), 10/5/1947.
42. F.O.371/67003 R6368: Inverchapel to F.O., 10/5/1947; F.O.371/67067 R6345: F.O. to Norton, 13/5/1947; *ibid.*, R6749: Inverchapel to F.O., 13/5/1947.
43. FRUS (1947): V, 174–5.
44. *Ibid.*, 850–60: Ethridge to Marshall, 12/5/1947; *ibid.*, 863–4: Ethridge to Marshall, 20/5/1947. The Report of the UN Commission in F.O.371/67069 R7244 and UNO/SC *Official Records*, 2nd Year, Special Supplement no.2. See also F.O.371/72240 R2576: Norton to Bevin, 18/2/1948: Annual Report for 1947; *Rizospastis* (Athens): 24/5/1947.
45. FRUS (1947): V, 865–89; UNO/SC *Official Records*, 2nd Year, nos 51, 55, 66, 69, 71, 74, 79, 89; UNOGA *Official Records*, 2nd Session, 1st Committee, Summary Record of Meetings, 16/9–19/11/1947, pp.14, 108, 114–15, 591, 597, 600; UNO/GA *Official Records*, 2nd Session, Plenary Meetings, I, pp.401, 461–2, UNO/GA *Official Records*, 2nd Session, Resolutions, 16/9–19/11/1947, p.12. For the story of the work of the UNO in Greece see A. Nachmani, *International Intervention in the Greek Civil War: The United Nations Special Committee on the Balkans, 1947–1952* (New York: 1990).
46. HC Deb., vol.438, col.2341.
47. F.O.371/67004 R8478: Norton to Bevin, 19/6/1947.
48. F.O.371/67003 R7553: Norton to F.O., 5/6/1947.
49. *Rizospastis* (Athens): 22 and 23/1/1947; 6, 12 and 18/2/1947; 1 and 23/3/1947; 4/4/1947.
50. KKE (es.) Archives, *Avgi* (Athens), 9/12/1979: Zachariadis's Memorandum to Stalin, 13/5/1947.
51. KKE (es.) Archives, *Avgi* (Athens), 7/12/1979: Zachariadis to Stalin, 12/1/1947; Ioannidis to Zachariadis, 1/2/1947.
52. KKE (es.) Archives, *Avgi* (Athens), 9/12/1979: Ioannidis to Markos, 2/4/1947; *Rizospastis* (Athens): 4/4/1947.
53. F.O.371/67090 R662: Norton to Bevin, 9/1/1947; F.O.371/66994 R185: F.O. to Dominions, 14/1/1947; F.O.371/67075 R7593: Southern Department to Embassy, 20/6/1947. For the activity of the Special Courts Martial see F.O.371/67075 R2317, R5212, R7591, R7593.
54. F.O.371/67049 R1795: Norton to F.O., 7/2/1947; *ibid.*, R2248: Norton to F.O., 17/2/1947; *ibid.*, R2950: Copy of Order by Minister of Public Order; *ibid.*, R4126: BPM to Embassy, 19/3/1947; *ibid.*, R5451: BPM to Embassy, 1/4/1947; F.O.371/67143 R7902: Norton to Bevin, 4/6/1947; F.O.371/72240 R2576: Norton to Bevin, 18/2/1948: Annual Report for 1947; HC Deb,

vol.434, col.933 (McNeil, 10/3/47); FRUS (1947): V, 102–3: MacVeagh to Marshall, 7/3/1947; *Rizospastis* (Athens): 5/3/1947.

55. *The Times* (London): 15/4/1947; *News Chronicle* (London): 13/6/1947; EPSV (1947): 130, p.1140: Statement by Konstantinos Rendis, 29/4/1947.

56. F.O.371/67127A R5486: Parker to Mayhew, 17/4/1947; EAM Press Bulletin, 4/4/1947; *ibid.*, R7900: Athens to Southern Department, 31/5/1947 and 8/7/1947.

57. EPSV (1947): 130, p.1210 (12/5/1947); F.O.371/67003 R6547: Norton to F.O., 14/5/1947; *ibid.*, R6649: Norton to F.O., 16/5/1947; F.O.371/67143 R7902: Norton to Bevin, 4/6/1947; F.O.371/67004 R8375: Norton to F.O., 19/6/1947.

58. KKE (es.) Archives, *Avgi* (Athens), 19/12/1979: KKE Memorandum to the Soviet CP on the belligerent forces in Greece, 12/6/1947; M. Vafiadis, *op.cit.* V, 134.

59. F.O.371/67064 R4206 Report by Mrs Fothergill-Payne (12–17 March 1947), 20/3/1947. For Mrs Fothergill-Payne, an employee of the British Consulate in Scopje, Yugoslavia, see F.O.371/66995 R481: F.O. Minute, 16/1/1947.

60. D. Zafiropoulos, *O Antisymmoriakos Agon* (Athens: 1956), pp.211–12; F.N. Grigoriadis, *Istoria tou Emfyliou Polemou, 1945–1949* IV (Athens: n.d.), 963–95; S.N. Grigoriadis, *Dekemvris–Emfylios Polemos, 1944–49: Synoptiki Istoria* (Athens: 1984), p.329; see also N. Margaris, *Istoria tis Makronisou* I–II (Athens: 1966).

61. F.O.371/67143 R11924: Reilly to Bevin, 28/8/1947; F.O. 371/72240 R2576: Norton to Bevin, 18/2/1947, Annual Report for 1947; *Rizospastis* (Athens): 16/2/1947; *To Vima* (Athens): 21/8/1947, 23/9/1947; *Eleftheria* (Athens): 23/8/1947.

62. F.O.371/58718 R18217: Norton to F.O., 12/12/1946. See also *ibid.*, R18337: Norton to F.O., 14/12/1946; Lord Montgomery, *The Memoirs of the Viscount Field-Marshal Montgomery of Alamein* (London: 1958), pp.427–8.

63. Ample documentation for the military operations in F.O.371/67075, F.O.371/67135, F.O.371/67143. For DSE accounts see M. Vafiadis, *op.cit.* V, 183–4, 275–342; D. Katsis, *op.cit.* I, 387–511; T. Psimmenos, *Andartes St' Agrafa (1946–1950): Anamniseis enos Andarti* 2nd edn. (Athens: 1985), pp.78–161.

64. FRUS (1947): V, 196–8: Greek Embassy to State Department, 7/6/1947; *ibid.*, 195: Memorandum by Henderson, 13/6/1947; F.O.371/67143 R11924: Reilly to Bevin, 28/8/1947.

65. KKE (es.) Archives, *Avgi* (Athens), 11/12/1979: Zachariadis's confidential directives to Markos, 17/4/1947.

66. For a similar analysis of the KKE gradualism and the Soviet connection, see P.J. Stavrakis, *Moscow and Greek Communism, 1944–1949* (Ithaca and London: 1989), pp.101–26, 135–46.

67. M. Vafiadis, *op.cit.* V, 151–2, 156. In 1957 Zachariadis claimed that his decision had been to leave Athens as early as summer 1946, but 'the c[omrades] who were assisting us [,] both small and big, objected'. See P. Dimitriou, ed., *I Diaspasi tou KKE* I (Athens: 1978), 96.

68. KKE (es.) Archives, *Avgi* (Athens), 9/12/1979: Zachariadis to Tito, 22/4/1947.

69. KKE (es.) Archives, *Avgi* (Athens), 14/12/1979: Zachariadis's Memorandum to Stalin, 13/5/1947; *ibid.*, *Avgi* (Athens), 12/12/1979: Ioannidis to Politburo (Athens), 4/6/1947. Zachariadis's memorandum appears to have been sent also

197

to the leadership of the Yugoslav CP, see S. Vukmanovič (Tempo), *How and Why the People's Liberation Struggle of Greece Met with Defeat* 2nd edn. (London: 1985), p.98.

70. N. Zachariadis, *Chroniko*, in P. Andaeos, *op.cit.*, p.199. For the charges against Zachariadis in 1956–7 see P. Dimitriou, ed., *op.cit.* I, 46, 52–4, 79–80; II, 561, 566–8.

71. KKE (es.) Archives, Avgi (Athens), 15/12/1979: Zachariadis's to Baranov, 5/6/1947.

72. KKE (es.) Archives, *Avgi* (Athens), 23/1/1980: Partsalidis to Ioannidis, 22/4/1947; Ioannidis to Partsalidis, 23/4/1947.

73. GAK: Tsouderos Papers, E (55): EAM Memorandum to Premier Maximos, 24/4/1947.

74. KKE (es.) Archives, *Avgi* (Athens), 20/1/1980: Extracts from the unpublished memoirs of Michalis Kyrkos.

75. F.O.371/67003 R6474: HM Consul-General (Thessaloniki) to Athens, 14/5/1947; Athens to F.O., 14/5/1947; Minutes by McCarthy (15/5/1946) and Selby (16/6/1947).

76. F.O.371/67000 R2733: Minute by Warner, 5/3/1947; F.O. 371/67001 R7553: Norton to F.O., 5/6/1947.

77. KKE (es.) Archives, *Avgi* (Athens), 23/1/1980: Partsalidis to Ioannidis, 19/5/1947; Ioannidis to Partsalidis, 13/6/1947.

78. FRUS (1947): V, 219–24: Marshall to Griswold, 11/7/1947.

79. KKE (es.) Archives, *Avgi* (Athens), 23/1/1980: Ioannidis to Partsalidis, 24/6/1947.

80. Speech in KKE: E.K., VI, Appendix, pp.440–3.

81. FRUS (1947): V, 260–1: MacVeagh to Marshall, 24/7/1947; *ibid.*, 238–42: State Department Memorandum, 17/7/1947; *ibid.*, 218: MacVeagh to Marshall, 10/7/1947; *Rizospastis* (Athens): 10, 11, 15/7/1947; F.O.371/67004 R9642: Reilly to F.O., 15/7/1947; F.O.371/72240 R2576: Norton to Bevin, 18/2/1948: Annual Report for 1947; KKE (es.) Archives, *Avgi* (Athens), 23/12/1979: Anastasiadis to Ioannidis, 9 and 10/7/1947; Ioannidis to Markos, 9/7/1947.

82. CAB 128/10/C.M.61 (47): 15/7/1947. On 2 July Maximos had sought US permission for the arrests and Marshall had granted it. FRUS (1947): V, 208–9: MacVeagh to Marshall, 2/7/1947; *ibid.*, 211: Marshall to MacVeagh, 3/7/1947; F.O.371/72240 R2576: Norton to Bevin, 18/2/1948: Annual Report for 1947.

83. F.O.371/67006 R10227: Reilly to F.O.,14/7/1947; F.O.371/67005 R10216: F.O. to Norton, 16/7/1947; F.O.371/67143 R11924: Reilly to Bevin, 28/8/1947.

84. FRUS (1947): V, 225–6: MacVeagh to Marshall, 11/7/1947.

85. KKE (es.) Archives, *Avgi* (Athens), 22/1/1980: Extracts from the unpublished memoirs of Michalis Kyrkos.

86. FRUS (1947): V, 250–2: MacVeagh to Marshall, 21/7/1947; *ibid.*, 217: MacVeagh to Marshall, 9/7/1947; *ibid.*, 219–4: Marshall to Griswold, 11/7/1947; FRUS (1947): IV, 547: Russell to Acheson, 27/3/1947; F.O.371/67005 R10070: British Embassy to State Department, Aide Mémoire, 16/7/1947.

87. F.O.371/67005 R10070: British Embassy to State Department, Aide Mémoire, 16/7/1947; FRUS (1947): V, 231–2: MacVeagh to Marshall, 13/12/1947.

88. FRUS (1947): V, 213–14: MacVeagh to Marshall, 7/7/1947.

89. *Ibid.*, 217: MacVeagh to Marshall, 9/7/1947.

90. F.O.371/67005 R10070: British Embassy to State Department, Aide Mémoire, 16/7/1947.

91. FRUS (1947): V, 251, n.2: MacVeagh to Marshall, 15/7/1947.

92. F.O.371/67006 R10227: Reilly to F.O., 14/7/1947; F.O.371/67005 R10070: British Embassy to State Department, Aide Mémoire, 16/7/1947.

93. F.O.371/67005 R10070: British Embassy to State Department, Aide Mémoire, 16/7/1947.

94. FRUS (1947): V, 243–4: Marshall to Athens, 18/7/1947; F.O.371/67005 R10191: Balfour (Washington) to F.O., 18/7/1947.

95. F.O.371/67005 R9991: Reilly to F.O., 20/7/1947; FRUS(1947): V, 250–2: MacVeagh to Marshall, 21/7/1947.

96. FRUS (1947): V, 250–2: MacVeagh to Marshall, 21/7/1947.

97. GAK: Tsouderos Papers, E (53): Five Articles in *To Vima*, 22–26/4/1947; *ibid.*, E (49): A Note on the Greek Question, n.d. [March 1947].

98. F.O.371/67005 R9991: Reilly to F.O., 20/7/1947.

99. F.O.371/67005 R9991: Minutes by Warner and Wallinger, 23/7/1947.

100. F.O.371/67005 R10068: Reilly to F.O., 22/7/1947.

101. F.O.371/67005 R9991: Minutes by Warner and Wallinger, 23/7/1947.

102. FRUS (1947): V, 245–6: MacVeagh to Marshall, 19/7/1947.

103. KKE (es.) Archives, *Avgi* (Athens), 16 and 18/12/1979: General Report of the KKE CC to the CPSU CC, 17 July 1947; T.D. Sfikas, 'O "Telefteos Peirasmos" tou KKE, Ioulios 1947', *O Mnemon* 14 (1992), 151–75.

104. F.O.371/72240 R2576: Norton to Bevin, 18/2/1948: Annual Report for 1947; FRUS (1947): I, 750751: Acheson to London, 17/5/1947; *ibid.*, 751758: Douglas to State Department, 11/6/1947; A. Bullock, *Ernest Bevin: Foreign Secretary 1945–1951* (Oxford: 1985), pp.411–13.

105. F.O.371/67006 R10513: Reilly to F.O., 30/7/1947; F.O.371/67007 R11218: Reilly to Wallinger, 22/8/1947, Wallinger to Reilly, 4/9/1947.

106. HC Deb., vol.444, col.814; CAB 129/16/C.P. (47) 34: Bevin's Memorandum, Policy towards Greece and Turkey, 25/1/1947; CAB 128/9/C.M. 14 (47) 4: 30/1/1947.

107. FRUS (1947): V, 79–81: British Embassy to State Department, Aide Mémoire, 4/3/1947; F.O.371/63195 J3634: Minute by Hankey, 29/5/1947.

108. F.O.371/67043 R10641: COS Committee, Extracts from Minutes of Staff Conference held at No.10 Downing Street, 28/7/1947. See also F.O.371/67045 R11390: Minute by Henniker, 16/8/1947.

109. F.O.371/67043 R10494: F.O. to Washington and Athens, 30/7/1947.

110. F.O.371/67043 R10641: Minutes by Sargent and Warner, 29/7/1947.

111. FRUS (1947): V, 268: Balfour to Marshall, 30/7/1947.

112. *Ibid.*, 271–2: Memorandum by Bohlen, 1/8/1947; F.O.371/67043 R10538: Balfour to F.O., 31/7/1947.

113. F.O.371/67043 R10539: Balfour to F.O., 30/7/1947.

114. FRUS (1947): V, 273–4: Marshall to Bevin, 1/8/1947; *ibid.*, 276: Marshall to Douglas, 1/8/1947.

115. *Ibid.*, 276: Marshall to MacVeagh, 2/8/1947; *ibid.*, 276–7: MacVeagh to Marshall, 2/8/1947.

116. F.O.371/67043 R10586: Minute by Bevin, 2/8/1947; FRUS (1947): V, 277–8: Douglas to Marshall, 3/8/1947; *ibid.*, 289–90: Douglas to Marshall, 9/8/1947; *ibid.*, 290, n.4 (Meeting between Douglas and Sargent, 15/8/1947); *ibid.*,

301–2: Bevin to Marshall, 20/8/1947.
117. W. Millis, ed., *The Forrestal Diaries* (New York: 1951), p.293.
118. FRUS (1947): V, 313: Marshall to Lovett, 25/8/1947; ibid., 317–18: Lovett to Royall, 27/8/1947.
119. *Ibid.*, 321–3: Douglas to Lovett, 1/9/1947. For the Pentagon Talks see *ibid.*, 485–626 and F.O.371/61114.
120. *Ibid.*, 327–9: Royall to Marshall, 5/9/1947; *ibid.*, 330–2: Marshall to Douglas, 8/9/1947.
121. Bevin Papers: F.O.800/468/GRE/47/34: F.O. to Washington, 12/9/1947; *ibid.*, F.O.800/468/GRE/47/35: Withdrawal of British troops from Greece, 15/9/1947; FRUS (1947): V, 334–5: Douglas to Marshall, 10/9/1947; *ibid.*, 337: Douglas to Marshall, 12/9/1947.
122. Records of the Pentagon Talks in Bevin Papers: F.O.800/476/ME/47/21 and FRUS (1947): V, 488–626.
123. F.O.371/67047A R14346: Minister of Defence to COS, 17/10/1947.
124. Bevin Papers: F.O.800/468/GRE/47/39: Meeting between Bevin and Tsaldaris, 31/10/1947.
125. F.O.371/67047A R15857: Extracts from Minutes of Staff Conference, 21/11/1947.
126. F.O.371/67045 R11390: Minute by Henniker, 16/8/1947.
127. FRUS (1947): V, 335–6: Royall to Marshall, 11/9/1947; W. Millis, ed., *op.cit.*, p.328: entry for 7/11/1947.
128. K. Morgan, *Labour in Power 1945–1951* (Oxford: 1985), p.239; A. Bullock, *op.cit.*, pp.394–400.
129. *Keep Left* (London: 1947), pp.37, 46.
130. L. Woolf, *Foreign Policy: The Labour Party's Dilemma* (London: 1947), pp.12–15.
131. *TUC Conference Report* (1947), pp.494–501; K. Morgan, *op. cit.*, pp.351–7; A. Bullock, *op.cit.*, pp.441–2, 452–5.
132. F.O.371/72240 R2576: Norton to Bevin, 18/2/1948: Annual Report for 1947.
133. F.O.371/72238 R757: Memorandum by David Balfour, 30/9/1947.
134. F.O.371/72238 R757: Wallinger to Norton, 15/6/1948.
135. Bevin Papers: F.O.800/509/UN/47/13: Bevin to McNeil, 15/10/1947.
136. FRUS (1947): V, 219–24: Marshall to Griswold, 11/7/1947.
137. Memorandum by the State Department to President Truman, 17/7/1947, Harry S. Truman Library (Independence, Missouri): Harry S. Truman Papers, quoted by V. Kondis, *I Anglo–Amerikaniki Politiki ke to Elliniko Provlima, 1945–1949* (Thessaloniki: 1984), pp.285–6.
138. F.O.371/67145 R11452: Bevin (Paris) to F.O., 2/7/1947.
139. FRUS (1947): V, 253–5: Memorandum by Jernegan, 22/7/1947; *ibid.*, 264–5: MacVeagh to Marshall, 28/7/1947; *ibid.*, 281–4: Memorandum by Villard to Marshall, 7/8/1947, *ibid.*, 284–5: Memorandum by Marshall, 7/8/1947; *ibid.*, 287–8: Memorandum by Villard to Marshall, 8/8/1947.
140. F.O.371/67145 R11654: Minutes of Conversation between Sargent and Tsaldaris, 18/8/1947.
141. FRUS (1947): V, 299–301: MacVeagh to Marshall, 19/8/1947; *ibid.*, 294–6: Griswold to McGhee, 14/8/1947.
142. F.O.371/72240 R2576: Norton to Bevin, 18/2/1948: Annual Report for 1947; FRUS (1947): V, 299–301: MacVeagh to Marshall, 19/8/1947; *ibid.*, 309–10: MacVeagh to Marshall, 23/8/1947.

143. FRUS (1947): V, 310–11: Lovett to MacVeagh, 24/8/1947.
144. *Ibid.*, 311–13: MacVeagh to Marshall, 25/8/1947; *ibid.*, 316–17: MacVeagh to Marshall, 26/8/1947; F.O.371/67007 R11718: Reilly to F.O., 26/8/1947.
145. F.O.371/67007 R11798: Reilly to F.O., 27/8/1947; *ibid.*, R11830: Reilly to F.O., 28/8/1947; *ibid.*, R11883: Reilly to F.O., 29/8/1947; FRUS (1947): V, 318–19: MacVeagh to Marshall, 27/8/1947.
146. F.O.371/67007 R11884: Reilly to F.O., 30/8/1947; *ibid.*, R11914: Reilly to F.O., 30/8/1947; FRUS (1947): V, 320–1: MacVeagh to Marshall, 30/8/1947.
147. F.O.371/67007 R11914: Reilly to F.O., 30/8/1947.
148. FRUS (1947): V, p.323, n.1: State Department to Athens, 28/8/1947.
149. *Ibid.*, 323–5: MacVeagh to Marshall, 2/9/1947; *ibid.*, 326–7: MacVeagh to Marshall, 4/9/1947; F.O.371/67007 R12241: Norton to F.O., 4/9/1947; *ibid.*, R12325: Greek Bulletin, 9/9/1947; F.O.371/72240 R2576: Norton to Bevin, 18/2/1948: Annual Report for 1947.
150. F.O.371/72240 R2576: Norton to Bevin, 18/2/1948, Annual Report for 1947; F.O.371/67007 R12204: Norton to Bevin, September 1947.
151. FRUS (1947): V, 9–11: Marshall to MacVeagh, 21/1/1947; *ibid.*, 299–301: MacVeagh to Marshall, 19/8/1947.
152. F.O.371/67007 R12591: Note by Sofulis to Henderson on Political Programme, 4/9/1947.
153. F.O.371/67007 R12325: Minutes by Balfour, 10–11/9/1947; also *ibid.*, R11885 and R12273: Minutes by Balfour, 2 and 9/9/1947.
154. *Rizospastis* (Athens): 10/9/1947.
155. F.O.371/67007 R12350: Norton to F.O., 8/9/1947; FRUS (1947): V, 332–3: MacVeagh to Marshall, 9/9/1947.
156. EPSV (1947): 130, pp.1470–2, 1492–4, 1507, 1514: 7, 8 and 10/9/1947; F.O.371/67007 R12411: Norton to F.O., 9/9/1947; *ibid.*, R12523: Norton to F.O., 11/9/1947; *ibid.*, R12692: Text of Amnesty Law, 10–12/9/1947.
157. F.O.371/67007 R12599: Norton to F.O., 13/9/1947.
158. F.O.371/67007 R12692: Southern Department to Athens, 29/9/1947.
159. F.O.371/67007 R12544: Norton to F.O., 12/9/1947.
160. F.O.371/67126 R12524: Moscow to F.O., 11/9/1947.
161. *Rizospastis* (Athens): 7/9/1947; F.O.371/67007 R12325: Extract from DSE Radio, 9/9/1947; F.O.371/72240 R2576: Norton to Bevin, 18/2/1948: Annual Report for 1947.
162. *Rizospastis* (Athens): 9 and 29/8/1947, 3/9/1947; KKE (es.) Archives, *Avgi* (Athens), 25/12/1979: Ioannidis to Markos, 5/8/1947.
163. KKE (es.) Archives, *Avgi* (Athens), 25/12/1979: Ioannidis to Markos, 7/8/1947.
164. KKE (es.) Archives, *Avgi* (Athens), 25/12/1979: Zachariadis to Tito, 12/8/1947.
165. KKE (es.) Archives, *Avgi* (Athens), 25/12/1979: Zachariadis to Zhdanov, 1/9/1947.
166. F.O.371/67146 R12364: F.O. to New York, 8/9/1947.
167. KKE: E.K., VI, pp.445–6: DSE GHQ Memorandum to UNO/GA, 5/9/1947; F.O.371/67146 R12391: F.O. to New York, 10/9/1947; *ibid.*, R12621: BBC Monitoring Service, DSE Broadcast and DSE Memorandum, 10/9/1947.
168. F.O.371/67146 R13326: New York to F.O., 30/9/1947.
169. *The Times* (London): 10/9/1947.
170. KKE (es.) Archives, *Avgi* (Athens), 1, 3 and 6/1/1980: Summary Minutes of

the 3rd Plenum; Summary Minutes of the meeting of the political and military leadership of the DSE; *Limnes* Plan; Resolution of the 3rd Plenum; Statement of the 3rd Plenum.

171. KKE (es.) Archives, *Avgi* (Athens), 10/1/1980: Anastasiadis to Ioannidis, 13/10/1947.

172. KKE: E.K., VI, no.773; *Rizospastis* (Athens): 8/10/1947.

173. *Rizospastis* (Athens): 17/10/1947; EPSV (1947): 131, pp. 877–8, 887 (17 and 21/10/1947).

174. KKE (es.) Archives, *Avgi* (Athens), 11/1/1980: Zachariadis to Tito, 20/9/1947; *Rizospastis* (Athens): 26/8/1947; *Avgi* (Athens), 30/1/1980: Interview with L. Eleftheriou; *Simioma me tis Apopseis tou Markou Vafiadi*, 15/11/1948, in P. Dimitriou, ed., *op.cit.* I, 24.

175. KKE: E.K., VI, p.444: Zachariadis's to Politburo, 18/9/1947.

176. KKE (es.) Archives, *Avgi* (Athens), 12/1/1980: Anastasiadis (Athens) to Ioannidis, 23/10/1947.

177. V. Georgiou, *I Zoi mou* (Athens: 1992), pp.532, 548–9; D. Partsalidis, *Dipli Apokatastasi tis Ethnikis Andistasis* (Athens: 1978), p.199. I am indebted to Professor Ole L. Smith for his detailed comments on this point (personal communications, 19/2/1990 and 23/12/1992).

178. O.L. Smith, 'The Greek Communist Party, 1945–1949', in D. Close, ed., *The Greek Civil War, 1943–1950: Studies of Polarization* (London: 1993), p.145.

179. F.O.371/67143 R11924: Reilly to Bevin, 28/8/1947; F.O.371/72240 R2576: Norton to Bevin, 18/2/1948: Annual Report for 1947; FRUS (1947): V, 388–9: Memorandum by Jernegan, 27–28/10/1947; *ibid.*, 402–4: Griswold to Marshall, 13/11/1947.

180. F.O.371/72240 R2576: Norton to Bevin, 18/2/1948: Annual Report for 1947; GAK: Tsouderos Papers, E (62): International Labour Office, Report of the ILO Mission to Greece, October–November 1947.

181. F.O.371/72240 R2576: Norton to Bevin, 18/2/1948, Annual Report for 1947; F.O.371/72238 R946: Copy of a Record of a Conversation between Rankin and Tsaldaris, 20/12/1947.

182. W.O. 292/893 (BMM): GNA – Review of the Anti-Bandit Campaign, October 1947.

183. H.S. Truman, *The Memoirs of Harry S. Truman*, II, *Years of Trial and Hope* (London: 1956), 115; F.O.371/67031 R9770: COS Committee, Joint Planning Staff, Greece: Defence Policy, 15/7/1947; W.O. 202/893 (BMM): COS to Commander-in-Chief: Greek Armed Forces, 16/7/1947.

184. FRUS (1947): V, 336–7: Keeley to Marshall, 2/9/1947; *ibid.*, 337–40: Griswold to Marshall, 15/9/1947.

185. *Ibid.*, 344–6: Memorandum of a meeting at the State Department, 17/9/1947; *ibid.*, 375–7: Chamberlin to Eisenhower, 20/10/1947; *ibid.*, 391–3, 398–400, 407–8.

186. F.O.371/67030 R8647: Norton to Sargent, Enclosure: Brigadier C.D. Steel to Norton, 31/5/1947.

187. F.O.371/67151 R10112: Commander, British Troops to Commander, BMM, 15/7/1947.

188. F.O.371/67160 R12152: Norton to F.O., 4/9/1947; Minute by Warner, 6/9/1947; F.O. to Athens, 6/9/1947.

189. F.O.371/67031 R10121: F.O. Minutes, 10/11/1947; HC Deb., vol.444, cols.815–16 (17/11/1947).

190. FRUS (1947): V, 419–20: Lovett to Marshall, 25/11/1947.

191. *Ibid.*, 433–4: Keeley to Marshall, 3/12/1947.

192. *Ibid.*, 452–3: Lovett to London, 11/12/1947; *ibid.*, 453: Douglas to Secretary of State, 13/12/1947; *ibid.*, 456–7: Douglas to Lovett, 17/12/1947.

193. W.O. 202/894: Agreement Defining Functions and Relationships of US Army Group Greece and British Military Mission, January 1948.

194. D. Zafiropoulos, *op.cit.*, p.88.

195. KKE (es.) Archives, *Avgi* (Athens), 12/1/1980: Zachariadis to Baranov, 6/10/1947; *ibid.*, *Avgi* (Athens), 13/1/1980: Zachariadis to Baranov, 10/11/1947.

196. KKE: E.K., VI, no.775: Resolution of the Second Commission of the Politburo of the CC of the KKE, 2/12/1947; *ibid.*, no.776: Letter from the Politburo of the CC of the KKE, 9/12/1947. Also in KKE (es.) Archives, *Avgi* (Athens): 15–16/1/1980.

197. KKE (es.) Archives, *Avgi* (Athens), 19/1/1980: Ioannidis and Markos to Anastasiadis, 11/12/1947; Anastasiadis to Ioannidis, 15 and 19/12/1947; V. Georgiou, *op.cit.*, p.551.

198. KKE: E.K., VI, Appendix, pp.452–4: Constitutional Act of the Provisional Democratic Government, 23/12/1947; FRUS (1947): V, 462–3: Rankin to Marshall, 24/12/1947.

199. D. Zafiropoulos, *op.cit.*, pp.301–15; D. Katsis, *op.cit.* II (Athens: 1992), 96–118.

200. *Simioma me tis Apopseis tou Markou Vafiadi*, 15/11/1948, in P. Dimitriou, ed., *op.cit.* I, 24.

V The Year of 'Doubt and Anxiety': 1948

The Athenians to the Melians

The path of justice and honour involves one in danger. And, where danger is concerned, the Spartans are not, as a rule, very venturesome ... It is hardly likely therefore that, while we are in control of the sea, they will cross over to an island.

Thucydides, V : 107, 109

The PDK and British Perceptions of Soviet Involvement

On Christmas Eve 1947 the Greek government and its patrons were plunged into further gloom. Civil war and economic crisis had shaken civilian morale, and the confidence of the faithful in the Populist-Liberal coalition had diminished. Norton appealed to his government to remain on guard:

> With all her faults she [Greece] is still ... a part of the Western World, where the liberty of the individual and freedom of thought and speech are regarded as an essential part of our heritage ... Whatever the strategic importance today of keeping Greece on the right side of the iron curtain, her disappearance behind it would be a major defeat for the Western Powers and for European civilization.[1]

Apocalyptic visions of what would happen if Greece fell to the communists were ten-a-penny in the 1940s; nevertheless, the implication that the establishment of the Provisional Democratic Government was a menace to European civilization is an adequate introduction to the reactions of the parties concerned.

The Greek government responded vigorously. With American approval, on 25–28 December 1947 650 suspected communists were arrested in Athens, and on 27 December emergency legislation outlawed the KKE, EAM and their offsprings. The nationalist dimension of the struggle against Communism was reinforced by the passing of severe sentences upon those who aimed at the detachment of Greek territory.[2] In its effort to isolate the KKE, the government tried to 'make it appear that the supporters of the Markos Government are very few'. In a confidential circular to regional Police and Gendarmerie Commands, the Liberal Minister of Public Order Konstantinos Rendis defined the objective as 'to break down this rise in morale and produce depression' among the KKE following. By way of appealing to republicans and leftists 'in a friendly manner' and 'extolling their patriotism', the authorities should try to extract from former EAM/ELAS members declarations

205

condemning the PDK and the 'bandit war'.[3] Backed by the British, Tsaldaris requested the despatch of US troops, but the Americans refused to be rushed into action before a careful examination of the situation.[4]

Though dismayed by the establishment of the PDK, Bevin was anxious to ascertain US reactions before committing himself to specific measures.[5] Attention initially focussed on Yugoslavia, the chief patron of the KKE and its army. On 25 December 1947 Cavendish Cannon, the US ambassador in Belgrade, inquired whether the Yugoslavs intended to recognize the PDK. Aleš Bebler, the Yugoslav Deputy Foreign Minister, replied that although such a decision rested with the Yugoslav Presidium, his country could not turn a blind eye to the Greek civil war. His reply was equivocal enough to prompt a warning from Washington that the recognition of the KKE 'government' would amount to a flagrant violation of the United Nations Charter.[6]

By then the Foreign Office had worked out its response. On 29 December 1947 Geoffrey Wallinger, Head of the Southern Department, informed the US Embassy in London that Britain would instruct its ambassadors in Belgrade and Sofia to make similar *démarches* to the Yugoslavs and the Bulgarians. Norton would urge the Greek government not to suppress indiscriminately parties other than the KKE, to drive a wedge between leftists and communists and get the former to denounce the PDK. The ambassador would also offer the Greeks some advice on the semantics of the issue: 'the Markos group' should not be referred to as '"free"', '"Greek"' or '"Government"', but as '"Communist"' or '"rebel"'.[7]

On 30 December London instructed its ambassador in Belgrade, Sir Charles Peake, to warn Bebler that the PDK did not qualify either for the grant of belligerent rights or for recognition as a government.[8] Following an unsatisfactory conversation between the two men, Peake asked his French counterpart to elicit Bebler's views in an informal talk. A 'hesitant' and 'depressed' Bebler offered the French ambassador categorical assurances that if Markos obtained a foothold, Yugoslavia would not regard his regime as extending throughout Greece but merely over the portion of it that he actually controlled. After hinting that his country might some time in the future maintain diplomatic relations with both the PDK and the Athens government, Bebler encapsulated the Yugoslav scruples:

> We are confronted by two tasks. We must give our moral support to Markos, with whom we are in sympathy, but at the same time we must do nothing to compromise the interests of peace as a whole. We must not therefore take up too decided a position and we shall in consequence have to manoeuvre.[9]

The Yugoslav government, according to Peake, was confident that by supporting the KKE as it had hitherto been doing, it could 'get its way' in Greece without risking a head-on collision with the West by recognizing the PDK.[10]

By the last day of 1947 Bevin had grown querulous over the sluggishness of the US reaction. He jibed that 'events might move quickly in Greece and that the Americans might also move very quickly if and when they once decide to move at all'. Though nothing should be done in advance of the United States,

Britain should be poised to take immediate supportive action. The Defence Secretary Albert Alexander told him that troops due to leave Palestine could be sent to Greece, and Bevin held that *all* lines of action should be examined 'urgently'.[11] That Bevin contemplated reinforcing the British troops, whereas only a few weeks earlier he had been adamant on their withdrawal, offers further proof that he was not particularly confident about the efficacy of American policy in Greece. His reservations were enhanced by the establishment of the PDK and the presumed implications for Soviet foreign policy. For the British Foreign Secretary, who had long before deemed his troubles in Greece as due to Soviet expansionism, the KKE 'government' seemed to have been set up at an opportune moment. The final conference of the Council of Foreign Ministers, held in London from 25 November to 15 December 1947, had ended in a complete breakdown between the West and the Soviet Union and with no date fixed for the next meeting. Bevin left the conference firmly convinced that since the Soviets were not genuinely interested in an understanding, Britain and the United States should proceed with the creation of 'a sort of spiritual federation of the West ... backed by power, money and resolute action'; that would make it 'clear to the Soviet Union that having gone so far they could not advance any further'.[12]

The Foreign Office accordingly endeavoured to assess the ultimate aims of Greek and Soviet Communism. Speculation had it that the KKE had been prevented 'from dressing the window of their new "government" with the familiar non-communist dummies' by the fact that the northern neighbours had rendered the provision of active aid conditional upon the annexation of Greek Macedonia to an autonomous Macedonian state. Although the Foreign Office welcomed the beneficial effect of this rumour inside Greece, in order to establish its veracity it sought the views of Sir Maurice Peterson, its ambassador in Moscow.[13] Peterson's analysis rested on the notion that the Soviets wished to deny Greece as a *'place d'armes'* to the United States and 'to acquire it as a springboard for their own expansionist purposes in the Mediterranean'. Their problem with Greece was that unlike states already under Soviet domination, where the communists 'were able to work from the centre outwards', in Greece the KKE scarcely had any chance of taking over at the centre; hence their best hope was that constant harassment and disruption in the north, coupled with the inefficiency and corruption of the Greek state, would lead to the collapse of the existing regime, 'dollars or no dollars'. In that eventuality the Kremlin deemed it useful to have an alternative government in store. However,

> that they do not at present rate the prospects of the Markos junta very high is suggested by the extremely cautious handling of the situation by the Soviet press.

The appearance of merely two leader comments, both couched in 'favourable but very restrained terms', indicated that the Kremlin would undertake no precipitate action vis-à-vis the PDK. The Soviets, Peterson concluded, 'cannot be reckoning on Greece taking its place at any very early date and territorially intact alongside its strong Communist neighbours'.[14]

In essence Peterson's assessment was a long way from confirming the speculation about would-be territorial concessions to the Slavs by the KKE, and it even hinted at Soviet reserves about the prospects of the Greek communists. Bevin, on the other hand, remained adamant that Greece's territorial integrity was at stake. On 8 January 1948 the Cabinet discussed a memorandum entitled 'Review of Soviet Policy', in which the Foreign Secretary asserted that the establishment of the PDK heralded a further communist effort to detach part of northern Greece and bring Soviet influence down to the Aegean. The ensuing discussion shows that he had some difficulty in persuading all his colleagues. One unnamed Cabinet member countered that

> The danger of pursuing a policy which concentrated on opposition to the
> Soviet Government was illustrated by events in Greece, where it had not
> been found possible to strengthen the influence of the Centre Parties.

Bevin's reply was inaccurate and misleading: in Greece, he said, 'every effort has been made to encourage the Centre Parties, but they had proved incapable of forming a stable government'.[15]

The perception prevailing at the Foreign Office with regard to the establishment of the PDK and the aims of world Communism was backed by the scare-mongering reaction from Athens and the reports of the British ambassadors from the capitals of eastern Europe. On 3 January 1948 the Greek ambassador in London handed Sargent a memorandum whereby the Greek government requested 'collective assistance' on account of the alleged concentration of two Yugoslav Armies, eight Albanian Divisions and the Fourth Bulgarian Army along Greece's northern frontier. Two days later the British Consul-General in Thessaloniki sent a report which knocked the bottom out of the Greek allegations. There was no information that the Fourth Bulgarian Army was where the Greek government wanted it to be, nor any sign of movements or reinforcement of troops in southern Yugoslavia; and it was impossible for eight Albanian Divisions to have massed on the Greek borders since the entire Albanian army consisted of three Divisions, of which only two were on active service footing.[16]

By making sensational allegations the Greek government was trying to elicit the despatch of US troops. The Embassy returned on 10 January with information 'as previously, based on communications of the Cominform to their secret Athens branch'. The second memorandum alleged that the recognition of the PDK was a matter of time, its delay being due to negotiations among Balkan governments for the creation of a Communist Balkan Federation. Military protocols had already been signed in Belgrade between the DSE Commander and representatives of Balkan states. The communist countries had placed at the disposal of the PDK eighty billion denars, with more aid about to come from Moscow; and the PDK would soon employ two submarines to organize the escape of leading communists out of Greece.[17] Unhappily for the Greek government, the KKE was not a member of the Cominform, as its humble application to join it in October 1947 had been ignored by Stalin.[18] Even so, on 8 January the British Embassy in Prague cabled London that, according to the Greek Chargé d'Affaires there, the Soviets 'informed [the] Greek Communists some time ago that they would only be allowed to set up a "Free Government" on condition that they had come to agreement with Yugoslavia and Bulgaria about the future of the Macedonia area'. The British noted that, 'unfortunately', the Greek Chargé 'does not reveal the source of his information'.[19]

Similar in outlook, though more sober in tone, was Peake's assessment from Belgrade. The British ambassador speculated that the Soviet directive to Bulgaria, Yugoslavia and Albania could be 'to put first things first', namely to establish a communist regime in Greece and *then* settle the future of Macedonia 'in comradely understanding'. As the KKE was in no position 'to do other than they are told', the decision for the establishment of the PDK was part of a 'coordinated programme'; if so, 'we must assume that Markos's chances were thought to be reasonably good, since the Slav bloc would hardly wish to risk the inevitable loss of face, which would be their lot if Markos failed'. 'In short', Peake summed up, Greece's northern neighbours 'are committed to doing all in their power to establish a communist regime in Greece'.[20]

Bevin stated his outlook on the problem at the House of Commons Foreign Affairs debate of 22 January 1948. Six days earlier he had informed the State Department of the line he intended to take: a public warning should be sent to the Communist bloc that 'they were playing with fire', and Tito and Dimitrov should be reminded that 'just as we had fought Hitler in defence of human liberties, so we would take a firm stand now against any new attempt to dominate free and independent countries'.[21] With Marshall's approval, Bevin told the House that 'this Markos business' was a 'ruthless' and 'constantly maintained' attempt to bring Greece into the Soviet orbit – 'a case of power politics'.[22] He only meant Soviet power politics.

Equally adamant that it knew what the KKE was up to was the Greek government, which continued to claim that it was intercepting communications from the Cominform to 'their Athens agents'. On 15 January the Foreign Office received another memorandum from the Greek Embassy, alleging that the two submarines were on their way, that the recognition of the PDK was 'now formally settled', that fourteen Soviet, Yugoslav and Bulgarian staff officers were assisting Markos, and, contradicting itself, that Zachariadis was in Moscow to arrange for the recognition of his 'government'.[23] Apart from the fact that the KKE was not a member of the Cominform, there is conclusive evidence that the entreaties of the PDK for recognition were ignored. On 1 January 1948 the 'Foreign Minister' Petros Rousos addressed a letter to his Rumanian 'colleague' Ana Pauker asking for the establishment of 'friendly relations'. The only reply he received came from the National Rumanian Committee for Assistance to the Greek People, which warmly saluted the formation of the PDK but failed to make any mention of formal recognition and diplomatic relations. The replies of the other communist states were similar.[24]

In the first ten days of January 1948 the reports of the British, French and US ambassadors from Eastern Europe fell short of indicating that the PDK was anywhere near recognition.[25] 'Perhaps an interesting straw in the wind', as the British Embassy in Moscow put it, came from the Soviet capital in mid-January, when the Yugoslav ambassador told the *Manchester Guardian* correspondent that Markos 'had a long way to go' before his government was recognized.[26] By the end of the month it appeared that the wind had subsided. The Yugoslavs claimed to be too busy with internal questions to be much interested in Greece, whilst the Bulgarians did not at present contemplate recognizing the PDK.[27] Peake and Cannon were right in arguing that Yugoslavia – and, by implication, the Soviet Union – would not risk a head-on collision with Britain and the United States over Greece. Tito assured Cannon that he would not indulge in dramatic or adventurous moves, for his principal concern was domestic development – 'and to achieve this we need peace'. In late January the Yugoslav leader intimated to the Czech ambassador in Belgrade that despite the attitude of the West towards Yugoslavia, he would not take any action which might endanger peace; the time was by no means ripe for the recognition of the PDK.[28] This was a major setback for the KKE, for the gamble which Zachariadis had taken on Christmas Eve 1947 looked increasingly unlikely to deliver the goods.

In Washington, however, the administration feared that if the United States did not show itself determined to claim Greece from the Soviet Union, the country 'and the whole Eastern Mediterranean and the Middle East, not to speak of Europe, will be lost to the Western World'.[29] The question of the despatch of US troops came to the fore again, but the Americans tried first to establish whether the allegations by the Greek government about the Macedonian policy of the KKE were true. On 20 January 1948 they asked the Foreign Office whether they had any evidence of the so-called 'Petritsi Pact', allegedly signed between Ioannidis and the Bulgarian Dusan Daskalov on 12 July 1943. The 'Pact', the subject of a pamphlet issued by the Greek government in June 1947 under the title *The Conspiracy against Greece*, was supposedly an agreement for the establishment of a Balkan Union of Soviet Republics with (Greek, Bulgarian and Serbian) Macedonia as an independent Republic within the Union, so that Bulgaria could obtain an outlet to the Aegean. The matter was a propaganda stunt by the Greek government, and the Foreign Office informed the Americans that despite its inquiries, it had been

> unable to establish the authenticity of this agreement ... it is a little too good to be true and it is perhaps improbable that Communist parties in fact draw up agreements in this form. This tended to render it suspect in our eyes, when first considered in Cairo in 1943.[30]

While the State Department was trying to work out a uniform approach to the new turn in the Greek question,[31] in February Norton advocated drastic action. If Greece was vital to Anglo-American interests, London and Washington should be prepared to send a joint force which could undertake 'offensive action' against the Democratic Army.[32] Bevin, who had been calling for a more concrete US military commitment, asked the American ambassador in London when his government was going to put 10,000 marines in Greece. He emphasized that he had kept his promise not to withdraw the British troops, but now the British felt they were a 'lone wolf'. Molotov's hope had been that Britain and the United States would grow tired of Greece, and that was why he had issued a warning during his Commons speech on 22 January. The US ambassador replied that President Truman would find it difficult to secure Congressional approval even for more appropriations, let alone for the despatch of troops.[33]

Bevin's demand was in harmony with the motives which had triggered the dispute with Marshall in July 1947, and which he now summed up as the 'lone wolf' syndrome. By April 1948, however, the US government had shifted against this 'militarily unsound' step which might 'precipitate overt action by Soviet satellites or USSR forces' in a country which was not strategically important enough to justify a US commitment to major operations.[34] None the less, while the Americans and the British were convinced that behind the KKE and its 'government' lay Stalin, the latter had more than two months earlier uttered a controversial verdict on the Greek uprising. In so far as it pertained to relations between the KKE and the Soviet Union, his pronouncement cast a negative light upon Western estimates of Soviet policy towards Greece.

Svernut and British Perceptions of Soviet Involvement

Following the formation of the Provisional Democratic Government, the guerrillas strove to seize urban centres and larger portions of territory in order to vest it with some authority. In 1948 the gradual transformation of the DSE into a regular army and the switch to positional warfare entailed its reorganization into brigades, battalions and companies and the introduction of a conventional command structure with proper military ranks and Commissars.[35] The morale of the guerrillas was high, but there were signs of friction between Zachariadis and Markos. On 2 December 1947 the Secretary-General of the KKE had accused the DSE Commander of exaggerating the numerical strength of his forces, and at a conference of the political and military leadership on 15–16 January 1948 Markos opined that the DSE was a guerrilla army and could not strike and occupy towns. Incensed, Zachariadis turned the matter into a question as to whether the decisions of the Third Plenum – which bore Markos's signature – had been correct. The DSE Commander, who was merely responding to criticism for the defeat at Konitsa, replied in the affirmative and the incident was laid to rest at that.[36] If 1948 appeared to be dawning unpropitiously for the KKE, it was because its 'government' remained unseated and unrecognized.

For the British the policy of the Greek communists was a perennial source of anxiety, yet at the same time they had to come to grips with the unremitting political crises in Athens. Whereas Tsaldaris was adamant that Sofulis was leading the country to the path of 'Kerenskyism', the British Embassy retorted that 'this was certainly a paradoxical complaint against a government which had already suppressed the communist papers, and enacted a law prohibiting strikes, and under which the Special Courts Martial had functioned with even greater severity than before'.[37] Rendis remained the black sheep, as he tried to exercise some moderation. Reilly wondered how many thousands Zervas would have arrested following the establishment of the PDK, whereas the Liberal Minister of Public Order had confined himself to 650. As for the 'lamentable' fact that the two "'historic parties"' of Greece could not produce 'a better team of ministers', the Embassy held the Populists to be the main culprits:

> The Greek Right are indeed quite unable to reconcile themselves to the truth that the dependence of Greece on foreign help means that she must in part suit her government to foreign public opinion and not only to her own.[38]

Once again Bevin lost patience. 'Increasingly disturbed' by the 'continuing failure' of the Greek politicians 'to come to grips with their problems in which we and the Americans are involved', on 6 February 1948 he sought Norton's recommendations for action.[39] The ambassador's thrustful reply, six days later, was based on the premise that the long history of British assistance to Greece gave the Labour government 'the right to suggest radical measures'. Britain and the United States should decide whether their strategic interests required an independent and non-communist Greece. If not, their hands would be strengthened in dealing with the Greek government by the fact that 'in the last resort they can use the sanction of withdrawal'; but if Greece was vital to Western interests, London and Washington should face the prospect of having to take action going far beyond anything hitherto contemplated – notably the despatch of an Anglo-American force which could take offensive action against the Democratic Army. Meanwhile,

> to stop the present rot, [the] first step is to disabuse the Sofulis Government's idea that they are indispensable and can snap their fingers at Allied advice. In practice it is most unlikely that if the US Government and HM Government jointly intervened with the same force that the former employed to install the present Government, they would refuse to comply with their demands. But in the last resort we must be prepared to compel them to resign. It is surely absurd when the issues are world-wide to stake everything on a Government which might in any case dissolve quite soon.[40]

In order to bring the Greek politicians into line Norton proposed a brand of intervention reminiscent of the Churchill-Leeper era. Since its advent to power, the Labour government had reserved such tactics for moments of great urgency, as in the case of McNeil's visit to Athens in November 1945. Taunted by his leftist critics, Bevin was reluctant to emulate the Churchill-Leeper pattern, while the Truman Doctrine often bailed him out in that the Americans had no qualms about exercising direct control over Greek affairs. Yet the cable to the Embassy and Norton's reply indicate that the transition from Churchill to Labour had not fundamentally affected perceptions of the means whereby British policy was to be enforced. That the Greek politicians were not expected to 'snap their fingers at Allied advice' was due to this continuity of ends and means and the fact that the regime in Athens owed its very existence to Anglo-American support. The unfolding of the Cold war, which had cast the domestic origins of the Greek Civil War into oblivion, and the 'world-wide issues' it raised, were additional potent reasons.

These issues were clarified on 11 February 1948, when Albert Alexander sent Bevin a report by the Chiefs of Staff. After studying Soviet policy towards Greece, the latter had come to the conclusion that 'in order to improve her political and strategic position, the USSR intends eventually to incorporate Greece as a Communist State in the Balkan bloc'. The immediate objective of the Kremlin was 'to gain control over Aegean ports and airfields, particularly those of Salonika, thus obtaining a dominant position in the Aegean Sea, outflanking the Dardanelles, and one from which to threaten Anglo-American communications in the Eastern Mediterranean'. To achieve these aims, the Kremlin would 'make full use of the Greek communists and rebel forces in reducing as much of Greece as possible to chaos'.[41]

While British perceptions of Soviet involvement in Greece were twisted to fit in with the exigencies of the Cold War, two days earlier Stalin had decreed otherwise. As tension between Yugoslavia and the Soviet Union had been building up for some time, in January 1948 Stalin summoned Georgi Dimitrov and the Yugoslavs Milovan Djilas and Edvard Kardelji to Moscow. During these talks it emerged that the wider developments in the Balkans had a powerful impact on the Soviet outlook to the Greek situation. Dimitrov had incurred Stalin's wrath for his public remarks on future federations in eastern Europe, while the Yugoslavs were brought to book for their independence both in domestic economic policy and in their foreign relations.[42] Stalin interpreted these initiatives as threatening to create a power centre in south-eastern Europe that would not be entirely dependent on Moscow, hence he told the Yugoslavs and the Bulgarian in no uncertain terms that their actions were inadmissible because they did not have his approval. Then, according to Djilas, on 9 February Stalin 'turned to the uprising in Greece':

> "The uprising in Greece has to fold up." (He used for this the word *svernut*, which means literally "to fold up".) "Do you believe" – he turned to Kardelji – "in the success of the uprising in Greece?" Kardelji replied, "If foreign intervention does not grow and serious political and military errors are not made." Stalin went on, without paying attention to Kardelji's opinion: "If, if! No, they have no prospect of success at all. What do you think, that Great Britain and the United States – the United States, the most powerful state in the world – will permit you to break their line of communication in the Mediterranean Sea! Nonsense. And we have no navy. The uprising in Greece must be stopped, and as quickly as possible."[43]

In view of the importance of Stalin's pronouncement for the prospects of the KKE and the British assessments of Soviet policy, it is worth examining the veracity of this account. Although he wrote after the Tito-Stalin split and after the Cominform had accused the Yugoslavs of betraying the KKE, Djilas has elsewhere proved a reliable witness with no special motive to pose as Tito's apologist. His story also corresponds with the subsequent accounts of Kardelji and Tito's biographer, Vladimir Dedijer.[44] Besides, after the Civil War Zachariadis asked Stalin whether he had indeed told the Yugoslavs that the uprising should stop, and though Stalin denied it, the KKE leader was not wholly convinced; he intimated to a top KKE cadre that 'what the Yugoslavs claim ... may be right, but in that period their relations [with Moscow] were tense and Stalin may have told them so deliberately in order to show them that he had nothing to do with our struggle'.[45]

If Djilas' account is reliable, the question arises whether Stalin's words genuinely reflected his view on the KKE uprising or they were aimed at clipping the wings of the increasingly independent Yugoslavs. The latter hypothesis may rest on a piece of information passed on by the Greek Chargé d'Affaires to the British Embassy in Prague. On 10 February 1948 the Chargé alleged that Zachariadis had recently met with Molotov and informed him of the 'desperate' military and economic position of his army and the dissatisfaction of the KKE with the lack of diplomatic support from 'supposedly friendly countries'. Molotov was said to have replied that it would soon be possible for the Soviet government and its friends to give Markos 'much stronger and more open support'; Molotov was waiting for Britain and the United States 'to give him an excuse by themselves adopting a more open and positive policy of support for the Greek government'.[46]

Given the Greek government's record in disseminating scare-mongering rumours, this piece of information must be called into doubt. In its endeavour to secure a greater Anglo-American commitment Athens alleged that wholesale aid to the KKE was imminent. Also, it is not clear how US and British assistance might have been more open, unless it implied the despatch of troops; but the Americans would not do this unless the communist countries attacked Greece. Finally, there is no reason to assume that Greek intelligence agencies were more competent than British and American ones. The Greek Embassy in Washington gave the same story to the State Department, but the latter did not know its original source and was unable to assess its reliability. The US Embassy in Moscow found it equally impossible to confirm or deny the allegation. Lord Inverchapel cabled the Foreign Office: 'The State Department tell me that in trying to track down these reports from various Greek representatives they often find themselves in a hall of mirrors containing many, and often distorted, images of the same story.'[47]

Thus the alleged meeting between Zachariadis and Molotov in February 1948 must be treated with circumspection. Yet there is still a point to be made that in 1948 the Soviets never told the KKE to end the uprising. The most reliable and better informed Greek communist accounts all converge on this point, with one of them stating explicitly that this did not happen until spring 1949.[48] This sequence of events would also tally with one source which claims that in September 1948 Zachariadis went to Moscow and received assurances of massive aid from the Soviet Union.[49]

The most plausible reconstruction of events would be that upon their return to Belgrade, the Yugoslavs informed the KKE liaison, Yiannis Ioannidis, of Stalin's verdict. Zachariadis was summoned to the Yugoslav capital, where Tito urged him to go to Moscow; the KKE leader reportedly replied that this was not necessary and that given time he would 'persuade' Stalin.[50] Be that as it may, the KKE would not abandon the endeavours towards a compromise, which had featured in its plans even after the Third Plenum of September 1947, and which was also Stalin's pursuit. In sum, in February 1948 Stalin told the Yugoslavs that the KKE uprising had to be folded up. Whether he meant it or not, his aim no doubt was to detach the Greek communists from the Yugoslavs and use the KKE as a lever in his dispute with Tito.[52] In any case, Stalin's motives were eminently different from those ascribed to him by the British.

It is not difficult to see, therefore, why the Foreign Office, enmeshed in rigid premises, was puzzled by the non-recognition of the PDK. In March 1948 Peake argued that the Soviets disapproved of the KKE 'government', for although they 'may have authorized or even inspired its establishment', now they 'have changed their views or decided that their orders had been bungled in execution.[53] In London Wallinger maintained that since Stalin did not as yet want an open break with the West,

> the Kremlin would probably prefer to write off Markos as a military factor rather than to allow Tito and Dimitrov to embark on any adventure which might lead to international war ... but the fundamental case continues to be that covert aid to Markos will in any case continue in increasing quantities so long as the rebellion assists in what is clearly the central factor of Moscow policy at the moment, namely the stabilization of chaos in the countries outside the Curtain.[54]

Having apparently come round from the confident belief that Stalin aimed at subjugating Greece, the Head of the Southern Department now rested on more modest premises. Yet the Foreign Office could not go as far as to discern that the Soviets were exploiting rather than creating opportunities.

On 20 February 1948 the Greek government proposed to the United States and Britain consultations between the British, Greek and US Staffs to clarify allied plans for the use of Greek forces and territory should large-scale hostilities break up. The Greek General Staff had decided to resist aggression and had worked out a defence plan based on the assumption that the Greek army would receive allied assistance.[55] The reaction of the Foreign Office was distinctly unfavourable, but it was the British authorities in Athens which perceived the Greek motives in pungent terms. The Embassy insinuated that the Greek government did not want the defeat of the guerrillas, which, it was held, would lead to an open Slav attack. The BMM Commander Major-General Down thought that the Greeks intended to 'keep the pot boiling, with the idea of involving both the British and the Americans in Greece and committing them to continuing intervention to hold that country against Communism. A defeat of Markos might mean an Anglo-American withdrawal from Greece!'. Down proposed that Britain and the United States threaten the Greeks with withdrawal – 'either Greece gets on, or we get out'. The counsels at the Foreign Office were divided; Wallinger agreed that the threat should be used, whereas other officials deemed it 'a dangerous bluff'.[56] The

US government, which shared British suspicions of the Greek motives, concurred that the Greeks would do better if they focussed on the defeat of the DSE.[57]

Yet Tsaldaris was determined to spare no efforts. On 15 March he handed the US ambassador in Paris a paper which reiterated the proposal for joint Staff talks and requested a guarantee of Greece's territorial integrity by Britain, the United States and France. Irritated by their conviction that the Greek government did not take its civil war seriously enough, the Americans held firm.[58] Tsaldaris then saw a second chance presenting itself when Britain, France, Belgium, Luxembourg and the Netherlands signed the Treaty of Brussels – a military alliance ostensibly directed against a revival of the German threat.[59] In April the Quai D'Orsay told the British that France was 'anxious' and 'nervous' at the possibility that events in Greece, where her interests were minimal, might end up by embroiling her in some quarrel she did not want and could ill afford; the French government had therefore 'coldly "taken note"' of the suggestion that an armed attack on British troops in Greece would involve the other signatories of the Treaty of Brussels.[60] Wallinger hinted that the whole issue might have been instigated by the Greek Foreign Minister:

> Tsaldaris, who is a thoroughly unscrupulous intriguer, was probably angling for some declaration which he might interpret to cover an attack on British troops by the rebels; but it is clear that the relevant article of the Treaty would only come into consideration if British troops were directly attacked by troops wearing the uniform of a foreign power.[61]

The British Embassy in Athens derided Tsaldaris as 'lacking that extra 10 per cent of grey matter that distinguishes the statesman from the politician'.[62] The more serious charge was that the Greek Foreign Minister regarded Greece's foreign relations as his personal fief. Sofulis asked to see Dwight Griswold to complain to him that the handling of foreign policy by his coalition partner was incompetent, and that Tsaldaris was 'always too anxious to go bustling off to foreign capitals'.[63]

Indeed, consistent with his professions of loyalty to Britain, on 16 March Tsaldaris sought Bevin's support for an initiative towards closer relations between Greece and Turkey. A few days later the Greek ambassador in London handed to the Foreign Office a draft declaration to be discussed by the Greek and Turkish Foreign Ministers, pledging the two states to defend their territorial integrity at all costs. Bevin approved the draft,[64] unaware that Tsaldaris's real aim was to secure a future treaty supported by Britain and the United States. On 16 April he told Bevin that the Turkish Cabinet had endorsed a declaration of solidarity, but Wallinger noted that this 'was an optimistic estimate of Turkish willingness to cooperate'; Ankara had expressed its scepticism to the British and requested Anglo-American support as 'a primary condition' for any pact.[65] With the full agreement of the Americans, who were reluctant to enter further commitments in the Middle East, Bevin and Sargent lectured the Greek ambassador in London that 'the mere making of paper pacts ... was of little value'.[66]

216

The resourceful and importunate Tsaldaris tried once more. His blandishments to Bevin that Britain 'had always assisted Greece in her worst moments and she ... naturally turned to us for advice',[67] showed where the Greek loyalties lay. On 4 June 1948 the Embassy in London sent Bevin a paper seeking 'immediate support' for an eastern Mediterranean pact between Greece, Turkey and Egypt on the grounds that the Near East was the only outlet for Greece's surplus population, economic needs, and the development of political activity and the 'creative capacities' of the Greeks.[68] The demand for Greek regional hegemony under British blessing was thinly veiled. The Greek government may have thought that since Greece was the only country in the region militarily involved in the crusade against Communism, she had a moral right to preponderance, which, as the memorandum unambiguously asserted, was also historically justified. Yet whatever the motives and aspirations of the Greek government, the reaction of the Foreign Office was one of uniform derision.

Wallinger was stunned by 'so brittle and egotistical a document'. Others jibed at a request which 'seems to go off into the fog of the Byzantium idea' and invited them to lend a hand with the imposition of 'Hellenism and Greek Orthodoxy' in the eastern Mediterranean at the expense of the Latin, Muslim and Slav element. Besides, R.M.A. Hankey, an expert on Soviet affairs, correctly pointed out that Stalin would hardly be impressed by a pact among Greece, Turkey, Egypt and the Arab States: 'What impresses the Russians is Power, and the power situation in the Middle East would only be affected if we and the Americans were brought in.'[69]

The task of admonishing the Greeks fell upon Norton. By mid-July the ambassador 'had to choke off Tsaldaris' from these 'Hellenistic-Byzantine' designs by way of telling him that 'a country in so poor a position as Greece had better keep off grandiose ideas'. This was typical of the contempt with which the British viewed their Greek protégés, while Tsaldaris's reply confirms that the latter sometimes did snap their fingers: 'this', he countered, 'might be an English way of looking at things but ... it was just when a Greek was in a poor way that he felt it necessary to show off'. Conspicuously enraged by this retort, Norton made a condescending appeal to London: 'Small countries like Greece are likely from self-interest, or fear, or excess of zeal, to go off the handle in International Affairs unless positive and concrete guidance is given to them by us and the Americans acting in concert'. The ambassador conceded that his diagnosis did not explain the Greek memorandum, but 'it may explain the psychology, or pathology, if you will, that produced it'.[70]

The British and the Americans were keen to stress where the priority lay. The position of the State Department, as stated by Loy Henderson on 18 February 1948, was that if the Greeks faltered, 'it would be extremely difficult for the UN or for any member of the UN to save Greece'.[71] In the same month the British Chiefs of Staff warned that the prolongation of the fighting beyond 1948 would lead to the political, military, and economic collapse of Greece.[72] Sceptical as to the efficacy of US policy, the British were not sanguine about the military prospect, they doubted whether Lieutenant-General James Van Fleet, head of JUSMAPG, could 'pull the show together', and they had also noted with discontent his reticence about the possibility of US marines being sent to Greece.[73] From Athens Down added to the gloom by warning that the defeat of the guerrillas within 1948 was 'very unlikely' because of the lack of offensive spirit in the army and the weariness of the people.[74]

The pessimistic estimates of the British military and his unhappiness with the division of responsibility – the 'lone wolf' syndrome – lent force to Bevin's desire for the despatch of US troops to Greece. Embarrassment came along when the Greek government stepped up the executions of leftists.[75] Following the assassination of the Justice Minister by the communists on 1 May 1948, the even more vigorous pace of executions appeared by way of state reprisals. On 5 May the Labour government declared that these 'wholesale executions will come as a grave shock to decent opinion', and that Norton had been instructed to make strong representations. The British view was widely publicized in the Greek press and was subjected to bitter attacks.'[76]

Bevin seized the opportunity to press for the despatch of US troops. On 12 May he told the US ambassador in London that the executions had created 'a very difficult situation' and had awaken 'dormant opinion' in Britain, therefore he feared that in the next Labour Party Conference he would face the demand to withdraw the troops from Greece. The United States should send forces not only because the burden had fallen upon Britain, but also because the civil war might otherwise not come to an end.[77] A few days later the Foreign Office tried to internationalize its request and present it as a Western Crusade. On 22 May the Embassy in Paris put out feelers on the French government about the idea of an international force to Greece, or at least the despatch of warships to Thessaloniki to boost Greek morale. The Quai D'Orsay held that the former would precipitate an attack by the other side, whereas the latter would be less risky but equally ineffective.[78] A week later a cable from Washington confirmed that the Americans were not prepared to send troops because their military disliked indefinite commitments, their public was unprepared for such action and also because the Greek army had scored some successes.[79] On the eve of the summer offensive against the Democratic Army the British Embassy in Athens produced a paper on 'Future Prospects in Greece'. The conclusion was, once more, that the Soviet Union aimed at establishing a Communist regime and bringing the country 'behind the Iron Curtain'. But there was not much change in British policy either. In peace, Greece should remain in the West and be 'sufficiently well-governed as not to be a reproach to Western ideas and a headache to HM Government'; in war, to ensure that Greek bases are not available to the Soviets, and 'that Britain is not involved in a war to which the United States might not immediately be a party, through the presence of British, though not American, troops'.[80]

This was a more elaborate version of what Leeper had in 1946 defined as the retention of Greece 'on our side of the fence'. The difference in 1948 was the fear lest Britain were once more entangled in a war without the participation of the Americans. By then, however, Washington had realized that Britain needed the United States more than the United States needed

Britain. The State Department held that as long as the situation remained unsettled, Britain relied 'on continued US co-operation and assistance in preserving peace and security in Greece'.[81] The Americans could thus afford to ignore the British appeal for the despatch of US troops. Despite Stalin's verdict and irrespective of its application, the pattern to follow was very much the same as in 1947. With the elimination of the Democratic Army regarded as the prerequisite to any solution, the Greek government would launch a major military offensive. The KKE would wave another olive branch.

Military Operations and Olive Branches (II)

By early 1948 it was clear that the US, British and Greek governments were bent on bringing the civil war to an end through the elimination or uncondi-tional surrender of the Democratic Army. Whereas the latter was unthinkable for the KKE, it is a moot point whether Zachariadis believed in the ability of his army to deliver the goods. Perhaps the KKE assumed that the longer the guerrillas remained undefeated, the more the morale of its opponents would be sapped and a compromise might be attainable. Stalin's pronouncement may, moreover, have sown seeds of doubt in the minds of the KKE leaders and thereby lent force to their peace initiatives.

In early January 1948 the small socialist party SK-ELD called for an end to the civil war, new elections and an agreement with the consent of the great powers for the independence and territorial integrity of Greece.[82] On 29 January the leader of the Left Liberals, General Neokosmos Grigoriadis, apparently sent a memorandum to Sofulis setting out measures for a compro-mise. Grigoriadis argued, with considerable justification, that the causes of the civil war would be removed if a new government including EAM were formed, the 'one-sided' Parliament were dissolved, a general amnesty were granted, and the repressive legislation were lifted.[83] No reaction to these terms is recorded, but interestingly enough, a copy of the memorandum is found in the Papers of Emmanuel Tsouderos; the hypothesis that it was sent to Tsouderos for transmission to Sofulis is reinforced by the rumours soon to emerge that '"certain liberal circles"' were planning a new appeasement move.[84] There is no hard proof that the KKE had a direct involvement in this, but it is known that Zachariadis was at least in touch with leftist circles in Athens.[85]

When it came, the KKE initiative was akin to that of July 1947. On 2 April 1948 the lawyer Konstantinos Despotopoulos, former legal adviser to the ELAS GHQ, dictated to Tsouderos a text which the latter translated into English and then handed it to the British and US Embassies. Tsouderos's translated typescript reads as follows:

A prominent member of the KKE made the following statement (word for word) to one of the leaders of the Centre:
  "The Party Offices of the Social Party participating in EAM has taken the following decision:
  The cessation of the internal strife is proposed under the three following conditions:

a. – That guarantee be given by UNO for the political and economic independence of Greece (departure of allied troops is hereby understood).
b. – That UNO guarantees Greece's integrity.
c. – Greece to be recognized [as] a neutral state inside UNO's framework.

Furthermore it is proposed that a Government of general confidence be brought into power; KKE's participation in this government is not a condition *'sine qua non'*.

Such a government would proceed toward [a] general amnesty and free elections; the KKE (i.e. government of the mountains) has taken cognizance of the above mentioned decisions and agrees to stop the rebellion if the proposed solution is accepted.

Financial and economic aid from abroad is accepted in principle (Marshall Plan or any other under UNO).[86]

It is striking that these proposals were more self-effacing than both those of July 1947 and those drafted by Balfour two months later. The KKE did not seek the participation of EAM in the government while, to quell fears of Slav encroachment, emphasis was placed on the role of the United Nations. In view of the Anglo-American objectives in Greece, however, this was unlikely to have any appeal in London and Washington, neither of which appears to have ever given the slightest consideration to the KKE proposal for neutrality.

On 28 April some Greek papers accused 'certain liberal circles' – Tsouderos and Lambrakis – of planning a new appeasement move. Sofulis told the press that he knew nothing of the rumoured desire of the Democratic Army to negotiate, adding that the issue would be resolved by force of arms. Tsaldaris, on the other hand, confirmed that there were '"indications of a camouflaged move"' to raise the issue of appeasement, and commented on the '"correlation between these rumours and other rumours from abroad according to which Moscow has recognized a reverse in the cold war and has been forced [to] change tactics."' In transmitting this information to the State Department, Karl Rankin, the US Chargé d'Affaires in Athens, dismissed the communist move as a 'trial balloon' or an attempt to throw the commencing military operations off the balance. Regarding appeasement as anathema, Rankin urged Washington to 'prevent growth of feeling [that] there is [an] easy way out of [the] present struggle'.[87]

Another reason for ignoring the KKE offer was the commencement of the campaign against the Democratic Army. All agreed on its importance, though not on its outcome. The US military forecast that the guerrillas would have been crushed by early summer,[88] but the British Chiefs of Staff doubted Van Fleet's ability 'to sort out the present Greek politico/military muddle'; they urged that their Greek colleagues should work out an adequate plan and establish an effective High Command system, whilst the Greek government would have to refrain from interfering with its execution. Yet at the same time they doubted the abilities of the Greek military and contemplated collaborating with the Americans in preparing the operational plan. In Athens the BMM Commander felt that the defeat of the DSE in 1948 was 'very unlikely' and jibed that a task which could be carried out by one British

Division required five Greek Divisions.[89] For their part, the Greek military conceded that they were fighting a peculiar war conducted in terrain that suited the guerrillas, who enjoyed the sympathy and support of part of the population. The First Deputy-Chief of the General Staff urged the government to ascribe to the struggle its proper content; it was not a civil war but one waged against 'foreign enemies', for 'it was not possible to consider the bandits and their fellow-travellers as Greeks because they speak Greek and have been born in Greece'.[90]

The plan of the Greek General Staff envisaged an orderly sweep from Attica to the north, the crushing of DSE units in the rear, and the destruction of their bulk on Mount Grammos. Operation *Haravgi* (Dawn) commenced on 15 April 1948 with the objective of clearing central Greece. Despite the correlation of forces (10:1 in favour of the government) and an outburst of desertions in the regional DSE ranks, the elimination of the guerrillas remained elusive as their bulk escaped to the north. The army scored valuable points only by seizing depots of arms and munitions and dislodging the local intelligence and support networks of the DSE through large-scale arrests of civilians.[91]

The involvement of JUSMAPG in the operations prompted Cyrus Sulzberger, who toured HQs of the Greek Army in mid-June, to note: 'The other thing that strikes me is the position of the Americans. Actually, they appear to be in charge of operations and there is not much disguising that fact, although everyone pretends it isn't so.'[92] The British were less impertinent. Having grasped the need for a speedy victory, they were substantially involved in military matters, yet more anxious than the Americans to keep up pretences. On the eve of *Haravgi* the BMM Headquarters sent the following directive to the Commanders of the British Liaison units attached to Greek army formations:

> You will endeavour to ensure that the plans which are ultimately adopted by the Greek Commanders are very closely similar to those recommended by the Greek General Staff, JUSMAPG and you. You will endeavour to ensure that the orders issued by Greek Commanders at all levels are given in a logical, clear and sound way ... You or your officers must ensure that Greek Commanders plan carefully and carry out energetically and in rapid succession operations ... As you have no executive powers over Greek Commanders or Staffs, nor any ultimate responsibility for operations, the method of consummating the instructions given in this paragraph will not be easy. Each individual must obtain the complete confidence of the Greek Commanders and Staff at all levels. This will require a high degree of tact, hard work and patience. No members of the Mission will in any circumstances: (a) take any executive part in operations (b) engage in political activities of any kind (c) assume any duties which will make them responsible to the Greek government.[93]

The opening of the campaign was hailed with optimism. Somewhat prematurely, Tsaldaris and Sofulis began to contemplate elections and agreed to establish a committee to revise the Constitution and prepare a new electoral law.[94] Confident that the army would 'this year break the back of the bandit menace', Norton felt free to speculate on Greece's political future. In a letter to Sargent, he reckoned that there might be a risk of dictatorship, and though an authoritarian regime might be best for Greece, Britain should press for the maintenance of parliamentary democracy while ensuring that communism would not revive again.[95] Sofulis was in tacit agreement, for by then he had abandoned all vestiges of appeasement. In May he assured the Americans that 'there could be no question of accommodation with the bandits until the latter had been crushed', and conceded that his erstwhile policies of releasing some deportees and offering an amnesty had been 'cardinal errors'. The British Embassy gleefully commented: 'It was well that neither Tsaldaris nor Zervas were there to hear these last remarks.'[96]

According to Vasilis Bartziotas, member of the KKE Politburo and Political Commissar at the DSE GHQ, throughout this period Zachariadis was in correspondence with leftist journalists in Athens, who regularly informed him of the disposition of the government circles. Bartziotas claims that Zachariadis allowed him to read his letters and the replies from Athens, which pointed out that pacification stumbled over 'the American bosses who aim at the solution of the Greek question by force of arms'.[97] Indeed, the unremitting aversion of the Americans to a compromise transpired yet again in early June, when the realization that the decisions of the Third Plenum of September 1947 was lagging behind prompted the KKE to renew its offers. On 31 May the DSE radio broadcast a declaration which, according to Norton, aroused 'great interest':

> The Provisional Democratic Government of Greece is always ready to accept and encourage any initiative from any side which would tend to assist Greece in finding herself and tranquillity with one condition: That the democratic life of the people will be unreservedly secured,that national autonomy and independence will be ensured without any foreign interference, that the people alone and free may decide for their future. In this direction the Provisional Democratic Government is ready to make every concession which the national and popular interest allows ... The popular democratic movement in our country never aimed nor does it aim today at violent and effective domination. It is always ready to discuss any proposal for the good of the people and the homeland.[98]

The US Embassy in Athens hastened to note that some insolent words in the text precluded the consideration of this offer, yet on 2 June the PDK broadcast a milder statement which emphasized the '"serious"', '"very sincere"' and '"honest"' nature of the proposal. Rankin speculated that this might be the prelude to a Soviet-sponsored move in the United Nations to intervene towards the cessation of hostilities; this would in turn provide evidence of the KKE's weakness and of the Soviet desire to salvage as much as possible from impending defeat, 'while continuing efforts by "peaceful" means to bring Greece into [the] position of Czechoslovakia'. In this spirit Rankin urged Washington to reaffirm 'that we are leading from strength not weakness and do not intend to be deterred from firm course'. Dwight Griswold, the Head of the AMAG, elaborated that there should be no contact between the Greek government and the PDK 'bilaterally or on an international level'.[99]

Confident that the KKE proposals aimed at buying time, the Greek government stated that no talks were possible with the communists, whose choice was only between surrender and elimination. British suspicion of the KKE was evinced in Norton's comment that the offensive diction of the original declaration, followed by the second 'much milder' statement, showed that the communists wanted to ensure that the government did not respond and then create the impression that a reasonable offer had been rebuffed.[100] It would certainly be a more modest hypothesis that, as in July 1947, the KKE could not afford to undermine the morale of its army with insinuations that the party leadership was desperate and docile. Moreover, the peace offers were consistent with the dual strategy as delineated at the Second Plenum of February 1946 and adhered to even after the decision to step up the armed struggle. They were also consistent with Stalin's objective to preserve communist influence in Greece through a negotiated settlement.

In anticipation of a Soviet initiative, the British and the Americans addressed the issue in forthright terms which left little doubt that the Greek Civil War was to be decided by force of arms. On 12 June 1948 President Truman declared that the Greek situation required no special negotiations, and that if the Kremlin wanted to make a contribution to world peace, it could prove it in Greece.[101] At the Foreign Office the prospect of talks with the Soviets was addressed by Geoffrey Wallinger on 24 May. The Head of the Southern Department argued that there were two ways of achieving a settlement:

> The first is to persuade the Kremlin to call off aid to the rebellion, when the Greek National Army might be able to cope single-handed; the second, that the Western Powers should put into Greece sufficient forces ... as would enable the Greek command to liquidate the rebellion ... All our information goes to show that we shall not be able to persuade the Kremlin to forego a cheap and effective weapon against us unless they can strike some kind of bargain and are convinced that the Western Powers intend to go in and clean up the situation anyway ... I am sure that we could not bluff Stalin into the abandonment of his Greek policy without convincing him that we really intend to use force to settle the Greek rebellion if it cannot be done by negotiation.

Hankey put it more succinctly: 'I feel that the Russians are really our enemies over Greece and that we should do better to keep them away, however difficult our position.'[102] Once more the portents boded ill for any Soviet initiative.

Until now it has been assumed, on the basis of US records, that the soundings for a compromise which took place in June 1948 were instigated by the Soviet Union. In early July Tsaldaris reported to the Americans that the Soviet Embassy had approached him with the proposal that the Soviet and Greek governments embark on talks for the settlement of outstanding difficulties; the precondition was that the Greek Foreign Minister would hold talks personally, in the greatest secrecy, and without mentioning the matter to anyone else in the Greek Cabinet. The Soviets were prepared to discuss both Greece's relations with the northern neighbours and the questions of Northern Epirus and Cyprus. Though Tsaldaris had taken a non-committal stance and sought American advice, he suspected that the Soviets aimed either at discrediting him, should he indulge in secret talks, or driving a wedge for Soviet mediation between the Greek government and Markos.[103]

It was indicative of the Americans' lack of enthusiasm that while the Embassy in Athens transmitted this information to Washington on 7 July, Marshall sought to ascertain Bevin's views two weeks later. Though no Soviet overture should be flatly rejected, the US Secretary of State deemed the Soviet motives 'justifiably suspect' and the method of the approach 'unacceptable'; he proposed to Bevin that Tsaldaris might undertake a commitment to talk with the Soviets only as a representative of the Greek government.[104] Bevin's priority was to ensure that there would be no talks on Cyprus. Then he agreed with Marshall and pointed out that the Soviet move might be a trap to discredit Tsaldaris and exacerbate his uneasy partnership with Sofulis; the former should therefore inform the Prime Minister at once. On 2 August Washington instructed the Embassy in Athens to convey a message to Tsaldaris on the above lines.[105] There is no record to show that Tsaldaris ever replied to the Soviets, but if he did, it would have probably been after 2 August – six weeks after the approach. With the ferocious battle of Grammos then raging, it was pointless to talk to them before the outcome on the battlefield was clear.

The British and US attitude towards this move stemmed from their determination to lead from a position of strength. The Soviet motives were consistent with their effort to retain a foothold in Greece by way of a diplomatic settlement, *and* with the KKE policy of keeping sight of the possibility of a compromise. The tantalizing question is why they chose Tsaldaris and were obsessed with secrecy. One obvious reason is that Tsaldaris was the Greek Foreign Minister and leader of the major component of the coalition government in Athens; besides, it is tempting to link this affair with subsequent leftist claims that in spring 1948 Tsaldaris indirectly tried to put out feelers on his Czech counterpart Jan Masaryk for mediation with Stalin. On the other hand, the recently published Soviet records explicitly state that in May–June 1948 it was Tsaldaris who sent intermediaries to the Soviet Embassy in Athens for negotiations. According to Nikolai Chernichev, the Soviet Chargé d'Affaires, the information on these contacts 'was top-secret and transmitted only to the responsible Centre'. Following instructions from that unnamed 'Centre', Chernichev communicated to Tsaldaris's confidants the Soviet view about the cessation of the civil war. Unfortunately there is no mention of what this view was; only the unhelpful piece of information that in June 1948 Chernichev was instructed by the 'Centre' to put an end to these contacts.[106]

If it was Tsaldaris who approached the Soviet Embassy, he could not admit this to Americans; hence the small liberties he took when reporting to their Embassy. Why he did so is hard to establish; in public the Greek government was optimistic about the campaign against the guerrillas, though it would seem that privately there might have been some lack of confidence among the domestic opponents of the KKE. Be that as it may, there is no reason to doubt that Tsaldaris reported fairly the Soviet position, which was tempting in so far as the Kremlin was prepared to discuss Greek claims in Northern Epirus and in Cyprus. Yet all the peace initiatives of early and mid-1948 stumbled over the resolve of the United States and Britain to impose the military solution.

Moreover, it was difficult to engage in peace-seeking manoeuvres while the critical phase of the army offensive was well under way. The ultimate objective of the government forces was to crush the DSE and occupy its stronghold on Mount Grammos. The first use of Napalm bombs by the Greek airforce presaged the ferocity of the confrontation, and Griswold warned Washington to be on its guard to counter communist propaganda against this novelty.[107] Then, in an interview to the *United Press* in mid-July, the Populist War Minister disclosed that the US government had 'promised' the Greek General Staff 'gas':

> To the question of whether the gas would be tear gas, he replied "no". He was then asked if it was poisonous gas. To this Mr. Stratos replied that the gas would not kill unless the subject remained in the contaminated area.

Reilly wrote to Wallinger that the Greek government had aspired to this weapon but 'the American Mission came down very heavily on the Greek request for gas'.[108]

The initial successes of the army inspired Norton with optimism that the guerrillas would soon be reduced from a menace to a nuisance. Feeling at liberty to speculate on the future of the KKE, the ambassador argued that communism must not revive again, hence Britain should advise the Greeks to refuse any negotiation with the rebels 'except for unconditional surrender'.[109] Bevin and the Foreign Office were less sanguine and had more immediate concerns. On 26 July Bevin told the Cabinet that his efforts 'to establish a stable democratic government in Greece had been hampered by communist interference', while the Foreign Office remained convinced that the Kremlin 'aims to control Greece'. For the British the fundamental objective of retaining that country on the western side of the fence was marred by the gloomy outlook of the overall position; Greece was 'a particularly weak bastion in the defences against Communism', and even in the event of a successful military offensive, 'the rebel menace will continue and there will be fresh infiltration by bandits'.[110]

Despite the persistent overtones of lack of confidence in the efficacy of American policy in Greece, it remained highly probable that in such a context any new appeal on the part of the KKE would fall on deaf ears. On 14 July the PDK reiterated its willingness to 'accept and encourage' any initiative towards a settlement. Sofulis replied that the only choice for the DSE was surrender or elimination, whereas the editor of *Kathimerini* asked himself 'Why don't we burn them?' and appealed for more American bombs and aircraft.[111] Yet the unity of purpose among Greek politicians did not match their unity of mind. In mid-July, while the crucial operation on Mount Grammos was in full swing,

Sofulis and Tsaldaris argued over the proposed electoral law, and a few days later some Liberal deputies withdrew their support from the government. Amidst rumours of manoeuvres within the Liberal Party by the followers of Plastiras and Venizelos, on 11 August some Populist deputies demanded the formation of a strong non-party administration; on the same day twenty-five Liberal deputies, supported by Venizelos, decided to recommend the withdrawal of their party from the coalition. To the great relief of the British, the crisis was eventually averted by the need to maintain the government until the conclusion of the campaign.[112] The Americans, on the other hand, who viewed the coalition primarily as a means of preventing 'Liberal flirtation with [the] Left', argued that Sofulis's party should be disabused of the idea that Washington regarded it 'sacred' enough to support any extravagance in which they might indulge.[113]

Evidently a lot depended on the outcome of the Grammos offensive, but the operations were hampered by a plan which Greek officers considered 'infantile'. Attacks on adequately fortified positions inflicted severe casualties on the government troops, while the British Embassy reported an 'idiotic weakness' in technique, reluctance to accept heavy casualties – 'possibly on instructions from high quarters' – and lack of drive 'due to the nature of this ideological war'.[114] In the Greek Parliament the initial jubilation was tempered on 7 August, when Tsaldaris and some deputies fell out over the question of who should claim the victory – the people or the government.[115] This irrelevance was obscured by the infinitely more cynical verdict of the British on the Grammos offensive. Reluctant to recognize either any military qualities in the Democratic Army or that the war was waged by Greeks against Greeks, the Embassy preferred to lay the blame on the Greek soldiers for not being as resolute as the British and US governments to bring the bloodshed to its desirable conclusion.

Soon the Greek government was alarmed by the heavy toll on its troops. In a memorandum addressed to the Foreign Office and the State Department on 10 August, it claimed that the Grammos operation was undertaken 'mainly at the pressing instance of our great friends', and that the 10% casualties might come to no avail if the Democratic Army crossed the border; the United States and Britain should therefore compel Albania to intern any guerrillas that might take refuge in her territory and secure the intervention of the Kremlin with Tirana.[116] The British questioned the high rate of casualties but were even more annoyed by what they perceived as an attempt by the Greek government to lay the blame on them and the Americans by presenting the operation 'as a matter of Anglo-American interest rather than as a primary Greek objective'.[117] As for the request to tackle Albania, it was abandoned because Washington feared that the allies would merely be 'pointing an empty pistol at their heads'.[118]

Meanwhile on 28–29 July the Fourth Plenum of the KKE Central Committee decided that in view of its lack of reserves and its inability to endure a protracted clash in the specific area, at the opportune moment the Democratic Army would manoeuvre from Mount Grammos to the adjacent Mount Vitsi. The wounded, auxiliaries, non-combatants and the supplies were gradually channelled into Albania, and on the night of 20–21 August 1948 the entire DSE force of Grammos, 8,500 guerrillas, made an orderly manoeuvre to Vitsi unscathed.[119] When the government troops occupied Grammos, they found nobody there, and in Reilly's words, 'an unduly optimistic impression spread' that the guerrilla movement in northern Greece had been crushed.[120]

On his return to Athens, in September 1948, Norton discerned a note of 'doubt and anxiety'. The morale of the army and the people was at a low ebb, for winter was approaching with no prospect of the war coming to an end. The ambassador was downcast. Upon succeeding Leeper, two and a half years earlier, he had felt that the 'optimum maximum' would be to turn Greece into 'a progressive democracy on western lines', and the minimum to keep her '"ticking over" and outside the Iron Curtain'; now, he argued, 'we should be content with something approaching the minimum'.[121] Norton's despondency was exemplified even by General Van Fleet, who complained to Sulzberger that the social and economic system of Greece 'sometimes makes him feel like a Communist'. Sulzberger himself was puzzled to notice that Greece was a poor country with 'too many rich people in it (or rich Greeks abroad who have milked it)'.[122] Howard K. Smith, Chief European Correspondent for CBS, found that behind the 'figureheads' of the Greek government, real power lay with the bureaucracy, the army and the police, 'and nothing has been done to purge these instruments even of the most vengeful pro-Nazis not to mention the reactionary fascists'. It did not take Smith long to realize that '"Democracy" in Greece is a paper façade, and beyond a quarter-mile radius of the hotel-district of Athens and Salonica where the foreigners live, not even that façade exists'.[123] This, of course, did not mean that life in Greece was a picture of uniform misery. Mount Grammos in the north might have been the scene of a seventy-day long and unrewarding carnage; but Athens, according to Norton, continued to be

> absurdly gay and social, with tennis matches, swimming parlours, visits by American ships and airplanes, etc. All this is in a way horrifying, but with strong nerves, a good digestion and a sense of humour one gets used to the contrast between appearance and reality.[124]

A Note of 'Doubt and Anxiety': September–December 1948

The military and political developments in the wake of the abortive Grammos operations suggest that Norton had understated the gravity of the situation. The DSE held back the renewed onset of the army on Mount Vitsi, and on 10 September 1948 launched its counter-attack, forcing the government troops to abandon positions they had occupied after more than two months of fighting. The vigour of the counter-offensive and the blunders of some officers led to the dissolution of two army battalions and the court-martialling and execution of some soldiers. The DSE even came within sight of capturing the town of Kastoria, but the army held firm and the guerrillas withdrew due to their lack of reserves.[125] The Greek government appealed to London and Washington for a naval demonstration against Albania, but the Foreign Office and the State Department rejected so premature and provocative an idea. The British, however, inquired of the Quai D'Orsay whether France would join in a would-be Anglo-American approach to Moscow concerning the situation on the Greek-Albanian frontier.[126]

The difficulties emanating from the precarious military situation were compounded by yet another political crisis in Athens. This time the occasion was the composition of the Greek Delegation to the UN General Assembly. Some Liberal deputies had been critical of Tsaldaris, who was now 'up in arms' and refusing to take any Liberal ministers with him. On 10 September an exasperated Bevin impressed on the Greek ambassador in London that the Delegation should be representative of the government and demonstrate the unity of the Greeks.[127] Although Sofulis temporarily kept a tight rein on his party, the British Embassy commented that the coalition was given 'yet another precarious lease of life'; it was unlikely to survive the conclusion of the General Assembly session, for the majority of Liberal deputies still intended to demand the withdrawal of their party.[128]

On 30 September Tsaldaris met Marshall in Paris and asked for the increase of the Greek army and additional US aid. Marshall's only concession was his promise to visit Athens shortly.[129] Bevin was anxious lest the ostensibly successful outcome of the Grammos campaign prompted the Americans to withdraw their Military Mission, in which case he anticipated an intensification of the attacks of the Labour left on his Greek policy. When Sir Oliver Franks, the new ambassador in Washington, conveyed these views to Marshall, the US Secretary of State assured him that the American Military Mission would remain until the situation in Greece was 'well stabilized'.[130]

Bevin conferred with Marshall in Paris on 28 September. He repeated that he was 'in constant difficulty' over the retention of British troops in Greece and that the military situation had to be brought to a speedy and successful conclusion. He embraced the Greek request for a larger army and pointed out that 'the victory in Grammos had misled many people: it was neither final nor conclusive.' Marshall explained that his difficulty lay in the disparity of opinion among US military and economic experts towards the question of appropriations, hence he would fly to Athens to ascertain the facts.[131] In a meeting with Tsaldaris on the same day Bevin took a non-committal attitude, while his Greek colleague pursued his tactics of appealing to Britain for whatever the United States was reluctant to agree to. His blandishments to Bevin that he was 'the best friend that Greece had' prompted Wallinger to comment that the Greeks suffered 'a bad attack of cold feet about the military situation', and that once they realized that there was much more fighting to be done, they wooed Bevin into asking Marshall for more appropriations.[132]

The increasing British anxiety was understandable. The Foreign Office continued to regard Greece as the weakest link in the Western defensive line in the Mediterranean, and abhorred the long-term and complex task of establishing her internal security and economic stability.[133] The Embassy in Athens chose to emphasize the attributes of the Greek leaders. Whereas the British concern was to bring the war to a speedy end, it was difficult to be sure of the Greek will to act decisively to that effect. The reason, according to the

Embassy, was that the political leadership was 'of very low order'. There was no inspiration, and as the party leaders lacked the personality or the sense of high endeavour to secure the support of their following, morale was 'brittle and subject to sudden changes either way'. This situation was exacerbated by the fact that Greece, blighted by war for nine years, had come to regard herself as a 'receiver nation' whose constant support was a matter of strategic importance to Britain and the United States. Time, in these circumstances, was crucial:

> If the end of the bandit war is not soon in sight, political jobbery and the feeling that the US and ourselves should do more and more to help, may so relax the will of the people to fight, that it will disappear altogether.[134]

The same, coupled by 'the tendency to shun responsibility at all costs', applied to the Greek military. An assessment of the situation by Henry F. Grady, the new US ambassador in Athens, reached identical conclusions.[135] Yet such overly simplistic interpretations only partially reflected the actual state of affairs. The Anglo-American anticipation of a speedy victory seemed to rest on the premise that the KKE owed everything to external support. Ironically, the only domestic reason for the stalemate they recognized was the ineptitude and party bickering of the Greek politicians, which of course had been anything but instrumental in the hitherto successful challenge of the KKE.

Marshall's visit to Athens on 16–18 October 1948 excited some short-lived optimism.[136] The US Secretary of State witnessed 'a rather depreciated state of morale' among the US Missions and in the Greek government, due to the incomplete training of the army (which sounded like an insinuation against the role of the British Military Mission), the fact that the officers were 'those of a distant past in all grades', the fatigue of the troops, and the lack of any prospect that the end of the war was in sight. An exceptionally nasty blow to the morale of the troops was the use by the Democratic Army of wooden shoe mines, which had claimed a formidable toll, principally in blowing off feet. The overall picture was one of 'impotence' and 'deterioration' prevailing among the Greek army as well as among the US authorities in Greece.[137]

As the Greeks continued to impress their demands on the British, Bevin became gravely alarmed by their bleak portrayal of the situation.[138] On 27 October the British Foreign Secretary anxiously asked Marshall whether the position was 'hopeless'; it was not, the reply came, provided that necessary measures were taken in time.[139] The British frustration came to a head on 23 October, when Norton instigated a meeting with Van Fleet, Down and Grady. There was mutual desire for a stronger political leadership, but the only stable alternative to the coalition would be a veiled dictatorship which would embarrass Greece's allies and endanger the position of the monarchy. The discussion turned to the possibility of General Alexandros Papagos, the Greek Commander-in-Chief during the Greek-Italian war of 1940–1941, resuming his command with wide powers. With King Paul and Sofulis favouring the appointment, the four men agreed to precipitate the issue, for if Greece was 'to get through the next six months without something near collapse', inspiration was urgently needed.[140]

Concerned lest the appointment turned into a military dictatorship, the British and the Americans asked for a written statement of Papagos's terms.[141] The General demanded an army of 250,000 men and a pledge by the BMM and JUSMAPG not to interfere with the organization of the army and the conduct of operations.[142] Stiff opposition was engendered by the intrinsic Anglo-American involvement in military matters and the fact that the British and US authorities were not used to the Greeks snapping their fingers. Yet it was indicative of the gravity of the situation that the two ambassadors were in favour of the appointment, though Norton regarded the terms (which encroached on the prerogatives of the BMM and JUSMAPG) 'unaccept-able'.[143] Grady agreed on the understanding that there would be no increase of the army and that Papagos would not act contrary to the advice of JUSMAPG.[144]

Hopes that Papagos might inspire the army were temporarily dashed by a new crisis. On 6 November 1948 Venizelos, who had rejoined the Liberals and become deputy-leader of the party, told the King that most of his deputies intended to withdraw their support from the coalition. In Paris Tsaldaris remained unruffled in his belief that the Populists would dominate a new Cabinet.[145] Sofulis resigned on 12 November and on the following day, upon Tsaldaris's return, negotiations resumed. Sofulis's terms were rejected by the Populists, and when Tsaldaris turned to Zervas and his ideological double General Stylianos Gonatas, the allies decided to bring the two leaders to reason. As Tsaldaris had already fixed a government with Zervas and Gonatas as Ministers for Public Order and War, Norton and Grady stepped in to abort the 'reactionary' set-up.[146]

Bevin's will was instrumental in the settlement of the crisis. 'Much disturbed', on 8 November he cabled Norton:

> The position as I see it is that whereas the rebels have a fixed policy and definite leadership, there is nothing but disunity on the Government side ... I feel that we are supporting a Coalition which is constantly threatening to fall into pieces and showing no resolution whatever to save the country. The Greek Government are making great difficulties for their friends. I am more alarmed by the dissension within the Greek Government ranks than by Markos and the rebels. You should emphasize [the] need for a really constructive effort ... for unity and determination to put an end to the rebellion.[147]

Four days later Norton suggested to Grady that they should offer 'constructive advice' on the composition of the new government. The British ambassador conceded that Sofulis was 'a figure-head', but he told Grady that the 'least bad' solution was to maintain the coalition and ensure that 'party hacks do not become Ministers'. The two ambassadors stifled Tsaldaris's hopes for a right-wing cabinet, Sofulis tempered his demands, and on 18 November the coalition was reconstituted.[148] The new government only just managed to obtain a vote of confidence in the Parliament – of the 335 deputies, 168 voted for and 167 against it – and Norton regretted that whether a new crisis erupted 'tomorrow or in a few weeks' the problem remained.[149]

The British ambassador accused the Populists and the Liberals of failing to provide inspiration, especially on the military plane, hence the Democratic Army was 'as strong as ever in the North and had now overrun the Peloponnese'. Venizelos had chosen to pose as the 'interpreter' of this view, calling for a government '"above parties"'; to that Sofulis had sagaciously retorted that such a government 'would have to be a Government of foreigners since all Greeks belonged to one party or another'.[150]

At this juncture the emergence of further Soviet overtures offered an alternative interpretation of Venizelos's motives and exposed the misguided British perceptions of Soviet policy in Greece. On 5 October 1948 the British Delegation to the UN General Assembly at Paris cabled the Foreign Office the following information. According to Venizelos, who accompanied Tsaldaris in Paris, Dimitri Manuilsky had told Sofianopoulos – the leftist Foreign Minister in 1945–1946 – that the Soviet attitude towards Greece would change if a representative government were formed, a general amnesty were granted, and Greece ceased to get involved in the differences between the Great Powers.[151] In trying to assess Venizelos's motives for provoking the government crisis, Norton dismissed stories that he was motivated by 'sinister intentions such as a desire to compromise with Markos'; it was 'more than possible that he was egged on by left-wingers in his own party who in Paris were in touch with Sofianopoulos'.[152]

The possibility, therefore, that some leftist fringe in the Liberal Party may have contemplated a compromise on the basis of the Soviet feeler cannot be discarded. On the other hand, the Soviets persisted with their efforts in the following month. On 7 November, during a Soviet reception in Paris, Vyshinsky told the British Minister of State that London was 'completely wrong in always assuming that a Communist Government in Athens was for Soviet Russia a "*sine qua non*" for co-operation in Greece'. The chat was taken up by some others present at the reception, including the Yugoslav Deputy Foreign Minister Aleš Bebler, and 'the proposition emerged that it [*sic*] might be value in having informal and private conversation with the four Powers plus … Yugoslavia upon an alternative government in Athens acceptable to all of us.'[153]

That the British took no notice of the second Soviet overture for a great-power settlement in Greece highlights their determination to have the Greek Civil War fought to the bitter end. Bevin's resolve is particularly important, for in 1948 the circumstances were rather discouraging for his Greek policy. The summer offensive had failed, while the reports piling up at the Foreign Office warned that the military situation was as precarious as ever and that Greek morale was being sapped by the prolongation of the war; and in the Commons the bothersome critics of Bevin's attitude towards Greece were active.[154] Yet 1948 was also the year which witnessed a dramatic turn of events in Europe, with the result that Bevin's policy of opposition to the Soviet Union seemed justified. The *Keep Left* group lost much of its momentum in the wake of the communist coup in Prague, the Soviet blockade of Berlin and the expulsion of Yugoslavia from the Cominform. In April the barrister John

Platts-Mills, one of Bevin's most formidable parliamentary critics over Greece, was expelled from the party on account of his pro-Soviet views; Konni Zilliacus and Leslie Solley were to follow. Also in March 1948 there was a move against communists in the Civil Service, with Attlee announcing that individuals belonging to, or associated with, the British Communist Party would be barred from employment in work vital to the security of the State.[155]

In a context where the Cold War had overshadowed the international situation and had even become a domestic political reality in many European states, receptiveness to communist overtures was bound to be a rare commodity. Bevin was more concerned with the conduct of the Greek politicians. His pungent cable to Norton on 8 November was instrumental in the reconstitution of the coalition and consistent with the pattern of selective intervention to secure the elusive unity among the anti-communist parties in Athens. Yet more trouble emerged in December, when sixty Labour MPs and other British personalities appealed to Attlee for a United Nations mediatory commission in Greece and invited the British government to take steps towards reconciling the Greeks. Attlee's reply was a far cry from his bold stance of December 1946–January 1947. On 6 December 1948 the Prime Minister told the Commons:

> HM Government does not intend to act upon this suggestion. The Charter of the UN expressly precludes interference in matters essentially within the domestic jurisdiction of any State. HM Government cannot, therefore, propose to the UN mediation between the Greek Government and the rebels ... [the] continued interference by Albania, Bulgaria and Yugoslavia in the internal affairs of Greece ... is at the root of that country's trouble.[156]

With the Foreign Office concurring that there was a 'clear distinction' between Greece's relations with her northern neighbours and the civil war,[157] the Under-Secretary for Foreign Affairs Christopher Mayhew took it upon himself to illuminate the House:

> So far as mediation goes between the Greek Government and the rebel bands, the Government having been elected under the supervision of a team of 1,000 international observers, the Greek Government's relations with the rebel bands are a matter for the Greeks and not for the UN.
>
> The basic cause [of the Greek Civil War] is the determination of the Communist northern neighbours of Greece to keep the flames alight.[158]

These public demonstrations of confidence were in marked contrast with the private frustration prevailing at the Foreign Office, where alarming reports on the 'depressingly low' civilian and military morale and 'utter irresponsibility' of the Greek politicians kept piling up. Sargent regarded the situation as so disturbing that on 7 December he contemplated full Anglo-American talks on all aspects of policy in Greece.[159] Probably the most perturbing and interesting was the report of John Tahourdin, an official at the British Embassy in Athens. Tahourdin diagnosed two forms of defeatism spreading all over Greece. One was the belief that victory was unattainable, and that since the present stalemate was disastrous for the country, the only course was a compromise with the KKE. The second was 'the attitude of sheer helplessness'. In areas under threat by the DSE, an increasing number of the population were beginning to say that if the army was incapable of beating the guerrillas, then there had better be some kind of a settlement. Even in the monarchist stronghold of the Peloponnese many people thought that if the 'rebel rule had come to stay, most of them would settle down under it more or less'. Beyond these 'treacherous elements', defeatism had already spread into the army, with 'discreditable episodes' where soldiers had refused to obey orders. Unable to see any end to the war, the officers and men felt that they were fighting not only for themselves but also for Britain and the United States. The Greeks criticized the Americans for providing '"too little and too late"' and measuring their aid 'from an eye-dropper'. Though Tahourdin upheld the British position that more US aid was needed, he castigated the Greek government's curious definition of the war:

> Although the present rebellion is foreign inspired, foreign aided and largely foreign directed, the fact remains that unlike the case of the Spanish Civil War, the actual fighting is being done on both sides by Greeks. Naturally this aspect of the situation is always glossed over by the Greek Government, who consistently refer to the rebels as Eamite Slavs or Slavo-Communists, and lull themselves into the comfortable belief that they are themselves in no measure responsible for the aggravation of the internal situation, and that more foreign aid rather than more strenuous exertion on the part of the Greeks is what is required.[160]

Tahourdin's report leaves no doubt that not only were the Greeks bordering on hopelessness, but also that the British authorities in Greece were scarcely more sanguine. The cumulative effect of such reports triggered off a forceful reaction from the Foreign Office. On Bevin's instructions, on 29 December 1948 the British Embassy in Washington asked the State Department whether it envisaged an increase of the Greek army. The answer was negative, and the Americans referred to reports that Bevin had gone too far in seeking alternatives: 'In his discouragement, he had even mentioned the possibility of getting out of Greece entirely, if things did not improve rapidly.' The Embassy assured them 'that this was not Mr. Bevin's considered view'.[161] Despite his genuine frustration, it is unlikely that Bevin saw withdrawal as an immediate alternative; the threat was deployed to achieve his twin objective – getting the Americans to pay for a bigger Greek army and getting the Greeks to pull themselves together. It was a moot point whether the threat could have a serious effect on US decisions, but it was bound to have a great impact in Athens.

On 29 December Bevin told the Greek Acting Foreign Minister, who was in London for his Christmas holidays, that the Greek situation was 'most unsatisfactory' and that the Greek political leaders 'seemed to be inept to the point of irresponsibility'. 'Had the Greek Government considered that the Americans ... might tire of their efforts to achieve a solution in Greece?'. The retention of British troops there was an 'embarrassment' which he would find difficult to defend to the Labour Party for much longer. Bevin summed up

233

with what he deprecated most in the Greek politicians: they held that 'what-ever they did, they could count on British and American aid ... and that they need not therefore make any sacrifices themselves by sinking their personal and party ambitions ... this was a mistaken idea.'[162]

As 1948 ended in military stalemate and political muddle in Greece, Bevin made no effort to conceal his frustration with Greek party politics and the American refusal either to bring in the marines or pay for a bigger Greek army. The British Foreign Secretary had even alluded to a withdrawal, while the Americans themselves had hinted that their resources were not inexhaustible. These, however, were no more than vague threats deployed for a specific purpose, and thus hardly amounted to a weakening of the Anglo-American resolve to assist the Greek government – at least in the short-term. What was languishing was the resolve of the patrons of the KKE and its army. A new and pivotal factor, which had already entered the picture, was bound to have a major impact not only on Anglo-Greek relations and the prospects of the KKE, but also on the entire position in the Balkans. It was the Yugoslav 'heresy'.

NOTES

1. F.O.371/72240 R2576: Norton to Bevin, 18/2/1948, Annual Report for 1947.
2. F.O.371/72201 R144: Norton to F.O., 4/1/1948; *ibid.*, R508: Norton to F.O., 8/1/1948; *The Times* (London): 27/12/1947; FRUS(1947): V, 461–2: Rankin to Marshall, 24/12/1947; EPSV (1947–1948): vol.133, pp.258–9.
3. F.O.371/72238 R946: Translation of Confidential Circular by the Minister of Public Order, 26/12/1947.
4. F.O.371/72236 R123: Norton to F.O., 27/12/1947; FRUS (1947): V, 464–6: Memoranda by Henderson, 26/12/1947.
5. F.O.371/72236 R100: F.O. to Washington, 24/12/1947.
6. F.O.371/67157 R16927: Belgrade to F.O., 26/12/1947, and Washington to F.O., 27/12/1947.
7. FRUS (1947): V, 475–6: US Chargé (London) to Marshall, 29/12/1947.
8. F.O.371/67157 R16927: F.O. to Belgrade, 30/12/1947.
9. F.O.371/72236 R101: Peake to F.O., 31/12/1947.
10. F.O.371/67157 R17045: Peake to Warner (personal), 30/12/1947.
11. Bevin Papers: F.O.800/468/GRE/47/46: Sargent to Attlee, 31/12/1947.
12. Bevin Papers: F.O.800/465/FR/47/31: Record of Conversation between Bevin and Bidault, 17/12/1947. Records of the CFM conference of November–December 1947 in F.O.371/64629, 64630, 64637, 64638, 64341, 64645, 64646; FRUS (1947): II, 676–829.
13. F.O.371/72237 R325: F.O. to Moscow, 2/1/1948.
14. F.O.371/72237 R474: Moscow to F.O., 5/1/1948.
15. CAB 129/23/C.P. (48) 7: Memorandum by Bevin, 'Review of Soviet Policy', 5/1/1948; CAB 128/12/C.M.2(48): 8/1/1948.
16. F.O.371/72236 R224: Greek Embassy to F.O., Memorandum, 3/1/1948; *ibid.*, R254: British Consul-General (Thessaloniki) to F.O., 5/1/1948.
17. F.O.371/72238 R814: Greek Embassy to F.O., Memorandum, 10/1/1948.
18. KKE (es.) Archives, *Avgi* (Athens), 12/1/1980: KKE letter to Baranov, 6/10/1947; P.J. Stavrakis, *Moscow and Greek Communism 1944–1949* (Ithaca and London: 1989), p.171, n.106; E. Barker, 'The Yugoslavs and the Greek

Civil War of 1946–1949', in L. Baerentzen, J.O. Iatrides, O.L. Smith, eds., *Studies in the History of the Greek Civil War 1945–1949* (Copenhagen: 1987), pp. 305–6; J.O. Iatrides, 'Perceptions of Soviet Involvement in the Greek Civil War 1945–1949', in *ibid.*, pp.247–8.

19. F.O.371/72237 R392: Prague to F.O., 8/1/1948.

20. F.O.371/72237 R473: Peake to F.O., 9/1/1948.

21. FRUS (1948): IV, 30: Inverchapel to Marshall, 16/1/1948.

22. HC Deb., vol.446, cols.420, 385; FRUS (1948): IV, 33: Marshall to Inverchapel, 20/1/1948.

23. F.O.371/72238 R926: Greek Embassy to F.O., Memorandum, 15/1/1948.

24. KKE (es.) Archives, *Avgi* (Athens), 19/1/1980: Rousos to Ana Pauker, 1/1/1948; V. Georgiou, *I Zoi mou* (Athens: 1992), pp.567–8. See also the commentary by the editor of the Archives, Filippos Iliou.

25. F.O.371/72237 R450: Minute by Wallinger, 2/1/1948; *ibid.*, R449: Sofia to F.O., 8/l/1948; *ibid.*, R932: Prague to F.O., 8/1/1948; *ibid.*, R513: Inverchapel to F.O., 10/1/1948; *ibid.*, R501: Minute by Wallinger, 10/1/1948.

26. F.O.371/72238 R911: Moscow to Wallinger, 13/1/1948.

27. F.O.371/72239 R1252: Paris to F.O., 23/1/1948.

28. F.O.371/72261 R170: Belgrade to F.O., 4/1/1948; *ibid.*, R1326: Belgrade to F.O., 28/1/1948.

29. FRUS (1948): IV, 9–14: Henderson to Marshall, 9/1/1948.

30. F.O.371/72238 R1025: US Embassy (London) to Peck (F.O. Southern Department), 20/1/1948; Peck to Coe (US Embassy, London), 2/2/1948.

31. FRUS (1948): IV, 2–37.

32. F.O.371/72239 R2032: Norton to F.O., 12/2/1948.

33. Bevin Papers: F.O.800/468/GRE/48/3: Bevin to Inverchapel, 19/2/1948; F.O.371/72240 R2434: Peck to Inverchapel, 19/2/1948.

34. FRUS (1948): I, 565–6: Memorandum by Forrestal to NSC, 19/4/1948.

35. Y. Kilismanis, *Apo tin Ionia sto Dimokratiko Strato* (Athens: 1989), pp.83, 90–2; S. Papayiannis, *Apo Evelpis Andartis: Anamniseis enos kommunisti axiomatikou* (Athens: 1991), pp.113–17.

36. V. Bartziotas, *O Agonas tou Dimokratikou Stratou Elladas* 3rd edn. (Athens: 1985), p.41; *idem*, *Exinda Chronia Kommunistis* (Athens: 1986), pp.278, 282–4; *Simioma me tis Apopseis tou Markou Vafiadi*, 15/11/1948, in P. Dimitriou, ed., *I Diaspasi tou KKE* I (Athens: 1978), 23; D. Gousidis, ed., *Markos Vafiadis: Martyries* (Thessaloniki: 1983), p.21; *Eleftherotypia* (Athens), 19/2/1980: interview with Markos Vafiadis.

37. F.O.371/72238 R946: Athens to F.O., 13/1/1948.

38. *Loc.cit.*

39. F.O.371/72239 R1769: Bevin to Norton, 6/2/1948.

40. F.O.371/72239 R2032: Norton to Bevin, 12/2/1948.

41. Bevin Papers: F.O.800/468/GRE/48/2: Alexander to Bevin, 11/2/1948.

42. W. Loth, *The Division of the World 1941–1955* (London:1988), pp.168–9.

43. M. Djilas, *Conversations With Stalin* (London: 1962), pp.181–2.

44. E. Barker, 'Yugoslav Policy towards Greece 1947–1949'; *idem*, 'The Yugoslavs and the Greek Civil War of 1946–1949', in L. Baerentzen et al., eds., *op.cit.*, pp.273, 306.

45. G. Vonditsos-Gousias, *Oi Aities yia tis Ittes, ti Diaspasi tou KKE ke tis Ellinikis Aristeras* II (Athens: 1977), 250.

46. F.O.371/72239 R1869: Prague to F.O., 10/2/1948.

47.	F.O.371/72239 R2241: Inverchapel to F.O., 16/2/1948.

48.	D. Partsalidis, *Dipli Apokatastasi tis Ethnikis Andistasis* (Athens: 1978), p.199. Also: *Politika* (Belgrade): 14 and 15/6/1982: interview with Markos Vafiadis; M. Djilas, *Vlast, Naša Reč* (London: 1983); both quoted by E. Barker, 'Yugoslav Policy towards Greece 1947–1949', in L. Baerentzen et al., eds., *op.cit.*, pp.276–7; G. Vonditsos-Gousias, *op.cit.* I, 440; L. Eleftheriou, *Synomilies me ton Niko Zachariadi* (Athens: 1986), pp.40–3. M. Vlandas, *Emfylios Polemos 1945–1949* III, part 2 (Athens: 1981), 87, claims that in March 1948 Stalin told Zachariadis to bring the civil war to an end. A. Papaioannou, *I Diathiki tou Nikou Zachariadi* (Athens: 1986), pp.40, 65–66, alleges that the order came in autumn 1948. Vlandas's memoirs are consistently unreliable, bitterly polemic and littered with wild and invariably unsubstantiated claims; Papaioannou's book is supposedly based on the notes he kept from his alleged meeting with Zachariadis in 1963. Both are of little value.

49.	G. Vonditsos-Gousias, *op.cit.* I, 440.

50.	L. Eleftheriou, *op.cit.*, p.41.

51.	V. Bartziotas, *O Agonas*, p.91.

52.	L. Eleftheriou, *op.cit.*, p.41; P. Stavrakis, *op.cit.*, p.170.

53.	F.O.371/72241 R3878: Belgrade to F.O., 15/3/1948.

54.	F.O.371/72241 R3484: Minute by Wallinger, 18/3/1948.

55.	F.O.371/72240 R2684: F.O. to Athens, 25/2/1948; FRUS (1948): IV, 56–7: Memorandum by Baxter, 2/3/1948.

56.	F.O.371/72241 R3484: Norton to F.O., 16/3/1948; *ibid.*, R4402: Record of Conversation between Maj.-Gen. Down and Wallinger, London, 23/3/1948; Minute by Wallinger, 24/3/1948; F.O. Minute, 25/3/1948.

57.	FRUS (1948): IV, 56–7,60–1: Memoranda by Baxter, 2 and 16/3/1948.

58.	*Ibid.*, 60–61: Memorandum by Baxter, 16/3/1948.

59.	P. Calvocoressi, *World Politics since 1945* 3rd edn. (London: 1977), p.120.

60.	F.O.371/72242 R5306: Minutes of a Conversation between Watson and Millard, Paris, 27/4/1948.

61.	F.O.371/72242 R5306: Wallinger to Ashley-Clark, Paris, 27/4/1948.

62.	F.O.371/72240 R2576: Athens to F.O., 25/2/1948.

63.	F.O.371/72242 R6553: Tahourdin (Athens) to Peck (F.O.), 20/5/1948.

64.	F.O.371/72349 R6576: Note by Wallinger, Greco-Turkish Declaration: Summary of Facts, 3/6/1948.

65.	*Loc.cit.*; F.O.371/72242 R4937: Minutes of a Conversation between Bevin and Tsaldaris, Paris, 16/4/1948; FRUS(1948): IV, 70–1: Lovett to Athens, 5/4/1948; *ibid.* 71–2: Wilson (Ankara) to Secretary of State, 8/4/1948.

66.	F.O.371/72349 R6576: Note by Wallinger, Greco-Turkish Declaration: Summary of Facts, 3/6/1948; Minutes by Sargent (3/6/1948) and Bevin (4/6/1948); *ibid.*, R7632: Bateman to Norton, 30/6/1948; FRUS (1948): IV, 70–1: Lovett to Athens, 5/4/1948.

67.	F.O.371/72242 R4937: Minutes of a Conversation between Bevin and Tsaldaris, Paris, 16/4/1948.

68.	F.O.371/72349 R7632: Greek Embassy to Bevin, 4/6/1948.

69.	F.O.371/72349 R7632: Minutes by Wallinger (8/6/1948), Hankey (21/6/1948), F.O. Minutes, 8, 15 and 16/6/1948.

70.	F.O.371/72349 R8527: Norton to Bateman, 15/7/1948.

71.	F.O.371/72240 R2631: State Department Confidential Release Note, 18/2/1948; FRUS (1948): IV, 54.

72. F.O.371/72240 R2405: Draft of Notes of Points which Chiefs of Staff might raise with Van Fleet, 16/2/1948.

73. F.O.371/72240 R2639: A.V. Alexander to Bevin, 18/2/1948; Bevin Papers: F.O. 800/468/GRE/48/2: A.V. Alexander to Bevin, 11/2/1948.

74. F.O.371/72241 R4402: Record of Conversation between Maj.-Gen. Down and Wallinger, London, 23/3/1948.

75. F.O.371/72203: Reports by the British Consul-General (Thessaloniki), 31/12/1947–15/7/1948.

76. F.O.371/72201 R6026: Norton to F.O., 13/5/1948; F.O.371/72203: Reports by the British Consul-General (Thessaloniki), 31/12/1947– 15/7/1948; HC Deb., vol.450, col.1390: C.P. Mayhew, 5/5/1948; S.N. Grigoriadis, *Dekemvris– Emfylios Polemos, 1944–1949: Synoptiki Istoria* (Athens: 1984), p.354; F.N. Grigoriadis, *Istoria tou Emfyliou Polemou 1945– 1949* IV (Athens: n.d.), 1137–8.

77. Bevin Papers: F.O.800/468/GRE/48/5: Bevin to Inverchapel, 10/5/1948.

78. F.O.371/72242 R396: Paris to F.O., 22/5/1948.

79. F.O.371/72243 R8421: Minute Sheet by Lord Jellicoe, 29/5/1948.

80. F.O.371/72242 R6553: Athens to F.O., 20/5/1948.

81. FRUS (1948): III, 1099–1100: Department of State Policy Statement – Great Britain, 11/6/1948.

82. F.O.371/72236 R270: Norton to F.O., 6/1/1948.

83. GAK: Tsouderos Papers, E (49): Memorandum by the Leader of the Left Liberals N. Grigoriadis to the Prime Minister, 29/1/1948.

84. FRUS (1948): IV, 80–1: Rankin to Marshall, 30/4/1948.

85. V. Bartziotas, *O Agonas*, pp.91–2.

86. GAK: Tsouderos Papers, E (54): Conditions for the Cessation of the Bloodshed, 2/4/1948.

87. FRUS (1948): IV, 80–1: Rankin to Marshall, 30/4/1948.

88. W.O.202/897: F.O. to Athens, 10/1/1948.

89. F.O.371/72240 R2405: Draft of Notes of Points which Chiefs of Staff might raise with Van Fleet, 16/2/1948; Brief for Discussion with Lt.-Gen. Van Fleet, note by W.O.14/2/1948; *ibid.*, R2639: Alexander to Bevin, 18/2/1948: Extracts from COS Minutes; F.O.371/72241 R4402: Record of Conversation between Maj.-Gen. Down and Wallinger, London 23/3/1948; Bevin Papers: F.O.800/ 468/GRE/48/2: A.V. Alexander to Bevin, 11/2/1948.

90. GES/DIS, *O Ellinikos Stratos kata ton Antisymmoriakon Agona (1946–49) – Ekkathariseis tis Roumelis ke i Proti Machi tou Grammou (1948)* (Athens: 1970), Appendix 1, pp.343–56: Extracts from the Report of Lt.-Gen. S. Kitrilakis, 26/2/1948.

91. *Ibid.*, pp.42, 45, 49–78; pp.357–60, Appendix 2: Operational Plan *Haravgi*, 5/3/1948; D. Zafiropoulos, *O Antisymmoriakos Agon* (Athens: 1956), pp.346–53; DSE Archives, *Eleftherotypia* (Athens), 5/2/1986: Circular by DSE Officer G. Vasilkos, 26/4/1948; F.N. Grigoriadis, *op.cit.* IV, 1125–33.

92. C. Sulzberger, *A Long Row of Candles: Memoirs and Diaries (1934–1954)* (London: 1969), p.356 (14/6/1948).

93. W.O.202/898: HQ BMM (Greece), Directive to Commanders of British Liaison Units attached to GNA, 14/4/1948.

94. F.O.371/72242 R5389: Norton to F.O., 30/4/1948; *ibid.*, R5668: Norton to F.O., 7/5/1948.

95. F.O.371/72242 R6174: Norton to Sargent (personal), 12/5/1948; *ibid.*, R7475: Norton to Bevin, 21/6/1948.

96. F.O.371/72242 R6553: Tahourdin to Peck, 20/5/1948.
97. V. Bartziotas, *O Agonas*, pp.91–2.
98. KKE: E.K., VI, pp.462–3: PDK Statement, 8/6/1948; FRUS (1948): IV, 100–1: Rankin to Marshall, 2/6/1948.
99. FRUS (1948): IV, 100–1: Rankin to Marshall, 2/6/1948; *ibid.*, 105–7: Rankin to Marshall, 12/6/1948; *ibid.*, 107–8: Griswold to Marshall, 16/6/1948.
100. F.O.371/72211 R6651: Athens to F.O., 2/3/1948; F.O.371/72203 R6954: British Consul-General (Thessaloniki) to F.O., 3/6/1948; F.O.371/72201 R7019: Norton to F.O., 3/6/1948.
101. *Public Papers of the Presidents of the US, Harry S. Truman, 1948*, pp.336–40 (12/6/1948), and FRUS (1949): VI, 323, n.4.
102. F.O.371/72243 R7560: Minute by Wallinger, 24/5/1948; *ibid.*, R7562: Minute by Hankey, 23/6/1948.
103. FRUS (1948): IV, 115–16: Marshall to London, 21/7/1948.
104. *Loc.cit.*
105. *Ibid.*, 117–18: Marshall to Athens, 2/8/1948.
106. Soviet Foreign Ministry Archives: Greek-Soviet Relations in 1946–1949, in P. Andaeos, *Nikos Zachariadis: Thytis ke Thyma* 2nd edn. (Athens: 1991), p.464. For the story involving Jan Masaryk see V. Bartziotas, *O Agonas*, p.91; S.N. Grigoriadis, *op.cit.*, pp.381–2. For a less plausible story of an alleged approach by Tsaldaris to the KKE leaders themselves in July 1948 see: D. Gousidis, ed., *op.cit.*, pp.32–4; G. Vonditsos-Gousias, *op.cit.* I, 37; V. Bartziotas, *O Agonas*, pp.89–91; M. Vlandas, *op.cit.* III, part 2, 86–7; and O.L. Smith, 'The Tsaldaris Offers for Negotiations, 1948: A Lost Opportunity or a Canard?', *Epsilon: Modern Greek and Balkan Studies* 1 (1987), 83–9.
107. FRUS (1948): IV, 107–8: Griswold to Marshall, 16/6/1948.
108. W.O.202/894: Memorandum for General Van Fleet by Colonel Nussbaum, 17/7/1948; F.O.371/72244 R9609: Reilly to Wallinger, 12/8/1948.
109. F.O.371/72243 R8116: Norton to Wallinger, 5/7/1948; F.O.371/72242 R7475: Norton to Bevin, 21/6/1948.
110. CAB 128/13/54 (48): 26/7/1948; Bevin Papers: F.O.800/502/SU/48/8: F.O. Memorandum, August 1948.
111. V. Bartziotas, *O Agonas*, pp.95–97; *Kathimerini* (Athens): 15 and 18/7/1948.
112. F.O.371/72243 R8451: Norton to F.O., 16/7/1948; *ibid.*, R8536: Norton to Bateman, 14/7/1948; F.O.371/72244 R8786: Reilly to F.O., 26/7/1948; *ibid.*, R9592: Reilly to F.O., 16/8/1948; F.O.371/72202 R9285: Reilly to F.O., 5/8/1948; *ibid.*, R9805: Reilly to F.O., 13/8/1948.
113. FRUS (1948): IV, 137–8: Marshall to Athens, 20/8/1948.
114. F.O.371/72243 R8688: Reilly to F.O., 23/7/1948; Th. Tsakalotos, *Saranda Chronia Stratiotis tis Ellados* II (Athens: 1960), 123; D. Zafiropoulos, *op.cit.*, p.429. For details on the operations see GES/DIS, *op.cit.*, pp.96–340; D. Zafiropoulos, *op.cit.*, pp.364–430; S.N. Grigoriadis, *op.cit.*, pp.368–80; F.N. Grigoriadis, *op.cit.* IV, 157ff; F.O.371/72201 R7601, R7895, R8199, R8478, R8783.
115. EPSV (1948): 134, pp.1234, 1254, 1284, 1311 (2–7/8/1948).
116. F.O.371/72244 R9624: Greek Embassy to F.O., Memorandum, 10/8/1948; FRUS (1948): IV, 122–4: Memorandum by Cromie, 10/8/1948.
117. F.O.371/72244 R8942: Minute by Peck, 11/8/1948.
118. F.O.371/72244 R9279: Franks to F.O., 19/8/1948.
119. DSE Archives, *Eleftherotypia* (Athens), 2 and 3/5/1979: Report by G. Vonditsos-

Gousias, 20–21/8/1948; V. Bartziotas, *O Agonas*, p.84; S.N. Grigoriadis, *op.cit.*, pp.373–80; F.N. Grigoriadis, *op.cit.* IV, 1169–70; GES/ DIS, *op.cit.*, p.325. On the battles of Grammos see S. Papayiannis, *op.cit.*, pp.104–5; D. Katsis, *To Imerologio enos andarti tou DSE 1946–1949* II (Athens: 1992), 235–409.

120. F.O.371/72202 R10073: Reilly to F.O., 24/8/1948.
121. F.O.371/72247 R11338: Norton to Bateman, 24/9/1948.
122. C. Sulzberger, *op.cit.*, p.501.
123. H.K. Smith, *The State of Europe* (New York: 1951), pp.225, 238.
124. F.O.371/72247 R11338: Norton to Bateman, 24/9/1948.
125. D. Zafiropoulos, *op.cit.*, pp.452–54; S.N. Grigoriadis, *op.cit.*, pp.386ff; F.N. Grigoriadis, *op.cit.* IV, 1174–83; F.O.371/72204 R11278, R11516, R11753: British Consul-General (Thessaloniki) to F.O., 1, 8, 15/10/1948.
126. F.O.371/72245 R10150: Paris to F.O., 28/8/1948; *ibid.*, R10161: Greek Embassy to F.O., 23/8/1948; *ibid.*, R10346: Reilly to F.O., 6/9/1948; *ibid.*, R10525: British Embassy (Paris) to French Foreign Minister, Aide Mémoire, 9/9/1948; *ibid.*, R10589: Minute by Bateman, 10/9/1948; *ibid.*, R10561: Washington to F.O., 10/9/1948.
127. F.O.371/72245 R10570: F.O. Minute, 'Greece', 9/9/1948; F.O. to Athens, 10/9/1948.
128. F.O.371/72245 R10600: Tahourdin (Athens) to Peck, 9/9/1948; F.O.371/72202 R10793: Reilly to F.O., 15/9/1948.
129. FRUS (1948): IV, 152–3: Grady to Marshall, 29/9/1948; *ibid.*, 154–5: Memorandum by Marshall, 30/9/1948; *ibid.*, 155–6: Minor to Marshall, 1/10/1948; *ibid.*, 156–7: Tidmarsh to Marshall, 1/10/1948.
130. *Ibid.*, 147: Memorandum by Marshall, 7/9/1948; F.O.371/72245 R10429: Washington to F.O., 7/9/1948.
131. Bevin Papers: F.O.800/468/GRE/48/8: Bevin to Franks, 28/9/1948, (see also F.O.371/72246 R11262); *ibid.*, F.O.800/468/GRE/48/9: Note by Roberts, 30/9/1948.
132. F.O.371/72246 R11230: Memorandum of Conversation between Bevin and Tsaldaris, Paris, 28/9/1948; *ibid.*, R11266: Minute by Wallinger, 28/9/1948.
133. F.O.371/72247 R11435: F.O. Minute, 4/10/1948.
134. F.O.371/72248 R12202: Athens to F.O., 14/10/1948.
135. FRUS (1948): IV, 168–70: Grady to Marshall, 22/10/1948.
136. F.O.371/72202 R11987: Norton to F.O., 20/10/1948; *ibid.*, R12255: Norton to F.O., 23/10/1948; F.O.371/72247 R11870: Norton to F.O., 16/10/1948.
137. FRUS (1948): IV, 162–5: Marshall to Lovett, 20/10/1948.
138. F.O.371/72247 R12018: Norton to F.O., 23/10/1948; F.O.371/72248 R12130: Bevin (Paris) to F.O., 21/10/1948.
139. Bevin Papers: F.O.800/468/GRE/48/10: Minutes of Conversation between Bevin and Marshall, 27/10/1948.
140. F.O.371/72248 R12095: Norton to F.O., 23/10/1948.
141. F.O.371/72249 R13117: Memorandum of Conversation between Sofulis and Grady, 25/10/1948; F.O.371/72248 R12127: Norton to F.O., 26/10/1948; F.O.371/72249 R13117: Memorandum of Conversation between Sofulis and Rankin, 26/10/1948; F.O.371/72248 R12301: Norton to F.O., 29/10/1948; *ibid.*, R12387: Minute by Wallinger, 27/10/1948; FRUS (1948): IV, 176–7: Grady to Marshall, 25/10/1948.
142. F.O.371/72249 R13203: Papagos to Premier, 11/11/1948.
143. F.O.371/72249 R12922: Norton to F.O., 16/11/1948.

144. F.O.371/72251 R13993: Norton to F.O., 7/12/1948; *ibid.*, R14112: Norton to F.O., 19/12/1948.
145. F.O.371/72202 R12497: Norton to F.O., 3/11/1948; *ibid.*, R12863: Norton to F.O., 9/11/1948; F.O.371/72248 R12357: Norton to F.O., 1/11/1948; *ibid.*,R12579: Norton to F.O., 6/11/1948; *ibid.*, R12540: Norton to F.O., 7/11/1948; *ibid.*, R12437: UK Delegation (Paris) to F.O., 4/11/1948.
146. F.O.371/72202 R13177: Norton to F.O., 17/11/1948; *ibid.*, R13356: Norton to F.O., 23/11/1948; F.O.371/72249 R12905: Norton to F.O., 15/11/1948; *ibid.*, R12922: Norton to F.O., 16/11/1948.
147. F.O.371/72249 R12662: Bevin to Norton, 8/11/1948.
148. F.O.371/72249 R12786: Norton to F.O., 12/11/1948; F.O. 371/72250 R13279: Norton to F.O., 19/11/1948; *ibid.*, R13126: Norton to F.O., 20/11/1948; F.O.371/72202 R13356: Norton to F.O., 23/11/1948.
149. EPSV (1948–1949): 136, pp.144–9, 181–2 (20/11/1948); F.O.371/72202 R13356: Norton to F.O., 23/11/1948; F.O.371/72249 R13155: Norton to F.O., 20/11/1948; *ibid.*, R13156: Norton to F.O., 21/11/1948; F.O.371/72250 R13280: Norton to F.O., 23/11/1948; *ibid.*, R13402: Norton to F.O., 24/11/1948.
150. F.O.371/72250 R13126: Norton to F.O., 20/11/1948; *ibid.*, R13155: Norton to F.O., 20/11/1948.
151. F.O.371/72247 R11622: Barnes (Paris) to F.O., 5/10/1948.
152. F.O.371/72249 R13126: Norton to F.O., 20/11/1948.
153. F.O.371/72248 R12657: UK Delegation (Paris) to F.O., 9/11/1948.
154. F.O.371/72249 R12794: Draft Paragraphs for Embassy Appreciation to Foreign Office, November 1948; HC Deb., vol.457, cols.1230–9, vol.458, col.852.
155. HC Deb., vol.448, col.1704; K. Morgan, *Labour in Power 1945–1951* (Oxford: 1985), pp.64–9; D. Childs, 'The Cold War and the "British Road", 1946–53', *Journal of Contemporary History* 23 (1988), 551–72.
156. HC Deb., vol.459, col.23.
157. Bevin Papers: F.O.800/468/GRE/48/11: F.O. to U.K. Delegation to UNO (Paris), 9/12/1948.
158. HC Deb., vol. 459, col. 790.
159. F.O.371/72251 R14135: F.O. Minute, 'Greece', 11/12/1948; *ibid.*, R13993: Sargent to Athens, 7/12/1948.
160. F.O.371/78393 R713: Tahourdin to Bateman, 22/12/1948.
161. FRUS (1948): IV, 220–4: Memorandum by Baxter, 29/12/1948.
162. Bevin Papers: F.O.800/468/GRE/48/12: Bevin to Norton, 29/12/1948; Enclosure: Conversation between Bevin and Pipinellis, 29/12/1948.

VI The Death Agony of the Democratic Army: 1949

> As for the gods, it seemed to be the same thing
> whether one worshipped them or not, when one
> saw the good and the bad dying indiscriminately.
>
> Thucydides, II : 53

With Stalin against Tito

In the early 1940s Britain's strategic interests in the eastern Mediterranean determined her interference in Greece, where the threat emanated from an indigenous left-wing resistance movement rather than from any transparent designs of the Kremlin. In 1945 the KKE acted independently, but in 1946 it embarked on a policy for which it sought the support of its ideological allies. In doing so, the Greek communists placed a certain portion of their interests with the Soviet Union and Yugoslavia and provided the former with a tempting opportunity to divert attention from eastern Europe. Whereas Stalin saw fit to exploit the opportunity, the decision of February 1946 for limited armed struggle aiming initially at a compromise was made by the KKE and was only subsequently endorsed by the fraternal parties. Later, as it became increasingly clear that the British, Greek and US governments were in no mood for a compromise, the KKE resolved to push matters to a head as the only alternative to capitulation.

It was in this process that the dependence on assistance from the Soviet Union and Yugoslavia was potentially hazardous, for the KKE could not have any control on the disposition of such exogenous factors. In order to elicit the necessary aid, Zachariadis endeavoured to present Stalin with a series of *faits accomplis*, but his efforts came to naught. Whereas the Athens government was receiving massive foreign support, the KKE at best received promises which proved hollow. The prolongation of this unrewarding state of affairs was bound to tilt the balance even further to the government's side and confine the KKE in a tight spot; in such a position, the Greek communists could ill afford a split between their chief patrons.

On 28 June 1948 the Prague newspaper *Rude Pravo* announced the expulsion of the Yugoslav Communist Party from the Cominform.[1] According to Markos, in spring 1948 Stalin sent a letter to him and Zachariadis detailing the charges against the Yugoslavs. The DSE Commander argued that in view of its need for Yugoslav assistance, the KKE should not take sides and that Zachariadis should in person explain to the Yugoslav and Soviet comrades the stance of the party. In apparent concurrence the latter went to Belgrade, where it was agreed that the KKE should itself determine its response to the dispute, and Yugoslavia restated its commitment to support the struggle. On

241

his way to Moscow, however, Zachariadis changed his mind and on arrival there proclaimed himself in agreement with Stalin's charges against Tito.[2]

Although Markos offers no explanation for Zachariadis's *volte face*, his story is partially confirmed by Djilas, who claims that just after the Cominform Resolution the KKE leader told the Yugoslavs that his party would be unable to stand on their side. The Yugoslavs anticipated this and hoped that the KKE would keep quiet or neutral; Zachariadis begged for the continuation of assistance and they agreed.[3] However, on 28–29 July 1948 the Fourth Plenum of the KKE Central Committee endorsed the denunciation of Tito, though the decision was not made public in view of 'the peculiar position of the KKE and our movement vis-à-vis Yugoslavia'.[4] This was proposed by Zachariadis, and it is quite important that in 1980 Markos revealed: 'For many reasons I also agreed.'[5] On 20 August, on the eve of the DSE manoeuvre from Grammos to Vitsi, Zachariadis ordered his Commander to withdraw for some rest. Recently Markos himself admitted that under the strains of the battle he experienced some 'exhaustion', while Bartziotas claims that he actually suffered something very much akin to a nervous breakdown; whatever his ailment, in September 1948 Markos was sent to Moscow for therapy.[6]

From there he sent a Note to the Politburo of the Soviet Communist Party, criticizing what he perceived as errors in the KKE policy since 1945. In October he sent a copy to the KKE leadership, and in the following month he was summoned to attend the KKE Politburo session of 15 November.[7] Though valid in several ways, Markos's views were laden with hindsight wisdom. He castigated the party leadership on a number of scores – notably the unrealistic decisions of the Third Plenum of September 1947 and the premature creation of the Provisional Democratic Government. Then he proceeded to assess the situation in the autumn of 1948. Propped up by the Americans, 'monarchofascism' had achieved 'a relative politico-military stabilization', while the Democratic Army could not muster the necessary numbers to capture towns; the KKE could not win the war unless the communist countries recognized the PDK and extended immediate aid, which was also unlikely. For Markos the best course was the 'continuation of armed struggle with intense partisan activity'; the war would thereby be prolonged beyond 1949 and the ensuing 'military and political haemorrhage' of the US and Greek governments would be the major negotiating weapon of the KKE.[8] The Politburo had already produced its own document dismissing Markos as a 'defeatist', 'panic-stricken factionist'.[9] According to his own account, Markos hung about in Vitsi until January 1949, when the Fifth Plenum expelled him from the KKE. He left for the Soviet Union and did not return to Greece until 1982.[10]

Markos's dismissal drew widespread attention and the interpretations placed upon it survived for far too long. The Greek press maintained that the purge was the result of pressure from Moscow to comply with Cominform directives, whereas Markos wanted to avoid opposition to Tito and thus ensure the continuation of Yugoslav aid.[11] At the Foreign Office the news raised spirits, for it was hoped that the Greek government would be able to benefit. The incident was interpreted as evidence of a 'serious rift' in the KKE ranks between a faction in favour of limited guerrilla activity and 'an extremist faction ready to pursue the civil war to the bitter end'. Though uncertain of the real reasons for Markos's purge, the Foreign Office reckoned that the immediate cause was the desire of the 'Deviationists' – '"heretics" on the Yugoslav pattern' – to come to terms with Tito in their search for more support, while 'the Moscow-trained Cominform Extremists' were opposed to Yugoslav aid.[12] The Yugoslav Deputy Foreign Minister Aleš Bebler voiced the view that the purge was 'a case of Titoism', surmising that Markos 'too had seen the light and had lost his post for that reason'.[13] The former Yugoslav ambassador to Prague assured Sir Charles Peake that Markos 'preferred the Tito brand of Communism to [the] Cominform variety'.[14] Even a member of the Hungarian Cabinet professed to know that the discharge of Markos was 'due to his having adhered to the Tito cause'.[15]

Markos's only relationship with 'Titoism' was his advocacy of guerrilla tactics as opposed to pitched battles. There are, in fact, three good reasons why he could not have been a convert: not only had he concurred in siding against Tito, but had he been a 'Titoist', his trip to Moscow in September 1948 would have probably been a trip to eternity. Besides, his Note was basically sound, but Markos himself was as much responsible for the policy he now deprecated as any other KKE leader.[16] For the Foreign Office and the Greek government a reflection of the Tito-Stalin break was obvious and desirable, but the true reasons for Markos's purge may have had something to do with the adverse prospects for the KKE. Markos had first submitted his Note to the Soviet Communist Party, hence its apologetic tone and the implicit attempt to blame the KKE leadership – that is, Zachariadis – for a course which in hindsight seemed to be leading to a dead end.

Whilst retaining his confidence, Zachariadis nonetheless embarked on a process of entrenching himself and defending his policy since 1945. On 6 October 1948 the Politburo dismissed the entire leadership of the Athens Party Organization for delaying 'the mass popular movement and the armed struggle' in the capital, and there were instances of DSE officers being executed for hardly plausible reasons.[17] Faced with adversity and criticism, in January 1948 the KKE leader had already introduced the concept of the DSE as a revolutionary army; now, in the Fifth Plenum of January 1949, he drastically recast the aspirations of the struggle by discarding the bourgeois-democratic goal and proclaiming the 'proletarian socialist revolution'.[18] He elaborated on this novelty in 1952, when he crudely argued that in the post-Varkiza era the party had bought time to regroup its forces and in 1946 had launched the 'socialist revolution'.[19] This source is little more than an ill-starred attempt by Zachariadis to convince the vanquished party of its commitment to the socialist revolution since 1945 – an anachronistic claim which the contemporaneous evidence defies. In his *apologia* of 1952 the KKE leader contradicts even himself when he argues that the party was also fighting for 'pacification', 'understanding' and 'reconciliation'.[20]

The re-examination of the character of the 'revolution' marks the beginning of an obsessive endeavour by Zachariadis to shake off personal responsibility for the abortive dual strategy. At the same time, however, it betrays an air of confidence about the prospects of the struggle. No doubt this was largely the result of his visit to Moscow in September 1948, when he received assurances of massive Soviet aid, including heavy artillery and aircraft for the supply of units in central and southern Greece.[21] If the past was anything to go by, Stalin's pledges would have been consistent with his aim to detach the KKE from the Yugoslavs through promises which he was neither willing nor able to redeem. For his part, Zachariadis continued to hope that a capture by the Democratic Army of the towns of Florina, Amyndaio, Naoussa and Edessa would enable the KKE to 'partially overthrow the correlation [of forces] and secure reserves', thus creating 'conditions for motorized armoured units, and perhaps a few airplanes'.[22] Though a subsequent claim, this is confirmed by the fact that in December 1948–January 1949 the Democratic Army twice attacked Naoussa and Edessa, and in February 1949 it launched a major attack on Florina.[23]

It is very likely, therefore, that in September 1948 Stalin kept the KKE subservient and rallied it against Tito through yet another hollow promise of aid.[24] There was clear proof now that the Greek communists were not the masters of their own fate. With the Greek government receiving massive assistance from the United States, the KKE could only have tilted the balance with commensurate foreign aid. Hence it had to repose its hopes in the Soviet Union and Yugoslavia, whose interests did not exactly match its own. The Greek communists were already in difficulties, but henceforth they would feel the ground slipping from under their feet.

An additional setback for the KKE was the attempt of its army at positional warfare. By late 1948 the DSE had been fully transformed into a regular army and launched a series of offensives on Edessa, Naoussa and other towns in northern and central Greece. Whereas in December 1948–January 1949 some relative successes seemed to vindicate Zachariadis's doctrine that his army could occupy and hold urban centres,[25] on 12 February 1949 came the major setback. A guerrilla force of 5,400 attacked Florina but was forced to withdraw after two days, with the number of wounded alone reaching 1,557. The DSE Chief Medical Officer noted that 'this battle resembled the exhausted wrestler who marshals his last impoverished strength and counter-attacks but licks the dust for good and all'.[26] The replenishment of such losses was impossible. After the elimination of potential recruits by way of deportations, incarcerations and, principally, the mass evacuation of the countryside by the government forces, in the winter of 1948–1949 the Democratic Army could only attack towns for forcible recruitment. Yet as these attacks were made by insufficiently equipped forces against fortified positions,[27] the DSE entered into a vicious circle in which in order to recruit, it inflicted purgatorial casualties upon itself. These difficulties were compounded in January 1949, when the Democratic Army came under the command of a War Council consisting of politicians with very little – if any – military experience, such as Zachariadis himself, Ioannidis, Bartziotas and Vonditsos-Gousias. After the end of the civil war the Foreign Office commented: 'No doubt some irreverent spirits had made a comparison with the disasters which overtook Germany when Hitler took over from his generals in the Russian campaign.'[28]

The adverse prospects lent force to the peace offers of the KKE. On 15 August, 20 September and 10 October 1948 the party appealed to the United Nations that it was willing to accept any initiative towards a 'democratic under-standing'. The Provisional Democratic Government reiterated its desire to send a representative to the General Assembly, but the reaction from Athens was that negotiations would be possible only after the guerrillas had laid down their arms. In December, when a number of Labour MPs urged the British government to undertake an initiative, the KKE welcomed the appeal and repeated its willingness to embrace any move conducive to a peaceful settlement.[29]

Yet the Fifth Plenum of January 1949 went further towards marginalizing the party. Zachariadis reintroduced the 1924–1935 thesis for an independent Macedonia, where the Slavo-Macedonians of northern Greece would 'find their full national rehabilitation'.[30] This decision was partly due to the fact that the Slavo-Macedonians of northern Greece were by this time the main source of recruitment for the DSE.[31] The KKE subsequently claimed that the temporary flirtation with this disastrous policy was also necessary in order to counter subversive propaganda by Yugoslav Slavo-Macedonians in the ranks of the Greek Slavo-Macedonians in the Democratic Army, this having led to desertions of the latter to Yugoslavia.[32] Defections of Greek Slavo-Macedonians to Yugoslavia had indeed taken place, for the Foreign Office knew that units of NOF (the National Liberation Front representing the Slavo-Macedonian minority in Greece) 'were in January withdrawn from active participation in the rebel struggle'.[33]

Norton interpreted the move as directed from Moscow in order to challenge Tito through the creation of a hostile coalition in southern Yugoslavia and furnish the Slavo-Macedonians who lived north of the Greek border with a pretext to fight for an autonomous state in Greek territory – that is, to join the Democratic Army.[34] The Foreign Office agreed that the move was orchestrated by the Kremlin in order to 'unseat' Tito but doubted whether a Macedonian state was actually in the offing. Wallinger, who believed that it was 'part of the war of nerves' against Yugoslavia, minuted that 'the Greeks have gone off the handle' and recommended 'a little soothing syrup' for the Greek ambassador and his government.[35]

The need of the KKE to retain the cooperation of the Slavo-Macedonian minority in Greece was evinced on 5 April 1949, when it was announced that the Provisional Democratic Government was reshuffled to include, among others, two Slavo-Macedonians representing NOF.[36] Evidently, as by early 1949 the odds were turning decisively against it, the KKE reacted spasmod-ically. Its self-inflicted estrangement was augmented by the flirtation between London, Belgrade and Athens, which further testified to the inability of the Greek communists to control the pace of events.

'Companions in Trouble': London – Athens – Belgrade

The flirtation was a corollary of the Tito-Stalin split in so far as it presented the Western powers with an opportunity to ensure the elimination of Yugoslav assistance to the Democratic Army. This possibility arose because the KKE found itself in the position of badly needing the continuation of Yugoslav support but potentially having to go against its own Stalinist grain in order to secure it. Tito had so far generously aided the KKE, but henceforth the state of diplomatic, political and economic isolation from East and West jeopardized the survival of his own regime. Gradually, as the split showed no signs of healing and their economy came on the verge of collapse, the Yugoslavs would realize that their total estrangement from the Soviet bloc left some sort of a *rapprochement* with the West as the only means of pulling through; for its part, the West was persistently alarmed by the Greek Civil War and bitterly resentful of Yugoslav assistance to the DSE. The two issues were bound to be connected and the potential opportunities were seen from the outset.

In mid-June 1948 the British and US ambassadors in Belgrade, Sir Charles Peake and Cavendish Cannon, noted that relations between the Soviet Union and Yugoslavia, as well as between the latter and the KKE, were strained, and that the Yugoslavs' inability to step up their 'unprofitable' investment in the KKE implied that Markos's fortunes were on the wane.[37] Two days after the expulsion of Yugoslavia from the Cominform, Peake speculated that the KKE was likely to side with Stalin, whereas the Slavo-Macedonians of NOF would probably stand by Tito. The ambassador welcomed this likely upshot, for 'divergencies between these two bodies will become even more acute and Markos's prospects even more gloomy'. Peake was tempted to address the question whether the Tito-Stalin split should necessitate a modification of British policy towards Yugoslavia: he advised against this, for the Yugoslav Communist Party remained hostile to the West and its capitalist system.[38] The Foreign Office was gratified that the Greek army could profit from the henceforth precarious position of the KKE, but with regard to Yugoslavia it preferred to refrain from taking sides. Any would-be overtures from Tito would have to be ignored until the position was clearer, in the hope that the split would 'widen more quickly and without our intervention'.[39]

One reason why the opportunity was not immediately seized upon was that British reactions conflicted. The Embassy in Belgrade held that Tito was likely to stick to his own brand of Communism and show that his policies would not be affected by the Cominform resolution. This, coupled by the need to satisfy Yugoslav Slavo-Macedonians in order to ensure the cohesion of his country, meant that there would probably be no immediate effect on Yugoslav support for Markos – 'unless the latter throws in his hand with the Cominform'.[40]

Bevin's initial reaction was one of scepticism. On 1 July 1948 he told the Cabinet that Yugoslavia and Bulgaria might move towards the establishment of a Balkan Federation. While the Soviet aim was 'to secure control of Greece by supporting the Communist movement in that country', Tito now provided the alternative course of securing an outlet to the south by way of such a Federation. These 'differences of method, not of ultimate aim, ... would not ease our problem of preventing Greece from being detached from the Western powers'.[41] Naturally, therefore, when the Embassy in Belgrade asked the Foreign Office to consider in advance its stance to would-be overtures from Yugoslavia, Bevin replied that he would view them 'with grave suspicion'. Tito remained 'a convinced Communist', hence the West 'cannot expect any change of heart'. Peake was instructed to 'hear willingly' but tell the Yugoslavs that British reactions to any approaches 'will be judged not on the professions of the Yugoslav Government but on their deeds'.[42] Though he did not specify what these deeds might be, Bevin seems at least to have expected the Yugoslavs themselves to do something to mollify Western opinion.

The State Department was amazed by the expulsion of Tito – 'the most highly favoured Soviet henchman' – but refrained from any gestures which might give the Kremlin a pretext for arguing that he 'was acting at the instances of capitalist America'.[43] Bevin agreed that the immediate objective should be to exploit the issue for propaganda against Stalin, who aimed at 'the liquidation of all local autonomy and ultimate absorption by Russia'. Britain and the United States should 'let the Communists quarrel among themselves', for if they now came out in support of Tito, they 'should create a situation where his people might be accused of being in association with the Western Powers'.[44]

Initially the attitude of the British was conditioned by their mistrust of Tito the Communist, but also their desire not to further exacerbate his position. This cautious approach was confirmed by their response to the first Yugoslav overture. On 8 July 1948 Wallinger received a letter from the US Embassy in London, claiming that a Yugoslav official, who 'apparently came to the conversation with the blessings of top Yugoslav authorities', inquired of the US Chargé d'Affaires in Belgrade 'what attitude Yugoslavia could expect from the US in [the] future', and especially whether she could get some aid from the European Recovery Programme. The Yugoslav official said that his country was 'extremely anxious to liquidate the Greek situation as quickly as possible in view of the burden placed by Greek refugees on [the] Yugoslav economy'. Even more significantly, he added that the Kremlin 'was now not particularly interested in Greece', and he insisted that Yugoslavia would give no more aid to the KKE and its army.[45]

Wallinger shared Bevin's scepticism on the grounds that Tito was still a communist and that the wrecking of the European Recovery Programme was 'a major objective of Communist policy'. The Foreign Office was disinclined to take the Yugoslav protestations at face value. If the British were approached, they would reply that their attitude towards Yugoslavia would change only when Yugoslav actions led to the improvement of relations with Britain. As for Greece, Wallinger's remark that 'the ball' was 'at Tito's own feet' demonstrates that the British would have liked a unilateral initiative by the Yugoslavs as an antecedent to a *rapprochement*. If they genuinely wanted the elimination of the Greek situation, they could of their own accord close down the PDK radio station which transmitted from Yugoslav soil, expel the Greek guerrillas who were receiving training in Yugoslavia, and seal the frontier against the DSE. Nevertheless, the Head of the Southern Department was not for lending a wholly deaf ear to Yugoslav entreaties, as it would be in the interests of the West to keep the Tito-Stalin rift open. He recommended, for instance, that a Yugoslav request to a British oil company for 20–30,000 tons of crude oil be granted, because 'oil is quickly expendable'.[46]

Though Wallinger did not want Britain to belie completely Yugoslav hopes, opinions within the Foreign Office remained divided. On 5 July the official G.T.C. Campbell recommended no more than the satisfaction of

Tito's crucial needs, for 'there should be no question of this barbarian being allowed to join western society, until he has shown by deeds that he has improved his ways'.[47] Yet on the same day that Wallinger received the letter from the US Embassy, Bevin told the Cabinet that 'it would be convenient if we could take advantage of this confused state of affairs in the Balkans to clear up the situation in Greece'.[48] Although he did not elaborate on how this might be done, the potential was transparent. The matter, however, ended there, for neither side pursued it any further. The British Embassy in Belgrade doubted whether a real overture had been intended, and on 10 July reported that the Americans had heard no more and would take no initiative.[49] The State Department agreed that no gesture should be made towards Tito, and on 15 July Bevin professed that Britain and the United States 'were not proposing to intervene in this family quarrel between the Communist States'.[50]

An additional reason for British circumspection may well have been the fact that the timing of these developments coincided with the major military offensive of the Greek government forces against the Democratic Army. Some optimism about its outcome, generated by the initial relative successes, may have persuaded the British that it was unnecessary to lure Tito into abandoning his commitment to the Greek guerrillas. From July to October 1948, therefore, Britain and the United States kept out of the 'family quarrel' while endeavouring to ascertain its impact on the KKE. Evidence gathered by the UN Special Committee on the Balkans (UNSCOB) showed that Yugoslav aid had 'definitely diminished', whereas the official paper of the Yugoslav Communist Party was adamant that nothing had changed. In Washington the information on relations between the KKE and Yugoslavia was regarded as 'mixed and inconclusive'.[51] The Foreign Office interpreted the evidence of UNSCOB as showing that Yugoslav aid to the DSE was on the wane, hence the obvious dilemma for the British was whether the West should offer Tito support conditioned on some sort of political bargain. On 8 October 1948 Sir Ivone Kirkpatrick noted that there was scarcely any possibility of reconciliation between Belgrade and Moscow, and proceeded to address the issue in the following terms:

> As it must be to our advantage to see a continuance of the state of tension behind the Curtain, we should not exclude the desirability of assisting the Yugoslav administration just enough to keep it going; but any *political* bargain must be extremely dangerous.[52]

The British held to this cautious attitude until in November 1948 the UN General Assembly adopted an Australian resolution for the establishment of a Conciliation Committee between Greece and her northern neighbours. Although the right-wing press in Athens claimed that an understanding was possible with Yugoslavia in view of her imminent secession from the Soviet bloc, the talks soon broke down because of Yugoslavia's reluctance to conclude a frontier agreement with Greece.[53] Besides, the equally circumspect attitude of the Greek government towards the Tito-Stalin break was not conducive to an agreement. Whether he was leading a schism or not, Tito remained the enemy of Greece, and Tsaldaris feared that he might now be asked to make concessions to Yugoslavia.[54]

Though by the last days of 1948 nothing tangible had emerged from the Tito-Stalin rift, the despondency generated by the military stalemate in Greece would soon change the position of the British and Greek governments. Already in October the Foreign Office had been tempted to consider the possibility of a political bargain with Tito. One reason for dismissing it was the fact that representatives of the Greek and Yugoslav governments had been brought together to discuss ways of improving bilateral relations. On 29 December 1948 Panayiotis Pipinellis, the Greek Acting Foreign Minister, disclosed to Bevin that the Yugoslavs had at one point been anxious to reach an agreement, but then 'something' had happened and they backed down. Pipinellis wanted Britain to exert pressure on Belgrade, but despite the recently signed British-Yugoslav economic agreement, Bevin held that 'there was no scope yet for political, as opposed to economic bargaining with Tito'. Towards the end of the meeting Hector McNeil suggested that a further approach should be made to the Yugoslavs through UN auspices, as that would provide Tito with a face-saving formula.[55]

For a disheartened Bevin this was an important meeting. The failure of the campaign against the Democratic Army and the political intrigue in Athens had tempted him to threaten to pull out of Greece entirely, yet now he found McNeil's idea promising.[56] On 6 January 1949 he sent Attlee a note as a basis for discussion of British policy towards Yugoslavia. The Foreign Office should be prepared for an approach from the Yugoslavs, 'to which we may need to respond with some urgency if we are to keep Tito afloat'. The course envisaged by Bevin was to seek the opinion of the ambassador in Belgrade as to whether the British government should inform the Yugoslavs that it would be willing to embark on negotiations for a long-term agreement between Yugoslavia and Britain.[57]

Peake replied on 28 January 1949. Bebler had confirmed Pipinellis's story that at one point he had hoped to enter into talks with the Greeks for the settlement of outstanding questions, but 'he had been confronted with "certain pressures" which were too strong for him'. The Yugoslav Deputy Foreign Minister emphasized the difficulties facing his country, but added that he now saw little prospect in a Greek-Yugoslav agreement mainly because of the 'both rotten and fascist' nature of the Greek regime. The Yugoslavs could negotiate only with a broadly-based Greek government, which did not necessarily mean the inclusion of the KKE but rather a scheme more representative of the Left. However, Bebler did not fail to mention that his government 'was sick and tired of supporting a rabble of Greek refugees of whom they were only too anxious to be rid'. Peake advised the Foreign Office that nothing should be done to compromise Tito with his followers. The lure for the Yugoslav leader to sign an independent agreement with the Greek government would be 'the belief that he could thereby gain something from the British and US governments which they would otherwise not let him have'. Yet a drastic deviation from the uniformity of Eastern bloc foreign policy in return for increased economic assistance from the West would be 'an act of the greatest political courage', hence the British ambassador recommended 'extreme caution'.[58]

In London Wallinger dismissed Bebler's hints for a broad Greek government, which could come only '*after* the rebels had been thoroughly defeated'. None the less, it was clear that the Yugoslavs were likely to seek a solution to the problem of the Greek-Yugoslav frontier 'if some sufficiently face-saving device could be found'. This was certainly an improvement, and given Tito's quandary, the British were not prepared to rush him off his feet. Wallinger endorsed Peake's call for caution: 'I do not think it would be in line with our objective of "keeping Tito afloat" to make any suggestion whatsoever about negotiations with the Greeks.'[59]

In January 1949 the background to these secretive contacts was bound to undergo a radical change. Yugoslavia was excluded from the Council of Mutual Economic Assistance (COMECON), while the KKE made public its alignment with Stalin. The possibility that Tito might veer more to the West – and *vice versa* – increased. In mid-February Bevin saw Bebler in London and explained to him what Britain would appreciate: 'If only other countries would stop interfering in Greek affairs she would be able to settle down to the task of healing her shattered economy.'[60] Pipinellis had already held exploratory talks with UNSCOB on the possibility of a Greek-Yugoslav *rapprochement*, and the Greek government considered prevailing upon the Yugoslavs to seal the frontier and hold informal meetings for the conclusion of a commercial agreement.[61] Athens was prepared to make some concessions in return, and Tsaldaris told Bevin that he did favour a Greek-Yugoslav commercial agreement.[62]

Now it was the Americans' turn to be sceptical. They argued that 'pending real Yugoslav change of heart', a conciliatory initiative on the part of the Greek government would be 'fruitless'.[63] The sluggishness of the contacts, however, was not so much the product of US reservations as a corollary of the need for caution on the part of the Yugoslav leaders and the British. This need was highlighted by the clumsy handling of such a delicate issue by the Greeks. On 11 March 1949 a right-wing Athens daily published an open letter inviting Tito to undertake the initiative for the restoration of Greek-Yugoslav friendship; Budapest Radio immediately seized the opportunity to charge Tito with 'Treason'.[64] A few days later the Yugoslav Chargé d'Affaires in Athens handed Pipinellis a document proposing the appointment of representatives to meet on neutral soil to discuss the possibility of an '*entente*'. Something of the sort happened, and by the end of March Bevin was cheered, for 'there had been a *rapprochement* between Tito and the Greeks, who were now companions in trouble'.[65]

Then in early April Tsaldaris's frivolity seemed to destroy the promising prospect. On 31 March the Greek Foreign Minister stated that Greece might be allied with Yugoslavia within a year. Despite the *démentis* issued by the Greek government, the Yugoslavs felt compelled to deny Tsaldaris's '"fictions"'; and despite the Yugoslav denial, Budapest Radio felt compelled to charge that Tito had now wholly seceded to the Western camp. The contacts between Greek and Yugoslav agents were maintained, though no progress had been made. Pipinellis thought that the Yugoslav leaders found it difficult to carry on talks because of Tsaldaris's rash statements.[66] Peake was irritated by the 'fatuous indiscretion' of the Greek Foreign Minister, which rendered the prospects for future talks 'pretty dim'.[67]

It was at this point that the Foreign Office changed tactics. The British had been reluctant to make any aid to Tito conditional upon a change of Yugoslav policy towards Greece, and as long as there seemed to be a prospect of a secret understanding between Athens and Belgrade, they could afford to hold off. By late April 1949, however, as the Yugoslav initiative in this regard seemed to have dried up partly because of Tsaldaris's frivolity, they decided to be more forthright. The Foreign Office thought that some gesture might now be 'timely' in order to show the Yugoslavs that 'we sympathize with them ... and that we are not out for their blood in all circumstances just because they are Communists'. A handy opportunity was in sight, for Brigadier Fitzroy Maclean, Head of the wartime British Military Mission in Yugoslavia and a personal friend of Tito's, was planning a visit to Belgrade. Peake made suggestions for an informal talk between the two men, and the Foreign Office came up with the idea that Maclean might insinuate to Tito that a change of his policy towards Greece could be the criterion for Western economic assistance to Yugoslavia.[68]

On 5 May 1949 Maclean lunched with Tito in Belgrade and discussed with him in detail Yugoslavia's relations with the West and Greece. Tito stressed his overwhelming need for credits and hoped that an agreement could soon be concluded. Maclean retorted that the British government would have to justify this to the Parliament and the British people – a difficult task since Yugoslavia was hardly popular in Britain; it was 'quite ridiculous' to have the Yugoslav press referring to the British and US governments as 'Fascist beasts and Imperialist warmongers'. Maclean warned Tito that London strongly deprecated the Yugoslav policy of allowing the Democratic Army to use Yugoslav territory for regrouping and refitting; then, seizing upon the decision of the KKE to align itself with Stalin, he ingeniously defined the Yugoslav quandary: Maclean could not grasp what gains they sought to reap by aiding the DSE, for 'it seemed silly to add to their existing troubles by actually helping to set up yet another hostile Soviet puppet state on their southern frontier'. Tito replied that in the past he had helped the KKE, but now the situation was different. It was difficult to initiate sudden changes, but certain steps had already been taken and a further 'gradual improvement' could be expected. Refugees from Greece were now being kept in Yugoslavia and would not be allowed to return to Greece, nor would any other help be given to the DSE; but he pleaded for his promise to be kept secret.[69]

Indeed, the conversation was kept secret for some weeks, even from the Americans.[70] Feeling that Tito's statements to Maclean had 'a ring of sincerity', the Foreign Office was gratified to see that the Yugoslav leader had himself admitted that the survival of his regime depended on Western aid. Anthony Rumbold minuted that the appeal for credits should be taken 'as the *cri de coeur* for which we have been waiting': 'I think we can take it that all Yugoslav help to the rebels has now ceased.' This was of crucial importance, for the Democratic Army would no longer be able to regroup and re-equip on Yugoslav soil, while units which maintained bases in Albania would not be able to draw supplies by rail and road across Yugoslavia from Bulgaria.[71]

Further Yugoslav professions came on 8 June 1949, when the Foreign Minister Edvard Kardelji and Bebler, his deputy, assured Cannon that material aid was '"not going over"' to the Democratic Army; Kardelji was 'unhappy and sick' with Yugoslavia's involvement in Greece.[72] This conversation, and the news that the British government had authorized Peake to offer Tito a £5m credit, prompted the State Department to inquire whether the time had come to secure some political concessions. The Foreign Office disagreed on the grounds that rendering economic aid conditional upon assurances over Greece would be tantamount to asking Tito to take a huge leap towards the West, which would in turn augment his domestic troubles and eventually defeat the objective of keeping him afloat.[73] On 30 June the British disclosed to the State Department Maclean's conversation with Tito and admitted that their decision to offer credits had been 'considerably influenced' by the latter's undertakings. Under the impression that Tito was sincere, the Foreign Office had instructed Peake to remind him of what he had told Maclean and to ask him squarely whether he was now aiding the DSE – though without necessarily suggesting that the grant of credits would depend on his answer.[74]

The *rapprochement* between Yugoslavia and the West had been brewing for some time, but the countdown started on 5 May 1949, when Maclean lunched with Tito in Belgrade. From then on it looked as if the Yugoslav leader would ponder over the political cost of accepting economic assistance from the West and ending his commitment to the KKE. The pondering took place against a bleak background. Yugoslavia's domestic and international position was marred by the economic blockade from the Cominform, bad relations with Austria and Italy over the Carinthian problem and Trieste, and even worse relations with London, Athens and Washington since the outbreak of the Greek Civil War. Eventually on 10 July 1949 Tito announced that he would accept a loan from the West and, more crucially, that he was closing the frontier with Greece; the pretext given was frontier incidents between the Greek and Yugoslav armies and a KKE allegation that Greek forces had made use of Yugoslav territory to attack the DSE with the consent of Yugoslav officers.[75]

The Foreign Office was gratified both at the closing of the frontier and at the pegs on which Tito hanged his decision.[76] Some officials were less sanguine, as they feared that the Greek guerrillas might not be completely crushed in the summer of 1949 but renew the war in 1950 from Albanian bases.[77] Nevertheless, the closing of the border deprived the Democratic Army of supplies stored on Yugoslav soil, while some 4,000 guerrillas who were injured and were being treated in Yugoslavia were not allowed to rejoin the ranks; and the reduction of the rear line of the DSE to the Greek-Albanian frontier severely curbed its ability to manoeuvre and exposed it to an enhanced danger of encirclement.[78] Despite their anxiety to bring the Greek Civil War to a speedy end, the British seized the opportunity provided by the Tito-Stalin break patiently and deftly. The gain was that Yugoslav policy moved in the direction desired by London, Athens and Washington. In consequence, the KKE would face the shoot-out of 1949 stripped of the assistance of its hitherto most genuine and generous supporter.

Throughout 1946–1949 two of the main thrusts of British and US policy were the attempts to liquidate foreign aid to the Democratic Army and refurbish Greece's image as a parliamentary democracy. By early 1949 the flirtation between London, Belgrade and Athens indicated that a breakthrough might soon be drawing near with regard to the former, but the latter still remained elusive. The permanently unsettled political situation in Athens had already generated domestic difficulties for Bevin, and these were bound to be aggravated when the Greek monarch manoeuvred in the direction of unconstitutional solutions. The threat to Greece's frail parliamentary legitimacy, a major embarrassment for the US and British governments, prompted them once more to step in and thwart the royal initiatives. As the Foreign Office put it, Greece continued to 'require outside advice and some degree of intervention to ensure that that advice is taken'.[79]

Influenced by the able and ambitious Queen Frederika, by January 1949 King Paul had decided to assume personal control over the situation through General Papagos, who was renowned for his devotion to the Crown. The King aimed at the establishment of a non-party government under the General and was prepared to dissolve Parliament if it rejected his scheme.[80] The royal design stumbled over the move by Sofulis and Tsaldaris to broaden their government with the inclusion of Papandreou and Kanellopoulos, and the determination of Norton and Grady to preserve parliamentary administration; the British ambassador was sufficiently alarmed to regard the initiative by Sofulis and Tsaldaris as Greece's '"last chance for parliamentary democracy"'.[81] The catalyst in changing the King's mind was pressure from Norton and Lord Mountbatten; the latter not only enjoyed the Greek monarch's full confidence, but also happened at the time to be staying at the Palace as his guest. On 18 January 1949 the two men urged him to stick to parliamentary procedures, whilst Grady sent to his Political Adviser a memorandum with the identical views of the State Department. King Paul was persuaded to abandon his plan[82] and on 20 January the government was broadened by the inclusion of Papandreou and Kanellopoulos. Bevin was hugely gratified that Norton and Grady had thwarted a development which would have led to a 'storm' in the House of Commons and probably forced him to withdraw all British forces from Greece.[83]

Though he did not escape domestic attacks for his 'squalid interference' in Greece,[84] it was the maintenance of parliamentary government which allowed the Foreign Secretary to retain his nerve. As his Greek policy remained unpopular with sections of the Labour Party and British public opinion, he saw that the best means of overriding the difficulty was to ensure the speedy conclusion of the civil war. Thus, once the government crisis had been settled, he addressed the particulars of the war effort. A step towards the improvement of the military situation was taken on 20 January, when Papagos was appointed Commander-in-Chief of the Greek armed forces, even though his demand for the increase of the army was turned down by the Americans.[85]

The size of the Greek army constituted only one facet of the military situation. A further complication lay in the friction between the British and

US Military Missions, which prompted Bevin's attempt to ensure that the former would not be relegated to a subsidiary role. On 12 January 1949 he minuted to Alexander that a would-be 'down-grading' of the BMM would be seen as a reduction of the British contribution to the joint effort, and as it might foreshadow a British withdrawal, it would be a blow to Greek morale. Bevin sought the establishment of a joint Anglo-American political and military team in Washington with the task of examining and co-ordinating all aspects of British and US policy in Greece, including the relationship between the BMM and JUSMAPG.[86] On 1 February he cabled Washington a request for the increase of the Greek army and his proposal for a joint team.[87]

Norton explained to the Foreign Office that although the lower echelons of the British and US authorities in Greece were able to cooperate, in the higher echelons the views of the US government prevailed. His assessment that this was due to a lack of consensus between London and Washington[88] appears correct. Grady admitted that the course of US policy in Greece 'was determined independent of British views and [is] not influenced by them': 'Greece more than any other country is a test of the American capacity for leadership of the new free world.' What was 'of vital importance' for the United States was agreement with the British 'on fundamentals'.[89] These could be summed up in the continuation of the British commitment to the elimination of the communist threat in Greece, whereas the particulars would have to be left with Washington. This division of responsibility furnished clear proof that the Americans were now beginning to acquire the confidence they lacked in their first steps towards a global policy of containing Communism. It was no surprise, therefore, that on 19 February Bevin wrote to Alexander that the Truman administration did not favour his proposal for an Anglo-American working team.[90]

Meanwhile the British Foreign Secretary continued to be at the receiving end of Tsaldaris's persistent demands.[91] Bevin obtained an authoritative assessment of the situation in March 1949, when Field-Marshal Sir William Slim, Commander of the Imperial General Staff, visited Athens. According to the CIGS, the need for a military success in the near future was overwhelming because Greece's economic rehabilitation could be embarked upon only after internal security had been achieved. The Field-Marshal recommended the increase of the army by 13,000 men and that of the airforce by two Fighter Bomber and one Reconnaissance Squadrons.[92] During a meeting with Bevin and his staff on 24 March, Slim argued that if his proposals were adopted, the Greek army could beat the DSE within the next twelve months; it was accordingly decided to communicate a copy of his report to Washington and ask the Americans to finance its implementation. Bevin was prepared to waive the Greek contribution to the cost of the British Missions (£437,500 annually) and make a free gift to the Greek government of fifty Spitfire aircraft. In his anxiety to get Slim's recommendations implemented, he wanted 'to have something in hand when approaching Mr. Acheson'.[93]

Shortly afterwards Bevin went to Washington and on 31 March gave Dean Acheson, Marshall's successor, a copy of Slim's report and requested the implementation of its recommendations; Acheson only promised to look carefully into it.[94] What the new US Secretary of State did was to send a synopsis to Grady and ask for his views. The ambassador's pungent comment confirmed that British consent was only sought 'on fundamentals': 'Being British it is cast in terms of Empire defence and being a British soldier's report it makes its recommendations without giving consideration to [the] cost either to US taxpayer or to US recovery programme.'[95] In this light, on 25 April Acheson told the British ambassador in Washington that there would be no increase of the Greek army or of US military aid to Greece.[96] Even so, in May Norton informed the Greeks that Britain would make them a free gift of twenty-two Spitfire aircraft, which would be delivered in June–July so as to play their part in the summer campaign.[97]

The Greek government would not relent on its endeavours to obtain a bigger army. In early April it submitted to the Foreign Office and the State Department a bold proposal. This time the request came in the closing paragraphs of a long memorandum prepared by a team headed by King Paul and Papagos. The Greeks were of the opinion that if the Cominform overthrew Tito, Greece, Yugoslavia, Turkey and Italy would be in grave danger. Since diplomatic action would then be to no avail, they proposed the naval blockade of Albania, subversive activity inside the country, persecution of the DSE forces that might flee there, and open military intervention by the Western powers; the ensuing collapse of Enver Hoxha's regime and the allied occupation of Albania would cover Tito's western flank as well as an important sector of Greece's northern frontier. The Greeks stressed the importance of Turkey's participation in this operation because should the Soviet Union descend to the Aegean through the creation of a Macedonian state, the Kremlin would then proceed to conquer the Straits and realize the dream of the Tsars to obtain an outlet to the Mediterranean through the Black Sea. As Greece would 'be called upon to play an important, perhaps the most important part', foreign aid to her 'should be adequately supplemented'.[98]

The motives of the Greek government in submitting these proposals lay with the resuscitation of the Macedonian question and the fact that Albania was the major supply base for the Democratic Army. Moreover, the memorandum was reminiscent of Tsaldaris's earlier plans for an *entente* with Turkey and smacked of an attempt to secure greater commitments and involvement from Britain and the United States. The request for increased military aid came as the logical consequence of an apocalyptic prognostication, but neither London nor Washington was willing to embark on impetuous initiatives. The Foreign Office noted that 'save a few characteristic Greek extravagances and inaccuracies', the appeal was 'well-argued and useful'. A naval blockade or military occupation of Albania was 'a tempting suggestion', but it would bring the West into direct conflict with the Soviets, who maintained a strong Military Mission in that country and regularly supplied her through ships unloading at Durazzo. The best course was the encouragement of subversive activities inside Albania by 'Titoist elements'. The possibility was even mentioned of encouraging the Greeks to pursue the DSE across the frontier, but 'the political and military consequences of such a step are not readily foreseeable'.[99] Bevin was prepared to consider 'in the near future' and 'in another context' the possibility of action against Albania, while the Foreign Office made the connection between the Greek memorandum and Tsaldaris's recent foreign policy pursuits: 'We may be sure that Greek pressure for a Mediterranean Pact will increase with the passage of time.'[100] Washington, too, discarded the military occupation of Albania and preferred a *rapprochement* that would compel Yugoslavia, Bulgaria and Albania to guarantee the Greek frontiers.[101]

The only profound impact of the memorandum was to expose the extent to which the KKE had lost control over its fortunes. By early 1949 the influx of foreign aid to the Greek government and the Tito-Stalin split had made these fortunes look dismal. Thus, despite the rhetoric, the launching of the 'socialist revolution' and Zachariadis's apparent confidence, the KKE continued to appeal for an understanding. On 25 January 1949 its 'government' proposed an armistice, the withdrawal of all foreign troops and Missions, a general amnesty, and a mutually acceptable government to hold elections within two months; if its opponents were interested, the PDK would send a delegation to Athens at once.[102] Although the offer was dismissed in Athens as an attempt to allow 'the Communists' Trojan Horse within the walls', a United Press report from London, dated 28 January, alleged that the Greek government was willing to accept a ceasefire 'sometime tonight or early tomorrow'. This story, allegedly disclosed by British sources, created an 'unfavourable impression' in Athens. The Foreign Office indignantly denied that there was a British source behind this 'offending message', whilst Norton reassured Tsaldaris that there was no change of British policy towards the KKE.[103]

Indicative of the determination of the Greek, British and US governments to impose the military solution was the fact that the operations of 1949 had been prepared in November 1948, and that in December of that year more than 40,000 troops were launched against the 3,000 guerrillas in the Peloponnese. Literally overnight, on 27–28 December 1948, the local intelligence and support networks of the DSE were dismantled by means of 4,500 arrests,[104] and in the following three months the outnumbered guerrillas were defeated; by April 1949 the Peloponnese was purged of the Democratic Army.[105] Next, 70,000 troops, supported by tanks, artillery and aircraft, took on the 4,500 ill-clad, ill-fed and ill-equipped guerrillas in central Greece. With heavy casualties the latter retreated northwards and broke into numerous small bands which were easy prey for the army. By the end of June 1949 central Greece was also clear, and the government mustered its army against Mounts Grammos and Vitsi, which the Democratic Army had recaptured in April.[106]

These victories of the government forces raised a number of questions about the future of the vanquished. Oddly, some concern was first shown by Reginald Leeper. In a letter to *The Times* on 6 April 1949, the former British ambassador to Greece suggested a new amnesty to be supervised either by UNSCOB or by Anglo-American observers. The Foreign Office rejected the proposal claiming that since no amnesty could be carried out fairly after a civil war, vendetta killings would not cease. The White Terror, which the British had doggedly refused to admit overtly, was now invoked as an argument against Leeper's suggestion. J.O. McCormick, a clerk at the Southern Department, remarked that even in 1945, when Leeper himself had been exerting an enormous influence on Greek affairs,

> we could not stop minor tyranny in outlying areas ... It would therefore be asking for trouble to guarantee something which we could not be sure of effecting. The prospect of parliamentary responsibility for every Greek murder should not be inviting to HM Government.[107]

Leeper's initiative foundered when Norton agreed that the supervision of an amnesty would be too burdensome a task.[108]

An additional obstacle was that the amnesty issue could undermine the morale of the army. By April 1949 the awareness that the KKE was in no position to make substantial demands had rendered the Greek government completely impervious to calls for a compromise. This was confirmed on 20 April, when the communists appealed to the United Nations that they were willing 'to make the greatest concessions'.[109] According to the State Department, this was the twenty-first peace offer made by the KKE since 1946, but the response from Athens was that the guerrillas would first have to lay down their arms.[110] A few days later Miltiadis Porfyrogenis, member of the KKE Politburo, applied to the US Embassy in Prague for a visa to go to New York to discuss at the United Nations the prospect of a settlement; the State Department informed the Embassy that he was 'inadmissible to the US in the absence of an official invitation from the UN'.[111]

There was a ring of desperation in these appeals of the KKE, and there was a good reason for it. Stalin feared that an indecisive prolongation of the Greek civil war, with the Democratic Army marching to and fro across the Albanian border, might spark off an allied invasion of the country which, through the Adriatic Sea, was his only exit to the Mediterranean. Thus in April 1949, only days after the Greek government had requested military action against Albania, Moscow informed Zachariadis that all DSE operations must be wound down by the beginning of May. Preparations began for withdrawal from the country, but then in early May Zachariadis informed his warlords that the situation had temporarily changed and that instead of withdrawal the DSE should embark on vigorous military activity.[112] This *volte face* was brought about by the emergence of another olive branch and the need to continue operations in order to prevent the impression that the KKE had shot its bolt and was now on its knees begging for peace.[113]

On 26 April 1949, while the Democratic Army was preparing to withdraw, Dean Rusk, the US Assistant Secretary of State, Hector McNeil, the British representative at the UN Security Council, and Andrei Gromyko, head of the Soviet Delegation to the UN, dined together in New York. Rusk asked Gromyko whether the three powers might use their influence towards a settlement in Greece, and the Soviets replied that they were prepared for further discussion.[114] The three men met again on 4 May. McNeil emphasized that he could not go into the merits of the question, while Rusk said that he 'had not intended to imply that we ... would be willing to change the form of discussion from existing channels, such as UNSCOB and diplomatic channels, to the great powers'. Gromyko proposed the cessation of hostilities and the holding of elections in Greece with the participation of 'the northern forces', hinting that the Soviet Union might take part in the implementation of these proposals. McNeil objected that the Greek government 'was a well-established, recognized independent government, and that the northern forces had no such status', but Gromyko insisted upon a reply. Rusk and McNeil were ambiguous, with the latter adding two more qualifications: that they should not infringe on UN responsibilities, and that Britain 'could not tell the independent government of Greece how to run its internal affairs'.[115]

The initial reaction in London and Washington was cautious. Rusk recommended a careful study of the issue, for this might both save the United States some of its annual spending on Greece and offer a better understanding of Soviet intentions. President Truman felt that they 'should not close the door' to Gromyko provided that no talks begin without the Greek government.[116] For Bevin the timing of the Soviet initiative coincided with an outburst of domestic pressure over Greece. In May 1949 seventy Labour MPs of the Union of Democratic Control appealed to him to support proposals for a peaceful settlement and provide for UN supervision of new elections; an impervious Bevin referred them to Attlee's statement at the Commons on 6 December 1948, that the UN Charter precluded meddling with the internal affairs of member-states. The UDC countered unavailingly that Britain 'has regularly intervened in the domestic affairs of Greece both before, during and since the liberation of that country; and that present British policy towards Greece can with difficulty be defined as one of non-intervention'.[117]

The conception of the Greek problem nursed by Britain and the United States remained incompatible with communist thinking. On 14 May Rusk and McNeil informed Gromyko that they could not discuss the issue without the participation of the Greek government, and that the real cause of the internal situation in Greece was the foreign assistance to the guerrillas. Gromyko explained that Moscow was willing to take part in the supervision of parliamentary elections in Greece and in controlling her northern border, but added that all foreign military assistance, including material and personnel, should be withdrawn. Rusk and McNeil again forbore to comment, stressing that their talks were 'informal and personal' and that any negotiations must include the Greek government.[118]

Bevin addressed the issue on 16 May, when he prepared a memorandum for Cabinet discussion. The Foreign Secretary found the Soviet terms 'quite unacceptable', for they 'place both parties to the civil war on a basis of equality' and would enable the KKE 'by means of renewed infiltration and trickery to retrieve their fortunes from the low level to which the determination of the Greek people has consigned them'. Nevertheless, he was against returning a completely negative answer, as the overture might reflect a genuine Soviet desire to settle their differences with the West over Greece, 'if only for temporary tactical reasons'. One obstacle was Gromyko's proposition for Soviet participation in the supervision of a ceasefire, which would give the Soviets 'endless opportunities of making a genuine and favourable settlement impossible'. What Bevin wanted was not an agreement between the Greek warring factions but the cessation of all foreign aid to the DSE; in this line, he would demand of the Kremlin to cease exerting pressure on Tito, Turkey and Cyprus, terminate Bulgarian aid to the Greek communists and agree to a settlement between Greece and Albania.[119] On 19 May the Cabinet invited Bevin to explore with Acheson the possibility of a satisfactory settlement in Greece and, if possible, of outstanding problems in the Balkans.[120]

The concern of the British and the Americans to include the Greek government in any talks meant that the fate of the Soviet initiative also depended on the mood prevailing in Athens. Under the fear that Greek interests might be sacrificed as part of a European settlement, the Greek government opposed a compromise. On 15 May the right-wing daily *Akropolis* invited party leaders to respond '"to fellow-travellers' efforts to bring about a new Varkiza"'. Tsaldaris replied that 'the country must not be cheated out of the fruits of [the] army's victories and there must be no new Varkiza. No Trojan Horses would be let inside national walls.' The Liberal Rendis took a more long-term view: 'the KKE had openly sided with [the] country's enemies and could not therefore exist in Greece even after [the] suppression of [the] rebellion.'[121]

This uncompromising stance was perfectly in step with the Anglo-American line. For the US government the main issue was foreign aid to the DSE, and the proper forum for its discussion was the United Nations. The United States and Britain should listen to the Soviets but no talks could commence without the participation of the Greek government; as for the guerrillas, since they had no status under international law, the extent of any negotiations with them would have to be decided by the Greek government.[122] The desire to discard the Soviet offer was inelegantly disguised by the insistence on a solution through the UN, where the fighting between the KKE and the Greek government could not be tackled. On 20 May Rusk assured the Greek ambassador that the issue was not Greece's domestic situation but foreign aid to the Democratic Army, while the ambassador maintained that his government would prefer no talks with Moscow; the guerrillas should first lay down their arms – 'amnesty and all that could come after'.[123]

The view of the Foreign Office was identical. Reckoned to be leading from weakness, the Soviet Union was unprepared to discuss a general Balkan settlement. British and US counter-proposals, 'if and when made', should therefore be designed to guarantee not only the end of communist interference in Greece, but also to secure advantages for the West in other fields. Since the consent of the Greek government was desirable, the Greeks should be invited to state their conditions for declaring a new amnesty and elections following the surrender of the DSE. British and US terms might be limited to the elimination of all foreign aid to the Greek guerrillas and their surrender with all their arms; the Soviets would no doubt reject them but they might be tempted to return with a less unacceptable offer: 'Meanwhile the Greeks will have derived further encouragement from our continued support and the disintegration of the rebels would continue.'[124]

The military solution clearly remained the top priority of the US, British and Greek governments. The latter yet again emphatically rejected the idea of talks which would undermine the morale of the army and might even allow Soviet meddling in the internal affairs of Greece. Grady supported the views of the Greek government, which was 'more democratic and more representative than at least half of UN members'.[125] When Bevin and Acheson met in Paris on 27 May, they agreed that an oral communication to the Soviets was preferable.[126] The Greeks had come to suspect that Bevin might be influenced by leftist pressure in the Commons, thus on 1 June the ambassador in London once more appealed to him that no talks be held with the Soviet Union, as that would undermine the morale of the army. With the appeal backed by Norton, the British agreed with the Americans not to press the Greeks on such internal matters as the international supervision of an amnesty and elections, or the lifting of the ban on the KKE.[127]

The Greek request was granted. On 20 July Rumbold wrote to Peake:

> If the Soviet initiative in New York had any demoralizing effect on the rebels, it probably had an even more demoralizing effect on the Greek Army and indeed it was largely for this reason that we turned it down so sharply and have not pursued the conversations started by Gromyko. On whichever side the Greek is fighting he is not going to fight any harder if he suspects that the quarrel may be composed at any moment as a result of the intervention by the Great Powers.[128]

For Britain and the United States there ought to be a military *dénouement* to the Greek civil war. The Soviets had misread western intentions. Soon after Stalin had ordered the withdrawal of the Democratic Army, Rusk had given the impression that the West had softened its attitude and contemplated a settlement. The Kremlin misconstrued this as its last chance of preserving a foothold in Greece. What transpired was that the British and the Americans – probably inspired by Tito's flirtation with the West – envisaged the elimination of all foreign aid to the DSE as a step which would facilitate the military solution. A settlement was aborted by the different perceptions of the two sides as to the causes of the Greek Civil War. The British and the Americans had been arguing that it was the foreign aid to the guerrillas, whereas the KKE and Moscow maintained that the origins were purely domestic. This discrepancy sufficiently accounts for Rusk's suggestion to Gromyko, its misreading by the Kremlin, and the Soviet initiative.

Despite the failure of the Soviet move, Zachariadis did not proceed with the withdrawal of his army. In 1956 he told Eleftheriou that 'in a war you do not retreat without a fight', to which his interlocutor poignantly remarked that the KKE leader, oblivious of the human toll, persisted with a war which had just been deemed impossible to pursue, let alone win.'[129] On 1 June 1949 a French delegation led by Paul Éluard reached the mountains of 'Free Greece'; the poet told the guerrillas that '"the Greeks have proved that the word freedom cannot be translated into English"',[130] but the aphorism failed to improve the position of the Democratic Army. After the clear-up of the Peloponnese and central Greece, the guerrilla forces mustered on Mounts Grammos and Vitsi. In late April Papagos ordered the immediate arrest and deportation of all those who had, or were suspected to have, any connection with the guerrilla movement in Macedonia. The continuation of the arrests throughout the summer dismantled the DSE supply and intelligence networks; many of those arrested were court-martialled and sentenced to death.[131] With the DSE unable to mount diversionary operations, an army of well over 100,000, supported by artillery, tanks and aircraft, took on the 12,000 guerrillas on Grammos-Vitsi. Against the support of the United States and Britain to the Greek government, the KKE was left with the support of Albania. General Tsakalotos, the ablest field-commander of the government army, commented that the closure of the frontier by Tito 'expedited the crushing of the bandits, otherwise no-one can tell for how long the struggle would have been prolonged'.[132]

In the night of 2–3 August 1949 the government forces unleashed a decoy attack on Mount Grammos, where they pinned down a DSE force of 5,000. On 11 August 60,000 troops carried out the main blow on Mount Vitsi, defended by 7,000 guerrillas. When the army penetrated their defensive positions, the peril of encirclement and annihilation forced the DSE to abandon Vitsi and wind its way to Grammos.[133] The forthcoming assault on Mount Grammos was likely to be the most crucial of the entire war. King Paul came to watch it. Accompanying him was Cyrus Sulzberger, who noted that the offensive was 'under General Van Fleet's guidance, if not his acknowl-edged direction'. The army had substantially improved since July–August 1948, and Van Fleet was confident that the communists had lost the war.[134] The offensive on Grammos began on 25 August. The IX Division outflanked the DSE positions and occupied the main passage to Albania. With the Yugoslav sanctuary denied to them, and with only a secondary passage into Albania still available, the KKE and its army had to move swiftly. On 29 August the Democratic Army of Greece and the leadership of the Communist Party fled across the border into Albania, never to return. All guerrilla resis-tance on Mount Grammos ended on 30 August 1949, when the entire Greek-Albanian frontier was occupied by the government troops.[135] In effect, the Greek Civil War was at an end.

The Aftermath

Soon after the retreat to Albania the KKE leaders grasped the impossibility of pursuing their solitary war. Zachariadis flew to Moscow, where he agreed with Stalin that the 17,000 DSE guerrillas would be transferred to the Soviet Union. Upon his return to Albania, on 9 October 1949 the Sixth Plenum of the Central Committee resolved to put an end to the armed struggle; the announcement was formally made one week later.[136] Nevertheless, by opting to maintain small guerrilla bands 'as a means of pressure … for the greatest possible democratic pacification', the KKE provided the Greek government with a pretext for perpetuating repression.[137] Concerned with their own survival rather than with pressing the government, these bands became easy prey for the army.[138] The KKE-in-exile was soon to be enmeshed in an ugly, and sometimes bloody, head-hunting for scapegoats, which led to the purging of Zachariadis in 1956–1957.

In President Truman's words, the Greek government was 'like any other dog who has been down in a fight and then gets on top'; the Americans were concerned lest victory was followed by 'the wholesale slaughter of prisoners'.[139] They prevailed upon the Greek government to abandon its threats to invade Albania,[140] and then suggested a lenient programme for the rehabilitation of former guerrillas, elections and a plebiscite on whether to lift the ban on the KKE.[141] An Australian proposal for the UN supervision of a possible repatriation of the guerrillas was rejected by the Foreign Office on the grounds that nobody could guarantee their safety. The British also abhorred the prospect of Soviet participation in such a scheme. The Foreign Office disagreed even with the idea of a plebiscite on the fate of the KKE: 'the referendum is a successful political institution in highly developed countries such as Switzerland and ... it has not been especially successful in Greece where the past referenda have been subject to manipulation'.[142]

The Greek government yielded to the military and continued the executions until UN pressure led to their suspension.[143] Even then, however, the Interior Minister warned 'against over-hasty concessions to the Communists', who might 'prepare for further rebellion when the word came from abroad'.[144] The propaganda of the victors was eminently encapsulated by the US ambassador:

> We should not permit revival of discredited theory that [the] Greek Communist rebellion reflected political and economic dissatisfaction of large number of Greeks and was not solely [a] Communist bid for power ... Despite [the] Greek Government's adherence to [the] Varkiza agreement and despite broad amnesties offered by Sofulis, [the] Greek Communist Party preferred recourse to sword.[145]

On 27 October 1949 the Labour government decided that the British troops should be withdrawn from Greece.[146] The last British soldiers left in early 1950, when it was clear that the country was safely anchored on the Western side of the fence. Considering that in the 1940s Greece's population was 7,000,000, the achievement had taken a gruesome toll. The number of Greeks who perished during the Civil War was well over 100,000 – perhaps as high as 150,000. Some 40,000 left-wingers were detained in concentration camps; 20,000 were sentenced for offences against the state, and of these at least 5,000 were put to death. Overall, 100,000 men and women fought in the ranks of the Democratic Army, whilst in the wake of its defeat between 70,000 and 100,000 Greek communists fled the country to live as political refugees in the Eastern bloc. More than 700,000 became 'displaced' persons within Greece; the overwhelming majority of them had been forced by the government troops to evacuate their villages in order to deprive the KKE of sources of supply and recruitment. By September 1949 the cost of living was 254 times higher than that of the prewar years, while no less than 2,400,000 Greeks were believed to be 'one step from starvation'.[147] For the victors the fighting was not entirely over. Until 1962 the Greek courts maintained that the 'rebellion' still continued. The emergency legislation of 1946–1949 outlived the Civil War by twenty-five years and was not repealed until 1974. In that year the ban on the KKE was also lifted.[148]

1. F.O.371/72579 R7653: Prague to F.O., 29/6/1948.
2. *Politika* (Belgrade): 14 and 15/6/1982: interview with Markos Vafiadis, quoted by E. Barker, 'Yugoslav Policy towards Greece 1947–1949', in L. Baerentzen, J.O. Iatrides, O.L. Smith, eds., *Studies in the History of the Greek Civil War 1945–1949* (Copenhagen: 1987), pp.275–6.
3. M. Djilas, *Vlast, Naša Reč* (London: 1983), pp.201–2, quoted by E. Barker, *op.cit.*, in L. Baerentzen et al., eds., *op.cit.*, pp.276–7.
4. KKE: E.K., VI, no.782: Resolution of the 4th Plenum; V. Bartziotas, *O Agonas tou Dimokratikou Stratou Elladas* 3rd edn. (Athens: 1985), p.86; *idem, Exinda Chronia Kommunistis* (Athens: 1986), p.299.
5. *Eleftherotypia* (Athens): 19/2/1980: interview with Markos Vafiadis.
6. D. Gousidis, ed., *Markos Vafiadis: Martyries* (Thessaloniki: 1983), pp.21–2; V. Bartziotas, *O Agonas*, pp.412, 66–9; *idem, Exinda Chronia*, pp.290–1; G. Vonditsos-Gousias, *Oi Aities yia tis Ittes, ti Diaspasi tou KKE ke tis Ellinikis Aristeras* I (Athens: 1977), 397–408 *passim*.
7. V. Bartziotas, *O Agonas*, p.42; D. Gousidis, ed., *op.cit.*, p.22.
8. *Simioma me tis Apopseis tou Markou Vafiadi*, 15/11/1948, in P. Dimitriou, ed., *I Diaspasi tou KKE* I (Athens: 1978), 19–28; also in KKE: E.K., VI, pp.482–9.
9. KKE: E.K., VI, no.788: Resolution of the KKE CC Politburo on the Opportunistic Platform of Markos Vafiadis, 15/11/1948. This Resolution was published in 1950.
10. *Ibid.*, no.795: Resolution, 5th Plenum, 31/1/1949; D. Gousidis, ed., *op.cit.*, pp.22–3.
11. F.O.371/78395 R1475: Norton to F.O., 8/2/1949.
12. F.O.371/78395 R2332: F.O. to Dominions, 23/2/1949.
13. F.O.371/78447 R2404: Minute by McNeil, 3/3/1949; *ibid.*, R2809: Minute by Wallinger, 5/3/1949.
14. F.O.371/78447 R1647: Peake to F.O., 10/2/1949.
15. F.O.371/78395 R1512: Budapest to F.O., 9/2/1949.
16. Markos's responsibility for the decisions he criticized (especially those of the Third Plenum of September 1947) is pointed out by V. Bartziotas, *O Agonas*, p.41; *idem, Exinda Chronia*, p.292. For the hackneyed myth of a 'Stalinists' vs 'Titoists' split in the KKE leadership see C. M. Woodhouse, *The Struggle for Greece, 1941–1949* (London: 1976), esp. pp.216–17, 231; and D. Eudes, *The Kapetanios: Partisans and Civil War in Greece, 1943–1949* (London:1972), esp. pp.264–8. This 'ideological fiction' is now persuasively exploded by P.J. Stavrakis, *Moscow and Greek Communism 1944–1949* (Ithaca and London: 1989), pp.197–202. Stavrakis argues that the 'split' was invented after the end of the civil war and may have been encouraged by Stalin in his attempt to isolate Tito.
17. KKE: E.K., VI, no.786. See also documents and letters in DSE Archives, *Eleftherotypia* (Athens): 13, 17/2/1986; 18, 19, 20, 23/3/1986; V. Bartziotas, *O Agonas*, pp.72–4.
18. V. Bartziotas, *O Agonas*, pp.86–7; *idem, Exinda Chronia*, p.301; D. Partsalidis's speech in *I Triti Syndiaskepsi tou KKE 10–14/10/1950* (Athens: 1988), p.77; N. Zachariadis, *Epilogi Ergon* (Athens: n.d.), pp.23ff.
19. N. Zachariadis, *Provlimata Kathodigisis sto KKE* (n.p.: 1952; reprint, Athens: 1978), pp.84–5.

20. *Ibid.*, p.137.

21. G. Vonditsos-Gousias, *op.cit.* I, 440.

22. A. Papaioannou, *I Diathiki tou Nikou Zachariadi* (Athens: 1986), p.65.

23. *Infra*, ns. 25 and 26.

24. *Cf.* P.J. Stavrakis, *op.cit.*, pp.169–85.

25. F.O.371/72202 R14380: Norton to F.O., 22/12/1948; *ibid.*, R14529: Norton to F.O., 25/12/1948; F.O.371/72251 R14236: Norton to F.O., 17/12/1948; F.O.371/78338 R707: Norton to F.O., 15/1/1949; *ibid.*, R1879: Norton to F.O., 16/2/1949; DSE Archives, *Eleftherotypia* (Athens), 6/5/1986:DSE 103 Brigade Report of Operation on Edessa, 2/1/1949; D. Zafiropoulos, *O Anti-symmoriakos Agon* (Athens: 1956), pp. 544–58; G. Blanas (Kissavos), *Emfylios Polemos 1946–1949: Opos ta Ezisa* (Athens: 1976), pp.171–2; Th. Tsakalotos, *Saranda Chronia Stratiotis tis Ellados*, II (Athens: 1960), pp.222–8; S.N. Grigoriadis, *Dekemvris–Emfylios Polemos 1944–1949: Synoptiki Istoria* (Athens: 1984), pp.393–4, 405; F.N. Grigoriadis, *Istoria tou Emfyliou Polemou 1945–1949* IV (Athens: n.d.), 1208–13, 1253–7; Y. Kilismanis, *Apo tin Ionia sto Dimokratiko Strato* (Athens: 1989), pp.116–18.

26. E. Sakellariou, *To Ygeionomiko tou Dimokratikou Stratou* (Athens: n.d.), pp.104–5. Also: G. Blanas, *op.cit.*, pp.173–6; S.N. Grigoriadis, *op.cit.*, pp.411–12; F.N. Grigoriadis, *op.cit.* IV, 1258–60; F.O.371/78338 R1879: Norton to F.O., 16/2/1949.

27. G. Blanas, *op.cit.*, pp.168–70.

28. F.O.371/78418 R10594: F.O. Minutes, 9/11/1949.

29. KKE: E.K., VI, pp.465–76: PDK Memorandum to UN/GA, 15/8/1948 *ibid.*, p.478: PDK Appeal to UN/GA, 20/9/1948; *ibid.*, pp.479–80: PDK Statement to UN/GA, 10/10/1948; *ibid.*, p.490: PDK Statement, 7/12/1948; F.O.371/72202 R10997: Norton to F.O., 22/9/1948.

30. KKE: E.K., VI, no.793: Resolution, 5th Plenum, 30–31/1/1949.

31. G. Vonditsos-Gousias, *op.cit.* I, 483; A. Papaioannou, *op.cit.*, p.53; F.N. Grigoriadis, *op.cit.* IV, 1265–76; *I Triti Syndiaskepsi tou KKE 10–14/10/1950*, pp.100, 289.

32. A. Papaioannou, *op.cit.*, p.52–3; V.Bartziotas, *O Agonas*, p.87; F.N. Grigoriadis, *op.cit.* IV, 1271–2; *I Triti Syndiaskepsi*, pp.100, 289, 384. The best discussion of this complex issue in E. Kofos, *The Impact of the Macedonian Question on Civil Conflict in Greece (1943–1949)* (Athens: 1989), pp.26ff.

33. F.O.371/78398 R3671: Minute by Peck, 1/4/1949.

34. F.O.371/78396 R2820: Norton to F.O., 12/3/1949. See also P.J. Stavrakis, *op.cit.*, pp.179–81.

35. F.O.371/78396 R3012: Minute by Wallinger, 10/3/1949.

36. F.O.371/78412 R3772: Extract from DSE Radio Broadcast, 5/4/1949.

37. F.O.371/72630 R7300: Peake to F.O., 18/6/1948; FRUS (1948): IV, 1070–2: Cannon to State Department, 8/6/1948.

38. F.O.371/72580 R7786: Peake to F.O., 30/6/1948.

39. F.O.371/72579 R7655: Minute by Campbell, 30/6/1948.

40. F.O.371/72581 R7867: Belgrade to F.O., 2/7/1948.

41. CAB 128/13/C.M. 46 (48): 1/7/1948.

42. F.O.371/72579 R7694: Belgrade to F.O., 29/6/1948; F.O. to Belgrade, 2/7/1948.

43. F.O.371/72579 R7690, R7753: Washington to F.O., 30/6/1948.

44. F.O.371/72579 R7655, R7769: Bevin to Washington, 30/6/1948.

45. F.O.371/72582 R8163: J.C. Sappington (US Embassy, London) to Wallinger, Most Secret Letter, 8/7/1948.
46. F.O.371/72582 R8163: Wallinger to US Embassy, London, 10/7/1948.
47. F.O.371/72583 R8234: Minute by Campbell, 5/7/1948.
48. CAB 128/13/C.M. 48 (48): 8/7/1948.
49. F.O.371/72583 R8252: Belgrade to F.O., 10/7/1948.
50. F.O.371/72163 R8363: Situation in the Balkans, Discussion with Mr. Chifley, 15/7/1948; F.O.371/72583 R8190: Minute by Roberts, 7/7/1948.
51. FRUS (1948): IV, 166–7: Lovett to Ankara, 21/10/1948.
52. F.O.371/73105 R28829: Minute by Kirkpatrick, 8/10/1948.
53. UNO: GA, *Official Records*, 3rd Session, Part I, First Committee, p.549; *Kathimerini* (Athens): 18/11/1948; CAB 129/35/C.P. (49) 113: Memorandum by Bevin, 'Greece', 16/5/1949.
54. F.O.371/72580 R7845: Norton to F.O., 3/7/1948.
55. Bevin Papers: F.O.800/468/GRE/48/12: Bevin to Norton, Enclosure: Record of Conversation between Bevin and Pipinellis, London, 29/12/1948.
56. *Loc.cit.*; FRUS (1948): IV, 220–2: Memorandum by Baxter, 29/12/1948.
57. Bevin Papers: F.O.800/522/YUG/49/1: Bevin to Attlee, Enclosure: F.O. Memorandum, 6/1/1949.
58. F.O.371/78447 R1067: Peake to F.O., 28/1/1949.
59. F.O.371/78447 R1095: Minute by Wallinger, 1/2/1949.
60. F.O.371/76436 C1520: Bevin to Peake, 18/2/1949.
61. FRUS (1949): VI, 253–5: Drew (UNSCOB) to Secretary of State, 19/2/1949.
62. Bevin Papers: F.O.800/468/GRE/49/2: Bevin to Norton, 21/2/1949, Enclosure: Record of Conversation between Bevin and Tsaldaris.
63. FRUS (1949): VI, 256, n.6; *ibid.*, 257–8: Acheson to Athens, 25/2/1949.
64. F.O.371/78447 R2965: Norton to F.O., 12/3/1949; *ibid.*, R2933: F.O. to Belgrade, 16/3/1949; *ibid.*, R3913: Extract from Budapest Radio, 12/3/1949.
65. FRUS (1949): VI, 267–8: Grady to Secretary of State, 18/3/1949.
66. F.O.371/78447 R3626: Norton to F.O., 2/4/1949; *ibid.*, R3821: Norton to F.O., 6/4/1949; *ibid.*, R3959: Draft Memorandum on Greek-Yugoslav Relations, n.d.; *ibid.*, R3909: Peake to F.O., 9/4/1949; FRUS (1949): VI, 268, n.3: Grady to Secretary of State, 18/3/1949.
67. F.O.371/78447 R4089: Peake to F.O., 8/4/1949.
68. F.O.371/78716 R4122: F.O. Memorandum, 'Policy Towards Yugoslavia', 24/3/1949; *ibid.*, R4734: F.O. to Norton, 10/5/1949; F.O. Minutes.
69. F.O.371/78716 R4734: Peake to F.O., 6/5/1949; *ibid.*, R5235: Maclean to Bevin, 7/5/1949.
70. F.O.371/78742 R6347: Minute by Rumbold, 24/6/1949.
71. F.O.371/78716 R4734: Minute by Rumbold, 9/5/1949; F.O. Minute, 9/5/1949.
72. FRUS (1949): VI, 355: Cannon to Acheson, 9/6/1949.
73. F.O.371/78725 R5930: Washington to F.O., 15/6/1949; F.O. to Washington, 17/6/1949; F.O.371/78742 R6347: Minute by Rumbold, 24/6/1949.
74. FRUS (1949): VI, 363: British Embassy to State Department, 30/6/1949; F.O.371/78742 R6347: Minute by Rumbold, 24/6/1949.
75. F.O.371/78725 R6714: Peake to F.O., 11/7/1949; F.O.371/78448 R6717: Belgrade to F.O., 11/7/1949.
76. F.O.371/78448 R6717: CRO to Commonwealth, 20/7/1949.
77. F.O.371/78691 R6880: Rumbold to Peake, 20/7/1949.
78. V. Bartziotas, *O Agonas*, pp.115–16; S.N. Grigoriadis, *op.cit.*, pp.416–17.

79. F.O.371/73105 R28829: Minute by Kirkpatrick, 8/10/1948.
80. C. Sulzberger, *A Long Row of Candles: Memoirs and Diaries (1934–1954)* (London: 1969), pp.380–3.
81. F.O.371/78346 R190: Norton to F.O., 6/1/1949; *ibid.*, R462: Norton to F.O., 14/1/1949; FRUS (1949): VI, 233–6: Grady to Acting Secretary of State, 5 and 12/1/1949.
82. FRUS (1949): VI, 240: Grady to Acting Secretary of State, 18/1/1949.
83. *Ibid.*, 256–7: Grady to Secretary of State, 21/2/1949; *ibid.*, 241–2: Grady to Secretary of State, 21/1/1949; F.O.371/78338 R101: Norton to F.O., 26/1/1949; EPSV (1948–1949): 136, pp.183ff, 248–50.
84. HC Deb., vol.460, col.1651 (2/2/1949).
85. F.O.371/78338 R101: Norton to F.O.,26/1/1949; D. Zafiropoulos, *op.cit.*, p.534; FRUS (1949): VI, 245–8: Grady to Acheson, 7/2/1949; *ibid.*, 248–9: Grady to Tsaldaris, 15/2/1949.
86. Bevin Papers: F.O.800/468/GRE/49/1: Bevin to Minister of Defence, 12/1/1949.
87. F.O.371/78346 R889: F.O. to Washington, 1/2/1949.
88. F.O.371/78348 R2119: Norton to F.O., 22/2/1949.
89. FRUS (1949): VI, 256–7: Grady to Secretary of State, 21/2/1949.
90. F.O.371/78348 R2165: Bevin to Alexander, 19/2/1949.
91. Bevin Papers: F.O.800/468/GRE/49/2: Bevin to Norton, 21/2/1949, Enclosure: Record of Conversation between Bevin and Tsaldaris.
92. F.O.371/78348 R3285: Report by the CIGS Field-Marshal Sir William Slim on the Greek Situation, 18/3/1949; *ibid.*, R3499: Norton to Bateman, 16/3/1949.
93. Bevin Papers: F.O.800/468/GRE/49/5: GREECE: Record of a Meeting with the CIGS on March 24, Minutes by Peck, 26/3/1949. For the endorsement of Slim's Report by the COS Committee see F.O.371/78348 R3503.
94. F.O.371/78348 R3537: Bevin to F.O., 1/4/1949; FRUS (1949): VI, 285 (ed.n.), 286–7: Bevin to Acheson, 31/3/1949.
95. FRUS (1949): VI, 290–1: Acheson to Grady, 5/4/1949; *ibid.*, 291–2: Grady to Acheson, 7/4/1949.
96. *Ibid.*, 300–301: Acheson to Sir Oliver Franks, 25/4/1949.
97. Bevin Papers: F.O.800/468/GRE/49/7: Bevin to Attlee, 13/5/1949; F.O.371/78339 R5579: Norton to F.O., 2/6/1949.
98. F.O.371/78398 R4018: Greek Embassy to F.O., 4/4/1949; FRUS (1949): VI, 287–8: Memorandum by Satterthwaite, 1/4/1949.
99. F.O.371/78398 R4018: Minute by Peck, 9/4/1949.
100. F.O.371/78398 R4018: Minute by Bateman, 19/4/1949.
101. FRUS (1949): VI, 294–5: Acheson to Austin (UNO), 12/4/1949.
102. KKE: E.K., VI, p.496: PDK Message, 25/1/1949; F.O.371/78338 R1368: Norton to F.O.2/2/1949; F.O.371/78395 R1882: DSE Radio Extract, 27/1/1949.
103. F.O.371/78395 R1064: Norton to F.O., 29/1/1949; *ibid.*, R1114: Norton to F.O., 31/1/1949, and F.O. to Norton, 1/2/1949; *ibid.*, R1203: Norton to F.O., 1/2/1949; *ibid.*, R1232: Norton to F.O., 1/2/1949.
104. F.O.371/78338 R193: Norton to F.O., 1/1/1949; Th. Tsakalotos, *op.cit.* II, 195–210.
105. For the operations against the DSE in the Peloponnese, see Norton's despatches in F.O.371/78338, F.O.371/78339; Th. Tsakalotos, *op.cit.* II,

195–210; Th. Svolos, *Andartis sta Vouna tou Moria: Odoiporiko (1947–1949)* (Athens: 1990), pp.105–6.

106. GES/DIS, *Ai Machai tou Vitsi ke tou Grammou 1949* (Athens: 1951), pp.9–19; S.N. Grigoriadis, *op.cit.*, pp. 409–14; D. Zafiropoulos, *op.cit.*, pp.569–80; F.O.371/78412 R3943: Minute by Peck, 5/4/1949; F.O.371/78366 R4040: British Consul-General (Thessaloniki) to Athens, 7/4/1949; F.O.371/78339 R4940: Norton to F.O., 7/5/1949; *ibid.*, R5184: Norton to F.O., 19/5/1949; V. Bartziotas, *O Agonas*, p.113; *idem, Exinda Chronia*, pp.305–6; T. Psimmenos, *Andatres St' Agrafa* 2nd edn. (Athens: 1985), pp.255–326.

107. F.O.371/78415 R3969: Bateman to Norton, 19/4/1949; *ibid.*, R4339: Amnesty in Greece, Note by J.O. McCormick, 14/4/1949.

108. F.O.371/78415 R4577: Norton to Bateman, 28/4/1949.

109. KKE: E.K., VI, pp.504–5: PDK Appeal, 20/4/1949; F.O.371/78412 R4360: Norton to F.O., 20/4/1949.

110. F.O.371/78412 R4360: F.O. to UK Delegation (UNO), 23/4/1949; *ibid.*, R4439: Norton to F.O., 27/4/1949; F.O.371/78338 R4500: Norton to F.O., 28/4/1949; FRUS (1949): VI, 305, n.3.

111. F.O.371/78412 R4786: Dixon (Prague) to F.O., 9/5/1949, and F.O. to UK Delegation (UNO), 5/5/1949; FRUS (1949): VI, 305, n.3.

112. G. Vonditsos-Gousias, *op.cit.* I, 500–503, 507, 516; L. Eleftheriou, *Synomilies me ton Niko Zachariadi* (Athens: 1986), p.42; D. Partsalidis, *Dipli Apokatastasi tis Ethnikis Andistasis* (Athens: 1978), p.199; V. Bartziotas, *O Agonas*, p.88.

113. G. Vonditsos-Gousias, *op.cit.* I, 516; D. Partsalidis, *op.cit.*, p.199.

114. FRUS (1949): VI, 301–3: Memorandum by Rusk, 26/4/1949; *ibid.*, 303–9: Memorandum by Rusk, 5/5/1949.

115. FRUS (1949): VI, 303-309: Memorandum by Rusk, 5/5/1949.

116. *Loc.cit.*; FRUS (1949): VI, 303, n.1: Acheson to Truman, 5/5/1949.

117. F.O.371/78412 R5095: UDC to Bevin, 13/5/1949, and Bevin to UDC, 19/5/1949.

118. FRUS (1949): VI, 320–1.

119. CAB 129/35/C.P. (49) 113: 'Greece', Memorandum by Bevin, 16/5/1949.

120. CAB 128/15/C.M.36 (49): 19/5/1949.

121. F.O.371/78412 R5014: Norton to F.O., 17/5/1949; FRUS (1949): VI, 322–3: Acheson to Athens, 19/5/1949.

122. FRUS (1949): VI, 324–5: Memorandum by Rusk, 19/5/1949; *ibid.*, 325–6: Annex A, Bevin to Washington, 19/5/1949; *ibid.*, 326–9: Annex B, State Department Paper, n.d.

123. *Ibid.*, 330–3: Memorandum by Cromie, 20/5/1949.

124. FRUS (1949): VI, 341–2: Millar to Rusk, 25/5/1949; *ibid.*, 342–3: Enclosure A, Paper by F.O., n.d.; *ibid.*, 343–4: Enclosure B, Paper by F.O., n.d.; *ibid.*, 344–5: Webb to Acheson, 25/5/1949.

125. *Ibid.*, 337: Acting Secretary of State to Athens, 24/5/1949; *ibid.*, 345–7: Grady to Secretary of State, 26/5/1949; *ibid.*, 347: ed. n.; *ibid.*, 348–9: Grady to Secretary of State, 28/5/1949.

126. Bevin Papers: F.O. 800/468/GRE/49/11: Bevin to F.O., 27/5/1949.

127. Bevin Papers: F.O.800/468/GRE/49/13: Bevin to Norton, 1/6/1949; FRUS (1949): VI, 353–5: Grady to Acting Secretary of State, 8/6/1949; *ibid.*, 356–7: Memorandum by Cromie, 17/6/1949.

128. F.O.371/78691 R6880: Rumbold to Peake, 20/7/1949.

129. L. Eleftheriou, *op.cit.*, pp.42–3.

130. F.O.371/78412 R5933: Extract from Free Greece Radio, 3/6/1949; V. Georgiou, *I Zoi mou* (Athens: 1992), pp.508–9.

131. F.O.371/78414 R4698: British Consul-General (Thessaloniki) to F.O., 7/5/1949; *ibid.*, R8586: British Consul-General (Thessaloniki) to Athens, 24/8/1949.

132. Th. Tsakalotos, *op.cit.* II, 217; FRUS (1949): VI, 379.

133. Th. Tsakalotos, *op.cit.* II, 261–6; S.N. Grigoriadis, *op.cit.*, pp.417–23; F.N. Grigoriadis, *op.cit.* IV, 1327ff; F.O.371/78339 R7826: Athens to F.O., 11/8/1949; *ibid.*, R8051: Athens to F.O., 18/8/1949; *ibid.*, R8294: Athens to F.O., 25/8/1949.

134. C. Sulzberger, *op.cit.*, p.411.

135. Th. Tsakalotos, *op.cit.* II, 266-278; S.N. Grigoriadis, *op.cit.*, pp.423–5; F.N. Grigoriadis, *op.cit.* IV, 1327–49; F.O.371/78339 R8775: Norton to F.O., 8/9/1949.

136. G. Vonditsos-Gousias, *op.cit.* II, 7–17; V. Bartziotas, *O Agonas*, pp.120–3; *idem*, *Exinda Chronia*, pp.314–18; FRUS (1949): VI, 434–5.

137. V. Bartziotas, *O Agonas*, p.122.

138. F.O.371/78339 R8775: Athens to F.O., 8/9/1949; *ibid.*, R8989: Norton to F.O., 15/9/1949. For the remarkable story of those left behind see G. Trikalinos, *292 Imeres Meta to Grammo-Vitsi* (Athens: 1987); T. Psimmenos, *op.cit.*, pp.327–423.

139. FRUS (1949): VI, 427–8: Memorandum by Webb, 1/10/1949.

140. F.O.371/78339 R8775: Athens to F.O., 8/9/1949; FRUS (1949): VI, 381–4: Memorandum by Crommie, 5/8/1949; *ibid.*, 385–6: Minor to Secretary of State, 6/8/1949; *ibid.*, 424–5: Webb to US Mission (New York), 23/9/1949; *ibid.*, 418: Grady to State Department, 11/9/1949; *ibid.*, 427–8: Memorandum by Webb, 1/10/1949.

141. FRUS (1949): VI, 409–12: Acheson to Athens, 10/9/1949.

142. *Ibid.*, 412–14: Memorandum by Cromie, 13/9/1949.

143. *Ibid.*, 424–5: Webb to US Mission (New York), 23/9/1949; *ibid.*, 465–6: Minor to Acheson, 16/12/1949; *ibid.*, 468–70: State Department to Athens, Aide Mémoire, 21/12/1949.

144. F.O.371/78414 R9345: Norton to F.O., 28/9/1949.

145. FRUS (1949): VI, 450–1: Grady to Acheson, 1/11/1949.

146. CAB 128/16/C.M. 62 (49): 27/10/1949.

147. F.O.371/78373 R11085: Athens to F.O., 14/11/1949. On the human toll of the Greek Civil War see: R. Clogg, *A Short History of Modern Greece* 2nd edn. (London: 1986), p.164; A. Laiou, 'Population Movements in the Greek Countryside during the Civil War', in L. Baerentzen et al., eds., *op. cit.*, pp.55–103; D. Zafiropoulos, *op.cit.*, p.670; F.N. Grigoriadis, *op.cit.* IV, 1355–9; S.N. Grigoriadis, *op.cit.*, pp.427–8; KKE CC, *Syndomi Istoria tou KKE, Schedio: Meros A, 1918–1949* (Athens: 1988), pp.285–6; G. Katsoulis, *Istoria tou Kommunistikou Kommatos Elladas* VI (Athens: 1977), 303.

148. N. Alivizatos, 'The "Emergency" Regime and Civil Liberties 1947–1950', in J.O. Iatrides, ed., *Greece in the 1940s: A Nation in Crisis* (Hanover and London: 1981), pp.220–8.

Such were the Events

> Such were the events connected with the plague
> … and the times were hard indeed, with men
> dying inside the city and the land outside being
> laid waste.
>
> Thucydides, II : 55, 54

The historical narrative has shown that the Greek Civil War was the product of the interrelation of two previously independent factors, the domestic and the international. The interwar economic, social and political divisions among Greeks were exacerbated by foreign intervention. The watershed marked by the Axis invasion and occupation was followed by the British intervention, motivated by the traditional requirements of British foreign policy in the eastern Mediterranean and the Middle East. Regional factors, relating to Balkan politics, and the widening rift between the United States and the Soviet Union entered the scene subsequently and contributed to the outcome rather than to the origins and initial escalation of the conflict.

The subject of Anglo-Greek relations in the late 1940s is a conceptually complex one: there can be no recapitulation of its main themes without reference to the period of the Second World War, an issue of equal complexity and therefore not amenable to concise treatment; and in the years of the Civil War the interconnection of wider international developments – relations between Britain, the Soviet Union and the United States, and the regional (Balkan) factor – compounds the complexity of the issue. If there is an element that eases the burden of the inquiry, it is the considerable degree of continuity which characterizes the strategic pursuits of the main actors.

The domestic potential for civil strife lay in the growing influence of the Left and the ensuing endeavours of the established order to protect its position. In 1936 a response had been possible by way of the Metaxas dictatorship, but five years later the occupation brought the old order on the road to ruin. Discredited by their attitude towards Metaxas, the bourgeois parties further demeaned themselves by their stance vis-à-vis the new reality. Opposed to resistance, they sat on the periphery of Greek politics and watched the growth of the communist-led EAM into a mass movement with genuine popular support; then, faced with the prospect of redundancy, they turned to foreign protection. However, the British factor did not enter the picture on invitation. The British objective with regard to Greece had been formulated well in advance of the rise of EAM, which in the main affected British tactics.

British policy in Greece aimed at the establishment of a regime that would guard imperial sea communications and the routes to the oilfields of the

Middle East. For Churchill the main pillar of such a regime was George II, the Anglophile monarch who had been discredited by the rigged plebiscite of 1935 and his complicity in the dictatorship. The British showed some flexibility which was only partly in response to the republican groundswell in Greece; their prime motivation was the neutralization of EAM. By 1944 they were convinced that the KKE intended to use EAM as a springboard for seizing power and subjugating Greece to Stalin, thereby disrupting their entire strategic position in the Middle East. Though from September 1943 Churchill was preparing for military intervention, priority was given to bringing EAM to heel by political means. Attracted by the prospect of resurrection, the traditional parties of Greece rallied behind Britain in an attempt to present EAM with a united bourgeois political front. By the autumn of 1944 the attempt had proved partially successful; EAM had entered a government as a minority partner but still retained its political and military strength inside Greece.

In the run-up to December 1944 two developments were instrumental in the clash. The case of Papandreou showed that by investing their hopes in Britain, the Greek politicians had forfeited their freedom to act independently of London's behest. Secondly, Churchill secured Stalin's assent to his having a free hand in trying to retain Greece in the British sphere of influence: an episode which suggests that Stalin had no room for Greece in his plans, but also one which testifies to Churchill's determination to crush EAM. The 'Percentages agreement' opened the way for the British military intervention of December 1944, for which Churchill had longed.

The Greek communists had evidently underestimated the determination of their opponents to achieve their aims. Because of the degree of popular unity it had attained, the KKE held that a political mobilization of the masses would enable it to impose its reformist political programme through the parliamentary road. Confronted with the intransigence of the British and Papandreou, in December 1944 the party resorted to a limited degree of military mobilization, confident that it would thereby strike a political compromise. The resolve of Churchill to deal a military blow against EAM, and of the Greek bourgeois politicians to re-enter the political arena through British arms, was a bitter revelation. For the KKE *Ta Dekemvriana* was a limited show of strength aimed at securing a political deal more favourable than the one offered by Papandreou and the British. Some continuity may be traced in the KKE tactics, for again in 1946–1947 the communists seemed to believe that a limited show of strength would suffice to secure a political compromise. In both cases they appeared unmindful of the possibility that their adversaries might prove intransigent, and the second time their oversight was to have far more catastrophic consequences; yet it is this continuity which indicates that on neither occasion did the KKE aim at the seizure of power through civil war.

Despite the partial military defeat of December 1944, EAM remained the best organized political force and one with a considerable political and moral potential. Thus in 1945 the British maintained their diplomatic and military involvement with a view to consolidating the anti-communist regime and bolstering the Centre parties. The undertaking was hazardous, for it denied representation to a substantial Greek political faction, and benign, for it aimed at dragooning Greece in the direction of an anti-communist parliamentary democracy, since the Greeks were deemed incapable of achieving this on their own. The British efforts were hampered by two impediments. The prewar erosion of the Centre's popular support had accelerated during the occupation and led to polarization between EAM and the monarchists. Then, soon after the Varkiza Agreement, along came the White Terror: the Right, devoid of any political programme, went out to smash the potential of the Left and ensure the return of George II.

Until July 1945 Churchill aspired to withdrawal once the location of Greece on the British sphere had been firmly established. Coupled with the British Prime Minister's preference for Greek collaborators, this precluded any diversion of British energies towards halting the White Terror. Thereafter the policy of the Labour government testified to the continuity of British objectives and methods of intervention. During the war, whenever they felt that their interests were under threat, the British intervened directly in Greek affairs; when the 'emergency' was over they devolved authority to a 'responsible' government. Direct intervention found its best expression in Churchill's policy; after Varkiza the British retreated to indirect methods of control whilst retaining their prerogative to intervene when the 'responsible' Greek governments were uncooperative.

Bevin's blend of intervention and non-intervention, discernible throughout 1945–1949, is explicable. The Labour government espoused the old axioms of foreign policy which had led to their predecessors' interference in Greece, yet at the same time they had to uphold some 'socialist' paraphernalia. As British influence in south-eastern Europe and the eastern Mediterranean remained sacrosanct objectives, Labour adopted a high moral tone in notional support of Greece's 'democracy' and 'independence'. Old pursuits of imperial defence came under the cloak of a fittingly moralistic rhetoric, exemplified in Bevin's assertion that by defending the eastern Mediterranean Britain was defending social democracy and the British way of life. No doubt if the loss of British predominance in the region would signal the end of social democracy, that would hardly affect Greece, which was anything but a social democracy. Bevin's motivation was encapsulated by Sir Orme Sargent as early as November 1945, when the conservative Under-Secretary for Foreign Affairs asserted that the new government would maintain the Greek commitment through 'other and more discreet methods', for it had to 'give it all the trappings of anti-Imperialist non-interventionist respectability'.[1]

Greek perceptions of relations with Britain became an embarrassment for London because the degree of British control had led most Greeks to hold Britain directly responsible for the state of affairs in their country. In perpetrating the White Terror and clamouring for the King, the Right assumed it had British approval, whereas the Left held Britain to blame for tolerating the situation. The economic chaos and the intransigence of the Right were playing into the hands of the Left and raised the prospect of civil war. In November 1945 Bevin addressed the economic situation by granting aid to be administered by Sofulis's Centre government, but this was a one-

271

sided form of intervention. Bevin and the British authorities failed to tackle the second problem in denying the Greek Prime Minister control of the army and the security forces, which were among the chief perpetrators of the White Terror. The reasons for this are to be found in the haste for the holding of elections, which for the British became an end in itself.

Sofulis's appeals for postponement were rebuffed because this would prolong the stationing of British troops in Greece and hamper Britain's chances to press for elections in other Balkan countries. Bevin was anxious to reduce his Greek burden, which exposed him to criticism from the Labour left; British prestige was at stake, for postponement of the polls would be tantamount to admitting that the British had been incapable of maintaining order. Yet the overpowering reason is to be found in the configuration of Greek politics and the British objective of retaining Greece in their sphere of influence. By early 1946 it was clear that the weakness of the Centre and the polarization between EAM and the monarchist Right presented the British with a stark choice: with EAM bent on abstaining, the Populist Party was the likely winner at the polls, but postponement would play into the hands of EAM. The British regarded the Populists as likely to set up an authoritarian regime and try to achieve the restoration of the King – and that, they feared, would lead to civil war. Nonetheless, Bevin did not postpone the elections because Britain had to retain Greece in her sphere of influence even if she was governed by a 'reactionary' and distasteful regime.[2]

Unaware of this conscious choice, the KKE had at first invested its hopes in peaceful evolution and made placatory gestures to the British. In 1945 EAM was the only party to publish a detailed political programme, and Zachariadis repeatedly proclaimed that the KKE sought friendly relations with Britain. The hopes engendered by Labour's victory evaporated when Bevin made it clear that he would follow in his predecessors' footsteps. The evidence shows that after Varkiza the KKE wanted to conform to legality, but as there was no background of equality and tranquillity, its policy must be seen in the context of the White Terror and British intervention. In late 1945 Zachariadis hardened his stance, but this was – in part at least – an attempt to mollify the grievances of the militants and the persecuted.

In 1945–1946 the KKE aimed at the establishment of a government that would include EAM, halt the repression and pave the way for elections. This goal was kept in sight even after the Second Plenum of February 1946, which opted for defensive action against the White Terror with a view to extracting concessions from the government. As in 1944, the KKE hoped that a limited show of strength could force a compromise; the possibility that its struggle might be construed otherwise, or that an intransigent attitude on the part of its foes could force the party over the brink, eluded Zachariadis.

This proved true in April 1946, when the 'representative' government took office in Athens. Bevin's hopes that he would be relieved of his burden collapsed. The political programme of the Populists consisted of rabid anti-communism and clamour for an immediate plebiscite. Instead of focussing on reconstruction, the new government embarked on a crusade against any Greek who was not a royalist and demanded from Bevin a speedy plebiscite.

Despite his claims that he did not wish to prolong the unsettled conditions in Greece and prevent the government from coming to grips with reconstruction, Bevin's consent to the Populist demand was spurred by international considerations.

In April 1946 the British Foreign Secretary agreed with his US colleague that the communists should at all costs be prevented from coming to power in Greece. An early plebiscite would enable him to withdraw the troops and bring pressure upon Stalin to do likewise elsewhere in Europe. In justifying this, Bevin revealed both his mistrust of the Populists and his largely clear idea of the actual situation. The British Cabinet reminded him that the restoration of the King could lead to civil war, but he would not budge; his determination to retain Greece on the British side of the fence led him to back willingly the only Greek political party that seemed up to the task.

The Populist government promptly became a source of incessant embarrassment for the British. Its response to the emergence of leftist armed bands was the introduction of inflammatory security measures. In summer 1946, as the plebiscite approached, state repression and the White Terror intensified in order to ensure a royalist victory. The British shared the objective of keeping the Left at bay, and even though they found the Populists' methods crude, they would not flinch from the task. At the same time the KKE, following a dual strategy which laid more emphasis on the legal aspect, made repeated proposals for an understanding, which the British and the Greek governments ignored. Instead, Populist repression thickened the ranks of the guerrillas by forcing thousands of Greeks to the mountains.

In September 1946 the restoration of George II marked the full resurrection of the prewar order, but this was hardly the last opportunity to avert civil war. From summer 1946 to January 1947 several opportunities for a compromise were squandered, for only the KKE showed willingness to take them in earnest. The Populists, the 'legitimate' government, would not relinquish power. The British, despite their economic difficulties and the prospect of Greece becoming a second Palestine, were bent upon maintaining their strategic position in the Middle East. Amidst open disaffection in Labour ranks, the most striking opportunity occurred in December 1946, when Attlee himself doubted whether 'backing a very lame horse' such as Greece 'was worth the candle'.[3]

The British Prime Minister eventually yielded to the resolve of Bevin and the Chiefs of Staff to retain the British position in Greece and the Middle East. Although it admitted the pitfalls of its Greek policy, the Foreign Office went out of its way to emphasize the far greater dangers in relinquishing it: apart from the destabilizing effect in the region, the underlying premise of the commitment was that Britain was still a great power with a legitimate claim to spheres of influence. The Labour leaders rigorously pursued this policy, even though the fear of economic collapse meant that British status could be maintained only with US dollars.

Economic and military dependence on the United States had a major impact on British policy. One of the main concerns of the Foreign Office was to show to Washington that Britain stood firm against the Soviet Union and thereby secure the continuation of American goodwill. There was no dissent between Attlee and Bevin over this. The Prime Minister only doubted whether it should be attained at all costs, arguing that no bastion of social democracy could support the Populists. Bevin had no scruples as to the moral capital to be sacrificed in the struggle to retain and protect the Middle East from possible Soviet encroachment. The British would continue to support the Populists because they saw no other alternative to a communist Greece.

The request that the Americans should take up the economic burden in Greece was in no contradiction of Bevin's resolute stance. The British had for long striven to get the United States involved, and in late 1946 they had succeeded in obtaining Washington's moral and diplomatic commitment. But what was needed in Greece was massive aid which Britain could not furnish. British economic difficulties, the incompetence of Greek politicians, the danger of full-scale civil war, the embarrassment caused by the Populist government, and Bevin's 'revulsion against all things Greek' account satisfactorily, but not wholly, for the British request. The main reason was that Greece's ranking in the list of British priorities was reconsidered. The devaluation of sea communications had decreased her importance as a Mediterranean watchdog. The real British interest was in the Middle East, and Greece lay only in the northern tier of that region. If the Americans came to sustain the eastern Mediterranean position, the long-term British strategic interests in the Middle East would be adequately safeguarded. The venture was successful.

The Truman Doctrine – whereby the United States picked up the torch of defending 'democracy' as construed by the Populists and the monarchist irregulars – neither erased British interests in Greece nor altered Greek perceptions of Britain's role. The Greek governments continued to look to Britain as the power with a time-honoured policy in the region and a long tradition of friendly bilateral relations. The leisurely touch-down of US aid, coupled with the American dislike for Tsaldaris, prompted the Greek governments to proclaim their attachment to Britain. For the British Greece remained a destitute country, in need of 'outside advice and some degree of intervention to ensure that that advice is taken'.[4] The deterioration of the military and economic situation would be a perennial source of dejection for Bevin, while the Americans would make it plain that in their first steps towards containing Communism, they counted on full British co-operation.

The Greek communists could now substitute 'Anglo-American imperialism' for their hitherto 'English imperialism' bogey. With hindsight it can be said that the KKE underestimated the implications of the Truman Doctrine. The Americans had come to Greece to halt the advance of Communism, not to make deals with it. The KKE was left with the choice either to capitulate or to step up its struggle in the hope that the Soviet Union would come to its support. Stalin failed to do so, and after 1947 the KKE pursued a solitary war in which the chances of military success looked increasingly slim. Its persistent offers for a compromise were made from a disadvantageous position and, therefore, were rebuffed.

From 1947 onwards developments inside and outside Greece demolished the benign dimension of the British objective. For reasons that had little to do with the domestic origins of the conflict, the British and the Americans were adamant that behind the Democratic Army lay Stalin's scheme to force Greece into his own empire. The 'optimum maximum' of British policy was to render Greece into a parliamentary democracy and ensure that in war Greek bases and resources would not be available to the Soviets. Yet the complexion of the Greek faction that showed itself up to the task, and the mounting tension between East and West, forced the British to be content with the minimum objective of keeping Greece '"ticking over" and outside the Iron Curtain'.[5]

For the Labour government not even that minimum could be achieved unless the guerrillas were militarily defeated. The Americans were in agreement, hence from spring 1947 a pattern is visible: with full support from London and Washington, the Greek government was launching military operations while holding out vague olive branches; the KKE did very much the same, but its olive branches were less vague. Having failed to strike a compromise, in the latter part of 1947 the communists opted for a full breach with legality. But before that, in July, they made a serious offer for a compromise which, despite British flexibility, was blown up by the Americans.

From the point of view of British policy, the last chance for a compromise occurred in the summer and autumn of 1947. Bevin's dispute with Marshall over the British troops in Greece disclosed the Foreign Secretary's discontent with the division of Anglo-American responsibility; and it is quite significant, in this regard, that Bevin's feelings echoed the views of his domestic critics that the Americans were fighting their battles with British soldiers. Whether or not the British government was genuinely embarrassed by the anti-communist line of US policy in Greece – and the American attitude towards the KKE offer in July 1947 may have had something to do with it – it remains true that the British had serious reservations about the efficacy of US policy.

In September 1947 these reservations, coupled with the failure of the Greek army to crush the guerrillas, prompted the Foreign Office to examine the chances of a compromise. The British overlooked the American aversion to a negotiated settlement and dismissed their scheme on account of the presumed Soviet objectives. Yet careful study of the Greek context shows that Stalin was exploiting rather than creating opportunities. It is ironic that the scheme was put in cold storage at a time when the Kremlin would hardly have been repelled by the prospect of an understanding that would have preserved a communist foothold in Greece.

Convinced that the cause of the Greek Civil War lay in the foreign assistance to the KKE, Britain and the United States chose a different course. Starting with the United Nations Commission of January 1947, they attempted to cast aside the domestic origins of the conflict and present world opinion with the picture of a small 'democratic' country at war with Stalin's local puppets. The second thrust of their policy was to patch up the embarrassing image of their Greek protégés. Since 1946 Bevin had hoped for the political isolation of the KKE through a coalition of all bourgeois parties. The unsavoury policies of the Populists, but mainly the fear that Sofulis harboured the ambition to become the Greek Kerensky, called for action. Opposed to direct intervention in cabinet-making in Athens, Bevin preferred to bring pressure on the Greeks through 'advice' offered by Norton. The establishment of the Populist-Liberal coalition clearly demonstrated that the Americans had fewer scruples.

The importance of the coalition lay in the inclusion of Sofulis, which deprived the Left of the most important politician available for overtures. This reinforced the militancy of the KKE, and as it diminished the chances of a compromise, led to the communists' full breach with legality. From late 1947 onwards the KKE embarked on the thankless task of trying to procure Soviet assistance and, at the same time, continuing the peace offers. The compromise-seeking thrust of this policy was of no lesser importance, for not only did it stem from the decision of the Second Plenum of February 1946, but it was also reinforced by the increasingly adverse prospects.

Both thrusts of the KKE policy collapsed. Stalin would not furnish aid, whereas for the British and the Americans a military victory remained the only solution. It is not irrelevant that the setting up of the KKE 'government' coincided with the complete breakdown between the West and the Soviet Union in December 1947. The domestic causes of the Greek Civil War were now irrevocably cast aside, and the effort to present the situation in Greece as a product of Soviet designs intensified. For Bevin there could be no doubt that 'this Markos business' was dictated by Soviet expansionism, whereas in February 1948 Stalin himself decreed against the struggle of the KKE.

The British would have been less ruffled if the presumed designs of the Kremlin had been their sole source of alarm over Greece. Throughout 1948 their doubts as to whether the Americans were doing enough were enhanced by the scare-mongering Greek memoranda requesting massive assistance; under domestic pressure, Bevin developed a 'lone wolf' syndrome and demanded from Washington a speedy victory through the despatch of US troops. The difficulties of the Foreign Secretary were compounded by the political squabbles in Athens. The Greek politicians were not supposed to 'snap their fingers', and Norton called for rigorous action to bring them to line. The transition from the Churchill-Leeper era to Labour had not altered British perceptions as to how their policy in Greece was to be enforced. The Labour government simply used the pattern of intervention more sparingly, in moments of great urgency and tantrum.

From late 1947 onwards the Greek government strove to secure a greater military commitment from Britain and the United States and strike an eastern Mediterranean treaty which would be supported by the two Western powers. Though for the Greeks the British connection remained more valuable, the Foreign Office dismissed the Greek aspirations and insisted on crushing the guerrillas. Greek records do not allow corroboration of the British charge that in 1948 the Greeks were keeping the pot boiling in order to perpetuate British and US assistance, but certainly in the wake of the Truman Doctrine the Greek governments had ascribed a special role to the British connection. This was manifested in the attempt to secure British patronage for Greek hegemony in the eastern Mediterranean, a scheme which collapsed in the face of undisguised British contempt.

The determination of the British and the Americans to see the Greek Civil War fought to the bitter end cannot be overstated. The rebuff of the communist offers in April–May 1948 shows that the insincerity of the KKE was invariably taken for granted. This was also the case with the Soviet overtures of June, October and November 1948. Aware of the predicament of the KKE, Stalin tried to preserve some communist presence in Greece by way of a negotiated solution. The Foreign Office and the State Department, on the other hand, continued to believe in a Soviet conspiracy and held firm to the view that the Soviet Union should at all costs be kept away from Greece.

This is particularly important with regard to the British attitude, for in late 1948 the prolongation of the military stalemate had driven many British and US officials to despair. In December Attlee and Bevin came under strong domestic pressure to take steps towards the reconciliation of the Greek warring factions. For the Foreign Secretary the retention of British troops was an 'embarrassment' which he would find difficult to defend to the Labour Party for much longer. Hence Bevin mentioned the possibility of withdrawal in the hope that he could secure greater US assistance to Greece and force the Greeks to pull themselves together.

In 1948–1949 there was little the British alone could do to achieve the common objective. It was indicative of their frustration that they attributed the stalemate to lack of inspiration among the politicians in Athens and to the Greek soldiers themselves for not being determined enough to win a war waged against other Greeks. All they could do was admonish the Greek government, press the Americans to step up their assistance, and allow the British Military Mission to get substantially involved in operations. Some effort was made to maintain a semblance of non-interference, but this was yet another example of British policy under Bevin – to force the Greeks to the desirable direction without incurring the charge of intervention.

In 1949 the split between Stalin and Tito held out the prospect of success with regard to one of the two thrusts of British and US policy. The two Western powers had invested a substantial part of their hopes in the elimination of outside assistance to the guerrillas. The possibility of a *rapprochement* between the West and Tito brought together western anxiety for the termination of Yugoslav support to the KKE with the Yugoslavs' need for western aid. The British handled the matter patiently and deftly, and the reward came in July 1949, when Tito closed the border.

The unflinching Anglo-American resolve to impose the military solution was manifested for the last time during the Soviet initiative of April 1949. Although this coincided with a fresh outburst of domestic pressure on Bevin, in May McNeil cynically claimed that Britain 'could not tell the independent government of Greece how to run its internal affairs'.[6] The Soviets, for their part, had underestimated Anglo-American fervour to crush the KKE. Inspired by Tito's flirtation with the West, the two powers were keen to eliminate foreign support to the DSE so that the Greek army could deal with it conclusively. The Kremlin misconstrued their motives as raising a last opportunity to preserve a communist foothold in Greece. A settlement was aborted because of the irreconcilably different perceptions of the two camps as to the causes of the Greek Civil War.

The Greek policy of the British Labour government was formulated on the basis of long-held wider assumptions concerning the requirements of imperial defence. This continuous trend of international conduct was underpinned by one conviction held by all Labour leaders but most augustly expressed by Bevin: that Britain's successful experimentation with democratic socialism at home rendered her 'the last bastion of social democracy' and allowed her to exert a unique moral and political influence throughout the world as a third force.[7] The unpalatable reality was that the configuration of international relations in the wake of the Second World War left little room for a third force. Though it did not take long to realise this, the Labour government remained committed to the foreign policy befitting a great imperial power, especially in the eastern Mediterranean and the Middle East. In Greece, the imperialistic overtones and diplomatic machismo which this policy assumed annoyed only the communists; the anti-communist faction was prepared to accept them as indispensable in the struggle against the common foe.

The Greek Communist Party's belief that the Civil War was imposed by the British and the Greek Right in 1945 is correct only in part. The exploits of the Right no doubt enabled the Left to take up arms in 1946. Britain, however, did not plot a civil war in which she could hardly afford to get actively involved. Nevertheless, once civil strife began to unfold, the Labour government, soon to be joined by the administration of President Truman, demanded that it be carried through to the bitter end, whereas the KKE strove until the autumn of 1947 to avert a fully-fledged confrontation. The British came to Greece in 1944 and left six years later, after nearly 100,000 Greek left-wingers had already fled the country in defeat. It was a case of 'socialism in one country', and that was definitely not to be Greece.

NOTES

1. Sargent Papers: F.O.800/276/GRE/45/10: Sargent to Leeper (private letter), 9/11/1945.
2. F.O.371/58676 R3032: Minute by Hayter, 21/2/1946.
3. Bevin Papers: F.O.800/475/ME/46/22: Attlee's letter to Bevin, 1/12/1946.
4. F.O.371/73105 R28829: Minute by Kirkpatrick, 8/10/1948.
5. F.O.371/72247 R11338: Norton to Bateman, 24/9/1948.
6. FRUS (1949): VI, 303–9: Memorandum of a conversation by Dean Rusk, 5/5/1949.
7. CAB 131/2/DO (46) 40: Memorandum by Bevin, 13/3/1946.

Appendix: Dramatis Personæ

Since most of the following individuals held various posts during the period under examination, in many cases I cite the one they held at the moment they appear in the narrative.

ACHESON, Dean: US Assistant Secretary of State; Secretary of State from January 1949.

ALEXANDER, Albert V.: Labour Defence Secretary.

ALEXANDER, Field-Marshal Harold: British CIGS.

ATTLEE, Clement R. (1883–1967): Leader of the Labour Party and British Prime Minister.

BALFOUR, David: Clerk of the Southern Department of the F.O.

BALFOUR, Sir John: British Minister in Washington.

BARTZIOTAS, Vasilis: Member of the KKE Politburo; from 1948 Political Commissar of the DSE GHQ.

BEBLER, Aleš: Yugoslav Deputy Foreign Minister.

BEVIN, Ernest (1881–1951): British Foreign Secretary.

BLANAS, Giorgis (Kissavos): KKE, ELAS and DSE cadre.

BYRNES, James F.: US Secretary of State until January 1947.

CACCIA, Harold: Minister at the British Embassy, Athens, 1945.

CANNON, Cavendish: US ambassador in Belgrade.

CLIVE, Nigel: Member of the wartime BMM in Greece, 1943–1945; from 1945 to 1948 he served at the Embassy in Athens.

DALTON, Hugh: Labour Chancellor of the Exchequer until 1947.

DAMASKINOS: Archbishop of Athens; Regent, 1944–1946.

DIMITROV, Georgi: Bulgarian communist leader.

DIXON, Sir Pierson: Principal Private Secretary to the British Foreign Secretary.

DJILAS, Milovan: Former Yugoslav communist leader.

DOWN, Major-General Ernest: Head of BMM from 1947.

ETHRIDGE, Mark: US Representative at the UN Commission of Inquiry in Greece, 1947.

FRANKS, Sir Oliver: British ambassador in Washington, 1948–1952.

GEORGE II (1890–1947): King of the Hellenes, 1922–1923, 1935–1941, 1941–1946 (in exile), 1946–1947.

GRADY, Henry F.: US ambassador to Greece from 1948.

GRIGORIADIS, Neokosmos: Leader of the Left Liberals.

GRISWOLD, Dwight: Head of AMAG.

GROMYKO, Andrei: Acting Head, Soviet Delegation to the UNO, 1946; then Soviet ambassador to the UNO.

HAYTER, William: Head of the Southern Department of the F.O., 1945–1946.

HENDERSON, Loy: Director of the Office of Near Eastern and African Affairs, State Department.

INVERCHAPEL, Lord (Sir Archibald Clark-Kerr): wartime British ambassador in Moscow; then in charge of the Embassy in Washington until 1948.

IOANNIDIS, Yiannis: With Siandos, he led the KKE during the occupation; then Zachariadis's second-in-command; from summer 1946 the KKE's liaison in Belgrade.

KAFANDARIS, Georgios: Leader of the Progressive Liberals; Deputy Prime Minister in Sofulis's 1945–1946 Cabinet.

KANELLOPOULOS, Panayiotis: Prime Minister, November 1945.

LASCELLES, Daniel: Counsellor of the British Embassy in Athens, 1945–1947.

LEEPER, Sir Reginald: British ambassador to Greece, 1943–March 1946.

McCARTHY, David: Clerk in the Southern Department of the F.O.

MACLEAN, Sir Fitzroy: Brigadier; head of the wartime BMM at Tito's HQ.

MACMILLAN, Harold: British Minister-Resident in the Mediterranean, 1944–1945.

McNEIL, Hector: Parliamentary Under-Secretary to the Foreign Office, 1945–1946; Minister of State, 1946; then UK spokesman at UN Security Council.

MACVEAGH, Lincoln: US ambassador to Greece until 1947.

MARKOS: See VAFIADIS, Markos

MARSHALL, George: US Chief of Staff; Secretary of State, 1947–1949.

MAXIMOS, Dimitrios: Governor of the Bank of Greece; Populist; Prime Minister, January–August 1947.

METAXAS, Ioannis (1871–1941): The Dictator, 1936–1941.

MOLOTOV, Vyascheslav: Soviet Foreign Minister.

MONTGOMERY of Alamein, Field-Marshal Bernard: British CIGS, 1946–1948.

MYERS, Brigadier E.C.W.: Head of the BMM to Greece until 1943.

NORTON, Sir Clifford: British ambassador to Greece from March 1946.

PAPAGOS, General Alexandros: Greek C-in-C, 1941, 1949.

PAPANDREOU, Georgios: Liberal; Prime Minister 1944–1945.

PARTSALIDIS, Dimitris (Mitsos): Member of the KKE Politburo, Secretary of the EAM CC; in 1949 Premier of the PDK.

PAUL, King of the Hellenes: Brother and successor of George II; he reigned from 1947 to 1964.

PEAKE, Sir Charles: British ambassador in Belgrade.

PETERSON, Sir Maurice: British ambassador in Moscow, 1948.

PLASTIRAS, Nikolaos: Specialist in republican coups; Prime Minister, January–April 1945.

PORFYROGENIS, Miltiadis: Member of the KKE Politburo.

RANKIN, Karl: Chargé d'Affaires at the US Embassy in Athens.

RAWLINS, Maj.-Gen. Stewart: Head of BMM, 1945–1947.

REILLY, Patrick D'Arcy: Counsellor at the British Embassy in Athens from 1947.

ROUSOS, Petros: Member of the KKE Politburo; foreign minister of the PDK; with Ioannidis, from summer 1946 the KKE's liaison in Belgrade.

RUSK, Dean: US Assistant Secretary of State, 1949.

SARAFIS, Stefanos: Military commander of ELAS; exiled throughout the civil war.

SARGENT, Sir Orme: Under-Secretary of State for Foreign Affairs until February 1946; then Permanent Under-Secretary.

SCOBIE, Lt.-Gen. Ronald (1893–1969): Commander of the British forces in Greece, 1944–1945.

SELBY, Ralph: Clerk in the Southern Department of the F.O.

SIANDOS, Giorgis (1890–1947): Secretary of the KKE CC, 1942–1945.

SLIM, Field Marshal Sir William: British CIGS, 1949.

SOFIANOPOULOS, Ioannis: Left-of-Centre, Foreign Minister in 1945–1946.

SOFULIS, Themistoklis (1860–1949): Successor of Eleftherios Venizelos as leader of the Liberal Party; Prime Minister, November 1945–March 1946, September 1947–June 1949.

SVOLOS, Alexandros: Socialist, Professor, President of PEEA.

TITO (Josip Broz): Yugoslav communist leader.

TSALDARIS, Konstantinos: Leader of the Populist Party; Prime Minister and Foreign Minister, 1946–1947; Deputy Prime Minister and Foreign Minister, 1947–1949; nephew of the prewar Populist leader Panayis Tsaldaris.

TSOUDEROS, Emmanuel: Liberal; Prime Minister, 1941–1944; Deputy Prime Minister in Sofulis's 1945–1946 government.

VAFIADIS, Markos (d.1992): Member of the KKE CC; ELAS Commander in Macedonia; from 1946 to his purge in 1948, DSE Commander.

VAN FLEET, Lt.-Gen. James: Head of JUSMAPG.

VARVARESSOS, Kyriakos: Minister of Supply, June–September 1945.

VELOUCHIOTIS, Aris (real name: Thanasis Klaras): KKE cadre; the fighting genius of ELAS; denounced by the party for his militancy in 1945, he committed suicide.

VENIZELOS, Eleftherios (1864–1936); Leader of the Liberal Party; Prime Minister, 1910–1915, 1917–1920, 1924, 1928–1932, 1933.

VENIZELOS, Sofoklis: Son of Eleftherios; Prime Minister, 1944; he left the Liberal Party to contest the 1946 elections with Papandreou and Kanellopoulos (EPE); in 1947 he returned.

VONDITSOS-GOUSIAS, Giorgis: KKE and DSE top cadre.

VOULGARIS, Petros: Admiral, Prime Minister in 1945.

WALLINGER, Geoffrey: Head of the Southern Department of the Foreign Office from 1947.

WARNER, Christopher: Head of the Northern Department of the Foreign Office until 1946; Under-Secretary of the Southern Department, 1946–1947; in 1947 Head of the 'Russia Committee' of the Foreign Office.

WICKHAM, Sir Charles: Head of BPM, 1945–1947.

WILLIAMS, Michael: Acting Head of the Southern Department of the Foreign Office, 1946.

WINDLE, Richard: Labour Party functionary; Head of the British contingent in AMFOGE and in the UN Commission.

WOODHOUSE, Christopher M. (1917–): Head of the Allied Military Mission to Greece, 1943–1944; temporary Second Secretary at the British Embassy, Athens, 1945.

ZACHARIADIS, Nikos (1903–1973): Secretary-General of the KKE; in Greek prisons from 1936 to 1941, in Dachau from 1941 to 1945; in 1956 he was deposed from the leadership of the KKE and in the following year he was expelled from the party. A highly controversial figure, he committed suicide in 1973 in Siberia.

ZERVAS, Napoleon: Military leader of EDES; Minister, 1946–1947; embarrassingly anti-communist.

Bibliography

Before providing an inventory of the sources consulted for this study, it is necessary to comment briefly on the available literature. The attempt is highly selective and confined to a few works almost all of which, irrespective of their outlook or problems, make essential reading.

For the period of the Axis occupation, J.L. Hondros, *Occupation and Resistance: The Greek Agony 1941–44* (1983), and H. Fleischer, *Stemma ke Svastika: I Ellada tis Katochis ke tis Andistasis 1941–1944* vol. I (1988) provide incisive analyses of internal developments in Greece and conclusively disprove the tedious argument of a communist conspiracy. Britain's attempts to neutralize the leftist challenge and restore her influence are superbly surveyed by P. Papastratis, *British Policy towards Greece during the Second World War 1941–1944* (1984). J.O. Iatrides, *Revolt in Athens: The Greek Communist 'Second Round'* (1972) remains an invaluable source which breaks away from conspiracy theories to produce the most balanced account of the events of December 1944.

By contrast, a book which has been the standard source of reference for British historians is *The Struggle for Greece 1941–1949* (1976), by the wartime Head of the British Military Mission in Greece, Colonel C.M. Woodhouse, whose hostility towards the Greek Left and understandable lack of primary sources raise not just a few problems. A more scholarly approach is that of G.M. Alexander, *The Prelude to the Truman Doctrine; British Policy in Greece 1944–1947* (1982), which draws heavily on Foreign Office records to produce 'a study of how the British interpreted the situation in Greece' (p.vi). This is an eloquent example of the hazards lurking in the preoccupation with a single point of view, for Alexander is restating Churchill's argument of the benevolent British intervention to thwart communist designs.

Different in outlook and impressive in detail is Heinz Richter, *British Intervention in Greece: From Varkiza to Civil War, February 1945 to August 1946* (1986). Extensive consultation of Foreign Office records and a survey of several Greek sources lead to a more balanced view, but Richter's account is weakened by a preconceived aversion to the 'ideological blindness' of the KKE leadership (p.539). Besides, a common attribute of these works is that British interests are defined and analysed superficially, leaving a lot to be desired in the way of the domestic and international considerations which shaped British policy.

The standard account of US policy is L.S. Wittner, *American Intervention in Greece, 1943–1949* (1982), while important aspects of the period of the Civil War are covered in three major collective volumes, L. Baerentzen, J.O. Iatrides, and O.L. Smith, eds., *Studies in the History of the Greek Civil War, 1945–1949* (1987); J.O. Iatrides, ed., *Greece in the 1940s; A Nation in Crisis* (1981); and D.H. Close, ed., *The Greek Civil War, 1943–1950: Studies of Polarization* (1993). V. Kondis, *I Anglo-Amerikaniki Politiki ke to Elliniko*

Provlima 1945–1949 (1984), is a scholarly Greek account which, nonetheless, makes minimal use of British sources and interprets KKE policy in 1945–1946 on the basis of post-1949 statements which were heavily distorted by the post-defeat internal turmoil and casting around for scapegoats. The tantalizing question of Soviet policy is impressively addressed in P.J. Stavrakis, *Moscow and Greek Communism 1941–1949* (1989), which offers a well-argued thesis of Stalin's 'prudent expansionism'. Stavrakis's seminal work, however, should be read while bearing in mind the domestic origins of the Greek Civil War and the British contribution to it. In his numerous publications Ole L. Smith provides detailed analyses of the main questions regarding the policy of the KKE, which is also the subject of H. Vlavianos, *Greece, 1941–1949: From Resistance to Civil War* (1992). The long-overdue correlation between developments in Greece and the European context is made in Y. Yianoulopoulos's major interpretative synthesis *O Metapolemikos Kosmos: Elliniki ke Evropaiki Istoria (1945–1963)* (1992).

A. PRIMARY SOURCES

I. Unpublished documents and manuscript sources

ATHENS

GAK: General Archives of the State

(i) The Papers of Emmanuel Tsouderos

(ii) Category K (Private Collections):

    a. K 116 (File F): Precise Extract from the Diary of Principal Events by K.D. Yiannoulis, Officer of EDES (1942–1945)

    b. K 163: The Papers of Iraklis Petimezas (Documents 1943–1953)

    c. K 197, K 205, K 210, K 215: The Papers of Michael I. Myridakis

    d. K 202 (The Papers of Michael I. Myridakis): The Diary of General Napoleon Zervas 1942–1945

LONDON

PRO: Public Record Office, Kew Gardens

(i) Cabinet Papers:

    a. CAB 128/1–16: Cabinet Minutes 1945–1949

    b. CAB 129/1–37: Cabinet Memoranda 1945–1949

    c. CAB 131/1 Minutes and Papers of the Cabinet Defence Committee 1945–1951

    d. CAB 133: International Conference Records

(ii) Foreign Office Papers:

    F.O. 371: General Political Files

(iii) War Office Papers: W.O. 202/235, 893–8

(iv) The Papers of Ernest Bevin:

F.O. 800/vols.446–9 (Conferences); 451–6 (Defence); 460 (Europe); 465 (France); 468 (Greece); 475–7 (Middle East); 492 (Politics); 501–3 (Soviet Union); 508–11 (United Nations); 512–17 (United States); 522 (Yugoslavia)

(v) The Papers of Sir Orme Sargent: F.O. 800/vols.272–9

(vi) The Papers of Lord Inverchapel: F.O. 800/vols.298–303

(vii) Papers of Private Secretaries: F.O. 800/vol.414

OXFORD

(The Bodleian Library)

The Papers of Lord Attlee

II. Published documents

GREECE

Archives of the Democratic Army of Greece (cited as DSE Archives). Excerpts published in the Athens daily newspaper *Eleftherotypia*, 12 December 1978 to 11 January 1979 and 20 January to 7 September 1986.

Archives of the Greek Communist Party (Documents in the possession of the Greek Communist Party of the Interior, cited as KKE (es.) Archives). Excerpts published by Filippos Iliou in the Athens daily newspaper *Avgi*, 2 December 1979 to 23 January 1980.

Dimitriou, P., ed. *I Diaspasi tou KKE: Mesa apo ta Keimena tis Periodou 1950–1975*. Vols. I–II. Athens: Themelio, 1978.

DSE. *Etsi Archise o Emfylios: I Tromokratia meta ti Varkiza, 1945–1947. To Ypomnima tou DSE ston OIE ton Martio tou 1947*. Athens: Glaros, 1987.

EAM. *Lefki Vivlos, Mais 1944–Martis 1945*. Trikala: 1945. (Cited as EAM: LV (I)).

EAM. *Lefki Vivlos: Paraviaseis tis Varkizas, Flevaris–Iounis 1945*. Athens: June 1945. (Cited as EAM: LV (II)).

EAM. *Lefki Vivlos: 'Dimokratikos' Neofasismos, Ioulis–Oktovris 1945*. Athens: October 1945. (Cited as EAM LV (III)).

Efimeris tis Kyverniseos. Athens: Ministry to the Prime Minister's Office, 1945.

Episima Praktika ton Synedriaseon tis Voulis (1946–1949). Athens: Ethniko Typografio, 1946–1949. (Cited as EPSV and followed by volume number in consecutive order).

KKE. *Episima Keimena*. Vol. IV: 1934–1940. Athens: Synchroni Epochi, 1975. (Cited as KKE: E.K., IV).

KKE. *Episima Keimena*. Vol. V: 1940–1945. Athens: Synchroni Epochi, 1981. (Cited as KKE: E.K., V).

KKE. *Episima Keimena*. Vol.VI: 1945–1949. Athens: Synchroni Epochi, 1987. (Cited as KKE: E.K., VI).

KKE. *To KKE apo to 1931 os to 1952: Vasika Dokumenta* N.p.: KKE CC, 1953.

KKE. *Voithima yia tin Istoria tou KKE*. N.p.: KKE CC, n.d.

KKE. *Saranda Chronia tou KKE: 1918–1958*. N.p.: Politikes ke Logotechnikes Ekdoseis, 1958.

KKE. *To Evdomo Synedrio tou KKE*. Vols.I–V. Athens: KKE CC, 1945.

KKE. *Deka Chronia Agones 1935–1945*. Athens: KKE CC, 1945.

KKE. *I Triti Syndiaskepsi tou KKE, 10–14/10/1950*. Athens: Glaros, 1988.

KKE (es.). *To KKE: Episima Keimena tou KKE ston Polemo ke tin Andistasi, 1940–1945*. Vol.V. N.p. [Scopje and Rome], 1973. (Cited as KKE (es.): E.K., V).

PEEA. *Archeio Politikis Epitropis Ethnikis Apeleftherosis (PEEA): Praktika Synedriaseon*. Athens: Synchroni Epochi, 1990. (Cited as PEEA Archives).

Siandos, G. *I Ekthesi Siandou yia ta Dekemvriana*. Athens: Glaros, 1986.

BRITAIN

British Sessional Papers (cited as BSP):

1941–1945: Vol.X, Cmd. 6592: *Documents Regarding the Situation in Greece*.

1945–1946: Vol.XXV, Cmd. 6733: *Financial and Economic Agreement Between HM Government in the UK and the Greek Government*.

Vol. XXV, Cmd. 6838: *Report of the British Legal Mission to Greece*.

Vol. XXV, Cmd. 6812: *Report of the Allied Mission to Observe the Greek Elections*.

Documents on British Policy Overseas. Series I. Vols.I–II. Ed. R. Butler, M.E. Pelly and H.J. Yasamee. London: HMSO, 1984. (Cited as DBPO).

House of Commons Debates. 5th Series. London: 1909 ff. (Cited as HC Deb.).

Report of the British Parliamentary Delegation to Greece, August 1946. London: HMSO, 1947.

Trades Union Congress: 77th Annual Report. London: 1945

Trades Union Congress: 78th Annual Report. London: 1946.

Trades Union Congress: 79th Annual Report. London: 1947.

Pamphlets:

[Keep Left Group]. *Keep Left*. London: New Statesman Publication, 1947.

Woolf, L. *Foreign Policy: The Labour Party's Dilemma*. London: Fabian Society Publication, 1947.

SOVIET UNION

Ministry of Foreign Affairs of the USSR. *Correspondence between the Chairman*

286

of the Council of Ministers of the USSR and the Presidents of the USA and the Prime Ministers of Great Britain during the Great Patriotic War of 1941–1945. Vols.I–II. Moscow. Progress Publishers, 1958. (Cited as Stalin et al.).

UNITED STATES OF AMERICA

A Decade of American Foreign Policy: Basic Documents, 1941–1949. New York: US Government Printing Office (GPO), 1950; reprint, 1968.

Chouliaras, G. and Georgakas, D., eds. 'Documents: Despatches of Lincoln MacVeagh', in *Journal of the Hellenic Diaspora* 12, no.1 (Spring 1985), 29–50.

(FRUS: *Foreign Relations of the United States*, followed by year and volume; published by the US GPO)

FRUS (1945): VIII. *The Near East and Africa*. Washington: GPO, 1969.

FRUS. *Diplomatic Papers: The Conferences of Malta and Yalta, 1945*. Washington: GPO, 1976.

FRUS. *The Conferences of Berlin (The Potsdam Conference), 1945*. Washington: GPO, 1976.

FRUS (1946): I. *General – The United Nations*. Washington: GPO, 1972.

FRUS (1946): III. *The Paris Peace Conference: Proceedings*. Washington: GPO, 1970.

FRUS (1946): VII. *The Near East and Africa*. Washington: GPO, 1969.

FRUS (1947): I. *General – The United Nations*. Washington: GPO, 1973.

FRUS (1947): III. *The British Commonwealth – Europe*. Washington: GPO, 1972.

FRUS (1947): IV. *Eastern Europe: The Soviet Union*. Washington: GPO, 1972.

FRUS (1947): V. *The Near East and Africa*. Washington: GPO, 1971.

FRUS (1948): I. *General – The United Nations*. (Part 2). Washington: GPO, 1976.

FRUS (1948): III. *Western Europe*. Washington: GPO, 1974.

FRUS (1948): IV. *The Near East and Africa*. Washington: GPO, 1974.

FRUS (1949): IV. *The Near East and Africa*. Washington: GPO, 1977.

FRUS (1949): V. *Eastern Europe: The Soviet Union*. Washington: GPO, 1976.

Iatrides, J. O., ed. *Ambassador MacVeagh Reports: Greece 1933–1947*. Princeton: Princeton University Press, 1980. (Cited as MVR).

Kimball, W.F., ed. *Churchill and Roosevelt: The Complete Correspondence*. Vols. I–III. Princeton: Princeton University Press, 1984. (Cited as Churchill–Roosevelt).

Public Papers of the Presidents of the US: Harry S. Truman Vols. III (1947), IV (1948), V (1949). Washington: GPO, 1963–1964.

UNITED NATIONS ORGANIZATION

UNO: *Security Council, Official Records*. First Year: First Series, Supplement no.1. London: 1946.

UNO: *Journal of the Security Council*. First Year. London: 1946.

UNO: *Security Council, Official Records*. Supplement no.5. First Year: Second Series. Lake Success, N.Y.: 1946.

UNO: *Security Council, Official Records*. Supplement no.10. First Year: Second Series. Lake Success, N.Y.: 1947.

UNO: *Security Council, Official Records*. Second Year. Special Supplement 2: Report to the Security Council of the Commission of Investigation Concerning Greek Frontier Incidents.

UNO: *General Assembly, Official Records*. Plenary Meetings, Third Session, Part 1 (1948).

UNO: *General Assembly, Official Records*. Plenary Meetings, Fourth Session (1948).

UNO: *General Assembly, Official Records*. Third Session. Supplement no.8: Report of the United Nations Special Committee on the Balkans.

III. Newspapers

GREECE

Akropolis	(right-wing)
Avgi	(left-wing)
Eleftheria	(liberal)
Eleftheri Ellada	(EAM)
Eleftherotypia	(left-wing)
Embros	(right-wing)
Estia	(right-wing)
Kathimerina Nea	(liberal)
Kathimerini	(right-wing)
Rizospastis	(KKE)
Ta Nea	(liberal)
To Vima	(liberal)
Vradyni	(right-wing)

BRITAIN

The Times

News Chronicle

IV. Memoirs – Diaries – Autobiographies

Acheson, D. *Present at the Creation: My Years in the State Department.* New York: Norton, 1969.

Amandos, K. 'Viografika Simiomata', ed. S.N. Fassoulakis, *Chiaka Chronika* 7 (1975), 69–80.

Attlee, C. *As It Happened.* London: Heinemann, 1954.

Bartziotas, V. *Ethniki Andistasi ke Dekemvris 1944.* 4th edn. Athens: Synchroni Epochi, 1983.

—— *O Agonas tou Dimokratikou Stratou Elladas.* 3rd edn. Athens: Synchroni Epochi, 1985.

—— *Exinda Chronia Kommunistis: Kritiki Aftoviografia.* Athens: Synchroni Epochi, 1986.

Berle, B. and Jacobs, T., eds. *Navigating the Rapids, 1918–1971: From the Papers of Adolf A. Berle.* New York: Harcourt Brace Jovanovich, 1973.

Blanas, G. (Kissavos). *Emfylios Polemos 1946–1949: Opos ta Ezisa.* 2nd edn. Athens: Kastaniotis, 1976.

Cadogan, A. *The Diaries of Sir Alexander Cadogan,* ed. D. Dilks. London: Cassell, 1971.

Chatzis, T. *I Nikifora Epanastasi pou Hathike (1941–1945).* Vols.I–III. Athens: Papazisis, 1977–9.

Churchill, W.S. *The Second World War,* Vol.V, *Closing the Ring.* London: Cassell, 1952; Vol.VI, *Triumph and Tragedy.* London: Cassell, 1954.

Clive, N. *Embeiria stin Ellada* (1943–1948). Athens: Elliniki Evroekdotiki, n.d. [1987].

Colville, J. *The Fringes of Power: Downing Street Diaries 1939–1955.* London: Hodder and Stoughton, 1985.

Dalton, H. *High Tide and After: Memoirs 1945–1960.* London: Frederick Muller, 1962.

Delaportas, P. *To Simiomatario Enos Pilatou.* 2nd edn. Athens: Themelio, 1978.

Dixon, P. *Double Diploma: The Life of Sir Pierson Dixon.* London: Hutchinson, 1968.

Djilas, M. *Conversations with Stalin.* Harmondsworth: Penguin, 1962.

Eden, A. *The Eden Memoirs,* Vol.III, *The Reckoning.* London: Cassell, 1965.

Eleftheriou, L. *Synomilies me ton Niko Zachariadi.* Athens: Kendavros, 1986.

Georgiou, V. *I Zoi mou.* Athens: Typoekdotiki, 1992.

Gladwyn, Lord. *The Memoirs of Lord Gladwyn.* London: Macmillan, 1972.

Gousidis, D., ed. *Markos Vafiadis: Martyries.* Thessaloniki: Epikerotita, 1983.

Hull, C. *The Memoirs of Cordell Hull.* Vol.II. London: Macmillan, 1948.

Ioannidis, Y. *Anamniseis: Provlimata tis Politikis tou KKE stin Ethniki Andistasi, 1940–1945.* Athens: Themelio, 1979.

Jones, J.M. *The Fifteen Weeks (February 21–June 5 1947).* New York: Viking, 1955.

Katsis, D. *To Imerologio enos Andarti tou DSE 1946–1949*. Vols.I–II. Athens: n.p., 1990–1992.

Kilismanis, Y. *Apo tin Ionia sto Dimokratiko Strato*. Athens: Synchroni Epochi, 1989.

Leeper, R. *When Greek Meets Greek*. London: Chatto & Windus, 1950.

Macmillan, H. *The Blast of War: 1939–1945*. London: Macmillan 1967.

Maltezos, G. *Dimokratikos Stratos Elladas*. Athens: n.p., 1984.

Matthews, K. *Memories of a Mountain War: Greece 1944–1949*. London: Longmans Green, 1972.

Millis, W., ed. *The Forrestal Diaries*. New York: Viking, 1951.

Montgomery, Lord. *The Memoirs of Field-Marshal the Viscount Montgomery of Alamein*. London: Collins, 1958.

Moran, Lord. *Winston Churchill: The Struggle for Survival, 1940–1965*. London: Cassell, 1966.

Myers, E.C.W. *The Greek Entanglement*. London: Hart-Davis, 1955.

McNeill, W.H. *The Greek Dilemma: War and Aftermath*. London: Victor Gollancz, 1947.

Papaioannou, A. *I Diathiki tou Nikou Zachariadi*. Athens: Glaros, 1986.

Papayiannis, S. *Apo Evelpis Andartis: Anemniseis enos Kommunisti Axiomatikou*. Athens: Synchroni Epochi, 1991.

Papandreou, G. *I Apeleftherosis tis Ellados*. Athens: Elliniki Ekdotiki, 1945.

Partsalidis, D. *Dipli Apokatastasi tis Ethnikis Andistasis*. Athens: Themelio, 1978.

Psimmenos, T. *Andartes st' Agrafa (1946–1950): Anamniseis enos Andarti*. 2nd edn. Athens: Synchroni Epochi, 1985.

Rousos, P. *I Megali Pendaetia*. Vols.I–II. 2nd edn. Athens: Synchroni Epochi, 1976–1978.

Sakellariou, E. *To Ygeionomiko tou Dimokratikou Stratou*. Athens: Afoi Tolidi, n.d.

Sarafis, S. *ELAS: Greek Resistance Army*. London: Merlin Press, 1980.

—— *Meta ti Varkiza*. Athens: Epikerotita, 1979.

Smith, H.K. *The State of Europe*. New York: Knopf, 1951.

Spais, L. *Peninda Chronia Stratiotis stin Ypiresia tou Ethnous ke tis Dimokratias*. Vols.I–II. Athens: n.p., 1970.

Sulzberger, C. *A Long Row of Candles: Memoirs and Diaries (1934– 1954)*. London: Macmillan, 1969.

Svolos, T. *Andartis sta Vouna tou Moria: Odoiporiko (1947–1949)* Athens: n.p., 1990.

Sweet-Escott, B. *Baker Street Irregular: Five Years in the Special Operations Executive*. London: Collins, 1965.

Trikalinos, G. *292 Imeres Meta to Grammo-Vitsi*. 3rd edn. Athens: Odigitis, 1987.

Truman, H.S. *The Memoirs of Harry S. Truman*, Vol.I, *Year of Decisions 1945*. London: Hodder and Stoughton, 1955; Vol.II, *Years of Trial and Hope*. London: Hodder and Stoughton, 1956.

Tsakalotos, Th. *Saranda Chronia Stratiotis tis Ellados*. Vols.I–II. Athens: n.p., 1960.

Vafiadis, M. *Apomnimonevmata*, Vol.III. Athens: Nea Synora, 1985; Vol.V Athens: Papazisis, 1992.

Vlandas, D. *Emfylios Polemos 1945–1949*, Vol.III, part 1 Athens: n.p., 1979; Vol. III, part 2. Athens: Grammi, 1981.

Vonditsos-Gousias, G. *Oi Aities yia tis Ittes, ti Diaspasi tou KKE ke tis Ellinikis Aristeras*. Vols.I–II. Athens: Na Ypiretoume to Lao, 1977.

Votsikas, D. *I Ipiros Xanazonete t' Armata (1946–1949): Dimokratikos Stratos Elladas*. Athens: n.p., 1983.

Ward, M. *Greek Assignments: SOE 1943–1948, UNSCOB*. Athens: Lycabettus Press, 1992.

Williams, F. *A Prime Minister Remembers: The War and Post-War Memoirs of the Rt. Hon. Earl Attlee*. London: Heinemann, 1961.

Woodhouse, C.M. *Apple of Discord: A Survey of Recent Greek Politics in their International Setting*. London: Hutchinson, 1948.

[Zafiris, Y. et al., eds.] *O Agonas tou Dimokratikou Stratou sti Samo*. Athens: Synchroni Epochi, 1987.

Zafiropoulos, D. *O Antisymmoriakos Agon*. Athens: n.p., 1956.

B. SECONDARY SOURCES

I. Books

Alexander, G.M. *The Prelude to the Truman Doctrine: British Policy in Greece, 1944–1947*. Oxford: Clarendon Press, 1982.

Andaeos, P. *Nikos Zachariadis: Thytis ke Thyma*. 2nd edn. Athens: Fytrakis, 1991.

Anderson, T. *The United States, Great Britain and the Cold War, 1944–1947*. London: Macmillan, 1981.

Auty, P., and Clogg, R., eds. *British Policy towards Wartime Resistance in Yugoslavia and Greece*. London: Macmillan, 1975.

Averoff-Tosizza, E. *By Fire and Axe: The Communist Party and the Civil War in Greece, 1946–1949*. New Rochelle: Caratzas, 1978.

Baerentzen, L., Iatrides, J.O. and Smith, O.L., eds. *Studies in the History of the Greek Civil War, 1945–1949*. Copenhagen: Museum Tusculanum Press, 1987.

Barker, E. *British Policy in South-East Europe in the Second World War*. London: Macmillan, 1976.

Bullock, A. *The Life and Times of Ernest Bevin*, Vol.II, *Minister of Labour 1940–1945*. London: Heinemann, 1967.

—— *Ernest Bevin: Foreign Secretary 1945–1951*. Oxford: Oxford University Press, 1985.

Calvocoressi, P. *World Politics Since 1945*. 3rd edn. London: Longman, 1977.

Clayton, A. *The British Empire as a Superpower, 1919–1939*. London: Macmillan, 1986.

Clogg, R. *A Short History of Modern Greece*. 2nd edn. London: Cambridge University Press, 1986.

—— *Parties and Elections in Greece: The Search for Legitimacy*. London: C. Hurst and Co., 1987.

Close, D.H., ed. *The Greek Civil War, 1943–1950: Studies of Polarization*. London: Routledge, 1993.

Dafnis, G. *Ta Ellinika Politika Kommata*. Athens: Ikaros, 1961

—— *I Ellas Metaxi Dyo Polemon*. Vols.I–II. Athens: Ikaros, 1955.

Darwin, J. *Britain and Decolonisation: The Retreat from Empire in the Post-War World*. London: Macmillan, 1988.

Dedijer, V. *Tito Speaks*. London: Simon & Schuster, 1953.

Deibel, T., and Gaddis, J.L., eds. *Containing the Soviet Union. Washington*: Pergammon-Brassey's, 1987.

Dilks, D., ed. *Retreat from Power: Studies in Britain's Foreign Policy of the Twentieth Century*, Vol.II, *After 1939*. London: Macmillan, 1981.

Dodds, N., Solley, L. and Tiffany, S. *Tragedy in Greece*. London: League for Democracy in Greece, 1946.

Eudes, D. *The Kapetanios: Partisans and Civil War in Greece, 1943–1949*. London: New Left Books, 1972.

Fleischer, H. *Stemma ke Svastika: I Ellada tis Katochis ke tis Andistasis, 1941–1944*. Vol.I. Athens: Papazisis, 1988.

—— and Bowman, S. *Greece in the 1940s: A Bibliographical Companion*. Hanover and London: University Press of New England, 1981.

Gaddis, J.L. *The United States and the Origins of the Cold War, 1941–1947*. New York: Colombia University Press, 1972.

—— *Strategies of Containment: A Critical Appraisal of Postwar American National Security Policy*. New York: Oxford University Press, 1982.

—— *The Long Peace: Inquiries into the History of the Cold War*. New York: Oxford University Press, 1987.

Gallagher, J. *The Decline, Revival and Fall of the British Empire*. London: Cambridge University Press, 1982.

GES/DIS. *Istoria tis Organoseos tou Ellinikou Stratou 1821–1954*. Athens: GES/DIS, 1957.

—— *Ai Machai tou Vitsi ke tou Grammou*. Athens: GES/DIS, 1951.

—— *O Ellinikos Stratos kata ton Antisymmoriakon Agona 1946–1949: To Proton Etos tou Antisymmoriakou Agonos, 1946.* Athens: GES/DIS, 1971.

—— *O Ellinikos Stratos kata ton Antisymmoriakon Agona 1946–1949: I Ekkathariseis tis Roumelis ke i Proti Machi tou Grammou.* Athens: GES/DIS, 1970.

Grigoriadis, F.N. *Istoria tou Emfyliou Polemou, 1945–1949 (To Deftero Andartiko).* Vols.I–IV. Athens: Kamarinopoulos, n.d.

Grigoriadis, S.N. *Dekemvris – Emfylios Polemos, 1944–1949: Synoptiki Istoria.* Athens: Kapopoulos, 1984.

Gritzonas., K. *O Aris Velouchiotis ke oi Angloi.* Athens: Glaros, 1983.

Harris, K. *Attlee.* London: Weidenfeld and Nicolson, 1982.

Heuser, D.B.G. *Western Containment Policies Towards Yugoslavia, 1948–1953.* London: Routledge, 1988.

Hondros, J.L. *Occupation and Resistance: The Greek Agony, 1941–1944.* New York: Pella, 1983.

Iatrides, J.O., ed. *Greece in the 1940s: A Nation in Crisis.* Hanover and London: University Press of New England, 1981.

—— *Revolt in Athens: The Greek Communist 'Second Round', 1944–1945.* Princeton: Princeton University Press, 1972.

Jones, H. *'A New Kind of War': America's Global Strategy and the Truman Doctrine in Greece.* New York: Oxford University Press, 1989.

Judt, T., ed. *Resistance and Revolution in Mediterranean Europe, 1939–1948.* London: Routledge, 1989.

Katsoulis, G. *Istoria tou Kommunistikou Kommatos Elladas.* Vols.I–VII. Athens: Nea Synora, 1977.

[KKE]. *Sta Saranda Chronia tou Dimokratikou Stratou Elladas.* Athens: Synchroni Epochi, 1987.

KKE CC. *Syndomi Istoria tou KKE, Schedio, Meros A: 1918–1949.* Athens: KKE CC, 1988.

[KKE/Centre for Marxist Studies]. *Symposio yia tin Istoria tis Ethnikis Andistasis.* 2nd edn. Athens: Synchroni Epochi, 1985.

Kofas, J.V. *Authoritarianism in Greece: The Metaxas Regime.* New York: East European Monographs, Boulder, 1983.

Kofos, E. *Nationalism and Communism in Macedonia.* Thessaloniki: Institute for Balkan Studies, 1964.

—— *The Impact of the Macedonian Question on Civil Conflict in Greece (1943–1949).* Athens: ELIAMEP, 1989.

Koliopoulos, J. *Greece and the British Connection, 1935–1941.* Oxford: Clarendon Press, 1977.

Kolko, G. *The Politics of War: The World and United States Foreign Policy, 1943–1945.* New York: Random House, 1968.

293

Kondis, V. *I Angloamerikaniki Politiki ke to Elliniko Provlima, 1945–1949.* Thessaloniki: Paratiritis, 1984.

Kousoulas, D.G. *Revolution and Defeat: The Story of the Greek Communist Party.* London: Oxford University Press, 1965.

Kuniholm, B.R. *The Origins of the Cold War in the Near East: Great Power Conflict and Diplomacy in Iran, Turkey and Greece.* Princeton: Princeton University Press, 1980.

Laquer, W. *Guerrilla: A Historical and Critical Survey.* London: Weidenfeld and Nicolson, 1977.

Loth, W. *The Division of the World 1941–1955.* London: Routledge, 1988.

Louis, W.R. *The British Empire in the Middle East, 1945–1951: Arab Nationalism, the United States, and Postwar Imperialism.* Oxford: Clarendon Press, 1984.

Loulis, J. *The Greek Communist Party, 1940–1944.* London: Croom Helm, 1982.

Lundestad, G. *The American Non–Policy Towards Eastern Europe.* Tromso–Oslo–Bergen: n.p., 1978.

Maddox, R. *The New Left and the Origins of the Cold War.* Princeton: Princeton University Press, 1973.

Margaris, N. *Istoria tis Makronisou.* Vols. I–II. Athens: n.p., 1966.

Mavrogordatos, G. *Stillborn Republic: Social Conditions and Party Strategies in Greece, 1922–1936.* Berkeley: University of California Press, 1983.

Meynaud, J. *Oi Politikes Dynameis stin Ellada.* 2nd edn. Athens: Bayron, 1974.

Miliband, R. *The State in Capitalist Society: The Analysis of the Western System of Power.* London: Quartet Books, 1973.

Milward, A. *The Reconstruction of Western Europe, 1945–1951.* 2nd edn. London: Methuen, 1987.

Morgan, K. *Labour in Power, 1945–1951.* Oxford: Oxford University Press, 1985.

Nachmani, A. *International Intervention in the Greek Civil War: The United Nations Special Committee on the Balkans, 1947–1952.* New York: Oxford University Press, 1990.

Nefeloudis, P. *Stis Piges tis Kakodemonias: Ta Vathitera Aitia tis Diaspasis tou KKE, 1918–1968.* 6th edn. Athens: Gutenberg, 1974.

O'Ballance, E. *The Greek Civil War, 1944–1949.* London: Faber & Faber, 1966.

Oikonomidis, F. *Oi Prostates: I Alithini Istoria tis Andistasis.* 2nd edn. Athens: Orfeas, 1986.

Ovendale, R., ed. *The Foreign Policy of the British Labour Governments, 1945–1951.* Leicester: Leicester University Press, 1984.

Owen, R. and B. Sutcliffe. *Studies in the Theory of Imperialism.* London: Longman, 1972.

Papastratis, P. *British Foreign Policy Towards Greece During the Second World War, 1941–1944.* London: Cambridge University Press, 1984.

Paret, P., ed. *Makers of Modern Strategy: From Machiavelli to the Nuclear Age*. Oxford: Oxford University Press, 1986.

Patatzis, S. *Ioannis Sofianopoulos: Enas Epanastatis Choris Epanastasi*. Athens: n.p. 1961.

Richter, H. *1936–1946: Dyo Epanastaseis ke Andepanastaseis stin Ellada*. Vols.I–II. 2nd edn. Athens: Exandas, 1977.

—— *British Intervention in Greece: From Varkiza to Civil War, February 1945 to August 1946*. London: Merlin Press, 1986.

Rothwell, V. *Britain and the Cold War, 1941–1947*. London: Macmillan, 1982.

Sarafis, M., ed. *Greece: From Resistance to Civil War*. Nottingham: Spokesman, 1980.

Sarlis, D. *I Politiki tou KKE ston Agona kata tou Monarcho fasismou*. 3rd edn. Athens: Synchroni Epochi, 1987.

Smothers, F., McNeill, W.H. and McNeill, E.D. *Report on the Greeks: Findings of a Twentieth Century Fund team which surveyed conditions in Greece in 1947*. New York: The Twentieth Century Fund, 1948.

Spriano, P. *Stalin and the European Communists*. London: Verso, 1985.

Stavrakis, P.J. *Moscow and Greek Communism, 1944–1949*. Ithaca and London: Cornell University Press, 1989.

Stavrianos, L.S. *Greece: American Dilemma and Opportunity*. Chicago: Regnery, 1952.

Svoronos, N. *Episkopisi tis Neoellinikis Istorias*. 9th edn. Athens: Themelio, 1985.

—— *Anallekta Neoellinikis Istorias ke Istoriografias*. 3rd edn. Athens: Themelio, 1987.

—— and Fleischer, H., eds. *I Ellada 1936–1944: Diktatoria–Katochi–Andistasi*. Athens: Agrotiki Trapeza Ellados, 1989.

Sweet-Escott, B. *Greece: A Political and Economic Survey, 1939–1953*. London: Royal Institute of International Affairs, 1954.

Thomas, H. *Armed Truce: The Beginnings of the Cold War, 1945–1946*. London: Sceptre, 1988.

Tsoucalas, C. *The Greek Tragedy*. Harmondsworth: Penguin, 1969.

Vlavianos, H. *Greece 1941–1949: From Resistance to Civil War*. London: Macmillan/St. Anthony's College, Oxford, 1992.

Vournas, T. *Istoria tis Synchronis Elladas: O Emfylios*. Athens: Afoi Tolidi, 1981.

Vukmanovič, S. (General TEMPO). *How and Why the People's Liberation Struggle of Greece Met with Defeat*. London: 1950; 2nd edn. London: Merlin Press, 1985.

Wittner, L.S. *American Intervention in Greece, 1943–1949*. New York: Columbia University Press, 1982.

Woodhouse, C.M. *The Struggle for Greece, 1941–1949*. London: Hart-Davis/MacGibbon, 1976.

Woodward, L. *British Foreign Policy in the Second World War*. 2nd edn. Vol.III. London. HMSO, 1971.

Xydis, S. *Greece and the Great Powers, 1944–1947: Prelude to the Truman Doctrine*. Thessaloniki: Institute for Balkan Studies, 1963.

Yergin, D. *Shattered Peace: Origins of the Cold War and the National Security State*. Boston: Houghton-Mifflin, 1977.

Yianoulopoulos, Y. *O Metapolemikos Kosmos: Elliniki ke Evropaiki Istoria (1945–1963)*. Athens: Papazisis, 1992.

Zachariadis, N. *Ta Provlimata Kathodigisis sto KKE*. (N.p.: 1952; reprint:) Athens: Poreia, 1978.

—— *Provlimata tis Krisis tou KKE*. (N.p.: 1962.) Reprinted as *I Paranomi Brosoura tou Nikou Zachariadi*. Athens: Glaros, 1987.

—— *Epilogi Ergon*. Athens: Protoporos, n.d.

II. Articles and Essays

Addison, P. 'The Political Beliefs of Winston Churchill', Transactions of the Royal Historical Society, 5th series (1980), 23–47.

Alexander, G.M. 'Perceptions of EAM/ELAS Rule in Thessaloniki, 1944–1945', *Balkan Studies* 21, part 2 (1980), 203–16.

—— and Loulis, J.S. 'The Strategy of the Greek Communist Party, 1934–1944: An Analysis of Plenary Decisions', *East European Quarterly* 15, no.3 (September 1981), 377–89.

Alivizatos, N. 'The "Emergency Regime" and Civil Liberties 1947–1950', in J.O. Iatrides, ed., *Greece in the 1940s: A Nation in Crisis* (Hanover and London: 1981), 220–8.

Baerentzen, L. 'The Demonstration in Syntagma Square on Sunday the 3rd of December, 1944', *Scandinavian Studies in Modern Greek* 2 (1978), 3–52.

—— 'I Afixi tis Sovietikis Stratiotikis Apostolis ton Ioulio 1944', in N. Svoronos, and H. Fleischer, eds., *I Ellada 1936–1944: Diktatoria–Katochi–Andistasi* (Athens: 1989), 563–97.

—— 'I Laiki Ypostirixi tou EAM sto telos tis Katochis', *O Mnemon* 9 (1984), 157–73.

Barker, E. 'Yugoslav Policy towards Greece 1947–1949', in L. Baerentzen, J.O. Iatrides, O.L. Smith, eds., *Studies in the History of the Greek Civil War 1945–1949* (Copenhagen: 1987), 263–95.

—— 'The Yugoslavs and the Greek Civil War of 1946–1949', in L. Baerentzen, J.O. Iatrides, O.L. Smith, eds., *Studies in the History of the Greek Civil War 1945–1949* (Copenhagen: 1987), 297–308.

Bouras, V. 'I Politiki Epitropi Ethnikis Apeleftherosis, Eleftheri Ellada 1944', in N. Svoronos, and H. Fleischer, eds., *I Ellada 1936–1944: Diktatoria–Katochi–Andistasi* (Athens: 1989), 327–35.

Boyle, P.G. 'The British Foreign Office View of Soviet–American Relations, 1945–1946', *Diplomatic History* 3 (1979), 307–20.

Childs, D. 'The Cold War and the "British Road", 1946–1953', *Journal of Contemporary History* 23, no.4 (October 1988), 551–72.

Clive, N. 'British Policy Alternatives 1945–1946', in L. Baerentzen, J.O. Iatrides, O.L.Smith, eds., *Studies in the History of the Greek Civil War 1945–1949* (Copenhagen: 1987), 213–23.

Darwin, J. 'British Decolonisation since 1945: A Pattern or a Puzzle?', *Journal of Imperial and Commonwealth History* 12, no.2 (January 1984), 187–209.

—— 'Imperialism in Decline? Tendencies in British Imperial Policy between the Wars', *The Historical Journal* 23, no.3 (1980), 657–79.

Elefandis, A. 'EAM: Istoria ke Ideologia. Proypotheseis yia mia epistimoniki theorisi tou EAM', *O Politis* 5 (September 1976), 63–8.

Fleischer, H. 'The "Third Factor": The Struggle for an Independent Socialist Policy during the Greek Civil War', in L. Baerentzen, J.O. Iatrides, O.L. Smith, eds., *Studies in the History of the Greek Civil War 1945–1949* (Copenhagen: 1987), 189–212.

Frazier, R. 'Did Britain Start the Cold War? Bevin and the Truman Doctrine', *The Historical Journal* 27, no.3 (1984), 715–27.

Gallagher, J., and R. Robinson. 'The Imperialism of Free Trade', *Economic History Review* 2nd series, 6, no. 1 (1953), 1–15.

Gerolymatos, A. 'The Role of the Officer Corps in the Resistance', *Journal of the Hellenic Diaspora* 11, no.3 (Fall 1984), 69–79.

—— 'The Security Battalions in the Civil War', *Journal of the Hellenic Diaspora* 12, no.1 (Spring 1985), 17–27.

Iatrides, J.O. 'From Liberation to Civil War: The United States and Greece, 1944–1946', *Southeastern Europe* 3, no.1 (1976), 32–43.

Iliou, F. 'I Synandisi mas me ton Stalin. Anamniseis tou Mitsou Partsalidi katagrammenes apo ton F. Iliou', *Avgi* (Athens) : 29/2–3/3 1976.

Kimball, W.F. 'The Cold War warmed over', *American Historical Review* 79 (1974), 1119–36.

Kitroeff, A. 'Continuity and Change in Contemporary Greek Historiography', *European History Quarterly* 19, no.2 (April 1989), 269–98.

—— 'I vretaniki politiki ke to Kinima sti Mesi Anatoli', in N. Svoronos, and H. Fleischer, eds., *I Ellada 1936–1944: Diktatoria–Katochi–Andistasi* (Athens: 1989), 541–52.

Kofos, E. 'National Heritage and National Identity in Nineteenth and Twentieth-Century Macedonia', *European History Quarterly* 19, no.2 (April 1989), 229–67.

Laiou, A. 'Population Movements in the Greek Countryside During the Civil War', in L. Baerentzen, J.O. Iatrides, O.L. Smith, eds., *Studies in the History of the Greek Civil War 1945–1949* (Copenhagen: 1987), 55–103.

297

Loulis, J.C. 'The Greek Communist Party (KKE) and the Greek-Italian War, 1940–41: An Analysis of Zachariadis's Three Letters', *Byzantine and Modern Greek Studies* 5 (1979), 165–85.

Lukač, D. 'I Synergasia metaxi ton Ethnikon Apeleftherotikon Kinimaton tis Elladas ke tis Yugoslavias', in N. Svoronos, and H. Fleischer, eds., *I Ellada 1936–1944: Diktatoria–Katochi–Andistasi* (Athens: 1989), 480–8.

Margaritis, G. 'Politikes Prooptikes ke Dynatotites meta tin Apeleftherosi', *O Mnemon* 9 (1984), 174–93.

Mark, E. 'American Policy toward Eastern Europe and the Origins of the Cold War, 1941–1946: An Alternative Interpretation', *Journal of American History* 68 (September 1981), 313–36.

Matloff, M. 'Allied Strategy in Europe, 1939–1945', in P. Paret, ed., *Makers of Modern Strategy: From Machiavelli to the Nuclear Age* (Oxford: 1986), 677–702.

Maude, G. 'The 1946 British Parliamentary Delegation to Greece: A Lost Opportunity?', *Journal of the Hellenic Diaspora* 11, no.1 (Spring 1984), 5–24.

Mavrogordatos, G. 'From Ballots to Bullets: The 1946 Elections and Plebiscite', in J.O. Iatrides, ed., *Greece in the 1940s: A Nation in Crisis* (Hanover and London: 1981), 181–94.

Mavromatis, P. 'Omilia pano sto proto thema tis Imerisias Diataxis', *Neos Kosmos* 4–5 (April–May 1957), 98–105.

Meissner, R. 'I Ethnikososialistiki Germania ke i Ellada tis Metaxikis Diktatorias', in N. Svoronos, and H. Fleischer, eds., *I Ellada 1936–1944: Diktatoria– Katochi–Andistasi* (Athens: 1989), 50–58.

Merrick, R. 'The Russia Committee of the Foreign Office and the Cold War, 1946–1947', *Journal of Contemporary History* 20 (1985), 453–68.

Mouzelis, N. 'I Ideologia tis Tetartis Avgoustou.' *To Vima* (Athens): 3/8/1986.

McFarland, S.L. 'A Peripheral View of the Origins of the Cold War: The Crisis in Iran, 1941–1947', *Diplomatic History* 4 (1980), 333–52.

Nachmani, A. 'Civil War and Foreign Intervention in Greece: 1946–1949', *Journal of Contemporary History* 25 (1990), 489–522.

Neumann, S., and Von Hagen, M. 'Engels and Marx on Revolution, War, and the Army in Society', in P. Paret, ed., *Makers of Modern Strategy: From Machiavelli to the Nuclear Age* (Oxford: 1986), 262–80.

Noutsos, P. 'Synistoses tis Ideologias tis Tetartis Avgoustou', in N. Svoronos, and H. Fleischer, eds., *I Ellada 1936–1944: Diktatoria–Katochi–Andistasi* (Athens: 1989), 59–69.

Ovendale, R. 'Britain, the United States and the European Cold War, 1945–1948', *History* 67 (1987), 217–36.

Papastraris, P. 'I Istoriografia tis Dekaetias 1940–1950', *Synchrona Themata* nos. 35–36–37 (December 1988), 183–187.

——— 'The Purge of the Greek Civil Service on the Eve of the Civil War', in L. Baerentzen, J.O.Iatrides, O.L. Smith, eds., *Studies in the History of the Greek Civil War 1945–1949* (Copenhagen: 1987), 41–53.

Petropoulos, J. 'The Traditional Political Parties during the Occupation', in J.O. Iatrides, ed., *Greece in the 1940s: A Nation in Crisis* (Hanover and London: 1981), 27–36.

Porter, P. 'Wanted: A Miracle in Greece', *Collier's* no.120 (20 September 1947).

Resis, A. 'Spheres of Influence in Soviet Wartime Diplomacy', *Journal of Modern History* 53 (September 1981), 417–39.

——— 'The Churchill–Stalin "Percentages Agreement" on the Balkans, Moscow, October 1944', *American Historical Review* 83 (April 1978), 368–87.

Richter, H. 'The Varkiza Agreement and the Origins of the Greek Civil War', in J.O. Iatrides, ed., *Greece in the 1940s: A Nation in Crisis* (Hanover and London: 1981), 167–80.

——— 'The Second Plenum of the Central Committee of the KKE and the Decision for Civil War: A Reappraisal', in L. Baerentzen, J.O. Iatrides, O.L. Smith, eds., *Studies in the History of the Greek Civil War 1945–1949* (Copenhagen: 1987), 179–87.

Robinson, R. 'Non-European Foundations of European Imperialism: Sketch for a Theory of Collaboration', in R. Owen, and B. Sutcliffe, eds., *Studies in the Theory of Imperialism* (London: 1972), 117–42.

Sfikas, T.D. '"The people at the top can do these things which others can't do": Winston Churchill and the Greeks, 1940–1945', *Journal of Contemporary History* 26, no. 2 (April 1991), 307–32.

——— 'O "Telefteos Peirasmos" tou KKE: Ioulios 1947', *O Mnemon* 14 (1992), 151–75.

Shy, J. and T. Collier. 'Revolutionary War', in P. Paret, ed., *Makers of Modern Strategy: From Machiavelli to the Nuclear Age* (Oxford: 1986), 815–62.

Smith, O.L. 'The Boycott of the elections 1946: A Decisive Mistake?', *Scandinavian Studies in Modern Greek* 6 (1982), 69–88.

——— 'On the Beginning of the Greek Civil War', *Scandinavian Studies in Modern Greek* 1 (1977), 15–31.

——— 'A Turning Point in the Greek Civil War, 1945–1949: The Meeting between Zachariadis and Markos, July 1946', *Scandinavian Studies in Modern Greek* 3 (1979), 35–47.

——— 'Review of "Die Kommunistische Partei Griechenlands 1941–1949", by Matthias Esche', *Journal of the Hellenic Diaspora* 11, no. 2 (Spring 1984), 60–70.

——— 'Marxism in Greece: The Case of the KKE', *Journal of Modern Greek Studies* 3, no.1 (1985), 45–64.

——— 'The Problems of the Second Plenum of the Central Committee of the

KKE, 1946', *Journal of the Hellenic Diaspora* 12, no.2 (Spring 1985), 43–64.

—— 'On Zachariadis's Theory of the Two Poles', *Scandinavian Studies in Modern Greek* 5 (1981), 29–35.

—— 'The Greek Communists 1941–1949: Review Article', *Epsilon: Modern Greek and Balkan Studies* 2 (1988), 77–101 .

—— 'The Tsaldaris Offers for Negotiations 1948: A Lost Opportunity or a Canard?', *Epsilon: Modern Greek and Balkan Studies* 1 (1987), 83–89.

—— 'Self-Defence and Communist Policy 1945–1947', in L. Baerentzen, J.O. Iatrides, O.L. Smith, eds., *Studies in the History of the Greek Civil War 1945–1949* (Copenhagen: 1987), 159–77.

—— 'Pos Vlepoun oi Xenoi tin Ethniki Andistasi: Kritiki tis Antikommunistikis Istoriografias', in *Symposio yia tin Istoria tis Ethnikis Andistasis*. 2nd edn. (Athens: 1985), 93–100.

—— 'Protes Meres tou '36'. *To Vima* (Athens): 7 August 1986.

—— 'KKE Reactions to the Truman Doctrine', *Journal of Modern Hellenism* 5 (1988), 1–8.

—— '"The First Round" – Civil War During the Occupation', in D. Close, ed., *The Greek Civil War, 1943–1950: Studies of Polarization* (London: 1993), 58–71.

—— 'The Greek Communist Party, 1945–1949', in D. Close, ed., *The Greek Civil War, 1943–1950 : Studies of Polarization* (London: 1993), 129–155.

Spais, L. 'Lathi–Pathi–Tafoi: Dekemvris 1944', *Politika Themata* no.125 (4–10/12/1976), 25–7.

Stavrianos, L.S. 'The Greek National Liberation Front (EAM): A Study in Resistance Organization and Administration', *Journal of Modern History* 24, no.1 (1952), 44–54.

Stringos, L. 'Omilia pano sto proto thema tis Imerisias Diataxis', *Neos Kosmos* 4–5 (April–May 1957), 82–8.

Svoronos, N. 'Greece 1940–1950: The Main Problems', in J.O. Iatrides, ed., *Greece in the 1940s : A Nation in Crisis* (Hanover and London: 1981), 1–14.

Tsakaloyannis, P. 'The Moscow Puzzle', *Journal of Contemporary History* 21, no.1 (1986), 37–55.

Vafiadis, M. 'O Markos Vafiadis Apanda ston Mitso Partsalidi yia ti "Synandisi me ton Stalin", ti Varkiza ke tin "Katagellia" Zachariadi', *Anti* 53 (4/9/1976), 30–5.

——'Omilia pano sto proto thema tis Imerisias Diataxis', *Neos Kosmos* 4–5 (April–May 1957), 45–72.

Vlavianos, H. 'The Greek Communist Party: in search of a revolution', in T. Judt, ed., *Resistance and Revolution in Mediterranean Europe 1939–1948* (London: 1989), 157–212.

Wittner, L.S. 'American Policy Toward Greece during World War II', *Diplomatic History* 3 (Spring 1979), 129–49.

Zachariadis, N. 'Deka Chronia Palis: Symberasmata–Didagmata–Kathikonda', *Neos Kosmos* 11–12 (November–December 1950). Reprinted in *I Triti Syndiaskepsi tou KKE 10–14/10/1950* (Athens : 1988), 61–72.

Index

and UN Commission of Inquiry: 159–160;
and Zachariadis's orders (April 1947): 165–166;
letter to *The Times*: 188;
dismissal of: 242–245
Marshall, George C., 144, 157, 168, 209;
and KKE peace proposals (1947): 172–175;
and dispute with Bevin: 175–182;
visit to Athens (1948): 229
Mavromichalis, Petros, 48–49, 112, 113, 115, 185
Maximos, Dimitrios, 136, 156, 167–168, 170, 184
Merkouris, Stamatis, 74–75
Metaxas, Ioannis, 20–21
Mikoyan, Anastas, 64
Molotov, Vyascheslav, 75, 77, 105, 118, 127, 214
Montgomery, Field-Marshal Bernard, 165
Myers, Brigadier E.C.W., 25
McNeil, Hector, 71, 80, 111, 117–118, 119, 125, 126, 143, 257–260, 277;
visit to Athens (1945): 59–61
McNeill, William H., 45

Norton, Clifford V., 82, 87, 88, 105, 109, 111, 114, 118, 129, 133, 143, 144–145, 158, 159, 164, 206, 222, 227, 229, 253, 276;
views on Greeks: 135, 217

OSS, 31

Papagos, General Alexandros, 229, 230, 253, 255, 260
Papandreou, Georgios, 19, 32, 87, 134, 184, 253, 270;
becomes premier: 27–29;
and demobilisation negotiations: 32–34
Partsalidis, Dimitris, 34, 43;
visit to Moscow (January 1946): 77–78

Paul, King of Greece, 115, 170, 192, 253, 255, 261
Peake, Charles, 206, 209, 210, 243, 246, 249, 250–251, 260
PEEA, 27, 65
Peterson, Maurice, 207
Plastiras, Nikolaos, 17, 18, 25, 43, 47, 50, 69, 115, 168, 226;
becomes premier: 36;
fall of: 51–52
Politt, Harry, 189
Popov, Lt.-Col. Grigori, 30, 35
Populist Party, 18, 67;
formation of government of (1946): 99–105;
and the KKE (1946): 105–117;
and coalition with the Liberals (1947): 184–187, 190–191, 211–212
Porfyrogenis, Miltiadis, 111, 169, 189, 257
Porter, Paul, 139
Public Security Committees, 107–108, 111

Rallis, Ioannis, 29;
trial of: 47
Rankin, Karl, 100, 222
Rawlins, Maj.-Gen. Stewart, 112, 113, 192
Rodionov, Admiral Konstantin, 77, 88
Roosevelt, Franklin Delano, 26;
and 'special mission' initiative: 64
Rousos, Petros, 122, 209
Rusk, Dean, 257–260

Sarafis, Stefanos, 23, 67, 69, 164
Sargent, Orme, 49, 54, 62, 79, 100, 175, 183–184, 232, 271
Scobie, Lt.-Gen. Ronald, 29, 32, 34
Siandos, Giorgis, 28, 31, 32, 43, 49, 63, 64, 66, 67, 87;
and *Ta Dekemvriana*: 63;
and presence of British troops (1945): 63;
and Eleventh CC Plenum (April 1945): 64–65

Slim, Field-Marshal William, 254
Sofianopoulos, Ioannis, 43, 61, 78, 231
Sofulis, Themistoklis, 20, 47;
  becomes premier (1945): 61;
  and 1946 elections: 81–88, 270;
  and 1946 plebiscite: 117;
  and appeasement statements: 136;
  and KKE peace proposals (1947): 169–175;
  becomes premier (1947): 185–186;
  and amnesty law: 186–187
Soviet Union, 22, 29, 64, 269;
  charges Britain at UNO: 76;
  foreign policy objectives (1944–1946): 76–77;
  and visit of EAM delegation to Moscow (January 1946): 77–78;
  and contacts with Tsaldaris (1948): 223–225;
  peace overture (November 1948): 231
Spais, Leonidas, 35
Stalin, Joseph, and meeting with Churchill (Moscow, October 1944): 30, 270;
  foreign policy objectives (1944–1946): 76–77;
  and Zachariadis's trip to Moscow (1946): 105–106;
  and Zachariadis's neutrality proposal: 122–124;
  and Zachariadis's visit to Moscow (1947): 165–167;
  and meeting with Djilas and Kardelji (Moscow, February 1948): 213–215
Sulzberger, Cyrus, 134, 261
Svolos, Alexandros, 27, 37

Tahourdin, John, 232–233
Theotokis, Spyros, 107–108
Thorez, Maurice, 105
Tito, 105, 106, 162, 241, 277;
  and meeting with Maclean (May 1949): 251–252

Togliatti, Palmiro, 105
Truman Doctrine, 9, 139–145, 158, 162, 167, 274
Truman, Harry S., 54, 103, 141, 142, 223, 262
Tsaldaris, Konstantinos,
  and formation of government (1946): 101–105;
  legislation of: 107–109, 115;
  Greek territorial demands: 118;
  British view of: 118, 127;
  US view of: 138;
  and Greek complaint at UNO: 134–135;
  and Truman Doctrine, 143;
  and coalition with Liberals: 185–186;
  seeks alliance with Turkey: 216–217;
  and plan for a Mediterranean Pact: 217;
  contacts with the Soviet Embassy (1948): 223–225;
  and Greek-Yugoslav relations: 250–252
Tsaldaris, Panayis, 18, 20
Tsatsos, Themistoklis, 47
Tsirimokos, Ilias, 43, 193
Tsouderos, Emmanuel, 25, 58, 61, 71, 75;
  becomes premier (1941): 22;
  resignation of: 27;
  views on White Terror: 47;
  and 1946 elections: 81;
  and KKE peace proposals (1947): 169–175;
  and KKE peace proposals (1948): 219–220

UNO, 76, 78, 133, 134–135;
  Commission of Inquiry (1947): 155–163;
  Special Committee on the Balkans (UNSCOB): 162, 248, 256
USA, 64, 68, 71, 81, 103, 269;
  early concern for Greece: 138–140;

307

Details of a selection of Ryburn books appear on the following pages.
For a complete list of Ryburn and Keele University Press publications
please write to
Ryburn Distribution, Keele University,
Staffordshire ST5 5BG, England

The British Government's China Policy 1945–1950

Zhong-Ping Feng

This carefully researched and well argued examination of a relatively neglected area of post-World War II British foreign policy represents an important contribution to historical scholarship. Showing how the British government viewed its interests and how it acted during the period, it begins with an historical background and then analyses Britain's principal economic concerns in China after the war, her attitudes towards the KMT-Communist conflict and the reasons for and consequences of American involvement following the opening of the cold war.

Dr Feng charts changes in attitude, policy and situation that followed, including the reasons for London's recognition of the PRC and its attempt to keep a 'foot in the door'. He also analyses factors which nevertheless led to the failure to establish normal diplomatic relations in 1950.

ISBN   1 85331 053 0

ISBN   1 85331 053 0

Class Formation and Popular Politics in Early Industrial Britain: Bolton 1825–50

Peter Taylor

This meticulously researched, lively and lucid examination of popular politics and labour-capital relations exposes how the transformation of both social and political relations in Bolton in the 1830s and '40s was in fact a gradual process of social stabilisation. The celebrated mid-Victorian 'consensus' in industrial Lancashire and Cheshire is a highly controversial subject, generally portrayed as a sudden and major shift in social relations around 1850 because of changes in the nature of work or shifts in the structure and ideology of the labour movement. By refuting such interpretations this book has wide implications.

Dr Taylor argues that political ideology played a crucial role in cementing links between reformers in the 1820s, '30s and '40s and that a combined attack on the aristocracy controlling power at the centre remained crucial to this process. He demonstrates the importance of conflicts within the middle class in determining class behaviour and argues that the national political framework, rather than the local economic sphere, shaped the working-class political response to industrial capitalism.

ISBN   1 85331 059 X

Class and Politics in a Northern Industrial Town:
Keighley 1880–1914

David James
Introduction by Asa Briggs

The reasons why the textile region of the West Riding of England was the heartland of the labour movement at the end of the 19th Century have been the subject of considerable debate among historians. By analysing the political and economic structure of the town as well as its politics, David James shows why Keighley in the 1890s had one of the largest and most active labour parties in the country (two of its leaders entering government, one – Philip Snowden – becoming Chancellor of the Exchequer). The work provides a specific study while at the same time suggesting more general reasons why British socialism developed in the way it did.

ISBN   1 85331 066 2

Drink and the Victorians
The Temperance Question in England 1815–1872

Brian Harrison

This new edition of a pioneering work, first published in 1971 and never previously available in paperback, studies the impact of nineteenth-century industrialization on drinking habits and attitudes to drink. The book had a major impact on the writing of nineteenth-century social history, and continues to be a much admired and constant source of reference. Although its overall argument and shape have not been changed, its expression has been improved, new material included and account taken of items published in the area since 1971. It also features a fresh introduction by Dr Harrison which assesses the book's current place in the understanding of Victorian social history.

Analysing the role of drink and the campaigns of the reformers who challenged that role, *Drink & the Victorians* deploys a rare combination of precise data, literary evidence and biographical detail for the purpose of illuminating Victorian values. It sheds fresh light on, among other things, Victorian attitudes to the state, patterns of recreation and above all the reforming mentality.

Dr Harrison is Reader in Modern British History at the University of Oxford.

ISBN   1 85331 046 8

European Papers in American History (EPAH)
No. 1   Reflections on American Exceptionalism
Edited by David K Adams and Cornelis A van Minnen

This is the first collection of conference and other papers to be produced in the EPAH series of volumes. The inaugural meeting of European historians of the United States, held in April 1993 at Middelburg in the Netherlands, attracted a diversity of papers. This selection has been shaped by the desire to provide internal cohesion around the theme of democratic republicanism as expressed domestically, reflected externally and articulated in particular foreign policy exercises.

It includes 'Concepts of Democracy and Republicanism in the Late 18th Century' (Colin C Bonwick); 'Transatlantic Radical Liberalism' (Owen R Ashton and Alun Munslow); 'James Bryce and Harold Laski' (William R Brock); 'The Turner Thesis Revisited' (Jan Willem Schulte Nordholt); 'The Exceptionalist Syndrome in US Continental and Overseas Expansionism' (Serge Ricard); 'The Anglo-American Discourse 1880–1920' (Anna Maria Martellone); 'Democracy Goes Imperial' (Sylvia L Hilton); 'World War One and Wilsonian Exceptionalism' (Daniela Rossini); 'The Principle of Self-Determination of Nations and American Policy in the Region of the Former Yugoslavia from Wilson to Roosevelt (Ivan Cizmic); 'The Myth of America in Poland from "Empire of Liberty" to the "Empire of Liberation"' (Zofia Libiszowska); 'The Gulf War and the New World Order' (Pierre Lépinasse); 'Soldiers and Citizens' (Manfred Berg) and 'Nationalism in International Law and Practice' (Knud Krakau).

ISBN   1 85331 074 3

Gender and Authority in Sixteenth-Century England

Amanda Shepard

This book looks at attitudes to women in early modern England as revealed in the writings of John Knox and his opponents. Its analysis of the ideas of leading Catholic noblemen challenges the view that Protestantism improved the status of women. The book also shows that it is within the aristocracy that we find the most radical ideas about women's right to participate in public life.

Dr Shepard sets the Knox debate in its historiographical and historical contexts and introduces the authors and their texts. She examines writings on resistance and the texts and views of defenders of women, theories about the nature of women and humanist attitudes to female education. Custom and precedent and the significance of the myth of the Creation and the Fall are also considered.

ISBN   1 85331 055 7

The History of the Social-Democratic Federation

Martin Crick

This book offers the first full analysis of the SDF's history and is essential reading for historians of the Labour Movement.

The SDF was the pioneer of the Socialist revival in the 1880s, Britain's first avowedly Marxist party and an important component of the Communist Party of Great Britain. As such it represents a crucial strand in late nineteenth- and twentieth-century English political history.

Although critical, Dr Crick dismisses the stereotype of a sectarian and dogmatic organisation attempting to force a foreign ideology onto an unreceptive audience. Blending the national picture with a detailed study of the party in Lancashire and Yorkshire, he reveals an organisation whose members contributed far more to the formation of local politics than is generally realised. They produced a generation of working-class militants, pioneered forms of social protest and made available for the first time in English a number of Marxist classics.

ISBN   1 85331 091 3

The Slave Trade and the
Economic Development of 18th Century Lancaster

Melinda Elder

Lancaster's development as a colonial port and commercial centre was inextricably linked with plantation slavery. During the 18th century the town changed from local agricultural centre to important transatlantic shipping port, the African slave trade representing a significant part of this commercial revolution, strengthening the whole town's potential to participate in the colonial operations and making Lancaster Britain's fourth slaving port.

Relatively little has been written about Lancaster's commercial development, and even less about its slave trade. This book relates it to the important historiographical issues which surround the trade in general. It examines the reasons for Lancaster's interest in the trade; looks at the structure and organisation of its typically small-scale enterprises, comparing them with those of its larger and similarly-sized competitors; analyses its participants and evaluates its impact on Lancaster's commercial and economic development.

ISBN   1 85331 030 1

Dominions Diary
The Letters of E.J. Harding 1913–1916

Edited by Stephen Constantine

'...exemplary editing by Stephen Constantine. This undertaking deserves the highest praise' — *Das Historisch-Politische*

'... a thorough apparatus of introduction and explanatory footnotes by Constantine, and a delightful collection of contemporary postcards ... As an evocative record of gracious long-distance travel, for their fascinating glimpses of the diverse societies which made up the British Empire, and for their revelations about the workings of a major public enquiry, E J Harding's letters make entertaining and informative reading' — *Archives Vol XX*.

From 1912 to 1917, E.J. Harding served with great distinction as secretary of the Royal Commission appointed to investigate ways of developing the natural resources of the Empire's white settler societies and their trade connections with Britain. His private letters home, published here for the first time with over a hundred contemporary postcards and photographs, provide a unique and entertaining description of the landscapes and journeys made to New Zealand, Australia, Canada, South Africa and Newfoundland and a frank and sensitive commentary on the major social and political issues.

Stephen Constantine, Senior Lecturer in History at the University of Lancaster, describes Edward Harding's career, the origins and consequences of the Commission and the extent and condition of the British Empire at the time of its tour. He also provides an extensive commentary, explaining Harding's references and amplifying his descriptions.

ISBN   1 85331 018 2

The RAF and Trade Defence 1919–1945:
Constant Endeavour

John Buckley

This dramatically illustrated book concerns the very real threat to British security posed by the RAF's lack of concern with trade defence from 1919–1945.

Dr Buckley examines the long- and short-term reasons behind the RAF's inability to defend British trade links and convoys during the Second World War and how these problems were conquered by mid-1943.

ISBN   1 85331 069 7

Belfast

W A Maguire

In 1800 Belfast was a market town and port of only 20,000 people. During the nineteenth century it became a great manufacturing city, with the largest linen industry, shipyard, ropeworks and tobacco factory in the world, and a major port. If more rapid, Belfast's economic development was in many ways similar to that of other British cities and its sudden expansion brought similar urban problems which were tackled in similar ways. But during its period of expansion Belfast developed patterns of ethnic conflict and division, based upon religion, which made it unique among the cities of the British Isles and which have culminated in the present troubles.

Dr Maguire traces the rapid nineteenth-century rise and long twentieth-century decline of industrial Belfast, and analyses social and political developments up to the present. The problem of sectarian division, which constantly proved to be far stronger than any movement towards compromise or cooperation, is a recurring theme of the book.

Town and City Histories

ISBN 1 85331 060 3 Paper
ISBN 1 85331 071 9 Buckram

Blackburn
The Development of a Lancashire Cotton Town

Derek Beattie

By 1914, and in just over a hundred years, Blackburn rose from near obscurity to become the cotton weaving capital of the world. Derek Beattie, Senior Lecturer in History at Blackburn College, considers the progress and profound consequences of such rapid change in thematically defined chapters to build a general analytical history of the town. A central issue is the way in which a small middle-class elite influenced, moulded and guided Blackburn's physical, social and political outlook. Dr Beattie also explores the way Blackburn has adapted to the present century. He looks at how it inherited 19th-century social and political traditions and has tried to come to terms with a declining economic base and new 20th-century pressures.

Town and City Histories

ISBN 1 85331 021 2

Bradford

David James

A concise, accessible and authoritative history of Bradford to the present day, this book is the first in Ryburn's *Town and City Histories* series, edited by Stephen Constantine, Senior Lecturer in History at the University of Lancaster. Archivist David James charts Bradford's growth from minor market town to worsted capital of the world, and the impact of the woollen industry on subsequent economic, social and political problems. He examines the changing economic foundations of the city and the ways they have affected its physical shape, built environment, employment, living conditions, urban character and politics. He analyses how power was structured, who wielded it, and its effects on the social behaviour of ordinary people.

'...initiating ... a valuable series with David James' coherently argued and clearly expressed account.' — *Industrial Archaeology Review*

Town and City Histories   ISBN   1 85331 005 0

Manchester

Alan Kidd

Manchester was arguably the first modern city and its history is more than the story of a town, it is a contribution to the history of the world. This well-illustrated work is the first general history to appear for over 20 years and it introduces many new interpretations and challenges several myths about the city's development.

After an introductory chapter on the centuries before the industrial revolution, it is divided into three sections: First Industrial City 1780–1850; Commercial Metropolis 1850–1914; and Within Living Memory: Manchester since 1914. Alan Kidd is Senior Lecturer in History at Manchester Metropolitan University.

'... A remarkable story and Alan Kidd tells it well' — *Gerald Kaufman, Manchester Evening News*

'... this is a very useful book with a lot to offer a wide range of readers. ...it is well-produced, well-written and conduces to a wider understanding of the remarkable rise of nineteenth-century Manchester' — *Dr John K Walton*

Town and City Histories   ISBN   1 85331 016 6

Sibirica:
The Journal of Siberian Studies

Edited by Alan Wood

The first issue of this important journal under the Ryburn imprint includes: 'An introduction to The New *Sibirica*' by Alan Wood; 'The Burden of the Far East: The Amur Railroad Question in Russia, 1866–1916' by Steven G Marks; 'The Chinese Eastern Railway Album at the New York Public Library' by Benjamin E Goldsmith; '"Amuria/Ussuria": The Russian Prize' by G Patrick March; 'The Russian Sloop "Apollo' in the North Pacific in 1822' by Glenn Farris and 'Siberian Regionalism Resurgent' by Alan Wood.

Volume 1 No. 2 will contain papers presented at a conference entitled *Facing the Future: An International Conference on the Indigenous Peoples of Siberia* and held at London University under the joint auspices of the School of Slavonic Studies and Survival International. It will consider a range of ethnic, historical, political and environmental problems of the region, with special attention to the conditions of the native peoples in present-day Siberia.

For details of this and other journals please write to:
Ryburn Booksellers, Keele University, Keele, Staffordshire ST5 5BG, England.